Birgit Schwelling (ed.)
Reconciliation, Civil Society, and the Politics of Memory

Erinnerungskulturen | Memory Cultures   Volume 2

Birgit Schwelling (ed.)
Reconciliation, Civil Society, and the Politics of Memory
Transnational Initiatives in the 20th and 21st Century

[transcript]

Bibliographic information published by the Deutsche Nationalbibliothek
The Deutsche Nationalbibliothek lists this publication in the Deutsche Nationalbibliografie; detailed bibliographic data are available in the Internet at http://dnb.d-nb.de

© 2012 transcript Verlag, Bielefeld

All rights reserved. No part of this book may be reprinted or reproduced or utilized in any form or by any electronic, mechanical, or other means, now known or hereafter invented, including photocopying and recording, or in any information storage or retrieval system, without permission in writing from the publisher.

Cover concept: Kordula Röckenhaus, Bielefeld
Proofread by Birgit Schwelling
Typeset by Hendrik Woicichowski
Printed by Majuskel Medienproduktion GmbH, Wetzlar
ISBN 978-3-8376-1931-7

Contents

Transnational Civil Society's Contribution to Reconciliation:
An Introduction
Birgit Schwelling | 7

RECONCILIATION AFTER THE ARMENIAN GENOCIDE

"A Question of Humanity in its Entirety": Armin T. Wegner as
Intermediary of Reconciliation between Germans and
Armenians in Interwar German Civil Society
Charlton Payne | 25

Mea Culpas, Negotiations, Apologias: Revisiting the "Apology"
of Turkish Intellectuals
Ayda Erbal | 51

RECONCILIATION AND HUMAN RIGHTS

Soldiers' Reconciliation: René Cassin, the International Labour
Office, and the Search for Human Rights
Jay Winter | 97

"A Blessed Act of Oblivion": Human Rights, European Unity
and Postwar Reconciliation
Marco Duranti | 115

RECONCILIATION IN THE AFTERMATH OF WORLD WAR II

Franco-German Rapprochement and Reconciliation in the
Ecclesial Domain: The Meeting of Bishops in Bühl (1949) and
the Congress of Speyer (1950)
Ulrike Schröber | 143

A Right to Irreconcilability? Oradour-sur-Glane, German-French Relations and the Limits of Reconciliation after World War II
Andrea Erkenbrecher | 167

From Atonement to Peace? *Aktion Sühnezeichen*, German-Israeli Relations and the Role of Youth in Reconciliation Discourse and Practice
Christiane Wienand | 201

RECONCILIATION IN POSTCOLONIAL SETTINGS

Apologising for Colonial Violence: The Documentary Film *Regresso a Wiriyamu*, Transitional Justice, and Portuguese-Mozambican Decolonisation
Robert Stock | 239

Facing Postcolonial Entanglement and the Challenge of Responsibility: Actor Constellations between Namibia and Germany
Reinhart Kössler | 277

INSTRUMENTS OF RECONCILIATION: COMMISSIONS IN EUROPEAN AND GLOBAL PERSPECTIVE

Political Reconciliation in Northern Ireland and the Bloody Sunday Inquiry
Melinda Sutton | 315

From Truth to Reconciliation: The Global Diffusion of Truth Commissions
Anne K. Krüger | 339

About the Authors | 369

Transnational Civil Society's Contribution to Reconciliation
An Introduction

BIRGIT SCHWELLING

The idea for this book has emerged out of the unease with developments in a field that since the 1990s we have become known to summarize under the neologism 'transitional justice'. Within a relatively short time, transitional justice became the standard formula for a broad range of concepts, instruments, and measures dealing with atrocities such as genocide, torture, civil conflict, disappearances, and other human rights violations.[1] Originally a label for legal instruments and mechanisms applied in transitions from authoritarian rule to democracy, the term by now is applied to fields beyond law, and therefore it covers a much broader terrain of attempts to deal with past violence. While transitional justice initially covered mechanisms such as trials, commissions of inquiry, vetting, restitution or reparation, the field

---

1 A burgeoning scholarly literature has emerged on the subject of transitional justice. For a sampling, see Elazar Barkan, *The Guilt of Nations: Restitutions and Negotiating Historical Injustices* (New York: Norton, 2000); Priscilla B. Hayner, *Unspeakable Truths: Transitional Justice and the Challenge of Truth Commissions*, 2nd ed. (New York: Routledge, 2011); Martha Minow, *Between Vengeance and Forgiveness: Facing History after Genocide and Mass Violence* (Boston: Beacon Press, 1998); *Transitional Justice: How Emerging Democracies Reckon with Former Regimes*, 3 vols., ed. Neil J. Kritz (Washington, DC: United States Institute of Peace Press, 1995).

now also includes non-judicial instruments such as apologies, healing circles, or forms of collective remembrance and commemoration. What is particularly striking about this development is the speed with which this development took place. As Christine Bell notes, the term 'transitional justice' "only came to be used in the mid-1990s" but already sometime after 2000 it was consolidated as a field of study and a set of practices.[2] One reason for what Elazar Barkan has called the "tidal wave of apologies, truth commissions, reparations, and investigations of historical crimes",[3] can be found in the establishment of a network of experts, international foundations, and non-governmental organizations, including the International Center for Transitional Justice (ICTJ), the Institute for Justice and Reconciliation (IJR), and the International Institute for Democracy and Electoral Assistance (IDEA). These experts and institutional bodies became quite powerful actors in the transitional justice process. As James Campbell notes, already their sheer number suggests "a fundamental shift in international political culture [and] an emerging consensus on the importance of confronting atrocious pasts".[4] An example here is the emergence of truth commissions. In her contribution to this volume, Anne Krüger convincingly argues that an "epistemic community" has developed that consists of practitioners in the field as well as academics, politicians, and policy consultants. Some of the members of this network are active in truth commissions, thereby contributing to the institutionalization of transitional justice as "a widely shared expectation in the context of regime transitions". With the adoption of the United Nations' "Basic Principles and Guidelines on the Right to a Remedy and Reparation for Victims of Gross Violations of International Human Rights Law and Serious Violations of International Humanitarian

---

2 Christine Bell, Transitional Justice, Interdisciplinarity and the State of the 'Field' or 'Non-Field', *The International Journal of Transitional Justice* 3 (2009), 5-27, here: 7.

3 Elazar Barkan, Introduction: Historians and Historical Reconciliation. AHR Forum Truth and Reconciliation in History, *American Historical Review* 114 (2009), 899-913, here: 901.

4 James T. Campbell, Settling Accounts? An Americanist Perspective on Historical Reconciliation, *American Historical Review* 114 (2009), 963-977, here: 965.

Law",[5] the codification affirming the importance of confronting past atrocities and recalling the resolutions of the International Humanitarian Law by the Commission on Human Rights in 2005, indicates that a global regime of transitional justice has been successfully established setting an international norm for dealing with past atrocities all around the globe. Or, as Susan Dwyer points out, "there appears to be a global frenzy to balance moral ledgers. Talk of apology, forgiveness, and reconciliation is everywhere".[6]

To be sure, the unease about this development that inspired this book does not root in a fundamental scepticism when it comes to prosecute and punish perpetrators, restore the dignity of the victims of atrocities or 'repair' the injuries suffered by them. It is not arguing in favor of a politics of forgetting, of amnesties and silence. Although it cannot be denied that there are possible dangers when past injustices are excavated, sometimes leading to even more conflict and violence, confronting past atrocities does lead to more balanced justice. It is a not only a politically, but even more so an ethically defensible position that the notion of transitional justice and the recognition of past suffering are given more serious consideration today. Fact is that perpetrators nowadays run a much greater risk of becoming subject to legal prosecution, and victims often are given a greater chance of having their suffering acknowledged and of being compensated for their losses. Moreover, it is more likely that their testimonies are being heard and recorded.

The unease about the developments briefly described above has other reasons. It is based on the impression that the current developments in transitional justice, both as a field of practice and research, tend to narrow the horizon and restrict the view of what coping with past atrocities means and contains. There is for instance a certain tendency to conflate democratization and transitional justice. Relevant research contends that coping with the legacies of repression of the old regime is a precondition of democratization. Leaving aside the fact that this fundamental assumption is fraught with multiple problems, for example the problem that we know cases of successful democratic consolidation based on silencing the past such as in

---

5 http://www.un.org/ga/search/view_doc.asp?symbol=A/RES/60/147, accessed 21 June 2012.
6 Susan Dwyer, Reconciliation for Realists, *Ethics and International Affairs* 13 (1999), 81-98, here: 81.

Spain, this assumption seems to somehow constrict our focus on societies in transition. However, coping with past legacies is not always limited to transitional periods; rather it is sometimes linked to older historical issues that inform contemporary crisis and political tensions. Take the example of historical injustices towards indigenous people who suffered from colonialism and who have been living in long lasting democracies such as Australia or the United States of America. It took several generations before attempts of dealing with these injustices emerged. Or, take the individual humanitarian payments to people who had to perform slave and forced labor in Germany during the period of National Socialism. The disbursement of these payments only commenced in 2001, no less than 55 years after the collapse of the National Socialist Regime. These are only two of many examples out of a great variety of cases that can be brought forward to show that coping with past atrocities is not always linked to processes of democratization. This book therefore decouples questions related to transitional justice from processes of democratization by arguing that transitional justice is not only about the sometimes rather short period of transition, but also about *longue durée*. Within this context, it was important to also integrate cases of transitional societies such as Ulrike Schröber's case study on Franco-German rapprochement and reconciliation in the ecclesial domain in the late 1940s and early 1950s. But, at the same time, we have broadened the spectrum of cases to be considered by including studies in which past atrocities became the focus of attention either long after transitions or even completely decoupled from such transitions.

Furthermore, this book takes issue with the practices that are considered as relevant in transitional justice discourse. With the establishment of networks of transitional justice experts, the tendency to formulate "best practices" of how to cope with past atrocities has emerged. An example is the International Center for Transitional Justice (IJTC) that provides "policy briefs and reports on best practice cover measures" such as reparations or vetting.[7] Experts not only formulate these standards of transitional justice but also are often involved themselves in these processes as third parties and some kind of mediators. This not only points to a certain tendency towards standardizing measures and instruments for coping with past atrocities but it moreover points to a concentration on processes in which experts

---

7 http://ictj.org/our-work/policy-relations, accessed 21 June 2012.

are involved. Against this backdrop, the articles in this book argue in favor of a differentiation of the field. This volume presents studies that examine cases beyond the support of experts and outside the sphere of standardized best practices of coping with past crimes. We are especially interested in cases were actors from within civil societies – dedicated personalities or engaged initiatives – developed often idiosyncratic means of dealing with the past. A case in point is the *Aktion Sühnezeichen* (literally: Action Sign of Atonement) analyzed by Christiane Wienand in her article for this volume. Founded in 1958, this organization developed a specific approach of hands-on reconciliation that was meant to atone for the atrocities committed under the National Socialist regime – a goal that is still being pursued today. Activities consist of practical reconciliation work performed by German volunteers in those countries that suffered the most from German crimes and include work assignments in various Kibbutzim in Israel or care for elderly Holocaust survivors in various countries. Within the scope of practical reconciliation work, it seems that approaches such as the one developed by the Protestant church functionary Lothar Kreyssig in the 1950s do not fit neatly into the rationale of best practices designed by transitional justice experts because they are to a great extent connected to particular local realities and specific cultural contexts. This book therefore argues in favor of studying cases of dealing with past atrocities that were established long before transitional justice developed as a paradigm. Moreover, it argues in favor of looking into initiatives that adopted approaches beyond the best practices designed by experts in the field of transitional justice, often idiosyncratic and born out of specific cultural prerequisites.

It can be stated that the broadening of the field beyond law has paradoxically caused a narrowing down of our perspective on actors, instruments, and measures involved in processes of coping with past atrocities. While, on the one hand, the initial focus on legal mechanisms has been broadened by including factors beyond law, the basic assumptions of transitional justice have, on the other hand, not been adjusted or codified accordingly. This observation serves as the point of departure for the contributions to this book. It is a plea for opening up opportunities for inquiry in the field of transitional justice by looking into relevant cases that do not fit neatly into the paradigm and that, to a large extent, have so far been overlooked.

Because this is a considerable challenge, we made some initial decisions concerning the case studies to be included and the research questions to be concentrated on. Firstly, we decided to integrate cases from the beginning of the 20th century up to the current day. The decision to cover this rather long period stems from the observation that transitional justice research seems to reflect a certain bias towards recent developments and cases to an extent that the invention of the term 'transitional justice' is somehow conflated with the beginnings of an increased sensibility for human rights violations and for questions of how to deal with them appropriately. An example is Joanna Quinn's textbook entry on transitional justice: "It was only in the 1990s that scholars and practitioners began to sort out how to deal with violent histories."[8] Contrary to such assertions, this book attempts to show that concerns about human rights violations and attempts at dealing with past atrocities can already be found at the beginning of the 20th century. We included case studies starting around 1919 with Armin T. Wegner's efforts of convincing his German and international audiences to look at images and listen to stories of the forced deportation of the Armenians from the Ottoman Empire.[9] We consider cases of early concerns with human rights, more precisely René Cassin's impressive engagement in favor of soldier's rights in the interwar period,[10] and the European Unity Movement's visions on human rights and reconciliation in the aftermath of the Second World War.[11] We proceed with three transnational initiatives developed by civil society actors since the 1950s that cover a broad range of ideas, instruments, and attempts of dealing with the atrocities committed under the National Socialist Regime. More precisely, these are attempts at Franco-German rapprochement and reconciliation in the ecclesial domain in the 1950s,[12] attempts at reconciliation between Germans and the French town Oradour-sur-Glane from around 1950 up to today,[13] and the already mentioned study on *Aktion Sühnezeichen*, founded in the late 1950s in the Federal Republic of Germany.[14] We furthermore included more recent ex-

---

8   Joanna R. Quinn, Transitional Justice, in: *Human Rights. Politics and Practice*, ed. Michael Goodhart (Oxford: Oxford University Press, 2009), 354-369.
9   See the contribution by Charlton Payne to this volume.
10 See the contribution by Jay Winter to this volume.
11 See the contribution by Marco Duranti to this volume.
12 See the contribution by Ulrike Schröber to this volume.
13 See the contribution by Andrea Erkenbrecher to this volume.
14 See the contribution by Christiane Wienand to this volume.

amples on civil society's engagement. With Ayda Erbal's chapter on the apology campaign initiated by Turkish intellectuals in 2008, we revisit the question of how to come to terms with the Armenian genocide around 90 years after Armin T. Wegner started his campaign in interwar Germany. Moreover, our recent examples include two case studies on the problem of dealing with colonial violence in postcolonial settings, both between Namibia and Germany[15] and Portugal and Mozambique.[16] Finally, we included two case studies on commissions in their function as rather new instruments of reconciliation and by now, the most commonly used restorative mechanism in processes of transitional justice.[17] With this long-term perspective on processes and dynamics of coping with past atrocities and human rights violations, we intend to present a more comprehensive and simultaneously more refined understanding of what transitional justice can mean in different socio-political contexts and time spans. At the same time, this approach allows us to gain comparative insights on similarities and differences emerging over a longer period.

Secondly, we decided to concentrate on civil society's involvement in processes of dealing with past atrocities. We are particularly interested in transnational engagement of civil society actors, ranging from dedicated personalities over institutionalized forms of engagement to societal elites. The decision to address the legacy of past wrongs from the perspective of transnational civil society's interventions is based on the observation that relevant research has mostly concentrated on major initiatives, either by national governments or by the international community. Except for nongovernmental organizations involved in these initiatives, the role of civil society has not attracted careful attention. Given the fact that actors from within civil society are active in processes of coping with past atrocities already since the beginning of the 20th century, the chapters collected in this book intend to contribute to this so far neglected aspect of transitional justice. That civil society became an active protagonist in the processes and dynamics of dealing with past atrocities is due to more general developments such as the increasing significance of society's involvement in public

---

15 See the contribution by Reinhart Kössler to this volume.
16 See the contribution by Robert Stock to this volume.
17 See the contributions by Anne K. Krüger on truth commissions and by Melinda Sutton on the Bloody Sunday Inquiry.

affairs. But it is also related to changing practices of warfare and state-sanctioned violence in 20th-century Europe and elsewhere. Just as total wars affected and mobilized whole societies, post-war processes also involved an unprecedented range of actors beyond the state. This involvement of large strands of the population into wars and atrocities as victims, perpetrators or bystanders led to a shift in the understanding of how power works. As Jeremy Sarkin and Erin Daly note, "until recently, political acts were likely to be seen as acts of single individuals or small cabals".[18] If justice after transitions was done, it was by trying and punishing the top leaders only. This slowly changed with "the recognition that political events are not the exclusive province of leaders, but implicate, and are implicated by, the population as a whole".[19] This fact carries implications "both for the new government's treatment of the past and for laying the foundations for the future".[20] Transitional justice is also an attempt at dealing with the involvement of society into the atrocities of past regimes, and building up a civil society after transitions is one of the main tasks in democratization processes. In addition, the question of contributions to these processes by actors from within civil society is here of fundamental importance. By focusing on civil society's involvement in processes of dealing with past atrocities, the chapters of this book refer to these developments.

Thirdly, we decided upon paying particular attention to reconciliation, both as a concept and a practice. On the one hand, "reconciliation has become a buzzword in the literature on […] transitional justice"[21] and "the darling of the transitional justice movement".[22] It is, as Jeremy Sarkin and Erin Daly note, "so easily evoked, so commonly promoted, and so immediately appealing".[23] Yet, at the same time, reconciliation remains a black box insofar as our knowledge is very limited with regards to the specifics of

---

18　Jeremy Sarkin and Erin Daly, Too Many Questions, Too Few Answers: Reconciliation in Transitional Societies, *Columbia Human Rights Law Review* 35 (2004), 661-728, here: 683.
19　Ibid., 684.
20　Ibid., 685.
21　Jens Meierhenrich, Varieties of Reconciliation, *Law and Social Inquiry* 33, 1 (2008), 195-231, here: 224.
22　Sarkin and Daly, Too Many Questions, 665.
23　Ibid., 664.

achieving and promoting reconciliation. We are not fully aware of the historical factors that contribute to the spread of reconciliation initiatives around the globe, the question of whether reconciliation can achieve the goals imputed to it, or what reconciliation actually means in different cultural contexts. In other words, there are still "too many questions, too few answers".[24] The chapters of this book intend to contribute to a better understanding of what reconciliation actually means when imbedded in processes of coping with past atrocities. The multitude of meanings generally associated with the term becomes more so obvious when looking at the actors in our case studies who refer within the context of their actions in various ways to 'reconciliation'. Yet, not only do they attach different meanings, goals, instruments, and strategies to the term, ranging from the Christian notion of reconciliation to versions that are more secular, but they themselves are at times uncertain about what this term might mean or what implications it might carry. In other words, continuing debates about the meaning of the term are not merely academic, but are already present within the initiatives under study here. We therefore do not start from a common definition of the term but rather ask what understandings of reconciliation are brought forward by the actors under consideration, what measures and instruments are used when 'reconciliation' shall be achieved, and what actually happens when actors become involved in processes they label as reconciliatory.

Taken together, the in-depth studies contained in this book analyze processes of coping with atrocities and human rights violations that were committed since the beginning of the 20th Century. The studies focus on the role civil society plays in processes in which reconciliation, both as an idea and a practice, plays a significant role. Special attention is given to situations where the actors and processes transcend national borders. The contributions describe actors and actor constellations involved in transitional justice, both as initiators and addressees. They ask for meanings attached to the concept of reconciliation and for the implementation of these ideas in practice. The contributions analyze strategies adopted and instruments utilized in attempts to repair historical injustices and to make whole what has

---

24 Ibid., 661.

been smashed.[25] In addition, they investigate expected and/or received outcomes of processes of reconciliation, hence ask both for successes and failures, potentialities and limits of intentional strategies and unintentional dynamics related to these processes.

What conclusions with regard to these research questions can be drawn from the detailed case studies contained in this volume? Firstly, the findings show that reconciliation by and large seems to be a utopian project. In all our cases, it is an unfinished, sometimes even a highly fragile endeavor in which a single ill-chosen phrasing, an inappropriate timing or the focusing on one group of victims or one atrocity instead of another can lead to even more dispute or hardening of positions. For example, take Wegner's attempts at reconciliation in interwar Germany, analyzed by Charlton Payne. Wegner's lecture in Berlin in 1919 and the accompanying presentation of pictures showing stages of the deportation and massacre of the Armenians in 1915 in graphic, sometimes brutal detail "was interrupted by the violent uproar among Turks and Armenians in the audience". As Payne shows, with the presentation of these pictures that was meant to create empathy for the fate of the Armenians, Wegner achieved just the opposite, namely the mobilization of feelings of partisanship instead of empathy. Or take the reactions to Tony Blair's setting-up of a judicial inquiry into the killings of thirteen unarmed civil rights demonstrators in Derry in 1972 that became known as Bloody Sunday. As Melinda Sutton shows, many Unionists interpreted the establishment of this inquiry "as indifference to the suffering sustained by the families of other victims of the Troubles". The example shows that acknowledgement of the pain and suffering of some victims can lead to bitter feelings on the side of other victims who interpret this recognition as a denial of their own trauma, suffering, and loss. It therefore points to the creation of some sort of competitive victimhood through measures aimed at reconciliation. In sum, these examples demonstrate how difficult and 'preconditionally dependent' these attempts at reconciliation are, e.g., how much they depend on an abundance of premises. They also raise the question of who is included in such endeavors, whose pain and suffering is left without public consideration, and who is entitled to make

---

25 I borrow this phrase from John Torpey, *Making Whole what has been Smashed: On Reparation Politics* (Cambridge, Mass.: Harvard University Press, 2006).

decisions within these processes. In other words, within the politics of reconciliation power may at times also play a significant role.

To state that reconciliation is a utopian project indicates an understanding of reconciliation as some kind of end state. In the case studies presented in this volume, this end state is hardly ever achieved. Against the background of a maximalist concept of reconciliation that calls for nothing less than an "ethics of caring for the enemy",[26] this seems not only plausible but in most cases probably an unrealistic expectation. As is convincingly argued in the contributions to this volume, reconciliation is not only an end state, but also constitutes a process. There is a *road* to reconciliation. It is made up of a great variety of gestures, symbols, instruments, and measures. Often it is taken in small steps, but it is those small steps that *can* make a difference. The case studies presented here may also be read as a plea to concentrate on those small steps and to adopt rather minimalist conceptions of reconciliation. Of course, sometimes already neutralizing issues of past conflicts in post conflict societies and initiating processes to move away from war requires a huge effort, as Jay Winter shows. At times, as Ayda Erbal in her contribution on the apology campaign by Turkish intellectuals in 2008 argues, even a rather unsuccessful attempt at apologizing can at least be "a step in the right direction for changing the lens of society by informing the public sphere of the necessity for recognizing that there is something grave to apologize for". Against this background, it seems plausible to not only shift the focus from an understanding of reconciliation as an end state to one as a process, but moreover to pay closer attention to related and probably less morally charged terms such as atonement, understanding, rapprochement, or redress. As Christiane Wienand points out in her contribution, the founder of *Aktion Sühnezeichen*, Lothar Kreyssig, had initially intended to call the organization *Aktion Versöhnungszeichen* (sign of reconciliation), "yet became convinced that *Sühnezeichen* (act of atonement) would be a more fitting term: atonement is offered by or on behalf of the one who has become guilty, whereas reconciliation already describes the next step of a mutual agreement between the two sides". To adapt less ambitious and morally charged concepts such as atonement, also seems to comply with the feelings of the victims. Asher Ben Nathan, the first Israeli ambassador in the Federal Republic of Germany, and one of the supporters

---

26 Meierhenrich, Varieties of Reconciliation, 211.

of German-Israeli youth exchange programs, nevertheless stated "instead of reconciliation I was talking about understanding". This and other examples in our volume show that the quest for reconciliation can be an unreasonable demand for the victims. Andrea Erkenbrecher draws our attention to the psychological barriers of some of the surviving victims of the massacre conducted on June 10, 1944 by a unit of the *Waffen-SS* in the French village of Oradour-sur-Glane. She argues that "reconciliation is not something that can rationally be decided upon", and that some victims just "*cannot* reconcile even if they would like to". Within the context of these findings, Erkenbrecher also states that the demand for reconciliation can be an all-to ambitious objective. The conclusion she draws is "a plea for a right to irreconcilability" on the part of the victims. This is only one of many examples that point not only to a certain scepticism when it comes to reconciliation but to its very limits.

The chapters of this volume convincingly show that there is no way around recognizing the power of experiences and memories related to conflict and war and that therefore one has to be very modest in expectations when it comes to reconciliation. In fact, in most of the cases described and analyzed here, only future generations might be able to reestablish "trustworthy and cooperative relationships"[27] and master the task of returning to some normalcy. This also leads to a conclusion of great significance: reconciliation is not just about a situation or moment, but rather, as stated previously, it involves rather long-term processes. Aside from this aspect of *longue durée*, the findings in our chapters point to another dimension of time being of importance, especially when asking at what time actors take initiative for reconciliation and within what time span these initial attempts take place. There are cases of rather immediate attempts at reconciliation such as Armin T. Wegner's activities described by Charlton Payne or the meetings of French and German church affiliates taking place as early as 1949 and 1950 analyzed by Ulrike Schröber. René Cassin's dedicated engagement for the war disabled presented by Jay Winter is another example

---

27 Veit Straßner, Versöhnung und Vergangenheitsaufarbeitung – Ein Vorschlag zur Begriffsbestimmung und Konzeptualisierung, in: *Amnesie, Amnestie oder Aufarbeitung? Zum Umgang mit autoritären Vergangenheiten und Menschenrechtsverletzungen*, ed. Siegmar Schmidt et al. (Wiesbaden: VS, 2009), 23-36, here: 29.

for initiatives being launched in temporal nearness to the experiences of war and violence they refer to. Nevertheless, other initiatives only start with a rather huge temporal distance to the events. The apology campaign by Turkish intellectuals analyzed by Ayda Erbal was set in motion nearly one hundred years after the genocide of the Armenians in the late Ottoman Empire. The cases of attempts at reconciliation connected to crimes committed under colonial rule analyzed by Reinhart Kössler and Robert Stock, also point to context variables that are of some importance here. Both in the case of Turkey's reluctance of dealing with the Armenian genocide in an open manner and in the cases of dealing with colonial atrocities, we are faced with the problem of silence and taboo that only lately began to slowly break down. In other cases such as in Franco-German relations, the environment was more supportive of these attempts at reconciliation, not least because of the political necessities imposed by the Cold War.

Furthermore, the findings of the investigations underline the importance of keeping alternatives in mind, both with regard to civil society's engagement and in terms of instruments utilized in processes of reconciliation. As Charlton Payne shows, Armin T. Wegner's attempt at reconciliation failed – at least as far as we can tell. What had a more positive effect was the trial against the Armenian student Salomon Teilirian who assassinated Talaat Pascha, one of the principle instigators of the Armenian genocide. After he had fled from Istanbul in 1919, Talaat Pascha had been living incognito in Berlin, where he was detected and assassinated by Teilirian in 1921. Teilirian's entire family had been massacred during the deportation in June 1915. A district court in Berlin had to decide whether this was a case of premeditated murder. Surprisingly, Salomon Teilirian was acquitted of the charge. As Payne argues, "this trial marks an instance of reconciliation between Germans and Armenians, and can be interpreted as contributing to the formation of an official cultural memory of the Armenian genocide. In this case, an authority sanctioned by the state […] became a conduit for the dissemination of witness testimonies as well as for a gesture of reconciliation, by issuing a verdict of not-guilty in favor of a victim of a massacre and thereby distancing itself from the previous foreign policy of supporting Germany's war-time ally responsibility for the forced deportations and massacres." This incident reminds us of alternatives to civil society's engagement. Here, the juridical system did find a more adequate response than was found by the civil society – not only from the perspective of Armenian victims living in Berlin but also in the view of some Germans. It is therefore of utmost importance to keep the interplay of different levels and actors – state, juridical system, civil society, dedicated personalities – in mind. Furthermore, this incident points to the distinction between restorative and retributive justice. While the latter includes forms of actively enforced measures such as trials und tribunals, the former describes ultimately voluntary instruments such as commissions, healing circles, or apologies. While the goals of measures of retributive justice are prosecution and punishment, restorative justice is commonly associated with reconciliation. The case presented by Charlton Payne complicates the picture of this often too clear distinction by showing that under certain circumstances, retributive rather than restorative justice can contribute to the dynamics of reconciliation.

Finally, the contributions to this volume point to the crucial and at the same time changing role played by mediators in processes of reconciliation. These mediators can be dedicated personalities as described in the chapters by Charlton Payne and Andrea Erkenbrecher, non-governmental organizations such as *Aktion Sühnezeichen* or various kinds of commissions as analyzed by Anne Krüger and Melinda Sutton. Even published texts, technical objects, or documentary films may be viewed as having mediating capacities as demonstrated by Robert Stock and Charlton Payne. Although not always with positive outcomes, these mediators fulfilled different functions. At times, they made people look at the pain of the victims and they created space for dialogue. They made efforts toward multiplying the number of circulating narratives and at complicating the language of all parties involved. The contributions also point to the changing role of mediators in the course of the 20th century. Methods and instruments utilized in the first half of the century have been rather idiosyncratic and mediators were sometimes in some – often unclear – way themselves involved in the events they had to cope with. In contrast, today we face the growing importance of standardized instruments of a culture of experts who advise countries all over the world in how to deal with past atrocities. It almost seems that by now a global regime of transitional justice has developed that might be a successor of the international humanitarian organizations having emerged in the first half of the 20th century. To look more closely into the question of whether these new global cultures of transitional justice are or will indeed be the successors to the international regimes of humanity described by Marco Duranti, Jay Winter and Charlton Payne in their chapters, will certainly be a challenging task for future research.

Acknowledgements

This book was conceived at the workshop 'Political Reconciliation and Civil Society in 20th-Century Europe' organized by the research group on 'History and Memory' at the University of Konstanz (Germany) on 9-11 December 2010. I would like to express my sincere gratitude to the Max Planck Society and the Alexander von Humboldt Foundation who provided funding in the framework of the Max Planck Research Award endowed by the Federal Ministry of Education and Research. I am also grateful to the research cluster on 'Cultural Foundations of Integration' for their financial support of both the workshop and this book. I also wish to thank Marco Duranti who has been a fellow of the 'History and Memory' group in 2010, and who helped developing the concept for the workshop. Our research assistant Hendrik Woicichowski was a great help in the editing process. My sincere thanks go to Anna Dowden-Williams who was an invaluable help in turning the manuscripts into much better English. I am also deeply grateful to my colleague Nina Fischer for her continuing personal and professional support. And last, but not at all least, I am grateful to thank the founder of the research group on 'History and Memory', Aleida Assmann, for her support and intellectual inspiration.

Reconciliation after the Armenian Genocide

"A Question of Humanity in its Entirety"
Armin T. Wegner as Intermediary of Reconciliation between Germans and Armenians in Interwar German Civil Society

CHARLTON PAYNE

Armin T. Wegner was a humanitarian writer and activist who witnessed the massacres and forced relocation of Armenian deportees while he was stationed in Ottoman Turkey during the First World War. This essay analyzes his efforts as an intermediary of reconciliation between Armenians and Germans within emerging conduits of civil society in Germany between 1919 and 1921. A look at the degree of apparent success, proximity to explicit political agendas, articulation and mobilization of narratives of suffering, and institutional sanction of his work is instructive for more general considerations about the role of intermediaries in acts of reconciliation in civil society.[1] The essay thus traces some of Wegner's activities within civil

---

1 I prefer the term 'intermediary' to that of 'mediator', and venture to follow here Michel Callon's definition of an intermediary as "anything passing between actors which defines the relationship between them"; hence, "actors define one another in interaction – in the intermediaries that they put into circulation". Whereas the term 'mediator' conforms to Wegner's self-presentation, the term 'intermediary' describes more aptly how his activities emerge out of processes of interaction between multiple agents and institutions, and with often unexpected results. Intermediaries include not only human agents but also published

society as well as the narrative and rhetorical contours of the interpretive framework within which these activities are set, and which they set-up, in the brief period of 1919-1921. Presenting himself as a mediator of reconciliation, Wegner explored ways of convincing his German and international audiences to look at images and listen to stories of the forced deportation of the Armenians. His work faced the difficult task, however, of how to navigate the heterogeneous terrain of personal witness testimony, contentious assertions of geopolitical identity by Germans and Armenians, and the normative claims of international humanitarian activism with which Wegner seems most strongly to identify. Despite Wegner's commitment to international humanitarianism and experiments with forms of narrative empathy, his attempts to mediate reconciliation were impeded by political circumstances and his own rhetorical associations of Armenian suffering with the legitimation for an independent Armenian nation-state.

EYEWITNESS OF THE DEPORTATION

Armin T. Wegner (1886-1978) was born in Wuppertal, Germany in 1886 to a socially well-connected family. He studied in Breslau, Zürich, and Berlin, before completing a doctoral degree in law. Yet he was more interested in the theatrical and literary arts, trying to make his way in the circles around Max Reinhardt's theater and as a writer of Expressionist poetry.[2] At the

---

texts and technical objects, such as Wegner's writings and photographs. Michel Callon, Techno-economic Networks and Irreversibility, in: *Sociology of Monsters: Essays on Power, Technology and Domination*, ed. John Law (London: Routledge, 1991), 132-164, here: 134-135.

2   For more details about Wegner's wider activities as a writer and not just as an activist for Armenian independence, I recommend Andreas Meier's informative podcast: http://podcast.uni-wuppertal.de/2008/09/04/politisch-literarische-abenteuer-armin-t-wegner/. See also: Martin Rooney, *Leben und Werk Armin T. Wegners (1886-1978) im Kontext der sozio-politischen und kulturellen Entwicklungen in Deutschland* (Frankfurt a.M.: Haag + Herchen, 1984). For a recent study on Wegner's wider literary writings on the Ottoman Empire, see Behrang Samsami, *"Die Entzauberung des Ostens": Der Orient bei Hesse, Wegner und Schwarzenbach* (Bielefeld: Aisthesis, 2011), 149-216.

outbreak of the First World War, he was initially stationed as a doctor's assistant on the Russian front. Thanks to his family's influence, he was then transferred in 1915 to the regiment of Field Marshall Colmar von der Goltz, where he served as the assistant to von der Goltz's personal doctor stationed in the region of the Ottoman Empire that is now Iraq. While stationed with von der Goltz, who was in charge of a Turkish regiment trying to fend off attacks by British soldiers, Wegner travelled from east to west within the Ottoman Empire. It was during this trip in the fall of 1915 and returning in 1916 that he crossed paths with the trekking Armenian refugees from the north heading southward into the Syrian Desert. In 1916, he spent time in the last refugee camp along the trek, where he talked to numerous refugees and documented in photographs and writing the suffering caused by the state-sponsored mass deportations and other brutal expatriation measures. After returning to Germany, he became a vocal activist on behalf of Armenian refugees. Due to censorship during the war, little information was disseminated within Germany about the Armenian genocide,[3] but following the November Revolution, Wegner was able to publish writings depicting the atrocities, overtly blaming them on the Young Turkish regime, and demanding a change in German foreign policy.

---

3   For a detailed and well-documented discussion about what was known within the German administration and what was silenced by the wartime censor, see Margaret Lavinia Anderson, Who Still Talked about the Extermination of the Armenians? German Talk and German Silences, in: *A Question of Genocide: Armenians and Turks at the End of the Ottoman Empire*, ed. Ronald Grigor Suny et al. (Oxford: Oxford University Press, 2011), 199-220; Dominik Schaller, Die Rezeption des Völkermordes an den Armeniern in Deutschland, 1915-1945, in: *Der Völkermord an den Armeniern und die Shoah*, ed. Hans Lukas Kieser and Dominik Schaller (Zürich: Chronos, 2001), 517-556, here: 522-531.

THE OPEN LETTER TO WILSON AND THE POLITICS OF INTERNATIONAL HUMANITARIANISM

With the publication of his "Open Letter to the President of the United States of America, Woodrow Wilson, On the Expulsion of the Armenian People into the Desert" in the *Berliner Tageblatt* on 23 February 1919, Wegner achieved fame and notoriety both at home and abroad as an activist for Armenian relief and national independence.[4] His appeal to Wilson makes clear that his ambition is "to right a wrong that no other people suffered like the Armenians [*ein Unrecht wieder gutzumachen, wie es keines dieser Völker erlitt*]" (5). Wilson had already announced his plan for the national independence of ethnic minorities within the crumbling Ottoman Empire. Hoping to garner support for the Armenians at the peace negotiations in Paris, Wegner announces in the letter his intention to speak on behalf of an Armenian nation – as "the mouth of a thousand dead ones" – justifying this speaker position on the basis of his eyewitness experience of the deportation, "as one of the few Europeans to have witnessed this nation's horrible demise" (2). He describes the letter as a "testament", at once an address "in accordance with the law of human community" and "a sacred promise" (5). Declaring that "no group of people has ever suffered an injustice to the extent the Armenians have", he casts responsibility and atonement simultaneously as "a question of Christianity" and a "question of humanity in its entirety" (2).

Wegner's appeal to Christian values here avers a common cause with the international evangelical lobby backing Wilson's foreign policy regarding Armenian independence. Evangelical missionary groups were some of the most vocal supporters of Armenian relief in the United States, for in-

---

4 I cite from the text published separately in book form, *Offener Brief an den Präsidenten der Vereinigten Staaten von Nord-Amerika, Herrn Woodrow Wilson, über die Austreibung des armenischen Volkes in die Wüste* (Berlin-Schöneberg: Buchdruckerei Alb. Sayffaerth [Otto Fleck], 1919). All translations from Wegner's texts in the following essay are my own. For more on Wegner's popularity among evangelical supporters of Armenians, as well as his troubles with the Foreign Ministry, following the publication of the letter to Wilson, see Martin Tamcke, *Armin T. Wegner und die Armenier. Anspruch und Wirklichkeit eines Augenzeugen* (Hamburg: LIT, 1996), 185-186.

stance. At the forefront of these activities was the Near East Relief organization, which had a long history of Protestant missionary activity dating back to evangelizing missions in the Ottoman Empire and the Middle East in the nineteenth century.[5] These U.S. missionaries were already present in the years before, during, and after the war, with some members supplying on-site relief work while others were concerned with bearing witness to the persecutions and launching a media campaign on behalf of the Armenians back in the United States – all in the name of a common Christian destiny. Granted a charter from Congress in 1919 and with James Barton appointed as its head, who would later participate in the treaty negotiations at the Lausanne Conference in 1922-23, Near East Relief became an important humanitarian relief organization and a vociferous lobby for Armenian independence.[6] The fact that Near East Relief could so successfully combine evangelism, philanthropy, and international politics was due in no small part to the close personal ties of some of its members to Woodrow Wilson.[7] Wilson's connection to the Protestant activists would not have been lost on Wegner, nor was Wegner unfamiliar with sibling networks of Protestant activism within Germany.

Yet Wegner's humanitarian agenda for reconciliation between Germans and Armenians is also staged here as a matter of concern for a presumed international community (hence the address to Wilson and the appeal to "humanity in its entirety"), and it consists of at least two parts. One concerns the commemoration of the dead: the creation of a cultural memory of the atrocities as a way to confer public recognition upon the dead as belonging to an imagined human community, in order to re-incorporate them into the world of the living.[8] This act of incorporating dead bodies into the memory of the living community involves the creation of empathy with the absent

---

5   Flora A. Keshgegian, "Starving Armenians": The Politics and Ideology of Humanitarian Aid in the First Decades of the Twentieth Century, in: *Humanitarianism and Suffering: The Mobilization of Empathy*, ed. Richard Ashby Wilson and Richard D. Brown (New York: Cambridge University Press, 2009), 140-155, here: 141.
6   Ibid., 143.
7   Ibid., 144-145.
8   Thomas W. Laquer, Mourning, Pity, and the Work of Narrative in the Making of "Humanity", in: *Humanitarianism and Suffering*, 31-57, here: 38.

dead. Furthermore, this story of mourning overlaps with the second project to ameliorate the suffering of the living in the present. And Wegner has concrete demands for how this should happen: through the founding of an independent Armenian nation-state, compensation for lost property, and the mandatory care of Armenian orphans. These measures, Wegner argues in a move which expands the issue of reconciliation beyond the confines of a matter solely concerning Germans and Armenians, would represent the international community's "recognition of our common guilt for the atrocities" (7-8). Armenian relief is thus no longer articulated solely as the objective of Christian missionary work, nor are distinctions between perpetrators and victims to be understood strictly in terms of national interest. Wegner presents the matter as entailing shared histories[9] by virtue of all participants being part of the common humanity underlying the international regime of nation-states.

Wegner's open letter to Wilson signals not only a shift in German humanitarian activism on behalf of Armenians, but also a recalibration of narratives about Armenia within discussions in German politics and civil society. Wegner's particular intervention in German debates about Armenians must be considered in light of changing attitudes in Germany toward Turks and Armenians since at least the time of the earlier massacres of 1894-96 during the rule of Abdul Hamid II in the Ottoman Empire. Whereas these deadly pogroms generated widespread international humanitarian outcry in Switzerland, France, Great Britain, and the U.S., a counter-discourse formed in Germany, which, as Margaret Lavinia Anderson has shown, "succeeded in diluting sympathy for the victims and shifting it to the perpetrators" of the massacres.[10] A conglomeration of arguments from diverse political directions were thus woven into effective geopolitical narratives aligning support for Armenians with support of either an expansionist England or tsarist Russia. These political arguments against Armenia and for

---

9 Elazar Barkan contrasts the notion of "shared narratives" to "national myths" in the efforts of civil society to achieve historical reconciliation. Elazar Barkan, Introduction: Historians and Historical Reconciliation. AHR Forum Truth and Reconciliation in History, *American Historical Review* 114 (2009), 899-913.

10 Margaret Lavinia Anderson, "Down in Turkey, far away": Human Rights, the Armenian Massacres, and Orientalism in Wilhelmine Germany, *The Journal of Modern History*, 79, 1 (2007), 80-111, here: 83.

Turkey were buttressed by "Orientalist" narratives that cast Turkey as an agent of secular progress and tolerance, in contrast to "backwards" Armenians abroad and Christian zealots at home, and were circulated even by the liberal German press.[11]

Wegner can thus be regarded as one of those alternative "spokesmen who could fit Armenians and Turks into a narrative in which listeners could imagine themselves".[12] He did so by appealing to a broad sense of suffering and re-inscribing notions of victims and perpetrators within a framework that cast matters in terms of international regimes of humanity and inhumanity. These rhetorical and narrative strategies are the main features of his work as an intermediary of reconciliation between Germans and Armenians from the time of his letter to Wilson and subsequent public lectures until the trial of Talaat Pascha in 1921.

The publication of the letter to Wilson in 1919, as well as of a programmatic statement the previous year demanding official acknowledgment of the Armenian massacre and support for the founding of an Armenian nation-state in German foreign policy,[13] cost Wegner his position as editor of *Der neue Orient. Monatsschrift für das politische, wirtschaftliche und geistige Leben im gesamten Orient*, a monthly publication of the Berlin Orient Institute supported by the German Ministry of Foreign Affairs. His public advocacy for the Armenians even cost him his contract with the Fleischel Verlag, his publishing company at the time.[14] Between 1919 and 1921, Wegner continued his public advocacy by aligning his activities with those of the international *Bund der Kriegsdienstgegner* in 1919, as well as by teaming up with organizations within Germany, such as the evangelical so-

---

11 Ibid., 93-102.
12 Ibid., 84.
13 Die Neugestaltung unserer Orientpolitik, *Der neue Orient* N.F. 4, Berlin 1918, 101-104. For a discussion and lengthy excerpts from this text, see Rooney, *Leben und Werk Armin T. Wegners*, 253-256, as well as Martin Tamcke, Armin T. Wegner's "Die Austreibung des armenischen Volkes in die Wüste". Einführung zum unveröffentlichten Vortragstyposkript vom 19. März 1919 in der Urania zu Berlin, in: *Orientalische Christen zwischen Repression und Migration. Beiträge zur jüngeren Geschichte und Gegenwartslage*, ed. Martin Tamcke (Hamburg: LIT, 2001), 65-71, here: 66-67.
14 Rooney, *Leben und Werk Armin T. Wegners*, 288.

cieties and the *Deutsch-Armenische Gesellschaft*.[15] Wegner's struggles for reconciliation between Germans and Armenians must be considered in the context of a pacifist proclamation of "a new law for the human" that entails the rejection of the centuries-old "law of violence" upheld by European political leaders, and the "complete and unconditional abolition of violence" as outlined in the manifesto of the *Bund der Kriegsdienstgegner*.[16] Wegner's language of rights and crimes in this context mirrors the terms deployed in his advocacy of Armenian aid and right to self-determination; in both contexts, normative prescriptions are elicited by Wegner's phrase of "righting a past wrong" (*ein Unrecht gutmachen*).[17] Wegner's interventions in civil society with the aim of reconciliation between Germans and Armenians are conducted under the banner of "righting a wrong".

"THE EXPULSION OF THE ARMENIANS": NARRATING SUFFERING, STAGING EMPATHY

One of his most impressive endeavors as an intermediary of reconciliation between Germans and Armenians was the presentation of his personal collection of pictures and reports, which he delivered between 1919 and 1921 as a public lecture accompanied by a slide presentation. The Institute for Popular Natural History at the *Urania* in Berlin had been founded in 1888 as an institution dedicated to the presentation of scientific knowledge to a

---

15 At the end of June 1919, Wegner founded the *Bund der Kriegsdienstgegner* with Robert Pohl, G.W. Meyer and Magnus Schwantje.

16 Armin T. Wegner, Die Verbrechen der Stunde – Die Verbrechen der Ewigkeit. Aufruf zur Gründung eines Bundes der Kriegsdienstgegner, in: *Das Ziel. Viertes der Jahrbücher für geistige Politik*, ed. Kurt Hiller (München: Kurt Wolff, 1920), 142-165, here: 143 and 152.

17 Wegner evokes this phrase in his discussion of the aims of the *Bund der Kriegsdienstgegner*, which he regards as a veritable alternative to the League of Nations, "a league of nations, whose provisions only entail a displacement, in the best case a reduction, of the instruments of power". He suggests that Germany could right one of the "the most disgraceful crimes of all time" by abolishing not only the institution of universal conscription but of military service in general. Ibid., 160.

popular audience. Its building contained an observatory, an exhibition space, and a theater – and, according to an expanded definition of intermediaries, which would include non-human actors, should as well be considered a potential intermediary of reconciliation within civil society, for it provides the physical site where participants might assemble to look at Wegner's images of suffering. The directors of the Urania Society agreed to schedule one or two personal lectures by Wegner on the topic of the Armenian massacres. Because, "the events that you depict have for some time now receded into the background", the directors write to Wegner in a letter from 1918, they questioned whether his presentation would have a strong "attraction" (*Zugkraft*) for the public.[18] Moreover, they expressed their disappointment at the poor quality of many of the diapositives for his slide show that he had sent along with his query letters, pointing out that many of them appear to be photographs of paper images and that their technological quality is substandard. Not until almost a year later, on March 19, 1919, did the plans for a public lecture at the *Urania* come to fruition.[19]

That the event was sponsored by the *Deutsch-Armenische Gesellschaft* reveals just how closely aligned Wegner had become to the efforts of the Protestant activists in Germany. The *Deutsch-Armenische Gesellschaft* had been founded in 1914 in Berlin by Pastor Johannes Lepsius (1858-1926), one of the most prominent German supporters of the Armenian cause, along with the journalist Paul Rohrbach and the Armenian writer Avetik Issahakyan. Lepsius' organization was an outgrowth of a conglomeration of mostly confessional non-governmental organizations such as the *Evangelische Hilfswerke, Der Hilfsbund für christliches Liebeswerk im Orient, Das Notwendige Liebeswerk*, and Lepsius' own *Deutsche Orientmission*. Lepsius' *Deutsche Orientmission* was founded in 1895 in response to widespread violence in cities and throughout the countryside targeting Armenians in the Ottoman Empire. A reaction to increasing resistance and unrest by Armenian populations due to decades of expropriation and mistreatment at the hands of paramilitary groups in regions along the Russian border, as well as to mounting perceptions of an international threat to Ottoman sovereignty,

---

18 Direktion of the Urania to Wegner, 20 February 1918, Deutsches Literaturarchiv Marbach (hereafter: DLA), Nachlass Wegner, A: Wegner.

19 Wegner delivered the lecture several times afterwards in Breslau and Vienna until 1924.

this wave of massacres between 1894 and 1896 claimed the lives of more than 100,000 Armenians. While the massacres were primarily conducted by Kurdish paramilitary groups, state authorities did little to protect the Armenian population.[20] News about the massacres reached audiences in Europe, resulting however in little more than notes of protest from the major state powers, yet sparking support for the Armenians within private relief organizations, such as Near East Relief in the U.S., or *Pro Arménia* in France. We thus find in conjunction with the early massacres against the Armenians an international history of humanitarian organization and assistance formed in explicitly non-state sectors. In the case of pre-war Germany, the channels of activity are primarily forged or pursued by confessional leaders such as Pastor Lepsius and the Frankfurt Pastor Ernst Lohmann.[21]

Strategy played a role in Lepsius' support for Wegner's lecture, for the event was scheduled to take place shortly before the issue of Armenian independence was to be raised at the peace negotiations in Paris, and tickets were reserved for representatives from the Foreign Ministry. It was hoped that Wegner's lecture would bolster support for Armenian claims for independence.[22] Not only did Wegner provide flesh and blood evidence as an eyewitness to the genocide, he also deployed his rhetorical prowess as a writer to help articulate the claims of Lepsius' humanitarian organization within a wider semantic framework than that of Christian charity. Around this time, Lepsius was also active as a compiler of documentary information concerning the state-sponsored Armenian massacres. Lepsius pub-

---

20 Annette Schaefgen, *Schwieriges Erinnern: Der Völkermord an den Armeniern* (Berlin: Metropol Verlag, 2006), 18-19.

21 Uwe Feigel, *Das evangelische Deutschland und Armenien. Die Armenierhilfe deutscher evangelischer Christen seit dem Ende des 19. Jahrhunderts im Kontext der deutsch-türkischen Beziehungen* (Göttingen: Vandenhoeck & Ruprecht, 1989). A work that critically situates Wegner's interventions within the wider context of the evangelical societies is Tamcke, *Armin T. Wegner*. For a discussion of efforts by the *Deutsch-Armenische Gesellschaft* to prevent the genocide during the war, see Anderson, Who Still Talked.

22 Martin Tamcke, Die Kamera als Zeuge. Armin T. Wegners Fotografien vom Völkermord 1915/16 in Armenien, in: *Das Jahrhundert der Bilder. Band I: 1900-1949*, ed. Gerhard Paul (Göttingen: Vandenhoeck & Ruprecht, 2009), 172-179, here: 178-79.

lished a revised version of his *Report on the Situation of the Armenians in Turkey*, originally published in 1916 but banned during the war, with the new title *The Passage to Death of the Armenians* in 1919.[23] He also edited a volume of diplomatic records commissioned by the German Ministry of Foreign Affairs, who hoped to thereby dispel notions of a German complicity and even removed passages that might have implicated German officials.[24] Although they are replete with numerous statistics, documentary sources, and factual reports, Lepsius' publications lack the narrative – sometimes lyrical[25] – eloquence of Wegner's writing.

Wegner's narrative eloquence faces the challenge, however, of how to move from the form of an open letter staging testimony in the first-person (i.e. the letter to Wilson) to the form of a public lecture in which those addressed view the images and hear the story of massacre as a communal event. The corollary question, moreover, is what type of communal event gets enacted in the process. Is it an act of looking at pictures or listening to stories together, in the hope of reconciliation between Germans and Armenians, or is it rather an act of myth-making and community-formation that solidifies geo-political identities and interests through a partisan foundational narrative? In the open letter to Wilson, Wegner still operates on the level of first-person address in the hybrid form of an open letter and an epistle.[26] He pens a self-aggrandizing eyewitness, who both "dares to grant

---

23 Johannes Lepsius, *Der Todesgang des Armenischen Volkes. Bericht über das Schicksal des Armenischen Volkes in der Türkei während des Weltkrieges*, zweite, vermehrte Auflage (Potsdam: Tempelverlag, 1919).

24 Johannes Lepsius, *Deutschland und Armenien 1914-1918. Sammlung diplomatischer Aktenstücke* (Potsdam: Tempelverlag, 1919); Schaefgen, *Schwieriges Erinnern*, 38-39. See also the reproduction of these and other documents by Wolfgang and Sigrid Gust at www.armenocide.de.

25 Upon witnessing the deportation during his trip through the desert, Wegner composed a poem in 1916 about the horror of what he saw, with the title, *The Expulsion*, which he tellingly also titled, *The Expulsion of Humanity*. DLA, Nachlass Wegner, A: Wegner.

26 Because the address to Wilson as a prominent representative of the U.S.A. is also published in the *Berliner Tageblatt*, it simultaneously seeks to inform a wider public; furthermore, the personal tone of the address "amplifies the credibility

myself the right to conjure before you these images of misery and horror"[27] and authorizes himself to serve as "the mouth of a thousand dead that speak through me".[28] This is no less than an inflated epistolary subject who assigns himself the moral authority to speak on behalf of Armenian victims in a German-language or international public sphere. A passage from the end of the slide presentation, on the other hand, describes the personal reaction of Wegner the public speaker to the images being presented, in a gesture that simultaneously affirms the amplified speaking self and hints at the dilemma of such a stance.

"Every time when I talk about the horrible pictures of misfortune of this group of people, from which your eyes have perhaps in horror often turned away from the screen, I imagine myself again among the starving and dying in the refugee camp, feel their supplicating hands in mine, summoning me to plead for them again once I return to Europe. And the bones of these abject ones, whose silent lament still cries over to us from these pictures, should become once again flesh in all of our hearts, in order to remind us of the hour of our deepest plunge. Yes, with the fervor of one who experienced the unthinkable ignominy of their suffering in his own tortured soul, I raise my voice for the surviving remnants of those abject ones for whom the benefit of life is no less precious than ours."[29]

While the passage affirms the aggrandized epistolary self by justifying his "fervent" speaker position with a description of his own reaction to the moving vividness of the images, the similarly presumptuous suggestion of an appropriate audience reception also raises the oratorical problem of how to create a shared reception of these images. The odd figure of the silent la-

---

and effect on the reader". Johanna Wernicke-Rothmayer, *Armin T. Wegner. Gesellschaftserfahrung und literarisches Werk* (Frankfurt a.M.: Lang, 1982), 188.
27 Wegner, *Offener Brief*, 2.
28 Ibid., 5.
29 DLA, Nachlass Wegner, A: Wegner. A comparison of the manuscript in Marbach with Tamcke's reconstruction of the manuscript indicates that Wegner apparently altered the passage after the presentation in the *Urania*. The figure of bones becoming flesh again in Wegner's heart and motivating him to testify on behalf of the dead is nonetheless already present in the older text. *Orientalische Christen*, 133-134.

ment of pictures of bones crying out at and becoming flesh in the hearts of the recipient is a riff on the rhetorical figure of *evidentia*, which denotes here the passage of images into voices that produce audience empathy for the victims.[30] While the text describes how the horrible images speak to Wegner, the question is what kind of images will be produced for the audience by Wegner's words as they present these images. Will the audience turn away in disgust, or hear the silent lament, and to what end?

Wegner opens by saying that the lecture tells "a story of death" of unprecedented scale either in the history of the Great War, or perhaps even in the history of humanity.[31] Wegner evokes the hearing of stories as a communal and even international phenomenon in the figure of the reverberating

---

30 Classified as an ornamental figure of thought ascribed to the domain of *elocutio* in, for instance, the rhetorical systems of Quintilian and Cicero, *evidentia* denotes the orator's ability to represent a case (*narratio*) in vivid, convincing images for the audience, as if all were eyewitnesses to the events. Such a compelling representation of the events should immediately convince the recipient of the veracity of the reconstruction. The clarity or liveliness (*enargeia*) of the illustration (*evidentia*) depends on the recipient's being emotionally affected, i.e. moved, by the mental images produced before his or her eyes in the reconstruction (*representatio*). For the discussion of the section in Quintilian, *Inst. Oratio*, VIII 3, 61, see Heinrich Lausberg, *Handbuch der literarischen Rhetorik. Eine Grundlegung der Literaturwissenschaft*, 3rd ed. (Stuttgart: Steiner, 1990), 400. Further research on the figure of *evidentia* has of course been conducted in recent years. I follow a similar approach to the one elaborated, for example, by Peter Schneck, The Laws of Fiction: Legal Rhetoric and Literary Evidence, *European Journal of English Studies* 11, 1 (2007), 47-63.

31 I cite an unpublished manuscript of Wegner's lecture from his papers at the DLA, Nachlass Wegner, A: Wegner. This manuscript resembles a palimpsest, for it is a later version that has been written over several times and that does not have identifiable consecutive page numbers. For a published version of the lecture see: *Die Austreibung des armenischen Volkes in die Wüste: Ein Lichtbildvortrag*, ed. Andreas Meier (Göttingen: Wallstein, 2011). Tamcke has published an attempt to reconstruct the lecture from the *Urania* in *Orientalische Christen*, 72-135 (hereafter: Wegner, Die Austreibung). Whenever possible, I will provide citations for the quotations which correspond to the page numbers in Tamcke's reconstruction. Here: 72.

echo, saying that this particular story of death's "echo reverberated across the borders of all countries even during the war, failing only to penetrate into the heart of Germany". The goal of the lecture, then, is to educate the audience about the devastating nature of what Wegner refers to as a "crime" by presenting "an unadorned [*schlichte*] representation of the events as such, because they alone speak such a strong language that they cannot be trumped [*überboten*] by any political explication".[32] Wegner's intended function is here neither that of plaintiff nor propagandist against Turkish people or culture, but instead that of a mediator of a moral admonition against the "terrible and disastrous demon" of violence. He strives to avoid a portrayal of the matter in terms of friend and foe distinctions between Armenians and Turks, or Christians and Muslims. In compliance with Wegner's desire to avoid partisanship, the narrative itself must not be adorned with either ornament or political explanation. An "unadorned" representation of the events, according to Wegner, will thus reveal the "truth" about the violence committed by a state against its own citizens in the interest of war. An underlying premise of his lecture is thus that "[t]he truth obligates him who knows it to speak".[33] Yet this is a form of speech that Wegner – and one could argue humanitarian narrative in general – has a difficult time negotiating. For the credibility of victimhood requires that narratives of suffering attest to the genuine innocence of a victim without too much interference by mediating instances. Wegner thus has to determine how to narrate this story of death in a way that enables the images to speak for themselves.

Wegner crafts a narrative out of his collected photographic materials and own eyewitness account from his tenure as personal assistant to Field

---

32 If Tamcke's reconstruction of the lecture at the *Urania* is accurate, then Wegner must have added this opening remark to a later version of the presentation. In any case, Wegner seems committed to the notion that truth can somehow speak for itself and that a politics of truth does not require further "political" explanation, as is apparent in his rather optimistic hope that "the politics of truth and humanity [*die Politik der Wahrheit und Menschlichkeit*]" could serve as a guide in these introductory remarks as well as in his denunciation of the propagation of lies and misinformation during the war. Wegner, Die Austreibung, 73.

33 "Die Wahrheit verpflichtet den, der sie kennt, zu reden". Wegner, Die Austreibung, 74.

Marshall von der Goltz in the region of the former Ottoman Empire that is now Iraq. Although Wegner photographed and talked to numerous refugees at that time, he does not elect to report his own experience in the form of an autobiographical narrative of his experience, but instead chooses first to introduce some historical background and then to *reconstruct* the expulsion of the Armenians with the aid of around 100 diapositives structuring the account. Because Wegner continued to collect materials from all sorts of sources, only around 24-26 of the pictures have been verified as actually taken by him.[34] The first thirteen slides show pictures of local color – geography, ruins, churches, Armenian women, etc. – while the following three show leaders of the Young Turkish revolution to supply political background to the account.

The account of the expulsions begins after such background information with a slide titled "Departure of the Refugees". The next slides and their accompanying text present stages of the deportation and massacres in graphic, sometimes brutal detail. Wegner's text surrounds the images with stories, including images and descriptions of groups of refugees, beaten individuals, corpses, and many Armenian women and children. Subsequent slides show packed wagons, families in tents, camps, and scenes from the Syrian Desert, including Kurdish horsemen, and the arrival of a transport in the desert. The remaining slides depict conditions in the desert camps, and, though interspersed with pictures of Armenian priests, they are overwhelmingly filled with additional images of women, children, and corpses.

The effectiveness of Wegner's narrative of the deportation is indicated by the response of his audience at the *Urania* in Berlin on March 19, 1919, although it was not the response he had sought. The presentation was interrupted by the violent uproar among Turks and Armenians in the audience.[35] Wegner was nonetheless able to conclude his lecture following an intermis-

---

34 Andreas Meier: http://podcast.uni-wuppertal.de/2008/09/04/politisch-literarische-abenteuer-armin-t-wegner/.

35 According to a newspaper report, "voices of protest were repeatedly raised by Turks present in the audience, which were then whittled down by the Armenians who were present". *Berliner Abendzeitung*, 20 March 1919, cited in Tamcke, Die Kamera als Zeuge, 178.

sion and the director's removal of the most disturbing slides.[36] The slides themselves thus played no small part as an intermediary of an unsuccessful attempt to bring people together to look at images of suffering. Despite his desire to articulate a narrative of human suffering at the hands of a particular logic of the nation-state at war – Wegner refers to a "megalomania of the concept of the nation-state and the bloodlust of armed force" – the violent response of the audience at the *Urania* suggests that his presentation of the events, through its focus on the production of a credible narrative of victimhood, mobilized feelings of partisanship rather than of empathy. This was the case for both Armenian and Turkish partisans in the audience, as well as for those eager to discuss the question of Germany's complicity with the persecution in the German press. The press reports focused predominantly on the conflict generated by the presentation and less on the actual topic of the lecture. Nationalist newspapers denounced Wegner as a charlatan, who either sought to discredit pre-republican Germany by suggesting its culpability or hoped to interfere in an internal affair that, as an article in *Die Verteidigung* from 22 March 1919 asserted, "could be settled between Armenians and Turks themselves".[37] Defending its ambitions to be an institution of civil society with a neutral stance toward partisan politics, the *Urania* consequently distanced itself from Wegner's lecture. The directors complain to him in a letter five days later that, "The Urania cannot permit itself to become a stomping ground for political oppositions and opinions.

---

36 "After the customary intermission the second part of the lecture was listened to in greater quiet; however, the director of the 'Urania' had run by meanwhile and removed the worst pictures of horror from the sequence of slides accompanying the lecture." *Berliner Abendzeitung*, 20 March 1919, ibid.

37 For an overview of press reports by both liberal and nationalist newspapers, see Tamcke, *Armin T. Wegner*, 196-197. Tamcke holds the "expressionist overload, the excess of affect", of the language of Wegner's lecture responsible for preventing "a more objective reception of what the audience heard". See Tamcke, Armin T. Wegner's "Die Austreibung", 69. Tamcke seems to believe that emotions are the source of conflict here and that there exists an appropriate form of representation that could bracket emotional factors in the pursuit of what he calls "political enlightenment" about the massacres.

Your lecture was a lesson for us that we have to steer more carefully here".[38]

One explanation for the failure of Wegner's lecture at the *Urania*, which had sought to provide an immediate forum for a shared experience of looking at the images and hearing this particular story of death, could possibly have been that the contested political situation at the time generated a pervasive environment of self-vindication and mutual recrimination. Wegner tries to carefully navigate the question of guilt. On the one hand, he avoids simple attributions of guilt by naming several international sites of war crimes,[39] and to no small extent, of German suffering. "Germany in Belgium, Russia in East Prussia, Rumania and France in the camps of German prisoners of war": these nations too are all guilty of committing heinous crimes against enemy combatants or local populations during the war. Yet he even goes a step further and distinguishes between the benevolent intentions of a majority of Turks or the Muslim religion and the nationalist ambitions of brutal Turkish political leaders. He makes a similar distinction when it comes to Germans. He asserts that while "Germany bears no small amount of complicity, due to its close alliance with Turkey during the war", the "mass of the German people that was shamelessly deceived knew nothing of this crime in which it was unwittingly implicated, because, as with everywhere else during the war, the public sphere, the voice of humanity, was suppressed". A key demarcation between innocent populace and culpable leaders underlies his efforts at reconciliation between Germans and Armenians. The implication is that if the Armenians are depicted here as

---

38 Direktion of the Urania to Wegner, 24 March 1919, DLA, Nachlass Wegner, A: Wegner.

39 His discussion of war crimes intersects with the discourse of international law around the time. At the Paris Peace Conference, this language of war crimes was used by the victors against Germany. For a discussion of this context with respect to international relations toward the Ottoman Empire, see Daniel Marc Segesser, Dissolve or punish? The international debate among jurists and publicists on the consequences of the Armenian genocide for the Ottoman Empire, 1915-23, in: *Late Ottoman Genocides. The dissolution of the Ottoman Empire and Young Turkish population and extermination policies*, ed. Dominik J. Schaller and Jürgen Zimmerer (London and NY: Routledge, 2009), 86-101, here: 96.

innocent victims, so too have the populations of warring European nations suffered at the hands of bellicose political leaders.

Yet a closer analysis of the rhetoric of Wegner's presentation reveals that the text also fails to escape a certain political logic of national myth. The final slide of Wegner's lecture contains a picture of a sunrise over Lake Van. Signifying life in contrast to death and darkness, optimism, awakenings, and new beginnings, the rising sun is a metaphor of the birth of an Armenian nation with Europe's help. It thus also figures the promise of reconciliation between Armenians and Germans as part of the international community of European nations. Europe, Wegner insists, has a duty to participate in the relief work, which according to him should include no less than the allocation of land, the supply of resources, and the founding of an internationally recognized independent Armenian nation-state.

"When, we finally ask, will the conscience of humanity rise up with such power that a crime will ultimately disappear from the earth, a crime, which for the last twenty-five years has tarnished the earth for the eyes of Europe. It is Europe's duty to assist earnestly and lovingly in this relief work so that the fate of Armenia does not take second place to the self-centered goals of large states. All of Europe, and not in the least Germany, adopted in the Berlin Agreement of July 1878 the most sacred guarantee to protect the peace and security of Armenia. Seduced by self-centered politics, it has to this day not honored this vow."[40]

Wegner's story thus does not end in the Syrian Desert, does not merely commemorate the deaths of many innocent Armenians, but signals the promise of a new beginning among the ruins of the Ottoman Empire. Humanitarian relief work is here coupled with the founding of an Armenian nation-state, which is no small demand and a very explicit political agenda that leads the search for a "transitional formula between suffering and relief"[41] back into the political logic of nation-states.

40　DLA, Nachlass Wegner, A: Wegner. The first sentence of the passage is not included in Tamcke's reconstruction of the manuscript. *Orientalische Christen*, 132.

41　The phrase is borrowed from Slaughter's analysis of grammars of humanitarian narrative in Joseph R. Slaughter, Humanitarian Reading, in: *Humanitarianism and Suffering,* 88-107, here: 99.

A second metaphor for the politics of the nation-state overlaps with that of the sunrise: the transmission of knowledge and the moral repercussions of the atrocity figured as the crime's echo across national borders. In the introduction of his lecture, Wegner refers to the reverberation of the crime's echo across national borders and its halting at the sound barrier in the heart of Germany. The moral imperative animating Wegner's project of reconciliation between Germans and Armenians is inseparable from recognition of the political responsibility of both Talaat Pascha and his accomplices and of the world powers that failed to intervene or are in a position now to redress this injustice. The previous distinction between the moral authority of innocent populations and the violent abuse of political authority by their leaders transforms into a newly claimed political authority for the victims pit against the immorality of political leaders. Wegner makes such a connection in the text accompanying a slide showing Talaat and Enver in their salons. The text briefly summarizes their plans for a pan-Turkism, which Wegner claims they strove to accomplish through the "regretless eradication of all that is not Turkish [*rücksichtslose Ausrottungn* (sic.) *alles dessen, was nicht türkisch ist*]".[42] Two slides later, the lecture presents a relief map of Turkey. In the corresponding text, Wegner explains that the consolidation of a Turkish nation-state went hand in hand with the transformation of entire regions, including not only the Russian front but also the territories historically populated by Armenians, as well as the coastal areas along the Mediterranean, into the "concept of the border [*der Begriff der Grenze*]". This "concept of the border" territorializes the notion of an ethnic nation-state by demarcating those areas, which might be susceptible to foreign invasion and providing a rationale for measures enacted to defend these borders in a time of war.[43] Wegner's sunrise metaphor reiterates, however, the logic of the border – though it temporalizes it by locating it on the horizon – and thereby legitimates semantics of the nation-state based on a story of common identity and geographical space ascribed to Armenia. What is more, his is a foundational myth tied to a vision of international reconcilia-

---

42 Wegner, Die Austreibung, 82.
43 Ibid., 87. A process analyzed by Jay Winter, Under Cover of War: The Armenian Genocide in the Context of Total War, in: *The Spector of Genocide? Mass Murder in Historical Perspective*, ed. Robert Gellately and Ben Kiernen (Cambridge: Cambridge University Press, 2003), 189-214.

tion and cooperation that is legitimated by an appeal to a normative sense of "humanity".

Wegner's audience would thus have cause to be wary of the reconciliation staged by his slide presentation. Even if his narrative was able to escape the solipsistic mobilization of the figure of *evidentia* that is characteristic of the Letter to Wilson, in order to encourage a situation of reception in which the vividness of his narrative slide show motivated his audience to look together at the images of mass brutality, such an act of communal hearing and viewing remained nevertheless subordinate to those very stubborn investments in the integrity of the nation-state that so often hinder the successful construction of shared histories. Although Wegner's slide show stages a scene of looking and hearing in the name of "humanity", the legitimation of an independent nation-state put forth in the narrative was too contentious for audience members caught up in the environment of political groups seeking to advance their interests at home and abroad during the negotiation of peace treaties and the consolidation of new political regimes in Turkey and Germany.

THE TRIAL OF TALAAT PASCHA: A UNILATERAL GESTURE OF RECONCILIATION

Two years later, on June 2 and 3, 1921, a trial was conducted before a sworn jury of the Third District Court of Berlin to decide the question of Salomon Teilirian's guilt for murdering Talaat Pascha, the former Minister of the Interior in Turkey between 1909 and 1917 and one of the principle instigators of the Armenian genocide. Talaat Pascha had been living incognito in Berlin since November 1918, after having fled there from Istanbul, along with other Young Turkish leaders, onboard a German torpedo boat with the help of the German General Hans von Seeckt.[44] Under pressure from the victorious allied powers, and in particular from Great Britain, the Ottoman regime conducted trials between 1919 and 1921 against politicians and officials responsible for the deportations of Armenians into the Syrian Desert. Talaat was sentenced in absentia to death on 5 July 1919.[45] He was

---

44 Schaefgen, *Schwieriges Erinnern*, 42.
45 Ibid., 31; Segesser, Dissolve or punish, 97.

thus either living secretly in Berlin as a refugee, or, depending upon one's perspective, as a fugitive. On March 15, 1921, the Armenian student and member of the Nemesis Group, whose avowed goal it was to assassinate such fugitive officials responsible for the Armenian genocide, shot Talaat Pascha in Berlin-Charlottenburg.[46] It was up to the jury to decide whether this was a case of premeditated murder.[47] After an hour of deliberation, the jury surprisingly acquitted Salomon Teilirian of the charge.

Remarkable for the topic of reconciliation and civil society is how this trial marks an instance of reconciliation between Germans and Armenians, and can be interpreted as contributing to the formation of an official cultural memory of the Armenian genocide. In this case, an authority sanctioned by the state, such as the district court of Berlin, became a conduit for the dissemination of witness testimonies, as well as for a gesture of reconciliation, by issuing a verdict of not guilty in favor of a victim of state-sponsored massacre and thereby distancing itself from the previous foreign policy of supporting Germany's war-time ally responsible for the forced deportations and massacres.

While the verdict was in strict legal terms to be decided by a twelve-member jury of laymen on the basis of expert testimony about the mental state of the defendant, whose entire family had been massacred during the deportation in June 1915, the shocking testimonies by eyewitnesses and German officials stationed in Ottoman Turkey during the war transformed the trial into a forum for the denunciation of the inhuman practices of a political regime toward the Armenians, in which victim transformed into perpetrator and vice versa. Armin T. Wegner had been commissioned as an expert witness for the trial by Counselor Johannes Werthauer due to his intimate knowledge of the massacres.[48] Though he never testified in court, he was involved in the proceedings and drafted an assessment of the trial, entitled "A Just Verdict" (*Ein gerechtes Urteil*), which was printed later in

---

46 Schaefgen, *Schwieriges Erinnern*, 42.
47 According to the *Eröffnungsbeschluß. Der Prozeß Talaat Pascha. Stenographischer Prozeßbericht mit einem Vorwort von Armin T. Wegner und einem Anhang* (Berlin: Deutsche Verlagsgesellschaft für Politik und Geschichte, 1921), 13. The publication of the court transcript was financed by the *Deutsch-Armenische Gesellschaft*. Tamcke, *Armin T. Wegner*, 214-215.
48 Werthauer to Wegner, 30 March 1921, DLA, Nachlass Wegner, A: Wegner.

1921 as the Foreword to the publication of the stenographic report of the trial. Wegner declares that the trial reveals "once again to the eyes of the world, and for the first time also to those of the German public [...] the systematic massacre of an entire people by the Young Turkish regime".[49] Wegner's synechdoche of the "eyes of the world" suggests that the path towards reconciliation was made possible by the trial's setting, which enabled both involved parties and an imagined international community to look together at the vivid and compelling images of the atrocity. This time the act of seeing together occurred within at least two frameworks that differ significantly from the previous ones in which Wegner was active.

The first setting was delineated by the institutional parameters of a local court of law. The district court in Berlin became, importantly and in contrast to Wegner's public lecture at the *Urania*, an opportunity for Armenian victims living in Berlin to bear witness to their own experiences of suffering. The testimony of witness for the defense Christine Tersibaschian, in particular, delivered a first-hand account of the horrors of the deportation from her hometown of Erzerum in July 1915. With the assistance of a translator, Tersibaschian recalled in explicit detail the deportation of the town's population in groups of four over the course of eight days.[50] Her twenty-one member family was part of the second group of five-hundred families to be deported; her testimony was especially moving for those present in the courtroom, because she testifies, "I have seen with my own eyes the loss of all but three of my family members", as well as the brutal deaths of many others who were drowned in a river or beaten to death at the hands of Turkish police and soldiers.[51] According to the court transcript, two statements from her testimony in particular caused "commotion" in the courtroom: The first was when she "swore" to have seen how the police and soldiers cut open the rib cages of pregnant women and threw away the fetuses. The second was when she explicitly attributed responsibility for the massacres to the Turkish leader Enver Pascha and described how Turkish soldiers forced the Armenian refugees to call out "Long live the Pascha!" for having spared their lives.[52]

---

49 *Prozeß Talaat Pascha*, vii.
50 Ibid., 53-55.
51 Ibid., 54.
52 Ibid., 55.

Additional eyewitness testimony combined with the accounts of expert witnesses, including extensive testimony by Lepsius, to make a damning case against Talaat Pascha and generate empathy for the defendant.[53] At the same time, the district court offered the German foreign ministry the opportunity to exonerate itself. For another expert witness called to testify at the trial was Limon von Sanders, the commander of the German military mission in the Ottoman Empire during the war, who explained for the record that neither the German government nor military officials had either participated in the deportations or been aware of the extent of the massacres.[54] Moreover, his account shifts the blame away from Talaat by emphasizing rather the role of unruly functionaries. For although he concedes that the Turkish regime ordered the mass deportations, he imputes the extent of their brutality to the undisciplined "bad elements" of the makeshift police placed in charge of conducting the deportations.[55] The presence of Limon von Sanders at the trial insured that reconciliation between Germans and Armenians was thus achieved at the expense of both vilified Turkish regime and functionaries. The trial thus conveniently allowed the German foreign ministry to participate in a gesture of reconciliation toward Armenian survivors while denying any responsibility as a former military ally of the Turkish regime and creating a measured degree of distance from those immediately responsible.[56] This in turn meant that the German public was also provided with an experience of hearing about the atrocities without being overly burdened by questions of complicity.

In addition to creating a setting invested with legal authority for the dissemination of survivor, eyewitness, and expert testimony about the massacre, the trial resulted predominantly in the scripting of an official public

---

53 Schaefgen, *Schwieriges Erinnern*, 42-49.
54 Sanders claims under oath: "everything was kept secret from us, so that we could not gain insight into the internal political affairs." *Prozeß Talaat Pascha*, 63.
55 Ibid., 61-62.
56 Nevertheless, the trial and question of German complicity or guilt for war crimes persisted as highly contentious issues within Germany, as the widely varying responses in the press show. Schaller, Die Rezeption des Völkermordes an den Armeniern, 531-538. Further remarks on the trial's reception are provided by Tamcke, *Armin T. Wegner*, 216-218.

record of the massacres within Germany, with no direct impact on Armenian political affairs. To be sure, Armenian survivors expressed their enthusiasm for the official recognition of the atrocities signified by the verdict, and their appreciation to Lepsius in particular for his efforts.[57] Yet the modest success of the trial as a unilateral gesture of reconciliation by Germans towards Armenians can be attributed to a large extent to its setting aside the question of material or political retribution through support of Armenian national independence. The Treaty of Sèvres from 10 August 1920 had recognized an Armenian Republic – the so-called "Wilsonian Armenia" – whose existence was under constant threat until finally being annexed by the Soviet Union in 1922, yet this political context was never thematized in deliberations at the trial. The trial might have served as a more congenial site for a gesture of reconciliation because its institutional conventions detached testimony from the explicit goal of Armenian independence that had been so important and contentious for Wegner's project of reconciliation.

Wegner's commentary to the trial attempts to re-frame the verdict within the international story of humanity that he had been advocating and narrating during the previous years. He insists on the political nature of the trial, asserting that it became a "tribunal of humanity" and that the verdict contains "world-historical significance".[58] Moreover, while he still advocates "empathy [...] on the side of the Armenian nation",[59] he casts the trial as a decision over "two other powers", those of "violence and law, crime and humanity". In other words, he casts the verdict as a "rejection of that politics which claims the right to treat entire peoples like animals for slaughter, or even worse, like unfeeling stones".[60] Wegner's text concedes here many of the concrete political goals that he had considered necessary

---

57 Schaefgen refers to a large file in the *Johannes-Lepsius-Archiv* in Halle containing positive responses to the verdict by prominent members of the Armenian diaspora community, 48, and to the study: Hermann Goltz, *Dr. Johannes Lepsius (1858-1926). Zu Leben und Werk des Potsdamer Anwalts der Armenier*. This essay is available alongside others on Lepsius, the genocide, Wegner, and German-Armenian relations at the website of the *Lepsiushaus* Potsdam: http://lepsiushaus.wordpress.com/aktivitaeten/publikationen/

58 Wegner, Vorwort, in: *Prozess Talaat Pascha*, vii.

59 Ibid., xi.

60 Ibid., x.

for the process of reconciliation between Germans and Armenians. His role has changed along with the different context of reconciliation from that of the humanitarian activist trying to inform the German public about the atrocity, and thereby garner political and material support for the Armenian survivors, to that of the passionate interpreter of a moment of symbolic reconciliation offered by a German court of law toward Armenian survivors.[61]

Nevertheless, Wegner continued his activism, trying in vain, for instance, to found a humanitarian relief operation in Armenia in cooperation with Fritjof Nansen, who was in charge of refugee aid under the auspices of the League of Nations.[62] In a gesture of appreciation for his work as an intermediary of reconciliation, an Armenian congregation granted him a generous stipend of 10,000 Reichsmark in 1922 to finance his attempt to write a great historical novel about the deportations called *The Expulsion*.[63]

---

61 Robert M.W. Kempner, the assistant U.S. Chief Counsel during the Nürnberg trials, interprets the trial as "recognition for the first time in legal history of the tenet" that foreign states can try to combat genocide without being regarded as interfering in the internal affairs of a sovereign state, and Wegner's role as consisting in "hammering the truth about this holocaust into the conscience of humanity". Robert M.W. Kempner, Vor sechzig Jahren vor einem deutschen Schwurgericht. Der Völkermord an den Armeniern, *Recht und Politik* 3 (1980), 167-69, here: 167.

62 Nansen to Wegner, 23 February 1923, DLA, Nachlass Wegner, A: Wegner. Continued attacks on the Armenians by nationalist Turks led Wegner to write another epistle, this time to the "regimes of the victorious nations", condemning the international failure to protect the newly-formed Armenian republic and the many displaced Armenians. Armin T. Wegner, Die Schrei vom Ararat. An die Regierung der sieghaften Völker. Aufruf zum Schutze Armeniens, *Die neue Generation* 18 (1922), 348-355, and again as: Die Schrei vom Ararat, *Die Weltbühne* 19 (1923), 122-126.

63 Meier, podcast. Despite fifty years of work, the novel was never completed. See also: Rooney, *Leben und Werk Armin T. Wegners*, 349. Exiled Armenians living in Germany expressed their appreciation for Wegner's work around 1920 and especially after the trial, as evidenced by publication of his writings in Armenian newspapers, the fact that many exiled Armenians bought his books, and letters of thanks in his archived papers, such as the one from the *Verein der Armenischen Kolonie* in Berlin from 2 July 1921. Tamcke, *Armin T. Wegner*, 205.

Moreover, in 1968, he was invited to Armenia by the Catholics of All Armenians and awarded the Order of Saint Gregory the Illuminator in recognition of his work on behalf of Armenians. Wegner's efforts as an intermediary of reconciliation between Germans and Armenians, which he always regarded as a project to be undertaken not only as a German but also as an international matter, explored with varying degrees of success strategies for getting people to look together at or listen to the pain of others. His activities remind us that while such acts of looking and listening are embedded within contentious frames of reference by a host of intermediaries within civil society, these mediating instances of acts of reconciliation are themselves defined by those very political circumstances and dynamics that they set out to discern, contain, and change.

Mea Culpas, Negotiations, Apologias
Revisiting the "Apology" of Turkish Intellectuals[1]

AYDA ERBAL

> "History is a nightmare from which I am trying to awake." Stephen Dedalus
> JAMES JOYCE, *ULYSSES*

The long nineteenth century of the Ottoman Empire's dismantling that started with the Serbian revolt of 1804 culminated in a series of events leading to the years 1915-1918 during which the Christian populations of the Empire, among them Armenians, Assyrians and Pontic Greeks, were annihilated in their homelands. Justified by the official narrative both as a response to the deportation and ethnic cleansing of Muslims from the Balkans and Russia and as a structural necessity to save the remains of the Empire, the last thirty years of Ottoman policies in the imperial territories that will become contemporary Turkey still remain a taboo.

Even though since the 1990s there has been considerable change in the Turkish state discourse and policy,[2] the Armenian Genocide and its institu-

---

[1] I thank Marc Mamigonian and Axel Bertamini Çorluyan for their valuable critiques and comments for several versions of this paper. I cannot thank Birgit Schwelling enough for her comments and patience during the editorial process. Lastly I would like to thank the participants of the Political Reconciliation and Civil Society in 20th Century Europe Workshop for their inputs.

tional and political/economic repercussions occupy the center-piece of this taboo. Among other things, contemporary street names and boulevards, schools and memorials honoring key figures in the planning and perpetration of the Armenian Genocide[3] offer testimony to the lack of the Turkish state's institutional commitments regarding gross human rights violations.

However, the Turkish state has not been the only enforcer of the taboo surrounding the issue of the Armenian Genocide. Turkish civil society and the academic and intellectual establishment within that civil society have also been either actively in denial or in some cases in service of a denialist state agenda or standing passively silent – another form of denial – for over 90 years. As a result, all late Ottoman historiography and the social sciences and related high school curriculum in Turkey[4] have been highly problematic in their evident obscurantism in both historical and economic data concerning the late Ottoman and early Republican periods. Historical sociologist Taner Akçam's pioneering work on the Armenian Genocide[5] has been the first crack in the long history of silence in Turkey, yet its trickling down to the popular journalistic discourse in Turkey is still very limited.

---

2   For an elaborate take on the history of the change of the Turkish state discourse since the 1970s see Seyhan Bayraktar, *Politik und Erinnerung: Der Diskurs über den Armeniermord in der Türkei zwischen Nationalismus und Europäisierung* (Bielefeld: transcript, 2010).

3   Ahmet İnsel, Katilden Milli Kahraman Olur Mu?, *Radikal*, 26 April 2004, http://www.radikal.com.tr/Default.aspx?aType=RadikalYazar&ArticleID=1047371&Yazar=AHMET%20%DDNSEL&Date=26.04.2011&CategoryID=99. Unless otherwise mentioned, all internet sources are accessed on 12 April 2012. All translations from Turkish by the author.

4   For an extensive debate on Armenian Genocide and Turkish high school curriculum see Jennifer M. Dixon, Education and National Narratives: Changing Representations of the Armenian Genocide in History Textbooks in Turkey, *The International Journal for Education Law and Policy,* Special Issue: Legitimation and Stability of Political Systems: The Contribution of National Narratives (2010), 103-126.

5   Taner Akçam wrote a series of books from *Turkish National Identity and the Armenian Question* (İstanbul: İletişim, 1992) to *The Young Turks Crime Against Humanity: The Armenian Genocide and Ethnic Cleansing in the Ottoman Empire* (Princeton: Princeton University Press, 2012).

The apology campaign initiated by four Turkish scholars in December 2008 and endorsed by over thirty thousand Turkish citizens, the subject matter of this chapter, might be considered as another "crack" in the long history of silence. I argue that despite the apology initiators' presentation of the apology as a purely "personal" gesture, framing it as a matter of "conscience", the campaign nonetheless cannot be viewed as falling outside the domain of political apologies. But their potentially important place in seemingly solving contemporary political crises aside, what are political apologies? Are they empty rhetorical tools with which states or citizens try to score public relations points in situations where there is neither the possibility of a direct remedy because of passage of time, nor the willingness to follow a transitional democratization process with direct economic and/or political consequences including retribution and reparation? Do contemporary apologies rather "signify the death twitches of expiring moral systems", and do those who complain about "disingenuous," "inauthentic" or "commodified" apologies suffer from nostalgia for a more principled age that probably never have existed"?[6] Are apologies new ways of "imagining", hence transforming the "nation"? What kind of institutional or civil societal normative commitments does the language of the state-to-state, state-to-many, or many-to-many apologies communicate, if any? What differentiates a successful apology from a pseudo or non-apology? What is the difference between *apologia* and apology?

In order to analyze the apology campaign with regard to these questions, I will first clarify the term apology by touching upon its evolution from the Greek word *apologia* (speech in defense) to the current word apology (a speech act of contrition), then very briefly go over the literature itself and possible political pitfalls both in the literature and actual acts of state-to-many and many-to-many apologies, the latter being a rarity itself. Secondly, I will also revisit the context and text of the Turkish intellectuals' *I Apologize* campaign to position and analyze it within the parameters of the present literature on apologies. I argue that although the *I Apologize*

---

6   Nick Smith, *I Was Wrong: The Meanings of Apologies* (Cambridge: Cambridge University Press, 2008), 2.

campaign is a move in the right direction for changing the lens[7] of society by informing the public sphere of the necessity for recognizing that there is something grave to apologize for[8], it falls short in too many aspects to be considered a successful apology that would lead to conciliation[9]. I also claim that the passive, unclear and negotiationist language of the text makes it more of an *apologia* in the old sense of word rather than an apology. While doing so I problematize the one-sided, top-down elitist/Jacobinist and preemptive/vertical politics of the preparation process of the "apology" text in which horizontal, large-scale deliberation clearly was lacking in at least two separate contexts: neither the necessity for nor the meaning of a personal apology, nor the wording of the text was widely discussed in the Turkish public sphere, nor were any Armenian representative organizations consulted about many issues ranging from whether they expected a personal apology to whether they approved the text of the "apology". I also posit that this preemptive public negotiation, lacking deliberative input from the offended party, is offensive itself in its re-creation of historical vertical power politics once again to the detriment of the offended party.[10] The non-

---

7   I thank Hella Dietz for the "changing the lens" metaphor she came up with during the discussions at the Political Reconciliation Workshop at the University of Konstanz.

8   This may not be a problem if one perceives apologies as repetitive performative actions to be bettered over time. In a parallel way Elazar Barkan argues in his *The Guilt of Nations: Restitution and Negotiating Historical Injustices* (New York: Norton, 2000), xxix: "An apology doesn't mean the dispute is resolved, but it is in most cases a first step, part of the process of negotiation but not the satisfactory end result. Often, lack of apologies, demands for apologies, and the refusal of them all are pre-steps in negotiations, a diplomatic dance that may last for a while, a testimony to the wish and the need of both sides to reach the negotiations stage."

9   I use the term conciliation instead of reconciliation in this context. Turks and Armenians never dealt with equal terms neither during Ottoman nor Republican times. The period leading to genocide recognition and post recognition will be the first where they will overcome animosity, hence conciliate.

10 Aaron Lazare dedicated Chapter 10 of *On Apology* (Oxford: Oxford University Press, 2005), 205-227, to the complex negotiation process between the offended and the offender before the actual apology gets publicized.

deliberated public nature of the apology is offensive in the present because if the offended party does not accept the apology, it will look non-cooperative and hostile. I finally argue that Armenians as a party not only disappeared from the historiography and the land itself but also from what should have been a non-preemptive, *dialogical* process of apology.

APOLOGIES IN PROCESSES OF (RE-)CONCILIATION

Apologia or Apology?

Most of the introductory courses in Western philosophy start with Plato's Apology – a philosophical work in which Socrates could not be farther from being apologetic, as the term has come to be understood later. Instead he provides an *apologia* as was customary in the classical Greek system in rebuttal to the prosecution's accusations. Its Greek root *apologos* means a story, from which *apologia*, an oral or written defense, will emerge and later be transformed into what we know as apology today. The *Oxford English Dictionary*[11] omits any reference to *apologos* as a story and begins from the Greek *apoloyia* (*apo*, away, off; *loyia*, speaking), which is defined as a defense or speech in defense. As we understand the term now, an apology is an encounter between two parties, the offender and the offended, where the offender acknowledges responsibility for an offense or grievance and expresses regret or remorse to the aggrieved party. There is an overall tendency, well studied by the literature, to confuse an apology with a perfunctory "sorry about that", which is merely a compassionate or empathetic expression where there is no offender or offended in the classical sense and, hence, no necessity for the acknowledgment of grievances.

The present literature dealing with political, philosophical, linguistic, as well as psychological issues related to apologies, mostly refers to the two works of Tavuchis and Lazare, and takes the following criteria as the basis of a successful apology:[12]

---

11 *Oxford English Dictionary*, 2nd ed., 20 vols. (Oxford: Oxford University Press, 1989).
12 Nicholas Tavuchis, *Mea Culpa: A Sociology of Apology and Reconciliation* (Stanford: Stanford University Press, 1991); Smith, *I Was Wrong*; Lazare, *On*

- Explanation of the offense
- Expression of shame/guilt/humility/sincerity
- Intention not to commit the offense again
- Reparations to the offended party

The first three are the standard criteria for a successful apology and the last criterion becomes all the more significant in proportion to the extent of the crime/offense. Nick Smith took the existing literature a step further and came up with several other criteria for a categorical apology in order to distinguish it from non-categorical apologies. For Smith, a categorical apology consists of the following:

- Corroboration of Factual Record
- Acceptance of Blame
- Possession of Appropriate Standing
- Identification of Each Harm
- Identification of the Moral Principles Underlying Each Harm
- Shared Commitment to Moral Principles Underlying Each Harm
- Recognition of Victim as Moral Interlocutor
- Categorical Regret
- Performance of Apology
- Reform and Redress
- Intentions for Apologizing
- Emotions[13]

Apology; Barkan, *The Guilt of Nations*; Elazar Barkan and Alexander Karn, *Taking Wrongs Seriously: Apologies and Reconciliation* (Stanford: Stanford University Press, 2006); *The Age of Apology: Facing Up to Past*, ed. Marc Gibney et al. (Pennsylvania: University of Pennsylvania Press, 2008); Danielle Celermajer, *The Sins of Nations and the Rituals of Apology* (Cambridge: Cambridge University Press, 2009); Roy Brooks, *When Sorry Isn't Enough: The Controversy over Apologies and Reparations for Human Injustice* (New York: New York University Press, 1999).

13 Smith, *I Was Wrong*, 28-108. Smith's work is not just limited to identifying categorical apologies and differentiating them from the non-categorical kind, he is also interested in the varieties of meanings that even non-categorical apologies transmit.

Hence, issues of linguistic and intentional clarity are paramount for a successful apology. A sentence such as "I apologize for whatever I may have done" is not an apology since it fails to acknowledge the offense; indeed, the offender may not even believe that an offense was committed. Similarly, what is called a conditional apology, i.e., "if you were hurt, I am sorry", is not an apology at all, because the implication is that perhaps it's the aggrieved party's sensitivity that is the problem. Another often cited example to illustrate the problems of an unclear language is President Nixon's resignation speech (1974) where he deeply regretted *any* injuries that may have been caused, or Senator Robert Packwood's "apology" for "alleged" offenses of sexually abusing female pages (1992). According to Aaron Lazare, "both failed to acknowledge definitively what the public believed to be true, thus insulting the intelligence of their respective audiences".[14] Although measuring sincerity is difficult in any given situation, with apologies the issue is not only vagueness but also sincerity. One also has to understand that it is possible to deliver a sincere but unsuccessful apology; hence, despite the fact that sincerity has been cited as one of the emotional components of a successful apology it is not indicative of success on its own.

Politics of Apologies

State, as well as non-state apologies from many-to-many, have proliferated especially since 1995[15] to the point where the Catholic Church had issued ninety-four apologies by 1998.[16] As Elazar Barkan pointed out, in the same period "questions of morality and justice" started to receive "growing attention as political questions. As such, the need for restitution to past victims has become a major part of national politics and international diplomacy".[17]

The literature dealing with institutional or state apologies for gross violations of human rights has grown tremendously within the last forty years,

---

14 Lazare, *On Apology*, 8-9.
15 Gibney et al., *The Age of Apology*, 2.
16 Ibid., 3. Not all of these apologies were directed towards the immediate victims themselves but "were apologies to God for the way the Church, or members of the Church, had behaved".
17 Barkan, *The Guilt of Nations*, xvi.

but more so since the Canadian government's official apology to their native citizens in 2008. It can be said that civil rights politics in the United States and Europe along with the continental institutional commitments of the post-Holocaust world gave way to a new wave of movements, both domestic and international, which tried to limit the way the powerful operated vis-à-vis the powerless.[18] Perhaps the apology of Queen Elizabeth II (1995) and of Jenny Shipley, the Prime Minister of New Zealand to the Maori people (1998) or Australian Prime Minister Kevin Rudd's recent apology "for the past wrongs caused by successive governments on the indigenous Aboriginal population"[19] (2008) have been informed by a world order more concerned about institutional impunity. It seems that "the problem of impunity became more and more of an issue, not only to new states but also to those still burdened by their colonial and world war pasts".[20] Or perhaps, scholars in memory studies as well as some victims of injustice are right in their suspicions of the usefulness of apologies themselves or the sincerity of several of these reconciliation policies in the 1990s. McLaughlin for example calls official apologies "symbolic and meaningless gestures made by leaders who have no intention of avoiding similar acts in the future".[21] Janna Thompson also refers to Aboriginal leader Patrick Dodson who thinks that "the only meaningful act an Australian government could perform is to guarantee the rights of indigenous Australians in the Australian Constitution". Thompson also reports that other Aboriginal leaders are highly critical of apologies they believe to be only a feel-good process for the apologizers that does nothing concrete to solve the issues of their communities.

---

18 Jean-Marc Coicaud and Jibecke Jönsson, Elements of a Road Map for a Politics of Apology, in: *The Age of Apology*, 77-93. Coicaud and Jönsson also mention the Latin American shift from dictatorships to democracies and several other regions, post-Soviet republics and African countries in transition that underwent significant institutional transformation in the years following the end of the Cold War.

19 Australia apology to Aborigines, 13 February 2008, http://news.bbc.co.uk/2/hi/7241965.stm.

20 Coicaud and Jönsson, Elements, 82.

21 Martin McLaughlin, Blair and the Potato Famine, *Socialist Equality*, 14 June 1997, quoted in: Janna Thompson, Apology, Justice, and Respect: A Critical Defense of Political Apology, in: *The Age of Apology*, 31-44, here: 32.

This is in line with Gibney and Roxstrom who criticize the West's highly selective and very ambiguous apologies mostly devised with an eye on preserving the international status quo.[22] De Laforcade also "notes that slavery memorial day, ironically, became an occasion for self-praise rather than for self-criticism since the commemorations focus on 'enlightened values, generosity of French liberals in 1830' rather than anti-colonial revolts and resistance movements in the Antilles",[23] and he suggests that by "declaring slavery 'a crime against humanity', legislators intended to divert migrant public opinion from measures against contemporary issues of discrimination".[24] Karen E. Till similarly argues that the commemoration of the abolition of slavery "positions France as a moral leader in a global order with 'good' nations acknowledging past actions. As tied to a neo-liberal agenda, acknowledging past crimes against humanity locates that legacy *in the past, not the present*, even in the face of stark anti-immigration laws and militant government responses to student and minority social unrest."[25] In a similar critical vein, after revisiting several selective political apologies Jenna Thompson argues that "political leaders are willing to apologize only when they think that there will be no serious political or legal repercussions".[26]

Political scientists have generally been less interested in apologies than philosophers, sociologists, linguists and anthropologists, perhaps because what state-to-state or state-to-many apologies achieve institutionally is not very clear. But although one can be conflicted about the meaning or function of collective apologies and acknowledge the validity of critiques of political apologies as diversions or fig leaves for regime crimes, especially if not accompanied with retributive and/or restorative justice measures, at the

---

22 Mark Gibney and Erik Roxstrom, The Status of State Apologies, *Human Rights Quarterly* 23, 4 (2001), 911-939. Accordingly, the West "wants credit for recognizing and acknowledging a wrong against others, but it also wants the world to remain exactly as it had been before the apology was issued".
23 Geoffrey De Laforcade, 'Foreigners', Nationalism and the 'Colonial Fracture': Stigmatized Subjects of Historical Memory in France, *International Journal of Comparative Sociology* 47, 3-4 (2006), 217-233, here: 229.
24 Ibid.
25 Karen E. Till, Memory Studies, *History Workshop Journal* 62, 1 (2006), 325-341, here: 339.
26 Thompson, Apology, 31.

same time one can see the existence (or in some cases the non-existence) of formal and informal political apologies as indicative of the direction of the normative commitments of the society in question.

As Nicholas Tavuchis argues in his path-breaking work *Mea Culpa*, "apologies [...] are potentially sensitive indicators of members' (and non-members') actual, if unspoken, moral orientations". Secondly, "as symbolic barometers, apologies register tensions and displacements in personal and public belief systems, that is, the contraction and expansion of interdictory motifs – what calls for an apology and what does not – that either precede or follow changes in social behavior and cultural expectations".[27] "We not only apologize *to* someone but also *for* something. The analytical focus of the former is on actors, agents, and social relationships; the latter, by contrast, directs attention to rules and meta-rules, that is, rules about the rules."[28]

In a parallel vein, the domestic and international demands of recognition have changed the way liberal theory classically thought about the social goods that the individual needed. Social recognition of present subaltern identities and the recognition of past sufferings were added to the traditional list until then headed by equality and liberty.[29] This also generated a critical discussion that exposed the Christian core of the politics of apology and made the parties more sensitive to local concepts, such as *ubuntu*, "which emphasizes restorative justice, including restored relations between perpetrators and victims, over retributive justice".[30] This was a novelty in the way the West positioned itself and its previously unchallenged and Eurocentric claims for truth.

Overall, it is not clear exactly what apologies accomplish in international or domestic politics or what other considerations within the domain of *realpolitik* make apologies necessary, not for their intrinsic value as sincere acts of contrition, but more for their value as one in a stash of self-

---

27 Tavuchis, *Mea Culpa*, 13.
28 Ibid.
29 For the new politics of recognition of "others" and minorities, see Michael Freeman, Historical Injustice and Liberal Political Theory, in: *The Age of Apology*, 45-60.
30 Rhoda E. Howard-Hassmann and Mark Gibney, Introduction: Apologies and the West, in: *The Age of Apology*, 2-6, here: 5.

serving diplomatic moves. Leonard Jamfa brings to our attention such a possible calculus behind the German statement of apology for the 1905-1908 genocide of the Herero people of Namibia, for example, and correlates the apology to the German fear of possible land invasions of white farms in Namibia akin to those in Mugabe's Zimbabwe.[31] This rather vigilant way of reading the process and the context of apology, without reducing it to the text, is one of the reasons why apology cases need to be approached not only from within a linguistic or philosophical framework but also from a political and economic perspective and calculus of *realpolitik*.

Notwithstanding an apology's timing and considerations of the political context in which the statement is written, apologies also are relevant to political theory since they lead to questions of membership in a community and responsibility stemming from such membership, i.e., citizenship. Besides, present apologies for injustices that happened in the recent or distant past are relevant for the domestic and international debates on institutional continuity and path dependency, and normative commitments and responsibilities of polities living in the present. What makes present political communities, whose members also may or may not include formally disenfranchised or discriminated-against citizens, responsible for past acts of transgression, for example? These discussions are not merely futile attempts at restoring what is perhaps impossible to restore. They also hint at possible ways of re-imagining domestic as well as international politics. For example, the debate within the Netherlands or Belgium regarding apologies to the peoples of their former colonies informs us about what is legitimate for future international endeavors of both countries since the political spectrum is divided between those who think that colonialism was beneficial – hence there is nothing to apologize for – and those who think that colonialism's detrimental effects far exceeded its benefits. In that sense, the politics of apology is another political issue mirroring the divide between the liberals and conservatives of almost any given country. Bearing these considerations in mind, I will proceed to examine both the official and non-official responses to the Turkish *I Apologize* campaign in an effort to contextualize and position it within the larger domain of Turkish politics and its actors.

---

31 Leonard Jamfa, Germany Faces Colonial History in Namibia: A Very Ambiguous "I am Sorry", in: *The Age of Apology*, 202-215, here: 206.

The I Apologize Campaign of Turkish Intellectuals

There has been an increase in the frequency of the usage of the term Genocide in the Turkish media and in the general coverage of the events of 1915[32] especially since the assassination of *Agos* newspaper's editor-in-chief Hrant Dink in January 2007. Yet the Armenian Genocide is still largely seen as a security issue and foreign policy obstacle to be brushed aside. As a result, a genuine intellectual quest to understand what genocide means for the Turkish state's institutional framework *and* the grammar of ethnic relations in Turkey is lacking. Thus, it is not surprising that current or former ambassadors are viewed as legitimate parties to the discussion; such was also in the discussions leading to the *I apologize* campaign. In an interview given to *Taraf*'s Neşe Düzel approximately three months before the Turkish intellectuals' "apology" campaign took off, and shortly after Turkish President Abdullah Gül's visit to Yerevan in the course of a series of events initiated by Armenian President Serge Sarkisian commonly referred to as 'soccer diplomacy',[33] Turkish former ambassador Volkan Vural clearly expressed the need for the state to apologize to Armenians.[34]

Thus, it is against this background of increased debate that the "apology" campaign launched by four scholars, Ali Bayramoğlu, Cengiz Aktar, Ahmet İnsel, and Baskın Oran, in December 2008 should be understood. The text of the campaign was translated as follows:

"My conscience does not accept the insensitivity showed to and the denial of the Great Catastrophe that the Ottoman Armenians were subjected to in 1915. I reject

---

[32] For a non-exhaustive coverage of the subject from year 2000 to 2011, see http://hyetert.blogspot.com/.

[33] For an extensive coverage of this particular process see Khatchig Mouradian, Soccer Diplomacy and the Road not Taken: An Alternative Perspective for building piece between Turkey and Armenians, ZNET, 13 April 2009, http://www.zcommunications.org/soccer-diplomacy-and-the-road-not-taken-by-khatchig-mouradian.

[34] Neşe Düzel, Volkan Vural: 'Ermeni ve Rumlar tekrar vatandaş olsun', *Taraf*, 9 August 2008, http://www.taraf.com.tr/nese-duzel/makale-volkan-vural-ermeni-ve-rumlar-tekrar-vatandas.htm#.

this injustice and for my share, I empathize with the feelings and pain of my Armenian brothers and sisters. I apologize to them."[35]

The first newspaper that broke the news of the campaign was the centerright *Vatan* via an interview with Cengiz Aktar, on December 3, 2008.[36] Nergis TV station (NTV) followed with the actual text of the apology on December 5, 2008,[37] and slowly all other major news outlets picked up the following week. The moderate Islamist *Zaman*, the highest circulating newspaper in Turkey did not cover the story until December 16, whereas its English edition *Today's Zaman* started to cover ten days earlier.[38]

The organizers first announced on NTV and other outlets their plan to launch the campaign via internet at the beginning of 2009 so that citizens could join them.[39] However, the online campaign began three weeks earlier than had been originally announced. Coincidentally, intellectuals from Armenia sent a letter to President Abdullah Gül on December 9, urging him to recognize the Armenian Genocide.[40] This letter was lost in the shuffle and largely ignored by the international and Turkish press. Addressing the Turkish President, the Armenian intellectuals challenged Ankara's vehement denial of any government policy to exterminate Ottoman Turkey's Armenian population:

"[…] here we deal with an appalling crime perpetrated against humanity which has no expiration date. This is not only a position held by all Armenians, but also an expectation shared by the World community. The Armenian Genocide is a crime

---

35 Özür diliyorum, http://www.ozurdiliyoruz.com/default.aspx.
36 Tülay Şubatlı, 'Ermenilerden özür diliyorum' Aydınlar, 1915'teki Ermeni tehciriyle ilgili imza kampanyası başlatıyor," *Vatan*, 3 December 2008, http://haber.gazetevatan.com/Haber/211898/1/Gundem.
37 Apology campaign of intellectuals for the Armenian deportation, http://arsiv.ntvmsnbc.com/news/468300.asp.
38 Ayşe Karabat, Turkish intellectuals give personal apology for 1915 events, *Today's Zaman*, 5 December 2008, http://www.todayszaman.com/news-160701-turkish-intellectuals-give-personal-apology-for-1915-events.html.
39 Apology campaign of intellectuals for the Armenian deportation.
40 For the full text of the Armenian intellectuals see: Open Letter to Abdullah Gül, http://asbarez.com/59724/open-letter-to-abdullah-gul/.

against humanity and against the values of modern civilization, and no individual, organization or even government can put a question mark on these events."

The letter further claimed that "[…] today's Turkish state has inherited this responsibility" and "[…] Your generation of Turkish leaders must accept the undeniable truth and recognize the fact of the Armenian Genocide […] Only then will both our nations be able to pursue a frank dialogue and achieve the true reconciliation so much desired."[41] This letter was particularly significant since it originated from Armenia and was an indirect response to the long-standing cliché that genocide recognition was important only for Diaspora Armenians, not for Armenians from Armenia.

In effect, by enlarging the scope of the campaign earlier than had been announced, the organizers of the campaign successfully, if not necessarily intentionally, blocked the Armenian text and the demand of the offended party. The historically powerless side's voice – the voice of those to whom the *I apologize* campaign was ostensibly directed – was thus muffled, and the historically asymmetrical character of the Turkish-Armenian relationship, itself a result of the Genocide, reasserted itself.[42]

The apology campaign led into a major backlash in Turkey – one that was hardly unexpected by those conversant with Turkish politics, but one that nonetheless went underreported in the international press or Turkish press in English: two major websites backed by several groups from the Turkish Republican left, center and the right appeared almost overnight, leaving the optimistic 13,000 number of the earlier days of the apology campaign pale in comparison.[43] At the same time, although the campaign

---

41 Ibid.

42 The letter was covered as short news by NTV website, Evrensel newspaper (Left), and Yeniçağ newspaper (Right), but completely ignored by mainstream news outlets, columnists and journalists alike, including the apology campaign organizers themselves.

43 As of September 19, 2011 anti-apology websites *özür bekliyorum* (Iamexpecting anapology.com) has 201,142 (http://www.ozurbekliyorum.com), *özür dilemiyoruz* (Wedonotapologize.biz) that also carries the public endorsement of main opposition party deputies has 87344 signatures (http://www.ozurdilemiyoruz.biz/index2.php). The main site of the *I Apologize* campaign *özür diliyorum* (weapologize.com) has 31003 signatures (http://www.ozurdiliyoruz.com/default.aspx).

organizers, among them Cengiz Aktar[44] and Baskın Oran,[45] and various other participants and journalists[46] reiterated that the apology was not for the genocide itself nor, technically speaking, for genocide denial per se, news outlets in English and French reported it as Turkish intellectuals "apologizing for the Armenian Genocide".[47] Nonetheless, on no occasion did the initiators of the campaign[48] offer a correction to this (mis)interpretation of the apology in effect, allowing this misunderstanding to flourish among audiences who would be receptive to such a (mis)reading. In this manner, the apology authors were frequently "credited" with apologizing

---

44 Tülay Şubatlı, 'Ermenilerden özür diliyorum', *Vatan*, 3 December 2008.

45 Baskın Oran, Verdiğimiz huzursuzluk için özür dileriz, *Radikal*, 16 December 2008, http://www.radikal.com.tr/Radikal.aspx?aType=RadikalEklerDetayV3&ArticleID=912867&Date=16.12.2008&CategoryID=42.

46 See Hadi Uluengin who vehemently argued that Great Catastrophe does not and cannot mean genocide. Hadi Uluengin, Özür ve imza, *Hürriyet*, 24 December 2008, http://hurarsiv.hurriyet.com.tr/goster/haber.aspx?id=10633079&p=2.

47 Robert Tait, Writers risk backlash with apology for Armenian genocide, *The Guardian*, 7 December 2008, http://www.guardian.co.uk/world/2008/dec/08/armenian-genocide-turkey-apology-petition.

48 See for example *Le Monde* coverage and its language equating "Grand Catastrophe" to Genocide. Des intellectuels turcs demandent pardon à l'Arménie, *Le Monde*, 20 December 2008 (http://www.lemonde.fr/web/recherche_breve/1,13-0,37-1063162,0.html) and another longer *Le Monde* piece aggregated by the website CollectifVan. Réveil des consciences, *Le Monde*, 19 December 2008 (http://www.collectifvan.org/article.php?r=4&id=24972). *Guardian* oscillated between alleged genocide and genocide, BBC Monitoring Europe did not use the term since it mostly translated and covered Turkish newspapers, which avoided the term. *The New Zealand Herald* was the only news outlet that got the avoidance of the term genocide correctly. See: Turkish Intellectuals Issue Apology for Past Atrocities Against Armenians, http://www.armeniandiaspora.com/showthread.php?154411-Turkish-Intellectuals-Issue-Apology-For-Past-Atrocities-Against-Arme#.TngVrnN3E5s. *The Independent* used genocide and ethnic cleansing interchangeably. Nicholas Birch, Turkish academics in apology to Armenians, *The Independent*, 15 December 2008, http://www.independent.co.uk/news/world/europe/turkish-academics-in-apology-to-armenians1067066.html.

for something which they explicitly stated elsewhere that they were not apologizing for.

I Apologize also received both official and unofficial reactions from the Turkish political elite, journalists and larger public alike. While it is impossible to give a full account of all unofficial reactions, an extensive coverage of several positions both for and against the apology among its endorsers and critics is paramount to understand the scope and variety of these arguments. It is also necessary to be able to soundly contextualize the endeavor and elaborate on the politics of both the text *and* the process leading to and following the campaign.

Official Reactions

The official reaction to the campaign was initially mixed. Prime Minister Recep Tayyip Erdoğan categorically rejected the idea of contemporary citizens apologizing for past deeds, whereas President Abdullah Gül did not condemn the campaign and framed it as an issue of citizens exercising their freedom of speech.

Although President Gül's reaction would change in the week following his press conference due to pressure and personal attacks from the main opposition party and its deputies, his approach to the campaign was more accommodating than the Prime Minister's. Gül[49] viewed the campaign as a sign of freedom of expression in Turkey along with the Ministry of Foreign Affairs that viewed both the apology and the counter apology campaigns launched by retired diplomats and others asking an apology from Armenians as part of the lawful exercise of freedom of speech.[50]

The main opposition Republican People's Party (CHP) condemned the campaign claiming that it was the Armenian side that needed to apologize for siding with and supporting a foreign country against Ottoman Empire,

---

49 Ayşe Karabat, Apology campaign triggers fierce debate, *Today's Zaman*, 18 December 2008, http://www.todayszaman.com/news-161594-apologycampaign-triggers-fierce-debate.html.

50 Turkish Foreign Affairs views apology campaign for "1915 incidents" as part of freedom of speech, *Today's Zaman*, 17 December 2008, http://www.todayszaman.com/news-161530-turkish-foreign-affairs-views-apology-campaign-for-1915-incidents-as-part-of-freedom-of-speech.html.

for massacring thousands of Azeri citizens and "for not persecuting or punishing ASALA terrorists who assassinated Turkish diplomats".[51] In the same week, CHP deputy Canan Arıtman besides calling the organizers of the campaign as traitors and asking for an apology for their deeds, also claimed that President Gül had not reacted negatively to the campaign because of his Armenian ancestry,[52] a claim President Gül would deny and later take to court. The leader of the second opposition party in the parliament, the ultra-nationalist Nationalist Action Party (MHP), Devlet Bahçeli, along with several other prominent figures from the party condemned the apology campaign along the same lines as CHP members.[53]

Two weeks into the apology campaign, the Turkish military also expressed its opinion during a General Staff meeting. General Staff Director of Communications Brigadier General Metin Gürak said: "We absolutely do not find the campaign right. Not only is apologizing wrong, it could also lead to detrimental results."[54]

In the same week, the Pro-Kurdish Democratic Society Party's (DTP) objected to a joint condemnation statement by CHP and MHP, and as a result deputies decided to issue condemnation notes on an individual basis. DTP deputy Sırrı Sakık supported the apology campaign further and argued that "the state's confrontation with its history would not be the end of the

---

51 Turkey's Main Opposition Party Condemns Apology Campaign For "1915 Incidents", 17 December 2008, http://www.turkishpress.com/news.asp?id=255909.
52 Ayşe Karabat, Critics of apology campaign turn to personal attacks, *Today's Zaman*, 19 December 2008, http://www.todayszaman.com/news-161691-critics-of-apology-campaign-turn-to-personal-attacks.html.
53 Bahçeli: Onlardan utanıyorum, 18 December 2008, http://hurarsiv.hurriyet.com.tr/goster/ShowNew.aspx?id=10594801; E.Bariş Altıntaş and Ercan Yavuz, Nationalists react to intellectuals' courageous apology, *Today's Zaman*, 6 December 2008, http://www.todayszaman.com/news-160813-nationalists-react-to-intellectuals-courageous-apology.html.
54 TSK: Ermeniler'den özür dilemek doğru değil, 19 December 2008, http://yenisafak.com.tr/Gundem/?t=19.12.2008&i=157194. For a critique of military's involvement in a civilian initiative see: Cengiz Çandar, Genelkurmay, sivil bireyler ve Ermeni tabusu..., *Hürriyet*, 20 December 2008, http://hurarsiv.hurriyet.com.tr/goster/ShowNew.aspx?id=10609505.

world".[55] Still, the main opposition MHP went ahead and issued a condemnation note later signed by the ruling Justice and Development Party (AKP) and CHP representatives.[56]

Canan Arıtman's personal attack on President Gül led to a massive reaction even from center rightist newspapers. Fatma Dişli Zıbak of *Today's Zaman* summarized the mainstream reactions both from center right and center left in her column under the title "Deputy's 'Fascist' Remarks Met with Criticism". Center-right journalist Ahmet Taşgetiren of *Bugün*, despite his disapproval of the apology campaign, argued: "What she (Canan Arıtman) said about Gül is very ugly and disgraceful. Even if Gül has Armenian origins, presenting this as a very negative feature could only be the reflection of a fascist mentality."[57] In spite of such support in the press, President Gül found it necessary to clarify that his family's roots were Muslim and Turkish for centuries.[58] Furthermore, the President took Arıtman to court where she was charged with "denigrating the reputation of a public persona".[59] A number of European deputies including Hannes Swoboda and Jan Marinus Wiersma, the two vice chairmen of the Socialist Group in the European Parliament, along with Joost Lagendijk, the Co-Chairman of EU-Turkey Joint Parliamentary Committee also harshly criticized both Arıtman and her party.[60]

By December 20 the earlier milder position of the Ministry of Foreign Affairs changed with Foreign Minister Ali Babacan claiming in Brussels

---

55 Press Roundup, *Today's Zaman*, 20 December 2008, http://www.todayszaman.com/news-161741-press-roundup.html.
56 MHP'den özür kampanyasına karşı bildiri, 18 December 2008, http://hurarsiv.hurriyet.com.tr/goster/ShowNew.aspx?id=10597947.
57 Fatma Dişli Zıbak, Deputy's 'fascist' remarks met with criticism, *Today's Zaman*, 20 December 2008, http://www.todayszaman.com/columnistDetail_getNewsById.action?newsId=161748.
58 Gül Arıtman'a cevap verdi, 21 December 2008, http://hurarsiv.hurriyet.com.tr/goster/ShowNew.aspx?id=10615884.
59 Cumhurbaşkanı Gül'den Arıtman'a dava, 22 December 2008, http://arsiv.ntvmsnbc.com/news/469808.asp.
60 Selçuk Gültaşlı, Arıtman should apologize or resign, say European leaders, *Today's Zaman*, 25 December 2008, http://www.todayszaman.com/news-162236-aritman-should-apologize-or-resign-say-european-leaders.html.

that the campaign may "negatively affect the Turkish-Armenian dialogue".[61] Indeed Gül's position also changed over the course of the month of December. In an interview he gave to *Aktüel* TV station (ATV) and *Today's Zaman* during the first week of January 2009, Gül said: "To be honest, it will affect the process negatively. Looking at the consequences and the latest debates, I don't think that it has made a positive contribution." While Gül insisted on freedom of speech, he nonetheless warned that the polarization that the campaign had triggered had brought negative consequences.[62] President Gül himself was criticized by CHP Parliamentary leader Hakkı Süha Okay for filing a symbolic 1 New Turkish Lira (YTL) lawsuit against Arıtman. Okay said that "[f]iling this lawsuit is an injustice to our citizens of Armenian roots", explaining that it implied that the president regards "Armenian ethnicity" as an insult. Emphasizing that "everyone's roots deserve respect", he added that Arıtman's words lacked "class", but that the president's action was inappropriate.[63]

Semi Official Reactions

As previously stated, former Turkish ambassadors hold a special position on the discussions of the Armenian Genocide because of the linkage between state security and foreign policy. In fact, the first organized non-official reaction came from retired ambassadors of Turkey, some of whom were actively on duty during the period of Armenian Secret Army for the Liberation of Armenia (ASALA) activity. But there were differences of opinion among retired ambassadors: for example, retired ambassador Temel İskit supported the apology campaign whereas ambassadors Şükrü Elekdağ and Korkmaz Haktanır were not only against the apology; they al-

---

61 Ayşe Karabat, State says 'no' to apology campaign, *Today's Zaman*, 20 December 2008, http://www.todayszaman.com/news-161807-state-says-no-to-apology-campaign.html.

62 Yavuz Baydar and Fuat Uğur, Gül says apology campaign hurts Armenia reconciliation bid, *Today's Zaman*, 2 January 2009, http://www.todayszaman.com/newsDetail_getNewsById.action?load=detay&link=162971.

63 CHP members react to racist remarks despite party inaction, 25 December 2008, http://www.todayszaman.com/news-162237-chp-members-react-to-racist-remarks-despite-party-inaction.html.

so were among those who started a counter declaration.[64] The group who came out against the campaign included former Foreign Ministry undersecretaries Korkmaz Haktanır, Şükrü Elekdağ and Onur Öymen,[65] who labeled the campaign "against Turkish national interests". In a public letter, the ambassadors repeated the CHP and MHP line, further linked the issue to the Nagorno Karabagh conflict and stated that Armenians should apologize.[66]

One-time Minister of Education, now columnist for *Radikal* newspaper, right-conservative Hasan Celal Güzel claimed that "this traitorous text, which includes the expression 'great catastrophe' in capital letters and has captured the signatures of some of our spineless intellectuals, hands everything over to those who prepared the text. Even the title of this text is perceived by both the diaspora and Armenia itself as a reference to 'genocide'. In other words, those who signed this traitorous text, no matter what they may insist on, are in fact accepting the allegations of genocide."[67]

Non Official Reactions

The non-official reactions can be categorized as protesters (left and right), supporters with reservations, and supporters.

Protesters

The State-Employees Union (*Memur-Sen*) and Public Employees Union (*Kamu-Sen*) protested the campaign, asking for an apology from Armenians for ASALA and "the Azerbaijan territory that is still under occupation". In

---

64 Abdülhamit Bilici, Let us set up our own historical committee independently of Armenians, *Today's Zaman*, 20 December 2008, http://www.todayszaman.com/columnistDetail_getNewsById.action?newsId=161764.
65 Ayşe Karabat, Apology campaign triggers fierce debate, *Today's Zaman*, 18 December 2008.
66 Zeynep Gürcanlı, Büyükelçiler isyan etti, *Hürriyet*, 15 December 2008, http://hurarsiv.hurriyet.com.tr/goster/ShowNew.aspx?id=10574633.
67 Hasan Celal Güzel, If you're all intellectuals, I guess I'm not!, *Today's Zaman*, 19 December 2008, http://www.todayszaman.com/news-161627-if-youre-all-intellectuals-i-guess-im-not.html.

a statement on behalf of a platform comprised of ninety-six labor and trade organizations, including Ankara Trade Chamber (ATO), Union of Agriculturalists and Turkey Workers Union (*Türk-İş*), Bircan Akyıldız, the leader of *Kamu-Sen* said: "Turkish Republic is always under attack openly or indirectly by cooperatives who have been sold." Atatürk University's senate not only opposed the campaign but also the president of the university read a statement that condemned the campaign as a "disrespectful act against the Turkish nation" betraying "our martyrs who lost their lives in Armenian terror".[68]

Although the apology text was signed by almost thirty thousand citizens, including two hundred academics and journalists in the first two months, there were prominent intellectuals on the left who refrained from signing the text. Some of these intellectuals withheld the reasons why they did not sign, but some spoke out early on and criticized either the endeavor, or the text, or both.[69] There also were instances of intellectuals critiquing the endeavor after having heard some of the campaign organizers' denialist public speeches.[70]

The coordinator of the Association for Facing History Aytekin Yıldız, criticized the campaign on three grounds: that the campaign was redundant in the sense that Armenians were aware that there were people of conscience in Turkey. Secondly, while admitting the campaign was a good start, Yıldız criticized usage of *Medz Yeghern* as "great disaster": "What do

---

68 Ayşe Karabat, State says 'no' to apology campaign, *Today's Zaman*, 20 December 2008.
69 One of those intellectuals is Ismail Besikci, "Büyük Felaket" mi, Soykırım mı?, 22 December 2008, http://www.gelawej.net/modules.php?name=Content&pa=showpage&pid=2711.
70 For Ragip Zarakolu's critique of Baskin Oran's populist denialist language see Özür o kadar kolay değil, *Özgür Gündem*, 12 February 2009, http://www.hyetert.com/yazi3.asp?s=&Id=394&DilId=1#.

they mean by 'great disaster'? Let's name it, it is genocide."[71] Finally, Yıldız also emphasized the fact that the state had to apologize.[72]

Historian Ayşe Hür, known for her work in popularizing the history of 1915 in newspaper articles, refused to sign the apology, criticizing both the idea and the implementation as elitist.[73] Hür also wrote a newspaper column, "I Apologize for not Apologizing", where she further clarified her position towards the apology campaign, explaining why she refused to apologize for the faults of Turkish nationalism with which she does not identify.[74]

Ismail Beşikci,[75] one of the most important figures in recent Turkish intellectual history with his pioneering research and discourse on the Kurdish issue, and a group of Kurdish intellectuals explicitly criticized the vague choice of wording in the apology and the problematic usage of the term Great Catastrophe.[76] These intellectuals signed a joint declaration explaining the reasons why the apology campaign falls short trying to satisfy several constituencies, including the state. Beşikci, while criticizing the campaign organizers' utilitarian calculus, said: "You can collect more signatures when you use a term such as 'Great Catastrophe' in order not to disturb the state. However, correctly understanding the content of factual connections is more precious than this. Quality (of the debate) must be more precious than the quantity (of the signers)."[77] In the same piece Beşikci also criticized the organizers for not referring to the "1915 Genocide against As-

---

71 At the initial stages of the "apology" campaign there were different translations for the term *Medz Yeghern*, here Aytekin Yıldız, is referring to one of them. See page 83 et seq. of this chapter for further information on the reactions to the usage of *Medz Yeghern*.

72 Ayşe Karabat, Turkish intellectuals give personal apology for 1915 events, *Today's Zaman*, 5 December 2008.

73 Ibid.

74 Ayşe Hür, I Apologize for Not Apologizing, *Armenian Weekly*, 20 April 2009, http://www.armenianweekly.com/2009/04/20/i-apologize-for-not-apologizing.

75 Ismail Besikci, "Büyük Felaket" mi, Soykırım mı?

76 Ortak Açıklama; Felaket Değil Soykırım, 26 December 2008, http://www.nasname.com/tr/2464.html.

77 Ismail Besikci, "Büyük Felaket" mi, Soykırım mı?

syrians, to the genocide against Kurds spread over time, and to the cultural and religious genocide against Alevis".[78]

In a lengthy article published in the popular news magazine *Aksiyon*, Taner Akçam, besides criticizing the close-ended character of the apology text and problematizing the issue of political responsibility like Hür and others, also criticized the avoidance of the term Genocide within the campaign by saying he found the arguments against the use of the term to be at a very low intellectual standard. While Akçam elaborately criticized the endeavour, he still found it important in its potential to start a debate on the issue and even could be considered a watershed moment for this reason alone.[79] This brings us back to the questions of what apologies are and whether this is really an apology or an *apologia* instrumentalizing the idea of apology for something else: A domestic "discussion starter" over the events of 1915 at the expense of Armenians?

Supporters with reservations

Emre Aköz of the center-right *Sabah*, Ahmet Hakan of center-right *Hürriyet* and Nuray Mert of center-left *Radikal* newspapers all agreed with the necessity communicating regret, but disagreed with the last sentence that included the actual "apology". They all claimed they found personal apology in the name of a nation politically problematic especially for something they did not take part.[80] Hakan and Mert signed the petition conditionally –

---

78 Ibid.
79 For a republished version of Akcam's article see Taner Akçam, Tartışalım ama bilgiyle, 26 December 2008, http://hyetert.blogspot.com/2008/12/tartisalim-ama-bilgiyle-prof-dr-taner.html.
80 Emre Aköz, "Özür" meselesi, *Sabah*, 11 December 2008, http://www.sabah.com.tr/Yazarlar/akoz/2008/12/11/ozur_meselesi; Center Right *Milliyet's* ex-editor in chief Mehmet Y. Yilmaz also argued along similar lines with a slightly different take asking why ordinary Turks will accept this, after all, he said, even the Holocaust is committed by Nazis and not Germans. Mehmet Y. Yılmaz, Bir rüşvet hikayesi! Muhalefet partileri nerede?, *Hürriyet*, 17 December 2008, http://hurarsiv.hurriyet.com.tr/goster/ShowNew.aspx?id=10584497.

up until the last sentence.[81] In an odd discriminatory tone Mert further reiterated a common stereotype in her column where she claimed she did not feel the necessity to apologize to well-to-do Armenians at all.[82]

Similarly, Murat Belge, a professor of English literature and one of the most prominent figures of the left, and Yıldırım Türker, columnist at the *Radikal* newspaper, also criticized the apologetic part of the apology on similar grounds to Mert, Hakan and Aköz. Belge further argued for a politically discriminatory approach to the surviving Armenians: "[...] if I am 'apologizing' or doing something else, it is neither possible nor meaningful to do this towards *all Armenians*. In the Armenian society, in the 'homeland' or in the 'Diaspora' there may be such persons that I may not even want to meet or greet, let alone apologize. Why should I apologize to an Armenian fascist because some Turks have done this act against Armenians in 1915?"[83] Türker, on the other hand, though he had initial reservations regarding the act of apologizing since this would mean his self-association with the denialists, ultimately decided to endorse it and condemned CHP parliamentarian Canan Arıtman in very strong language.

"Arıtman was not satisfied with implying that President Abdullah Gül's mother might be of Armenian descent, but she also declared Armenians are the element that should be sought after every catastrophe and be labeled our eternal enemy. Arıtman is proud. She is not only unapologetic but also brags about how many supporters she has. Is there anyone left who still doubts that this is exactly the right time for the campaign [of apology to Armenians by intellectuals] that we have been debating for a long time at a time when Arıtman and those who like her proudly commit this crime in Parliament and declare a segment of the country's population the national

---

81 Ahmet Hakan, Aferin Cem Yılmaz, *Hürriyet*, 17 December 2008, http://www.hurriyet.com.tr/yazarlar/10584434.asp?yazarid=131.
82 Nuray Mert, Özür Değil, Paylaşma, *Radikal*, 16 December 2008, http://www.radikal.com.tr/Radikal.aspx?aType=RadikalYazar&ArticleID=912950&Yazar=NURAY%20MERT&Date=16.12.2008&CategoryID=98.
83 Murat Belge, Ermeni Kıyımı üstüne metin, *Taraf*, 14 December 2008, http://www.taraf.com.tr/makale/3097.htm.

enemy, creating threats against their lives? Arıtman and those like her are the strongest reason we have to apologize to the Armenian community."[84]

While Belge (along with Aköz, Hakan, Hür and Mert) expressed legitimate concerns about the uneasy relationship between individual responsibility regarding past crimes and apologies, a tension problematized within both communitarian and liberal theory,[85] his political categorization of Armenians who *deserve* an apology as only non-fascists shows that he completely misses the point of apology and gross human rights violations which are quite different than discriminatory politicides. On the other hand, Türker's lengthy take on why they should apologize only shows the kind of anti-intellectual corner in which the Turkish liberal left is trapped: as can be clearly seen from the CHP-MHP-ex-ambassadors episode, the Turkish center and right were able to hijack the discourse and reduce the entire discussion to being pro or anti apology, without an informed and substantial debate on the kind of issues that are paramount in a dialogical process involving gross human rights violations and political responsibility.

The majority of the non-official reactions in English were published by the moderate Islamist *Today's Zaman* that has a number of non-Islamist liberal scholars and journalists as columnists. One such liberal scholar close to the ruling AKP is İhsan Dağı, an International Relations' Professor at Middle East Technical University. Dağı criticized the ultra-nationalist discourse used to justify the massacre of Armenians in the name of survival of the state then argued:

"We do not have to, and should not, accept that the 1915 events constituted genocide, but we must stop trying to find excuses for the massacres of Ottoman citizens of Armenian origin. Otherwise, we can find excuses for the suppression of the

---

84 Yıldırım Türker, What if we are all Armenian?, *Today's Zaman*, 23 December 2008, http://www.todayszaman.com/newsDetail_getNewsById.action?load=detay&link=161978&bolum=130.

85 Freeman, Historical Injustice and Liberal Political Theory.

Kurds, of Islamic dervish orders, of the girls who wear the headscarf, etc. If we allow the raison d'état to reign, then everything will be explainable and justifiable."[86]

Dağı's position is indeed important in that it shows that even individuals close to government circles do not deny the massacres but refuse to acknowledge that the massacres constitute genocide.

Another columnist close to government circles, Hüseyin Gülerce, supported the endeavor as expressing the will of citizens, something that should not be condemned as traitorous. Yet he was critical of the timing of the campaign, claiming that because of the climate of animosity it generated among the citizenry, the campaign may disrupt an otherwise successful process of rapprochement between Turkey and Armenia.[87] He also criticized the text of the campaign, asking why it was silent on the issue of Turks massacred by Armenians or the Ottoman losses in Balkans. A position claiming reciprocity of massacres that is common among Turkish conservative circles.[88]

Supporters

It will be extremely difficult to cover the arguments of all initial two hundred campaign supporters since a good number of them either in print or on

---

86 İhsan Dağı, From Apology to Reconciliation, *Today's Zaman*, 22 December 2008, http://www.todayszaman.com/columnistDetail_getNewsById.action?newsId=161892.

87 Hüseyin Gülerce, Apology is Valuable If It Works Out, *Today's Zaman*, 19 December 2008, http://www.todayszaman.com/columnistDetail_getNewsById.action?newsId=161695.

88 See the links below for a more extensive response from centre-right journalists Enis Berberoğlu, Söz kılıçtan keskin, *Hürriyet*, 20 December 2008, http://hurarsiv.hurriyet.com.tr/goster/ShowNew.aspx?id=10609508, Tufan Türenç, Gençler için bazı gerçekler, *Hürriyet*, 19 December 2008, http://hurarsiv.hurriyet.com.tr/goster/ShowNew.aspx?id=10600787, Rahmi Turan, Ağacın kurdu içinde olur, *Hürriyet*, 18 December 2008, http://hurarsiv.hurriyet.com.tr/goster/ShowNew.aspx?id=10592881, Bülent Keneş, Yes, but who will apologize to my grandmother and grandfather?, *Today's Zaman*, 17 December 2008, http://www.todayszaman.com/columnistDetail_getNewsById.action?newsId=161457.

TV defended their position. However, the following support without a signature is meaningful since it exemplifies a very common misrepresentation of both the critiques and context of the campaign.

Although he neither signed nor disclosed why he withheld his signature, Yavuz Baydar of the center-Islamist *Today's Zaman* newspaper wrote favorably about the campaign while criticizing what he called the response from Armenia and Armenian diaspora – though without making it clear which Armenian authors or organizations he had in mind:

"It is encouraging that the international press gives it broad coverage. Reactions from the West are mainly positive, though the 'response' from Armenia and the Armenian diaspora was rather scarce, mainly because of the apparent discontent over the wording of the text, which, to them, falls short of calling it 'genocide'. The shying away of Armenian support seems to have deviated from the focus that the individual apology addresses the consciences and exclusively highlights the (in)human dimension of what happened in 1915, rather than 'minimizing it to a legal term that functions as a stumbling block for reconciliation and dialogue'."[89]

Baydar's portrayal of Armenians as a group hung up on a "minimizing" legal term – i.e., genocide, which "functions as a stumbling block for reconciliation and dialogue", as opposed to the representation of Turkish individuals' as attentive to "the '(in)human' dimension of 1915", is in line with the mainstream representations of diaspora Armenians in the Turkish press. In the same article Baydar quoted University of Michigan Professor Fatma Müge Göcek as one of the pioneers of Turkish-Armenian dialogue in academia. Göcek argued:

"I think this is a very significant step forward that needs to be congratulated and fervently supported for two reasons. First, it is an initiative occurring within the public sphere free of state intervention, unhindered by state interests and the denialist stand the state has promoted for so long. It actually openly counters it, trying to build a social movement against it. Second, it tries to do so with a very simple grass roots aim of acknowledgment, which comprises the first step in addressing a social problem.

---

89 Yavuz Baydar, Public Apology Stirs Controversy, Angers, Breaks New Ground, *Today's Zaman*, 17 December 2008, http://www.todayszaman.com/columnistDetail_getNewsById.action?newsId=161419.

In a country where the state has for so long officially denied that there has been such a problem, its acknowledgment would indeed be the first step forward and it could only be done through the public sphere. One therefore has to first get society to acknowledge there is a problem in order to start working on it: Since one relates to a problem interpersonally as an individual, through one's own interpretation, ideas, feelings, emotions, experiences or recollections, the best way to do this is to transform all those who individually acknowledge into a social group."[90]

Baydar's asymmetrical presentation of the "Turkish side" and "Armenian side" of the discussion and Göcek's argument need to be problematized separately. Although Baydar chose to frame the Armenian response in very general terms and as devoid of agency while framing and (mis)representing their critique in his own terms, he chose to feature prominently, and hence legitimize, a Turkish scholar's argument, all in service of praising an initiative that he calls "yet another strong signal of Turkey's undefeatable conscience".

In actuality, Armenian or other protesting responses were neither unified nor did they focus solely on the omission of the word genocide; indeed, although some Armenian responses did offer such a criticism this was by no means unique to Armenians. Much of what was expressed by Armenian and other critical scholars in the Armworkshop discussion list, an outlet of which Yavuz Baydar was a longtime member, was also later expressed at length by Marc Mamigonian,[91] Khatchig Mouradian,[92] Bilgin Ayata,[93] Seyhan Bayraktar and myself[94] on several occasions. These critiques were

---

90 Ibid.
91 Marc Mamigonian, Commentary on the Turkish Apology Campaign, *Armenian Weekly*, 21 April 2009, http://www.armenianweekly.com/2009/04/21/commentary-on-the-turkish-apology-campaign/.
92 Khatchig Mouradian, From Yeghern to Genocide: Armenian newspapers, Raphael Lemkin, and the Road to the UN Genocide Convention, *Haigazian Armenological Review* 29 (2009), 127-137.
93 Bilgin Ayata, Critical Interventions: Kurdish Intellectuals Confronting the Armenian Genocide, *Armenian Weekly*, 29 April 2009, http://www.armenianweekly.com/2009/04/29/kurdish-intellectuals-confronting-the-armenian-genocide/.
94 For a review of a critical panel discussion on the *I Apologize* campaign, see Ayşe Günaysu, Silenced but Resilient: A Groundbreaking Panel Discussion in

similar to those expressed during the first days of the campaign and showed variety and depth, as opposed to being simply 'hung up' on a term. Thus, a historical discursive asymmetry was further exacerbated through Baydar's editorial choice.

Göcek, in her remarks, reframes the debate as if the usage (or lack thereof) of the term genocide is completely irrelevant to the discussion and/ or as if Great Catastrophe is equivalent to genocide – which it is not – either in linguistic or in historico-legalistic terms (something that will be discussed in length later in this chapter). Göcek also reduces genocide recognition (a term she refuses to use) to an interpersonal affair where individuals will decide with their own "interpretation, ideas, feelings, emotions, experiences or recollections". For this reason, she sees the apology campaign as a "significant step" towards "acknowledgement". Acknowledgement of what? Presumably of what Baydar terms Armenian "suffering" and what the apology statement calls "pain".

However, what has been denied by the Turkish state and the public in general has not been whether Armenians suffered in 1915. The proponents of the Turkish state discourse, such as former ambassador and Turkish Armenian Reconciliation Committee member Gündüz Aktan, never denied that there was "suffering" or large numbers of Armenian deaths;[95] rather, the discussion has revolved around whether this "suffering" and these deaths were the result of a deliberate policy or policies, and thus whether the term genocide can be applied. Finally, Göcek's remarks remain silent to the following socio-political question: "if individuals should decide on their own, as individuals, how to confront 'the events of 1915', why did intellectuals decide to mandate a text and a term *from above* without considering an open-ended, transparent and horizontal campaign along the lines of the Australian *Sorry Books*".[96]

Istanbul, *Armenian Weekly*, 3 August 2010, http://www.armenianweekly.com/2010/08/03/gunaysu-silenced-but-resilient-a-groundbreaking-panel-discussion-in-istanbul/.

95 For further discussion about Gündüz Aktan's position see David Phillips, *Unsilencing the Past: Track two Diplomacy And Turkish-Armenian Reconciliation* (New York: Berghahn Books, 2005).

96 The Sorry Books project was an initiative of the group *Australians for Native Title* (ANT), which was formed in June 1997. They were seen as an opportunity

The Armenian Responses

The several Armenian responses were marred by similar kinds of problems, ranging from vagueness to lack of wide-scale deliberation. The two largest representative American-Armenian organizations, the Armenian National Committee of America (ANCA) and the Armenian Assembly of America (AAA), both hailed the apology campaign by *reframing* it in their own way. Whereas the campaign organizers explicitly refrained from using the term genocide in the text of the apology and they also explicitly said they are neither claiming responsibility nor apologizing for the Armenian Genocide, the ANCA's statement said:

"The efforts of those courageous parliamentarians and historians in Turkey who have placed the Armenian Genocide center-stage must be commended. [...] By the same token, the campaign by Prime Minister Erdoğan and other Turkish leaders to quash honest discussion of the murder of 1,5 million Armenians from 1915-1923 must not be rewarded. Silence by the international community will be misinterpreted by Turkey's leadership as support for their genocide denial agenda."[97]

Even though the voices in Turkey themselves did not send a clear message of neither responsibility, nor showed any incentive for formal recognition of genocide, ANCA communications director Chouldjian said, "Only by formally recognizing the Armenian genocide can the United States and democratic countries around the world send a clear message that they stand with the voices of truth in Turkey".[98] The AAA's Executive Director Bryan

---

for ordinary Australians who wanted to do something in response to the Federal Government's refusal to make a formal apology to the Stolen Generations. For more see The Australian Institute of Aboriginal and Torres Strait Islander Studies' website, http://www.aiatsis.gov.au/collections/exhibitions/sorrybooks/introduction.html.

97 Armenian National Committee of America, ANCA Statement on Recent Efforts in Turkey to Confront the Armenian Genocide of 1915-1923, press release, 22 December 2008, http://www.anca.org/press_releases/press_releases.php?prid=1641.

98 Ümit Enginsoy, US Armenian group hails 'apology', *Hürriyet Daily News*, 26 December 2008, http://www.hurriyet.com.tr/english/domestic/10644886.asp.

Ardouny's words also clearly indicated a reframing of reality, despite the fact that AAA's statement was more tuned to the difference between Great Catastrophe and genocide:

"Over 12,000 people in Turkey want history to be recorded truthfully, having already signed the Internet-based petition apologizing for what they call the 'Great Catastrophe' that befell the Armenians of Ottoman Turkey in 1915. This public apology is a first step in that direction and will inevitably lead to Turkey coming to grips with its genocidal past."[99]

A letter of support initially signed by 21 Armenian individuals, mostly Canadian and French Armenians involved in arts, was circulated in Armenian newspapers in mid January 2009. These Armenians seem not to have been aware of the kind of political discourse that surrounded the apology campaign other than its limited accounts in British and French newspapers, nor did they command the same kind of political clout that the apology campaign organizers and initial signers did. Whereas the campaign organizers wrote and acted within a consistent national political sphere in which they have been prominent political actors at least for the last ten years, the Armenian respondents lacked the same kind of national discursive space and have not been involved in active politics themselves.

Indeed this power asymmetry led to a scandalous event at the beginning of February 2009 when Armen Gakavian, an Armenian academic in Australia's Macquarie University, gave an interview to the Turkish daily *Radikal* which quoted him as saying, "Armenians should apologize to the Turkish nation for killing several thousands of Turks in the early 20th century and for the actions of ASALA".[100] Later Gakavian would issue a correction letter where he claimed his words were distorted by *Radikal* and that he

---

99 Ayşe Karabat, Critics of apology campaign turn to personal attacks, *Today's Zaman*, 19 December 2008.

100 Erhan Üstündağ, Armenian Diaspora Reactions to Apology Campaign, 4 February 2009, http://bianet.org/english/english/112323-armenian-diaspora-reactions-to-apology-campaign; Adnan Gündoğan and Ertuğrul Mavioğlu, İki "özür" den sıkı bir kardeşlik doğar mı?, *Radikal*, 2 February 2009, http://www.radikal.com.tr/Radikal.aspx?aType=RadikalDetayV3&ArticleID=919479&Date=01.02.2009&CategoryID=97.

never spoke for all Armenians nor did he state that Armenians should apologize.[101]

Finally on February 2, 2009 the European Armenian Federation issued a statement that read:

"We have noted the development of a new campaign in Turkey by which the Armenian people would need appeasement provided by certain strata of Turkish society, thereby solving the Armenian question without causing too much damage to Turkey. While being fully receptive to genuine expressions of sympathy and outreach by Turkish individuals who choose to speak out against their own government's policy of denial of the Armenian Genocide, we must also make clear that the cause of justice with regard to this mass crime cannot be 'apologized' away by populist initiatives, however well-intentioned such actions might seem to be. The recently publicized 'apology' campaign in Turkey is, indeed, a populist initiative, which deliberately avoids the term 'genocide' and which, by so doing, intends to de-criminalize the destruction by the Ottoman Turkish government of 1,5 million Armenians, as precisely claimed one of its initiators, Mr. Baskın Oran in a Turkish newspaper (Milliyet, December 19, 2008)."[102]

All in all the Armenian side was underinformed regarding the intricacies of the Turkish politics. Both linguistic barrier and information asymmetry worked against the Armenians. Especially the initial statements from representational organizations show that the Armenian side heard what they wanted to hear notwithstanding what the Turkish intellectuals said.

---

101 Armenian Academic Reacts To Apology Speculations, 4 February 2009, http://bianet.org/english/world/112343-armenian-academic-reacts-to-apology-speculations. The first distorted version of Gakavian's initiative was not publicized by anybody but one of the initiators of the campaign, Baskın Oran, on February 1, 2009. See Oran's article on the incident: http://www.agos.com.tr/index.php?module=corner&status=old&author_id=5&corner_id=1079&cat_id=22.

102 Armenians still demand recognition and reparation of their genocide by Turkey, 2 February 2009, http://eafjd.eu/spip.php?article521.

CONTEXTUAL CONSTRAINTS OR POLITICAL STRATEGIES? AN ANALYSIS OF THE "APOLOGY" TEXT

2012 is the twentieth anniversary of the publication of Taner Akçam's first book.[103] Akçam, the first historian from Turkey to openly acknowledge the Armenian Genocide without resorting to euphemisms did not use the term genocide in this early work and later explained the kind of psychological barriers he overcame in the years to follow.[104] Akçam and others published several books and dozens of newspaper and scholarly articles on the issue and appeared frequently on TV since then. Hence, although the debates surrounding the Turkish apology campaign suggested or stated outright that as a result of the campaign Turkish society at large encountered the issue of Armenian Genocide the first time, this is not the case.

It is true that the Turkish public has not had many opportunities to receive a good education on the subject of the Armenian Genocide, and the Turkish press, on this issue, is either willfully denialist, completely unaware or ill-informed or simply politically biased. Nonetheless, the Turkish public at large is familiar with the fact that Armenians and others[105] are demanding the recognition of a particular kind of crime, that of genocide. Elsewhere in Turkey the term genocide has been non-problematically used for cases such as Bosnia, Algeria, and at times for Gaza or Palestine. Moreover a number of recent scholarly works have clearly established that the Turkish state never entirely denied the "tragic events" of 1915 as such. The core argument of the Turkish Republic has always been that the mass killings during and as a result of forced deportations were not a result of an intentional policy by the Young Turk regime to eliminate the Armenians, thus these events cannot be defined as genocide according to the UN Convention of 1948.

The apology text, the choice of the term *Medz Yeghern* and the campaign itself did not appear out of nowhere but exist in a historical and polit-

---

103 Akçam, *Turkish National Identity and the Armenian Question*.
104 See the introduction of Taner Akçam, *İnsan Hakları ve Ermeni Sorunu: İttihat Terakki'den Kurtuluş Savaşı'na* (Ankara: İmge Kitabevi, 1999).
105 See the letter of International Association of Genocide Scholars addressed to Prime Minister Erdoğan, 6 April 2005, http://eo.tchobanian.org/en/communique00010086.html.

ical context; thus they must be the subject of a political, philosophical and linguistic analysis taking into account this context. In order to do so, one needs not only take into consideration the limits of the public sphere in Turkey and the place the left and the liberals occupy in it, but also to challenge and expose the ways in which the progressive discourse fails to deliver what it promises to do, i.e., acknowledgement of a particular crime against humanity in the full extent of the international legal framework. Since the text is the work of four writers, Ahmet İnsel, Ali Bayramoğlu, Baskın Oran, and Cengiz Aktar, all known as public intellectuals in Turkey, it is safe to assume that they are, as Marc Mamigonian says, "acutely aware of the effects of language, that they chose their words with great care, and thus that the apology text was not arrived at by accident or in haste".[106] For this purpose we need to read the text of the apology campaign closely, in addition to revisiting the speeches and writings of the campaign organizers as well as the way the campaign was publicized and managed in the public sphere. As is established in the literature primarily by Nick Smith[107] but also by others, non-categorical apologies or even non-apologies transmit meaning that may still inform us about intentions, offense, regret, shame, humility or the lack of any of these.

The first sentence of the text: "My conscience does not accept the insensitivity showed to and the denial of the Great Catastrophe that the Ottoman Armenians were subjected to in 1915" acknowledges that there is an insensitivity towards the Great Catastrophe that the Ottoman Armenians were subjected to in 1915, and that there is a denial of the same Great Catastrophe. Also the sentence posits that this is an issue of conscience. The second sentence: "I reject this injustice and for my share, I empathize with the feelings and pain of my Armenian brothers"[108] rejects *this* injustice and claims to personally empathize with the feelings and pain of Armenian brothers. The third sentence: "I apologize to them" claims to apologize to them.

---

106 Mamigonian, Commentary on the Turkish Apology Campaign.
107 Smith, *I Was Wrong*, 17-27.
108 Following various critiques, "Armenian sisters" was added to the text after its first publication in the newspapers and the website.

The full extent of the political, philosophical and linguistic issues at stake here are beyond the scope of this chapter. Yet they need to be analyzed, even if briefly.

Linguistic Issues: Translatability, Clarity, Agency

Aaron Lazare,[109] among others, cautions us to the first issue, that of translatability, which, in this case is not just a simple issue of translation between different languages and cultures. To begin with, the Armenian term *Yeghern*, the usual word for "pogrom", cannot be translated to any other language as catastrophe for three reasons: As indicated by Marc Nichanian, "it seems that its root is the past form of the verb to be, as though Yeghern was the Event par excellence".[110] *Yeghern* embodies an element of agency, in the sense that there cannot be a *yeghern*, slaughter, without a *yegherna-gorts*, slaughterer. In contrast, neither the word Catastrophe nor its Turkish "equivalent" *Felaket* includes the element of agency.[111] However Boğos Levon Zekiyan used the poetic license to translate *Medz Yeghern* as Great

---

109 Lazare, *On Apology*, 34.
110 Marc Nichanian and David Kazanjian, Between Genocide and Catastrophe, in: *Loss: The Politics of Mourning*, ed. David Eng et al. (Berkeley and Los Angeles: University of California Press, 2003), 125-147, here: 127.
111 Catastrophe is the translation of *Aghed* – one of the words used by Armenians to describe both 1915 and several pogroms and massacres before 1915, such as the Adana massacres of 1909 or 1895-96 massacres. Besides the issue of impossibility of translation for linguistic reasons, the term is also non-translatable from a cultural perspective, since it's not a categorical proper name, but rather one that corresponds to a particular experience within Armenian history. Just as there is no *Yeghern* that means Catastrophe in the Armenian language, there also is no *Medz Yeghern* that means Great Catastrophe. So the Turkish intellectuals came up with a brand new concept Great Catastrophe that would have been the translation of *Medz Aghed*, and not that of *Medz Yeghern*. For a much elaborate discussion on the issue of impossibility of translation and further philosophical considerations such as impossibility of categorizing that which is uncategorizable and unimaginable see Marc Nichanian, Catastrophic Mourning, in: *Loss*, 99-124; Nichanian and Kazanjian, Between Genocide and Catastrophe.

Catastrophe in order to avoid the legal repercussions of Article 301 of the Turkish Penal Code[112] and Turkish intellectuals referred to his translation.

The second linguistic issue, that of clarity, is not exclusively linguistic and has both political and philosophical implications. This dimension is well problematized in the literature under the subtitle of pseudo or failed apologies. Lazare cites eight – some slightly overlapping – ways that the statements of offense can fail. The following are relevant for our purposes since the *I Apologize* text does all: "offering a vague and incomplete acknowledgment; using the passive voice; [...] minimizing the offense; using the empathic 'I'm sorry'; [...] apologizing for the wrong offense".[113]

It is necessary to revisit the terminology used in the Armenian language use to describe 1915, in order to clarify what we mean by vagueness in this particular context. Armenians use *Medz Yeghern* (Great Pogrom), *Darakrootioon* (Deportation), *Ahksor* (Exile), *Chart* (Chopping), *Aghed* (Catastrophe), *Vojir* (Crime), *Medz Vodjir* (Great Crime), and several other terms, and most commonly *Tseghaspanootioon* (Genocide). The Turkish terms *Tehcir* (Deportation), *Sürgün* (Exile), and *Kıtal* (Massacre) are even used within official Turkish discourse, though with some variety: For example, Turkish official sources and historians close to the Turkish official position prefer to use *Mukatele* (Mutual Massacre) instead of *Kıtal*.

By adopting the more sanitized and literary term Great Catastrophe the authors of the apology, firstly, introduced, via this campaign a brand new term to the Turkish public sphere. Even if the term meant something for Armenians, it certainly did not mean anything for the larger public in Turkey who heard the term *Buyuk Felaket*/Great Catastrophe or its Armenian "equivalent" *Medz Yeghern* for the first time. One of the campaign organizers, Baskın Oran, explicitly claimed on more than one occasion that *Medz Yeghern* was the only term Armenians used until 1965 when they "discov-

---

112 Boğos Levon Zekiyan, Tehcir ve Soykırım: Bağdaşmaz Görünümden Tamamlayıcı İşleve; Büyük Ermeni Felaketi 'Medz Yeğern' üzerine Düşünceler (Lecture, New Approaches to Turkish-Armenian Relations, Türk Ermeni İlişkilerine Yeni Yaklaşımlar Sempozyumu, İstanbul Üniversitesi, 15-17 March 2006, 9).

113 Lazare, *On Apology,* 86.

ered" the political value of genocide.[114] Not only is the normative implication of Oran's words problematic for its chastising of Armenians for using the term genocide, but also his argument is historically baseless, as shown earlier: Armenians used over a dozen terms besides *Yeghern* and started using genocide almost immediately after its being coined by Raphael Lemkin.[115]

Secondly, the authors of the apology text avoided the politico-legal aspect of genocide by divorcing the naming of the crime from its legal/political repercussions and pushing it, on the one hand, into the sphere of the parochial,[116] as opposed to the positive legal, and on the other hand, into the sphere of the past. By only partially acknowledging earlier generations, who expressed their experience via a dozen terms other than genocide and by choosing to obscure the ongoing political struggle of subsequent generations embodied in the term genocide, the "apology" authors managed to keep the past confined within a private sterilized linguistic terrain while attempting to avoid any current political or institutional consequences. Indeed Ali Bayramoğlu explicitly argued for a divorcing of several aspects of 1915 from each other and came up with the term "understanding by differentiating", claiming that "understanding by differentiating" is simultaneously the indicator of a democratic culture, democratic maturity, democratic ethics and indeed of understanding itself. Bayramoğlu claimed the legal/poli-

---

114 See Mamigonian, Commentary on the Turkish Apology Campaign, for Oran's interview with Canadian Broadcasting Company and the text of his election campaign pamphlet where he publicly repeated his position on Armenians' politicizing their pain.

115 Mouradian, From Yeghern to Genocide.

116 Indeed one of the campaign organizers, Cengiz Aktar, argued for this kind of romanticized parochialism vying for an Anatolian exceptionalism in his post-campaign *Agos* and *Radikal* piece. Soykırım ötesi Büyük Felaket, *Radikal*, 26 April 2009, http://www.radikal.com.tr/Radikal.aspx?aType=RadikalEklerDeta yV3&ArticleID=933179&CategoryID=42. Aktar claimed that the narrow "cold" term genocide is not able to capture the full scope of "the Anatolian tragedy", and that a more humane term is needed. The entitlement to speak for the Armenian experience on the one hand, the odd aestheticization of a crime against humanity by reducing it to a parochial exception on the other is extremely puzzling to say the least.

tical dimensions and human dimensions of the catastrophe can be divorced and this divorce can contribute to their understanding of Armenians' pain.

Thirdly, the authors politicized a formerly non-political term, by instrumentalizing the term *Yeghern* for their own multidimensional utilitarian calculus to be discussed below. The irony of this is that some of the organizers have been extremely critical of the term genocide on the basis of its "politicized" nature. Seemingly unaware that any term used to refer to a historical crime of this nature is necessarily always already "politicized", when used in this context, just as when President Obama used the same term as a means of avoiding the word genocide, *Medz Yeghern* ceases to be a private term of communal mourning for Armenians, it becomes something else: a political instrument in the hands of others.[117]

Finally, the authors arbitrarily shifted the terrain of denial by redefining denial of "Great Catastrophe" as a general denial by the Turkish state and society of any Armenian suffering, which has not historically been the case. Using denial without a qualifier itself can easily become an instrument of denialist discourse, since even the most notorious denialists in parallel contexts, such as David Irving, for example, do not deny that something terrible happened. They deny that it happened the way and to the extent established historiography says it happened – that the resulting deaths were the product of intentional actions and policies. In this debate, denial means

---

117 Mamigonian, Commentary on the Turkish Apology Campaign, points to a similar issue: "On April 24, 2005, President George W. Bush issued a statement reading, in part, 'On Armenian Remembrance Day, we remember the forced exile and mass killings of as many as 1,5 million Armenians during the last days of the Ottoman Empire. This terrible event is what many Armenian people have come to call the 'Great Calamity'.' The official Armenian-language version of the statement translated 'Great Calamity' as Mets Yeghern. It is unreasonable to suppose that during the reportedly two years that the apology was being pondered, the authors did not notice that Medz Yeghern/Great Catastrophe/Great Calamity was becoming the 'not g-word' of choice when a political agenda disallows the ineffable g-word. Unfortunately, rather than openly acknowledge this concession to political expediency, an imaginary history has been conjured in which this usage is the only one Armenians knew before they were tainted by political agendas and started insisting on 'genocide'."

genocide denial alone and not the denial of anything and everything. To reiterate a point, even the state discourse itself and pro-state historians do not deny that Armenians were massacred.

Lack of Offense, Lack of Agency

The vagueness is not limited to the issue of denial alone. One of the central aspects of any successful apology, even for smaller offenses that concern the public, is the clear acknowledgement of responsibility for the offense or grievance and expression of regret or remorse to the aggrieved party. Here the first sentence acknowledges *some* offense but neither specifies any agency nor takes any responsibility for the said offense. The use of the passive voice is instrumental in hiding both the agency and responsibility. One could read the statement and have no idea who subjected the Ottoman Armenians to the "Great Catastrophe."

Lack of Responsibility in the Past

The organizers have chosen a language that neglects to specify agency for the historical crimes whose denial they are criticizing. Instead, a vague description of 1915 is used that neither addresses individual and collective responsibility nor steps in any significant way outside the politics of the state with regard to 1915.

It is true that the Turkish state has never apologized for Armenian suffering and in that sense the apology attempt is a novelty. Yet the new Turkish foreign policy discourse under Ahmet Davutoğlu is willing to acknowledge Armenian suffering within a certain safety zone.[118] Similarly, we note the comparatively mild reaction to President Obama's use of the term *Medz Yeghern* starting with his Presidential Statement on Armenian Remembrance Day of April 2009. There were no threats of cutting diplomatic ties, no burning of American flags in the streets of Turkey, nor were there threats of trade reduction as has been the case with the French Parlia-

---

118 Foreign Minister Ahmet Davutoğlu acknowledges the Armenian pain – to a point in his Harvard speech of 28 September 2010, http://www.iop.harvard.edu/Multimedia-Center/All-Videos/A-public-address-by-Ahmet-Davutoğlu,-Minister-of-Foreign-Affairs,-Republic-of-Turkey.

ment's acknowledgement of Armenian Genocide. Although the far right reacted strongly – as it reacts strongly to any mention of "the events of 1915" – the state appeared to regard *Medz Yeghern* as an acceptable and basically harmless variation on its own retooled, more humane policy of denial.

Lack of Responsibility in the Present

An additional dimension of vagueness is the reason why many journalists, both domestic and international, intellectuals, politicians and lay people were confused about what exactly people were apologizing for. As indicated by Marc Mamigonian the text is not an apology for the events of 1915, but a meta-apology for "insensitivity towards and denial of Medz Yeghern",[119] which brings us to a different kind of lack of responsibility, the one situated in the present.

In this sense the "apology" text not only does not identify agency for past crimes but also fails to identify agency in the present: Who is responsible for the denial? The state? The intellectuals? Lay people? All? To the same extent? And denial of *what* exactly? Is an apology text what everybody makes of it? Is it the place to start (and end) a negotiation over terminology? If so, how are we sure that this negotiation over terminology is not a sophisticated form of validating denialist discourse frames and minimizing the legal political extent of the crime?

Indeed one of the campaign organizers, Professor of International Relations Baskın Oran, said on December 19, 2008: "The Prime Minister should be praying for our campaign. Parliaments around the world were passing automatically resolutions. These are going to stop now. The diaspora has softened. The international media has started to no longer use the word genocide."[120] While Oran's words should not cast doubt on the intentions of thirty thousand citizens, his take coupled with Cengiz Aktar's take on the term genocide (see footnote 116) gives one ample reason to rethink about the intentions of the campaign organizers. This concern was emphasized by longtime human rights activist Ayşe Günaysu, who wrote:

---

119 Mamigonian, Commentary on the Turkish Apology Campaign.
120 Quoted in Mamigonian, Commentary on the Turkish Apology Campaign.

"We now hear some of the initiators of the campaign trying to use the apology as a means to fight the use of the word genocide and hamper the work of those who seek the recognition of the Armenian Genocide. They portray those seeking recognition as the twin sisters and brothers of the Turkish fascists, and they present the 'diaspora' as the enemy of any reconciliation [...]. [By] their discourse, they contribute to the demonization of those who do use the word genocide."[121]

Obviously, a comprehensive critique of Turkish intellectuals in the past and the present is beyond the scope of this chapter. However, one can speculate via the apology campaign's text and the nature of the debate surrounding it, that either the intellectuals themselves did not give serious thought to the connection between the responsibility of intellectuals and genocide denial, or that they thought about it extensively but consciously wanted to avoid responsibility. Since the intellectuals' responsibility must be greater than regular citizens', their silence has been more deafening than if they were "the man in the street". This brings us to the close-ended, non-deliberative nature of the apology text also briefly problematized by Taner Akçam as cited earlier.

Jacobinism vs. Horizontal Deliberation

Although the campaign looks like a participatory endeavor where citizens could individually decide on their own whether to sign or not, since the terms of the apology were defined by the intellectuals from above, it was rather mock-deliberative in character. The signers did not necessarily agree with the text, indeed a number of intellectuals, some referred to in this paper, signed the text while either disagreeing with the content publicly or criticizing it privately. Some did not agree with the idea of apologizing for the crimes or the denial altogether; some said they can only be sorry and cannot apologize for something for which they are personally not responsible. We are not even sure whether the signers agreed with the idea of apologizing. In stark contrast, several counter-"apology" campaigns were more horizontally deliberative in their being open-ended. Citizens who expected a counter-apology from Armenians or expressed their anger at the "apology" campaign signed their opinions individually with their own words.

---

121   Ibid.

The campaign is not only Jacobinist in its nature, since the preparation process was not transparent even to the majority of intellectuals, but also Jacobinist in its approach to both the offended and the offender party. In the case of Turkish citizens, both the idea of apologizing for denial and the text are dictated from above without any attempt to broaden the base of participants in drafting or pre-apology deliberation regarding the terms of the apology. The organizers did not strive for inclusiveness and the involvement of as many people as possible in the process itself – unlike the very horizontal experience of *Sorry Books* in Australia where many took part in an apology campaign personally by writing their own apologies (or refusals) in empty notebooks.

Regarding Jacobinism towards Armenians, which is worse, comparatively speaking, the organizers made no effort to get in touch with *representative* bodies of the Armenians to gain an insight into what they really want or need from an apology, or whether they need an apology from individual Turkish citizens at all. Instead, by mandating the term, hence normalizing the discourse at a lower equilibrium point than what genocide entails, by pre-emptively authoring a *public* apology on whose terms the offended and the "offender" did not agree, the campaign organizers created a de facto setting wherein if the offended party (Armenians) rejected the "apology", they would be cast in a negative light and end up being portrayed as the hostile and aggressive party, despite the fact that preemption of this kind is a symbolically violent endeavor to begin with – this was the case in Yavuz Baydar piece cited earlier. Symbolic violence stems from the fact that the public negotiationist character of the text itself lacks the kind of humility that is expected from any apology, let alone an apology for gross human rights violations. In short, the campaign commands an enormous amount of preemptive power over the offended party: this is its most politically, to say nothing of ethically, problematic aspect. The Armenians not only disappeared from the land but they also disappeared from a process that is supposedly intended to bring them "healing" or "closure"; instead, they were treated as bit-players in someone else's drama instead of being a party whose century-old quest for political justice and equality before international law is treated with respect.

The pre-apology process, then, was not transparent; and during the post-apology process, the domestic backlash, hence politics, hijacked the discussion and an apology for Armenians became a public terrain of fighting among the political spectrum of Turkey.

Conclusion

The Turkish intellectuals' "apology" initiative promised to start a debate on the Armenian Genocide and according to the campaign organizers strived to remain within the domain of individual citizens' conscience. However, it is obvious from the kind of reaction it provoked among citizens that it could never stay outside of the domain of politics since the calamity itself is the immediate result of a political decision with constitutive political and economic results. As we have seen, the attempt to compartmentalize the issue of genocide recognition into public and private spheres is an evasive tactic that is far from establishing the kind of trust that any conciliation process would require. So despite the fact that the campaign informed the general public that there is something to be apologized for, it failed to go beyond the discursive mechanisms that are remnants of denialist politics. Far from opening up the debate to substantial arguments regarding the legitimacy of genocide recognition, the apology campaign gave way to a rather odd discursive space in Turkish civil society in which citizens are encouraged to empathize with the "pain" of Armenians, sometimes called Anatolian pain. Accordingly, the events of 1915 should be understood through emotions without necessarily calling a spade a spade. Individual citizens are given decision-making agency over how to qualify the events of 1915 while not being properly educated on the events or the legal framework that emerged out of the international debates following the events of 1915. A vague language of common pain is substituted instead of demanding common post-genocidal institutional norms on which both Turkish and Armenian citizens and societies can base their future both as individuals and as neighbours.

In this sense the campaign does not constitute any meaningful challenge to the official Turkish stance and is also far from a novel move away from the perspective of the societal discourse about 1915 in Turkey. To be clear on this: it is not the refusal or lack of courage to call the forced deportation and massacres a genocide that has been central to my take. Instead I mainly critiqued the balancing act of the organizers trying to appeal to a wide range of internal and external audiences. It is this strategy that tries hard not to alienate any group involved in the Turkish-Armenian conflict over the history that makes the text and the endeavor a patchwork rather than a critical assessment of the discourse in Turkey on coming to terms with 1915. Last but not least, the total omission of much earlier attempts at apology by Kurdish politicians and citizens both in exile and in Turkey by the campaign organizers is also indicative of the limits of the apology endeavor that claimed to remember the distant past while conveniently forgetting the recent past itself.

Armenians and Turkish citizens need a more substantial, horizontal and deliberative dialogical process where the historically disadvantaged party is not further forced into pre-emptive public negotiations on whose terms it has absolutely no power.

Reconciliation and Human Rights

Soldiers' Reconciliation
René Cassin, the International Labour Office, and the Search for Human Rights

JAY WINTER

Reconciliation is the search for an alternative way of configuring hostile parties, locked in the hatred and bitterness unleashed by war and violence. One set of identities – that of soldiers killing other soldiers on the other side of the line – is muted by the construction of another set of identities, coming out of combatant status but moving away from war. Here the moral authority of soldiers, as men who know what Walt Whitman termed the red business of war, is decoupled from the conflict which brought them into uniform in the first place. Thereafter the door is at least ajar, leading to other encounters with those whom they would have tried to kill on the battlefield. Those post-combat meetings help engender solidarities, an unlikely alliance of former enemies determined after the end of hostilities to make another murderous war unthinkable.

I want to tell the story of one such effort. To be sure, in the short term, it failed, but in the process of creating a new kind of veterans' politics, a series of ideas emerged which had long-lasting consequences. These are the interests former soldiers had in constructing a norm of international affairs above that of the nation state. States, Raymond Aron tells us, are those institutions defined by their right to wage war. Veterans in the interwar years challenged the absolute sovereignty of states precisely because of the lethal consequences of decisions to go to war for everyone caught up in them. Veterans had rights that superceded the writ of the states, which had sent them to war; those rights were human rights, shared by men without limbs or eyes or faces or minds, all over the world. They deserved pensions and prosthetic devices and a new start in life not because of their nationality but because of their individual and collective dignity. This turn from charity to entitlement is one of the key preliminary stages in the creation of a new kind of social movement, a human rights movement, which took shape in the Second World War, and which after 1970, has mushroomed into a significant social, political, and moral force all over the world.[1] Reconciliation after one war led to reconciliation after a second, and even more embittering and devastating calamity.

In this chapter, I want to trace this crooked path of reconciliation, a twisted journey leading in directions no one in 1918 had ever imagined. To do so, I will tell the story of René Cassin, who would go on to frame the Universal Declaration of Human Rights and win the Nobel Peace Prize in 1968. In 1914, he was almost killed in combat, and joined with other disabled veterans to create the French veterans' movement.[2] In the interwar years, René Cassin became a soldier in another kind of war, one waged against war itself. His point of entry into international politics was the international veterans' movement, launched with the aid of the International Labour Organization (ILO) in Geneva in the early 1920s. There too, between 1924 and 1938, he served as a member of the French delegation to the League of Nations (LON). His place at the table in Geneva was as the official representative of the French veterans' movement. Year after year, the *Union fédérale des anciens combattants et mutilés de guerre* (UF) formally nominated him for this post. Indeed, Cassin himself drafted the letter signed by the Federation's president, making this request, and dispatched it to the Prime Minister's office. And each year until 1938, Cassin travelled to Geneva and spent the month between about the 10th of September and the 10th of October at work on League of Nations' business. After the disas-

---

1   Samuel Moyn, *The Last Utopia: Human Rights in History* (Cambridge, Mass.: Harvard University Press, 2010). My interpretation differs from Moyn on the significance of pre-1970 developments, but on the later period, his book is now the standard work.

2   Jay Winter and Antoine Prost, *René Cassin et les droits de l'homme. Le projet d'une generation* (Paris: Fayard, 2011).

trous Munich accords of 30 September 1938, he decided not to return to the LON, which to all intents and purposes, had collapsed.

Over the years he spent in Geneva, he was joined by a remarkable assembly of men, in the ILO, in its early days under Albert Thomas, and in the LON itself. In 1926, for instance, Aristide Briand, Louis Loucheur, and his old friend from student days in Paris, Marcel Plaisant, served on the League's first commission, devoted to juridical questions. Léon Jouhaux, the designated representative of the French trade union movement, served on the second commission, devoted to economic questions. In the same year – 1926 – Cassin joined Paul-Boncour, Jouhaux and Henri de Jouvenal on the third commission, which focused on disarmament. In other years Cassin also served on the fifth commission, devoted to humanitarian matters, and on the sixth commission, responsible for what were termed political questions.

In Geneva, he also served alongside and formed friendships with distinguished jurists and politicians from many other countries. It was in Geneva that he met Eduard Beneš, foreign minister of Czechoslovakia, and Nikolas Politis, foreign minister of Greece. Both were pillars of the League, and dominant figures on the commissions on which Cassin served. Both made important contributions to the development of notions of human rights and state sovereignty at the very time Cassin began to write substantially about these matters. He presented his thinking to the Institute of International Law in Geneva and The Hague Academy of International Law. It is evident that his work in these years prepared the ground for the effort he made alongside many others during the Second World War and after to frame a new international rights regime.[3]

In Geneva, Cassin saw why the theory of absolute state sovereignty was in need of fundamental revision. The League sought collective security, but rested on the premise that its members enjoyed absolute state sovereignty. This contradiction ultimately tore it apart. In the 1920s, in the glow of the Locarno agreements, there seemed to be a commonality of interest among sovereign states in finding alternatives to war as a means of settling conflicts between states. But after the economic crisis of 1929, that consensus – always precarious, though palpable enough in the Kellogg-Briand Pact of 1926 – evaporated. The Japanese invasion of Manchuria in 1931 opened a

---

3   Ibid., chapters 5-6, and 9.

decade of disasters for the League of Nations, a sorry spectacle Cassin saw at first hand. While he and his colleagues continued to work on disarmament and other matters of common concern, the League crumbled, and then collapsed after the Munich accords of 1938.

In this chapter, I tell the story of Cassin's engagement in international affairs in the ILO and the LON in the hopeful years of the 1920s. His leadership in a veterans' effort of reconciliation rested on a second tier of the identities of millions of soldiers: that of mutilated men, men wounded or disabled who had a claim – moral, political, and financial – on the countries which had called on them to fight. The rights of disabled men to care, treatment, prosthesis, and a living pension was not a national right; it was a human right, one that was independent of the nationality of the legless, armless, eyeless, or brain-damaged men. By shifting veterans' politics from the level of international reconstruction to the level of transnational rights, they formed one of the first effective bridges between the two sides in the Great War.

That wounded men had the right to care was inscribed in the work of the Red Cross ever since the Battle of Solverino in 1859. But that association was an effort of charity, conducted by those who had not fought. The veterans' movement I discuss here was led by disabled men themselves, and their struggle for recognition provided a basis for what we now term rights talk. Twenty five years later, when the Second World War required a second effort of reconciliation, veterans were there too, making human rights the project of a generation, the war generation of 1914-18.

THE THIRD WAY, THE INTERNATIONAL LABOUR ORGANIZATION, AND VETERANS' POLITICS 1919-25

For veterans, there were three paths out of the Great War. The first was towards communism. Henri Barbusse's war novel *Under fire* (1917) had won the *Prix Goncourt*, international acclaim and a wide readership. Royalties helped launch Barbusse's *Association Républicaine des Anciens Combattants* (ARAC) which took heart from the hopes of social transformation kindled by the Bolshevik Revolution. The second path was that of battle-hardened nationalism, of the kind the *Union Nationale des Combattants* (UNC) expressed, thereby keeping alive the spirit of camaraderie and bitterness towards Germany. Cassin helped forge a third way, an internationalist veterans' movement aligned with the League of Nations and committed towards reconciliation between the two enemy camps after the war.

From the start, Cassin was a League of Nations man. He helped the nascent organization create its working library of books and official statistics and reports, and gathered support among those who saw in the League the only hope against communism on the left and strident nationalism on the right. It is this middle-of-the-road, progressive line that he forged in the UF. He did so with other men like Henri Pichot, who had suffered in combat with German forces, but who came to be committed to transcending the iron bitterness of the war.

Cassin was not at all averse to joining the inter-Allied veterans' organization, *La Fédération Interalliée des Anciens Combattants* (FIDAC). But he was against a political and cultural quarantine of German and Austrian veterans. Why should justified contempt for the old guard of the *Kaiserreich* pollute the atmosphere long after those responsible for the war had been overthrown? This is a question Cassin and Pichot, through their service and their suffering, had earned the right to ask. They were moral witnesses to the war, men who had faced the enemy, and had bled for their country.[4] What they said commanded respect. Pichot had spent eleven months in a German prisoner-of-war camp, and another six months at home recuperating from wounds received at the end of August 1914, wounds and the maltreatment of which, almost cost him his left leg.[5] He was initially convinced that German culture and the German people were rotten through and through, but abandoned his initial *amertume* and used his fluent German to argue in both Germany and France for reconciliation.[6]

As we have noted, Cassin had been fortunate to survive his combat experience, and had cried *Vive la France*, when hit by enemy fire on 12 October 1914. The defeat of Germany was a moral victory to him, a victory for the right. But his unshakable view was that the only way to prevent the return of war was to forge an international order which would block the de-

---

4 Avishai Margalit, *The Ethics of Memory* (New York: Basic Books, 2000).
5 Fond Pichot, Archives Nationales, Paris (hereafter: AN), AS 43 1 and 2.
6 Fond Pichot, AN, AS 43 2. Pichot's account of his military service and his extraordinarily detailed account of the treatment of his wounds contain all the venom of a die-hard nationalist.

scent into armed conflict, when international tensions rose. His was the view of Lord Grey, the British Foreign Secretary, who said time and again that had in the summer of 1914, had there only been a League, a place for the Great Powers to bring their grievances, the war would never have occurred.[7] After 1918, that conviction made Cassin and many other veterans turn towards Geneva, the seat of the new League of Nations.

By no means did all French veterans share Cassin's and Pichot's views. But what is remarkable is the degree to which their internationalist position became the middle way, the dominant position among French veterans in the inter-war years. From the spring of 1920 on, Cassin joined inter-allied meetings of veterans, where he and others put the case that the best defense of France was the strengthening of the democratic forces represented in the Weimar Republic.[8]

The man who forged the links between the UF and the LON was Adrian Tixier. Tixier like Pichot was a teacher. Tixier had lost his left arm in the Battle of the Frontiers in 1914, and like Cassin, he had won the *Médaille Militaire* and the *Croix de Guerre* for bravery. Tixier returned to the classroom in 1915, and served as president of one of the early veterans' organizations, the *Fédération des mutilés du Tarn*. He joined the UF, and then in 1920, accepted the invitation offered by Albert Thomas, director-general of the ILO, to come to Geneva and take up the post of secretary responsible for disabled veterans in the new organization.

From the outset, Tixier worked to make the ILO a meeting point for veterans from countries on both sides of the war. The advantage he had was that the ILO, an independent satellite of the LON, could offer a venue for the discussion of purely technical questions of interest to veterans: questions concerning different approaches to retraining and reeducating wounded veterans, as well as different developments in prosthetic surgery and technology going on all over Europe and beyond. The political arena was elsewhere, a few streets away in the League of Nations. Thus from mid-1920 on, Tixier did everything he could to point out to British, French or Belgian veterans the benefits arising from an exchange of information and

---

7   Que fait la Société des nations?, 1, League of Nations Archives, Geneva, Mantoux papers.
8   Antoine Prost, *Les Anciens combattants et la société française, 1914-1939*, vol. 1 (Paris: Fondation Nationale de la Science Politique, 1977), 75.

experience with disabled men and their representatives in Germany or Austria, whose wounds and whose difficulties in coping with disability and with finding and keeping a job were very similar to their own.

There is no doubt that this was a sleight of hand. Tixier wanted the ILO to provide the venue for regular meetings of veterans from all combatant nations, both to forge an international organization with its own voice, and to imbed this large and influential population in the culture and overall work of the LON. The problem was, though, that there were many veterans' groups in Britain, France, and elsewhere unwilling to sit down together with their former enemies. The question was how to get around them.[9]

Discussing technical matters was one way to do so. Already in 1920, an inter-allied veterans' meeting was held in Brussels, during which a *Centre de prothèse internationale* was born. At the same meeting, the Allied veterans decided to enter into discussions with the ILO "pour les questions internationales intéressant les mutilés". This confirmed an earlier resolution at the 1920 UF Congress at Nancy to work towards an international meeting of veterans at Geneva.

In January 1921, Tixier wrote to the UF, asking if it would participate in such a meeting to discuss "législation internationale des victimes de la guerre". Cassin as secretary-general of the UF, replied favorably, since this request was in line with the *Conseil d'administration's* decision to discuss technical matters among other veterans' organizations; such a meeting would in no way constitute the creation of "une Fédération internationale des victimes de la guerre".[10] So much for Allied veterans' sensibilities. Cassin insisted that the initiative had to come from the ILO, not from the UF. A majority of the *Conseil d'administration* supported Cassin's position, giving him a

"mandat de représenter éventuellement l'Union Fédérale à toutes conferences internationales qui pourraient être organisées pour le BIT de Genève, en vue de l'étude

---

9 See Tixier's reports to Albert Thomas, Historical Archives of the International Labour Organization, Geneva (hereafter: ILO Archives), as well as articles in *Après la bataille*, 25 August and 5 September 1920, as cited in Prost, *Les Anciens combattants*, vol. 1, 76, n. 131.

10 Tixier papers, ILO Archives, MU/7/3/1 et seq.

d'une unification des mesures de protections édictées par les different pays en faveur des mutilés, réformés et veuves de guerre".[11]

The first such meeting was held on 12-14 September 1921, when delegates from the UF, the British Legion, and the Italian veterans' movement sat down in Geneva with representatives of the German *Reichsbund* and the Austrian *Zentralverbund*. Pichot and Gaston Rogé were unable to attend; Cassin was the sole spokesman for the UF. He felt some apprehension, he wrote, in starting down this path, sensing

"la conscience des grands devoirs à accompli envers tous les invalides, toutes les familles victimes de cette guerre, envers aussi notre France ravagée, dont les devastations, dont l'effort de relèvement et l'esprit pacifique, si souvent ignorés ou méconnus, devaient être mis au première plan dans une conférence visant aux soulagement des souffrances".[12]

Tixier and the head of the ILO Albert Thomas welcomed the delegates. Among them was General Sir Frederick Maurice, representing the British Legion. There were delegations from Italy and Poland in Geneva, alongside German and Austrian delegates. Both countries had participated in the work of the ILO since 1919.

This very first encounter of veterans' representatives from both sides was a delicate moment. And yet Cassin saw this meeting as the right time and the right place to begin to construct a different kind of veterans' *internationale*. Surely, he said, disabled men should benefit from developments in care and treatment, whatever their origin. If they lived outside their country of origin, they had to have the right to receive pensions and to obtain medical assistance. Cassin knew that there were employers' organizations alongside trade union groups attached to the ILO: here was the natural place to discuss retraining and job placement. From these points of mutual interest, he argued that veterans could construct a common front, based on the view that the Treaty of Versailles had opened the way towards a peaceful future.

---

11 Entente internationale, *La France mutilé*, 26 January 1921.
12 René Cassin, La Réunion de Genève, *La France mutilé*, 25 September 1921.

Cassin himself witnessed the way the German delegate to the meeting, Schumann, representing the *Reichsbund*, took up the challenge, and

"responded by making a declaration which everyone listened to with rapt attention, especially by the French delegation. He said he came not only to *manifest* a pacific spirit, in denouncing war and revenge, but in order to *recognize* the debt in reparations that Germany owes to our country. They were committed to take all steps to ensure that the German government pays this debt, and also to struggle against all those efforts to overthrow the Weimar Republic and to resurrect the imperialist principles of the pre-war period."[13]

Here was the opening Cassin had hoped for: a public commitment by German and Austrian veterans to accept the terms of the peace treaty and to work together with their former enemies on matters of mutual interest. Deeds, to be sure, had to follow words, and Cassin expressed a certain reserve in reporting to French veterans what had happened in Geneva. His aim was clear: "To remember so that we do not fall into a trap; to act everywhere to lessen the suffering and to see justice done."[14]

Not all Allied veterans were persuaded that they could work with German and Austrian veterans. Suspicions were still set in stone; it would take time, Cassin believed, to dissolve them. A second step towards building an international veterans' movement took place in Geneva in March 1922, which was the convening of the first ILO-sponsored meeting of experts on problems of war disability. Tixier and Cassin worked hand-in-hand to prepare this meeting. Cassin suggested names of possible delegates, and hoped that labour and employers' leaders could be persuaded to come; perhaps, Cassin suggested, someone from the *Comité des forges*.[15] That was not possible, but others accepted the invitation. One was Dr Ripert, an expert on prosthetic medicine who had worked at the *Centre de prothèse de St Maurice*, and joined Cassin in the French delegation in Geneva.[16]

Between 2 and 4 March 1922, Albert Thomas himself presided over the meeting of delegates from Austria, France, Britain, Germany, Poland, Italy

---

13 Ibid.
14 Ibid.
15 Cassin to Tixier, 26 November 1921, ILO Archives, MU/7/3/1.
16 Pichot to Tixier, 31 January 1922, ILO Archives, MU/7/3/1.

and Germany. Their recommendations were uncontroversial: veterans should have the right to treatment and care wherever they resided; there should be a center of documentation on developments in prosthetic and orthopedic medicine – a point on which Cassin insisted – and a fully international exposition on the care of disabled men; veterans' organizations should work closely with other associations, including the Red Cross and the *Comité d'hygiène* of the LON.

The only bone of contention concerned how this initiative cut across the work of the *Centre de prothèse internationale*. Here Tixier was clear. The Brussels meeting of 1920, including an exhibition of prosthetic appliances, was part of the work of the permanent Inter-Allied committee on medical care of the disabled; they rejected the idea of a fully international association to deal with these questions. That is why they did not participate in the March 1922 meeting in Geneva; it was therefore necessary, Tixier felt, that the ILO move into the area they refused to inhabit. Cassin seconded Tixier: there were matters on which the Inter-Allied committee was the competent authority; and others, fully international matters, on which the ILO was the competent authority. They should work in parallel.[17]

This was easier said than done. Six months later, Tixier took the next step, once again in tandem with Cassin. On 26 September 1922, he wrote on behalf of the ILO inviting the UF and other veterans' groups to come to Geneva the following year for a second meeting of experts. On 3 October 1922, Cassin, then President of the UF, stated that, after consultation with the Executive Committee, his organization was happy to accept the invitation. Such a programme, he said, "fits perfectly the ideas of the Union Féderale". Cassin asked Tixier further to send him any information he had about "the legal and economic organization of the supply of prosthetics through cooperatives in Austria and Czechoslovakia". Following his line of argument in March, Cassin added that the UF's decision was without prejudice to the work of the *Centre de prothèse internationale* in Brussels. It was time, Cassin wrote, to seize the moment, one which was "exceptionnellement favorable à tous points de vus".[18]

---

17 Meeting of committee of experts, March 1922, Procès-verbaux, 11, ILO Archives, MU/7/3/2.
18 Cassin to Tixier, 3 October 1923, ILO Archives, MU/7/3/3.

Getting other associations to join the meeting was not so simple. On 10 November 1922, Tixier wrote to Albert Thomas in no uncertain terms: "I will not deny that establishing cordial relations among veterans of the Great War on both sides is a delicate matter." There were those who would not sit down with German veterans, but he believed that after "negotiations, perhaps protracted, we will be able to establish a formal programme and fix a specific date acceptable to all the major associations of men wounded in the Great War".[19] The UNC refused to go, but other Allied groups, like the British Legion, accepted the invitation.

The ILO did indeed convene a second meeting of experts on disabled veterans' matters in Geneva in July 1923. This time the focus was on job placement, and on the conditions disabled men faced on the job in many different countries.[20] Delegates attended from South Africa, Germany, Australia, Austria, Belgium, Canada, France, Britain, Italy, New Zealand, Poland, Czechoslovakia, Yugoslavia, and the Red Cross. Cassin was joined by Pichot and Rogé from the UF, as well as Monsieur Gauthier, head of *L'office regional de la main d'oeuvre de Paris*. The deliberations, Cassin later noted, were helpful in negotiations on French legislation passed a few months later on the mandatory employment of disabled veterans.[21]

These discussions, while intrinsically useful to veterans, were eclipsed by the increasingly tense reparations crisis. In January 1923, French and Belgian troops had occupied the Ruhr Valley. German inflation assumed astronomic proportions. In January 1922, the exchange rate was roughly 200 Deutschmarks to the dollar; in July 1923, the rate was 350,000 to the dollar; month after month the spiral continued. In this atmosphere, little could be done to promote international understanding. Though Tixier kept trying to find common ground among veterans' groups, he knew he had to await the end of the crisis.[22]

The parallel efforts of the new German Chancellor Gustav Stresemann in Germany and the new French Foreign Minister Aristide Briand created

---

19 Tixier to Drummond, 10 November 1922, ILO Archives.
20 Meeting of 31 July to 2 August 1923, Procès-verbaux, ILO Archives, MU/7/4/2/2.
21 Rapport de René Cassin à la Commission de la Paix sur la C.I.A.M.A.C, 3, AN, Fonds Cassin, 382 AP 10.
22 Tixier to Cassin, 16 March 1923, ILO Archives, MU/7/5/1.

the conditions for rapprochement. Currency stabilization, through the Dawes Plan, and greater Franco-German understanding, leading to the Locarno Treaties of 1925 broke the log-jam in Geneva as elsewhere. Here was the moment Tixier had been waiting for. But once again, it took a parallel effort by Cassin and the UF to bring about the creation of CIAMAC, the first fully international association of veterans of the Great War.

CIAMAC

In effect, improved relations between and among the Great Powers still left many ex-soldiers and other nationalists suspicious of the LON in general and the ILO in particular. For that reason, Tixier, identifed unalterably as a League of Nations man, could not himself convene a meeting of veterans' groups without alienating many potential delegates; that job was done by Cassin and the UF.

Here begins a story of eight years of work both in the field of international veterans' affairs and in the corridors of the League of Nations itself. From 1924 on, Cassin served as a French delegate to the League. At the same time, he launched, with the assistance of the Secretariat of the ILO, la *Conférence internationale des associations des mutilés et d'anciens combattants*, known by its acronym, CIAMAC. Since the two sides to Cassin's Geneva years form one integral story, we first deal with his work with *anciens combattants* in this organization in the years before 1933, before turning to his parallel activity within the League itself. Both show his broadening and deepening approach to the difficult task of healing the wounds of war, an approach, which prepared the ground for his work on human rights during and after the Second World War.

Cassin was fully aware of the differences between the UF and other French veterans' groups on questions of working with old enemies. He and Tixier reached the unavoidable conclusion that they simply had to go ahead on their own with the plan to create a body in which old soldiers from both the Allied and the Central powers could come together to discuss issues of mutual interest and to defend the peace.[23]

---

23 Tixier to Cassin, 15 October 1925, ILO Archives, MU/7/9/5.

On 7 August 1925, Paul Brousmiche, then President of the UF, wrote to Albert Thomas, asking him to provide a venue for an international meeting of all veterans' groups to be held later that year in Geneva. With Thomas' support, Tixier wrote back to the UF saying that the good offices of the ILO were at the disposal of the organizing committee of CIAMAC. Tixier found two rooms in the University of Geneva, on the ground floor, to enable disabled men to attend the meeting without difficulty. The ILO provided translators and secretarial staff, who gathered in the *salle d'attente des professeurs* of the University, adjacent to the rooms set aside for the meeting, whose date was set as 18-19 September 1925. The ILO provided no financial support, save negotiating a fee of 2 francs for the rent of the meeting rooms. This was formally a UF affair.[24]

On 18 September 1925, Brousmiche welcomed delegates from eleven countries to Geneva. He saw the meeting as a reflection of the growing power and confidence of veterans, who felt impelled to speak out on a broad range of domestic and international issues. Disabled men, in particular, had to voice their views on war and peace. After the formalities were over, the delegates got down to business. And business was not easy. Tixier explained to Thomas that it took five to six hours of negotiation before a text was agreed, committing all delegates, including the German delegation, to support unequivocally the Covenant of the League and the obligatory arbitration of future international disputes. Tipping the balance towards agreement was the rapport developed between Rossmann, the German delegate and Socialist member of the *Reichstag*, and Pichot, whom Tixier termed "the most convincing speak and also the best journalist in the UF".[25]

The next day the delegates were greeted formally by Eric Drummond, the Secretary General of the LON, by the president of the League's Assembly, the Canadian Raoul Dandurand, and by Joseph Paul-Boncour, the French President of the Council, with whom Cassin worked in the French delegation.[26] The publicity was good for CIAMAC, but some journalists tried to reduce this initiative simply to an LON public relations exercise. Tixier took care, with Thomas' prodding, to distance himself from

---

24 File on September 1925 meeting of CIAMAC, ILO Archives, MU/7/9/5.
25 Tixier to Thomas, 22 September 1925, ILO Archives, MU/7/9/5/1.
26 Drummond to Thomas, 25 September 1925, ILO Archives, MU/7/9/5/1.

CIAMAC, which thereby became one of the first of a breed of political groups we now term 'non-governmental organizations'.

The originality of CIAMAC was that it was a political group speaking up on behalf of ex-soldiers, people with rights. They had no intention of taking or giving charity, and hence were at one remove from the Red Cross and its allied organizations. They were also at one remove from the governments of their members, and were emphatically not paid by nor responsible to the states from which they had come. "The role of CIAMAC", wrote Cassin in 1930, "is not to stand in the place of governments, but to make known to them popular sentiment" in more than one country.[27] Their responsibility was to all the men who had fought in the war, and those whose courage and whose suffering gave them the moral authority to speak out on a whole range of issues. They were non-denominational, and hence had none of the advantages nor any of the disadvantages of the Vatican. They represented a generation of men in uniform, their families, their widows, their orphans, their dependents. They spoke for those millions of men and women for whom the war of 1914-18 was a catastrophe. And for whom was it not? For disabled men like Cassin, Pichot and Tixier, theirs was a moral crusade, a crusade against war. From the outset, their primary aim was to help build a durable peace, and to work to strengthen the League of Nations.[28]

This pacifist voice is what Cassin and his colleagues in the UF transferred to CIAMAC. It was a forum for the discussion of matters of common interest, in the same way as the experts' committees had been. But it was also a voice for understanding across the divide between former enemies, and throughout the later 1920s, before the onset of the world economic crisis undermined the fragile democracies of Germany and the rest of Europe, CIAMAC pressed its campaign to ensure that no future generation of young people would know the ravages of war. Even before Germany was admitted to the League of Nations in 1926, German delegates came to Geneva, to CIAMAC, to prepare the way for their country's re-entry into the community of nations.

CIAMAC met for a second time in Geneva on 30 September to 2 October 1926: 80 delegates from 10 nations and 20 organizations attended. The

---

27 Cassin on CIAMAC, 1930, 15-16, AN, Fonds Cassin, 382 AP 10.
28 Ibid., 4.

hope was that Col. G.R. Crossfield, the British president of FIDAC, could attend and open the meeting, but he was barred from doing so by nationalists within his own organization.[29] As before, the UF, as an allied veterans' group, participated in FIDAC; but FIDAC refused to have anything to do with CIAMAC, tainted by the presence of former enemy soldiers. These tensions erupted within the French delegation as well. Some who attended, Tixier learned, probably from Cassin, aimed to disrupt the meeting and destroy the organization.[30] They wanted to force the German delegates to state publicly their acceptance of the war guilt clause of the Treaty of Versailles, article 231; this would have compromised them at home. Pichot got around this, by asking for a majority vote, yes or no, on the matter within the French delegation. The no's won the vote; the French delegation spoke with one voice. They did not raise the issue, and the storm faded away. For Cassin, as much as for Tixier, five years of slow and steady work had paid off. How moving it was, Tixier told Albert Thomas, to stand together at this meeting, with all these old soldiers, and feel the emotion of the moment of silence they observed to pay their respects to the dead of the war.[31] CIAMAC was launched.

Cassin saw the association as reflecting the interests of a wide body of veterans. In terms of membership, the French, German, and Polish associations predominated. The first service they offered was to bring the experience of other veterans to the aid of individuals in different countries dealing with laws and regulations concerning disability payments, services, and pensions. In addition, its independence from all other bodies – including, Cassin insisted a bit disingenuously, from the LON – enabled it better to work "towards a rapprochement of the countries divided by the war".[32]

In 1927, CIAMAC's annual congress was held in Vienna. Cassin was there together with Brousmiche, Viala, and a priest who was very active in the UF, Bernard Secret. He was a prominent member of the Catholic social movement, was apparently a particular favorite among Austrian Catholics. In Vienna there were 17 delegations in attendance, all, in Tixier's opinion, "resolutely pacifist". The absent organizations were the American Legion,

---

29 Ibid., 5.
30 Tixier to Thomas, 5 October 1925, ILO Archives, MU/7/9/5/1.
31 Ibid.
32 Cassin on CIAMAC, 1930, 6, AN, Fonds Cassin, 382 AP 10.

the British Legion, and the fascist association of Italian veterans. The profile of CIAMAC was centre-left. Half were socialists, radical socialists, or social democrats. What mattered most, Tixier wrote, was their power to challenge ardent nationalists who claimed to speak for the war generation.[33] Here was the pacifist alternative.[34]

In the following year, 1928, CIAMAC met in Berlin, from 9-11 August. Now there were 100 representatives in attendance, coming from 25 delegations. Secret introduced a motion, passed by acclamation, affirming that all disabled men had a right to reparation for the wounds they had incurred in the service of their country. Once more, their position was to demand justice, not charity. The one ticklish moment in the meeting was a complaint by a Polish delegate about certain "incessant aggressive tendencies among German nationalists". This potential embarrassment was defused by Rossmann who said that "the commitment to the principles of the renunciation of war and obligatory arbitration of international conflicts applies to all countries including Poland, and the German people will never permit the use of force to modifier the status quo in Europe".[35] If only that had been true. Unbeknownst to the delegates, the years of hope were coming to an end. The economic crisis of 1929 put paid to the vision that CIAMAC could help forge from soldiers' solidarity a weapon to defend the peace. Meetings in Warsaw in 1929 and in Paris in 1930 showed how braided together in substance were the efforts of CIAMAC and the work of the LON. Its International Commission, established in 1929, was in constant contact with Geneva, as well as with national commissions in each member state of CIAMAC. In the annual meetings in Paris in 1930 as well as in Prague in 1931, Cassin and Rossmann were joint *rapporteurs* on progress and impediments in the path towards a system of arbitration, collective security, and disarmament. But despite all their efforts, the tide had turned. Just after the Prague meeting, in September 1931, the Japanese invasion of Manchuria became the first of the major shocks that were to destroy the foundations of the LON, and of CIAMAC as well.

Throughout its early years, CIAMAC's leaders had hoped to preserve a kind of peace in its dealings with FIDAC, the old Allied veterans' organiza-

---

33 Tixier to Thomas, 15 October 1925, ILO Archives, MU/7/9/5/1.
34 Correspondence and papers on CIAMAC, AN, Fonds Cassin, 382 AP 10, dos. 1.
35 Tixier to Thomas, 17 August 1928, ILO Archives, MU/7/9/5/4.

tion. In 1932, the gap between them became unbridgeable. CIAMAC met in Vienna on 1-3 September 1932; FIDAC chose precisely the same day to hold its annual convention in Lisbon. The British veterans chose FIDAC; then in 1933, the Nazis came to power, and promptly arrested a number of men who had attended CIAMAC meetings. With the major Italian veterans' organizations refusing to come, the entire *raison d'être* of CIAMAC vanished rapidly. The vision Cassin and Tixier had had of a powerful pacifist veterans' association, bringing former enemies together, had been a chimera. The group soldiered on until 1939, but it was – like the peace itself – doomed to destruction.[36]

CONCLUSION

Cassin knew what had been lost, but he also enumerated what had been gained, in particular in defence of the rights of disabled men and their families to decent treatment and adequate pensions. In Danzig, the work of CIAMAC had helped bring sightless veterans under the aegis of the LON, with a subsequent increase in their pensions. The same had been true in Bulgaria. The centre for documentation on the treatment of disabled men was a source of reference for those working on behalf of disabled men everywhere. These were small gains, but real ones. They established in microcosm what CIAMAC stood for in general: the notion that veterans everywhere had rights, defined not only by their nationality but by their humanity. They were not supplicants, but citizens, men who had fought and bled for their countries, and whose well-being was a matter not of charity but of natural justice.[37] What they demanded went beyond citizenship, and by moving in that direction, they presented an option of solidarity, which offered an alternative to the sterile nationalism of the interwar years. Their failure was palpable, but out of it came a precedent central to a later reconciliation with which we are still living today.

---

36 Files on CIAMAC meetings in the 1930s, ILO Archives, MY/7/9/5/13-17.
37 Cassin on CIAMAC, 1930, 9-11, AN, Fonds Cassin, 382 AP 10.

"A Blessed Act of Oblivion"
Human Rights, European Unity and
Postwar Reconciliation

MARCO DURANTI

In a now celebrated address delivered at Zurich in September 1946, the British Conservative politician and former prime minister Winston Churchill launched an ambitious transnational campaign to "re-create the European family in a regional structure called, it may be, the United States of Europe". He urged his audience to lift the opprobrium cast upon those complicit in the crimes committed by the Axis powers during the war. "The guilty must be punished. Germany must be deprived of the power to rearm and make another aggressive war", Churchill conceded. The Nuremberg trials were coming to a conclusion and few believed that the top Nazi leaders deserved to be spared. "But", he continued,

"when all this has been done, as it will be done, as it is being done, there must be an end to retribution. There must be what Mr. Gladstone many years ago called 'a blessed act of oblivion'. We must all turn our backs upon the horrors of the past. We must look to the future. We cannot afford to drag forward across the years that are to come the hatreds and revenges which have sprung from the injuries of the past. If Europe is to be saved from infinite misery, and indeed from final doom, there must be an act of faith in the European family and an act of oblivion against all the crimes and follies of the past."[1]

Invoking the nineteenth-century Liberal statesman William Gladstone's address to the British House of Commons on the question of Irish Home Rule, Churchill had called for a deliberate act of forgetting in the name of social peace and a new Franco-German understanding as the basis of restoring harmony within the "European family" – a community that was "the fountain of Christian faith and Christian ethics" and now aspired to live according to the democratic principles of Franklin Roosevelt's Four Freedoms.[2] Churchill ended his speech with an extraordinary appeal for Franco-German reconciliation. "The first step in the creation of the European family must be a partnership between France and Germany", he declared. "There can be no revival of Europe without a spiritually great France and a spiritually great Germany."[3]

Just as Gladstone had miscalculated the depth of feeling against Home Rule in 1886, Churchill underestimated just how deep the scars of the war and occupation were in France, where the trials of collaborators were still underway and fears of a resurgent Germany were the overriding factor in shaping French foreign policy. The French government had no official comment, while the speech "dumbfounded" and "shocked" French opinion by ignoring the intensity of their fears of reviving German power, according to British reports.[4] Centrist newspapers such as *Le Monde* and the MRP organ *L'Aube* expressed skepticism or polite bemusement regarding Churchill's lack of realism, pointing to France's need for definite guaran-

---

[1] Winston Churchill, Zurich speech, 19 September 1946, in: *Documents on the History of European Integration*, Vol. 3, ed. Walter Lipgens and Wilfried Loth (Berlin: Walter de Gruyter, 1988), 664-665.
[2] Ibid., 663, 665.
[3] Ibid., 665.
[4] An Ill-Timed Speech?, *Manchester Guardian*, 20 September 1946, 5; Franco-German Partnership, *Birmingham Post*, 20 September 1949; French Take Time to Think, *Yorkshire Post*, 20 September 1949; Churchill and Germany: Speech May Arouse Storm, *Liverpool Daily Post*, 20 September 1949.

tees on its eastern borders among other delicate questions.[5] The Socialist party organ *Le Populaire* ignored the speech altogether. Pierre Courtade of the communist daily *L'Humanité* claimed that Churchill spoke of "Europe" as a "smokescreen" for the formation of a "western bloc", another step in the process that had begun in 1925 with the Locarno accords.[6] Such views were not limited to the French alone. In Britain, *The Times* not only thought it unlikely that Churchill's plan was feasible given current French attitudes towards Germany but it feared that the proposal would jeopardize British relations with the Soviet Union: "Many will see in his speech a call, not for a United States of Europe but for a United States of Western Europe."[7] The *News Chronicle* reported that Churchill had given delegates at the ongoing international conference in Paris "new ground for mistrust and suspicion" and that the "early reactions are that nobody is happy about it. [...] There is a widely expressed view that Mr. Churchill has picked a curious time to advocate a policy which was certain, as he must have known, to embarrass the hard and uphill effort which 21 nations are now making in Paris to hold together the victorious war alliance."[8]

In the months to come, Churchill and other advocates of European unity rearticulated their calls for Franco-German cooperation through European unity in a new idiom: the language of international human rights norms. Human rights discourse had entered the vernacular during public discussions over Allied war aims before becoming the subject of intense negotiations at the United Nations Human Rights Commission from 1947 onwards. The human rights projects of the European unity movements would catalyze the adoption of the European Convention on Human Rights by the member states of the Council of Europe in November 1950 and the subsequent establishment of a European Court of Human Rights in Strasbourg.

---

5   Les idées de M. Churchill, *Le Monde*, 20 September 1946, 1; La France et l' Allemagne devront faire les Étas-Unis d'Europe, *L'Aube*, 20 September 1946, 1.
6   Pierre Courtade, Le coup des grands sentiments, *L'Humanité*, 20 September 1946, 3.
7   A Voice from Zürich, *The Times*, 20 September 1946, 5.
8   Denis Weaver, Churchill speech perturbs Paris, *News Chronicle*, 20 September 1946, 1. See also: Mr. Churchill Accused of 'Belligerence', *Newcastle Journal*, 20 September 1949.

This chapter examines three moments in which European unity movements inflected their visions of international reconciliation with the idiom of human rights: the May 1948 Congress of Europe in The Hague, the February 1949 conference of the European Movement in Brussels and the summer 1949 session of the Council of Europe in Strasbourg. In all three instances, transnational networks of civil society elites and opposition politicians fashioned an ideational basis for future reconciliation efforts by imagining the form of community that needed to be created – or in their words, recreated – for reconciliation to be achieved. This initiative, it will be argued, was backward-looking as well as forward-looking, retrospective as well as prospective. European unity movements invoked the language of human rights in order to recall a lost European civilization, one that had supposedly existed before the First World War. The temporal orientation of rights-based reconciliation pointed away from the divisions and crimes of the recent past and towards a Christian and liberal Europe of the deeper past. Moreover, although rights-based visions of reconciliation after 1945 distinguished themselves from *fin-de-siècle* visions of "Peace through Justice" by employing democratic rhetoric, they continued to be fundamentally elitist projects. Both early twentieth-century efforts to create a legal and institutional framework for Franco-German reconciliation and postwar rights-based reconciliation were rooted in a profound fear of the nationalist or radical ideological impulses of mass politics.

THE 1948 CONGRESS OF EUROPE AND THE ANTI-POLITICS OF INTERNATIONAL LAW

The Congress of Europe was one of the greatest transnational meetings of European elites witnessed in modern times. It was not sponsored by any state but rather had been organized by a transnational network of European unity movements coordinated by the Joint International Committee of the Movements for European Unity. The national delegations that this international non-governmental organization had invited to the Congress of Europe corresponded to the sixteen member states of the Organization for European Economic Cooperation: Austria, Belgium, Denmark, Eire, France, Greece, Iceland, Italy, Luxembourg, the Netherlands, Norway, Portugal, Sweden, Switzerland, Turkey, and the United Kingdom. The western zones of Germany, Liechtenstein and the Saar were also represented. In addition to this official first tier of participants, the Congress hosted a number of unofficial "observers" without voting privileges – many of them émigrés – from Bulgaria, Canada, Czechoslovakia, Finland, Hungary, Poland, Rumania, Spain, the United States and Yugoslavia. The largest contingents of delegates came from Britain and France, which combined made up almost half the total presented at the Congress. Each national contingent was composed of politicians and representatives from the arts, humanities, sciences, law, industry, trade unions, women's movements and religious organizations. Among those present at the Congress were twenty-two former prime ministers and twenty-eight former foreign ministers.[9]

The stated objective of this gathering was to develop a blueprint for progress towards greater European cultural, economic and political unity. Before the convening of the Congress, there had been much disagreement amongst the participants over a united Europe's institutional framework and political boundaries. The organizers believed that agreement on the ideal or "spiritual" bases of their project would facilitate the realization of an accord on such temporal matters. They hoped that a common affirmation of human rights and democratic principles would encourage Congress delegates to transcend national and party differences while delimiting the frontiers of a united Europe. In the name of securing the moral foundations of European unity, the Congress organizers proposed that these principles be enshrined in international law. Delegates obliged by calling for the establishment of a supranational court empowered to adjudicate claims brought by individuals or groups against states for alleged violations of a binding human rights charter.

When, during the opening ceremonies of the Congress of Europe on May 7, Churchill touched on the controversial subject of German participation in the European unity project, his words were received with mixed applause.[10] This contrasted with the sustained ovation given to Churchill when he affirmed, "The Movement for European Unity, as our Draft Report declares, must be a positive force, deriving its strength from our sense of common spiritual values. It is a dynamic expression of democratic faith

---

9 Action Awaited, *News Chronicle*, 13 May 1948; Richard Vaughan, *Twentieth-century Europe: Paths to Unity* (London: Croom Helm, 1979), 85.

10 Mr. Churchill's Day at the Hague, *Manchester Guardian*, 8 May 1948, 5.

based upon moral conceptions and inspired by a sense of mission. In the center of our movement stands the idea of a Charter of Human Rights, guarded by freedom and sustained by law."[11] Churchill implicitly compared the system of human rights guarantees proposed by the Congress organizers to the "Grand Design" that Henry IV of France and his advisor Sully had devised during the first decade of the seventeenth century, using the analogy of the religious warfare that had wracked Europe at that time. He focused in particular on Henry IV's plans for a pan-European council, which was, in his words, a "permanent committee representing fifteen – now we are sixteen – leading Christian States of Europe. This body was to act as arbitrator on all questions concerning religious conflict, national frontiers, internal disturbance, and common action against any danger from the East, which in those days meant the Turks."[12] As he would do throughout the address, Churchill hinted at the identity of the "danger from the East" without addressing it by name.

The Congress of Europe's final resolutions recommended that the states of Europe establish a supranational European human rights court, i.e. one that could adjudicate on claims lodged by both state and non-state actors. This constituted a radical challenge to the Westphalian order and has rightly been regarded as an important milestone in the twentieth century's 'human rights revolution'. The requirement that all member states be democracies contrasted with the absence of such criteria in interwar schemes for European federation. The Congress of Europe did not, however, represent a complete sea change in the ideational framework of international law or European unity projects. The Congress's human rights proposals marked a recasting of the elite anti-politics that had long shaped the cultural underpinnings of these fields. It was the residue of this elite anti-politics at the Congress that enabled the emergence of an ephemeral political consensus.

Nearly fifty years before the Congress of Europe, The Hague had been the site of a peace conference that catalyzed the construction of a spectacular Peace Palace that housed the new Permanent Court of Arbitration and later the Permanent Court of International Justice. This Peace Palace anchored the culture of international law in the ideals of ancient Rome and

---

11 Congress of Europe, Vol. 1., Plenary Sessions, 6, Sandys Papers, Churchill Archives Centre, Cambridge (hereafter: CAC), 9/1/8.

12 Ibid.

medieval Christendom. Its irenic utopias gave no purchase, however, to democratic principles and the defense of human rights. Instead, they masked the weak legal prerogatives of its courts, which remained bound to the Westphalian system of sovereign states. Their cosmopolitan, aristocratic sensibility suited well those Good Europeans who saw themselves as above politics and yet remained fearful of those political and social changes that threatened to sweep their class from power. Although the First World War witnessed a refashioning of the international legal field, the Peace Palace continued to embody that depoliticized vision of 'Peace through Justice' where culture and conciliation provided the surest foundations for a Europe of perpetual peace.[13]

The community of international law had long positioned itself defiantly above politics. Just as civilizational discourse had demarcated membership in the society of sovereign states, so had social class provided the shared cultural sensibility that structured the rules for participation in the international legal field. This field had crystallized social distinctions across national boundaries, discouraging diplomats and international lawyers from being tempted by the "petty" nationalism embraced by lower social orders. Such elitism had been meant to inoculate international relations from the ideological struggles that the rise of mass politics had engendered. Even after the advent of the First World War and the Bolshevik Revolution, when civilizational discourse became infused with democratic rhetoric and the League of Nations coordinated a system of minority rights protections, there continued to be no universal requirement that members of international organizations be democracies or respect fundamental rights. Although some advocates of European unity insisted that the member states of a European federation respect certain fundamental rights, even they defined the criteria for entry on the longstanding mores of European elites rather than on democratic principles.[14]

---

13 Geoffrey Best, Peace Conferences and the Century of Total War: The 1899 Hague Conference and What Came After, *International Affairs* 75, 3 (1999), 619-634; Arthur Eyffinger, *The 1899 Hague Peace Conference: 'The Parliament of Man, the Federation of the World'* (The Hague and Boston: Kluwer International Law, 1999).

14 Martti Koskenniemi, *The Gentle Civilizer of Nations: The Rise and Fall of International Law 1870-1960* (Cambridge: Cambridge University Press, 2002);

Churchill's strategy for achieving Franco-German reconciliation through appeals for the "spiritual" unity of Europe anchored in the defense of human rights contrasted with that of Aristide Briand, who had alternated roles as French foreign minister and delegate to the League of Nations from the mid-1920s to the early 1930s. In September 1929, Briand had made a dramatic appeal in front of the League Assembly for new measures to promote international peace.[15] In addition to touching on subjects such as disarmament, Briand had told his audience "I am convinced that, of those peoples that are grouped geographically, such as the peoples of Europe, there must exist a kind of federal bond."[16] Briand's rhetoric had alluded to twentieth-century theories of solidarism, which posited that interlocking networks of communities would eventually break down barriers between peoples, whether erected by class distinctions or states. His scheme had been purportedly inspired in part by the Pan-American solidarist writings of the Chilean diplomat Alejandro Alvarez.[17] Briand's language had also echoed that of nineteenth-century liberals who believed that peace would emerge from closer contacts between peoples without infringing on the sovereign prerogatives of the Great Powers.

Most striking was Briand's insistence on preserving the principle of absolute sovereignty, or as he put it, "without affecting the sovereignty of any nations that could be part of such an association".[18] This wording had left ambiguous the question of which "nations" would be admitted to the proposed "association". Briand had implied that "bonds of solidarity" would emerge primarily through economic exchanges. He had spoken of the need for "a federal bond" arising from geographical proximity and "common interests" without specifying those attributes that formed the basis of a common European civilization. As European culture had long framed the international diplomatic and legal field, Briand had felt no need to articulate its

---

James J. Sheehan, *Where Have All the Soldiers Gone? The Transformation of Modern Europe* (Boston: Houghton Mifflin Co., 2008); Paul Laity, *The British Peace Movement, 1870-1914* (Oxford: Clarendon Press, 2001).

15 Discours du M. Briand du 5 septembre 1929, in: *L'Union Européenne*, ed. B. Mirkine-Guetzevitch and Georges Scelle (Paris: Librarie Delegrave, 1931), 34.
16 Ibid.
17 Koskenniemi, *The Gentle Civilizer of Nations*, 342.
18 Discours du M. Briand, 34.

qualities. They were implicit in the aesthetics of The Hague's Peace Palace, relying more on cultural sensibility than on a precise set of characteristics that could serve as criteria for admission into a European regional organization.

None of this should obscure Briand's primary objective, which had been to contain the rising power of Germany by embedding its relations with France within a broader regional framework. His stress on economics had stemmed from the enthusiasm for European unity projects amongst French and German industrialists who wished to form a continental customs union in order to protect their business concerns from competition with the United States. Briand's proposal had also been warmly received on the part of British businessmen and advocates of Imperial Preference who wished to undermine the free-trade system favored by both the United States and the dominant political factions in Whitehall.[19] The loudest criticisms of Briand's scheme had stemmed from the perception that, first, it would undermine the authority of the League and, secondly, that it would be directed against "non-European" powers, particularly Turkey, the Soviet Union and the United States.[20]

The stunning results of the German legislative elections of September 1930, which made the National Socialists the second-largest party in the Reichstag, had made the failure of the Briand initiative all but inevitable. Whereas the Nazi party had appealed to the primordial racial bonds that united the German *Volk*, the Briand memorandum had not rooted its vision of a European union in a shared history or culture. His proposed European union had no means of defining its external and internal frontiers other than

---

19 Cornelia Navari, Origins of the Briand Plan, in: *The Federal Idea*, ed. Andrea Bosco (London: Lothian Foundation Press, 1991), 211-212; Robert Boyce, British Capitalism and the Idea of European Unity Between the Wars, in: *European Unity in Context: The Interwar Period*, ed. Peter Stirk (London: Pinter Publishers, 1989), 78-81.

20 Memorandum sur l'organisation d'un régime d'Union Fédérale Européenne, in: *L'Union Européenne,* 60-61; Raymond Léonard, *Vers une organisation politique et juridique de l'Europe: Du projet d'Union Fédérale Européenne de 1930 aux Pactes de Sécurité*, published doctoral thesis (Paris: Rousseau, 1935), 198; see, in particular, the responses of Estonia, Germany, Greece, Hungary, Italy, Latvia, Lithuania, and Luxembourg in: *L'Union Européenne*.

fall back on the criteria of geography and mutual interests, which in practice corresponded to the existing organization and membership of the League.

Briand's distinctly temporal vision of Franco-German reconciliation through European unity contrasted distinctly with his collaborator Richard Coudenhove-Kalergi, the Czech count who had founded the transnational Pan-Europa Movement shortly after the First World War. Coudenhove-Kalergi had been the most prominent proponent of a rights-based approach to European unity in the interwar period. He was an outspoken opponent of National Socialism from its inception, writing at length on the fallacies of its racial and anti-Semitic theories. The Czech nobleman was, however, no democrat. Although he often cited contemporary Switzerland as a template for a future European federation, his writings strongly implied that the most salient historical model was the "cosmopolite and polyglot" Austro-Hungarian Empire, whose aristocratic political class had formed a "supernational" government that for many years checked the nationalistic tendencies of the middle classes.[21] He justified his contacts with dictators such as Benito Mussolini and Engelbert Dollfuss by claiming that Europe was above all a "cultural community" that should be governed by its "greatest geniuses," those "really educated statesmen" who would save Europe from the "half-educated" masses swayed by populist agitators of the extreme left and right.[22] Mussolini's reputation as an uncultured demagogue did little to deter Coudenhove-Kalergi from courting the Duce's favor, as the Count believed that Bolshevism and Nazism were greater evils than what he perceived as "moderate" authoritarianism.[23]

Coudenhove-Kalergi believed that a comprehensive and enlightened solution to the minorities question was essential for the peace of Europe. In 1923, he proposed in his book *Pan-Europa* "a true protection of minorities by the universal enforcement of a national edict of toleration – a Magna

---

21 Richard Coudenhove-Kalergi, *Crusade for Pan-Europe: An Autobiography of a Man and a Movement* (New York: G. P. Putnam's Sons, 1943), 46-47.
22 Richard Coudenhove-Kalergi, *Europe Must Unite* (Glarus: Paneuropa Editions, 1939), 130-131.
23 Richard Coudenhove-Kalergi, *The Totalitarian State Against Man* (London: Frederick Muller, 1938), 118-120.

Carta of all European nations".[24] This "Pan-European edict of toleration deprives the state frontiers of their national meaning" and thus "inter-European points of friction which might lead to another war disappear", he wrote.[25] Shortly before the outbreak of the Second World War, Coudenhove-Kalergi's issued a new program for his Pan-Europa Movement that required "all European states, regardless of differences in their constitutions, to respect the rights of the human personality and the equality of their citizens belonging to ethnic or religious minorities". Coudenhove-Kalergi explained, "Only if this principle of national human rights is accepted can there be European reconciliation and perpetual European peace."[26]

Coudenhove-Kalergi's program had been drafted in conjunction with a committee of British notables organized by the Conservatives Leo Amery and Duff Cooper. He had initially placed Britain outside the frontiers of a united Europe.[27] In the late 1930s, however, he began to look across the Channel. In June 1938, he told an audience at Chatham House in London that they should view Europe as a second Commonwealth or "the *Lebensraum* of England", as British rule was preferable to German domination of the continent.[28] In 1939, Coudenhove-Kalergi wrote, "[O]ur common European culture is today rooted in a humanist education, in a Christian morality, and in the spirit of chivalry now incorporated in the civic ideal of the English gentleman."[29]

Coudenhove-Kalergi's address at the opening ceremonies of the Congress of Europe echoed Churchill's speech by embedding a future European organization in a broader rapprochement between peoples. "I hope that our Congress will serve not only the cause of European Union, but also that of European reconciliation", he announced. Though Coudenhove-Kalergi insisted that "Europe needs a thorough reeducation and denazification," he

---

24 Richard Coudenhove-Kalergi, *Pan-Europe* (New York: Alfred Knopf, 1926), 166.
25 Ibid., 170.
26 Coudenhove-Kalergi, *Europe Must Unite*, 120.
27 Coudenhove-Kalergi, *Pan-Europe*, 35-50.
28 Andrea Bosco, *Federal Union and the Origins of the 'Churchill Proposal': The Federalist Debate in the United Kingdom from Munich to the Fall of France, 1938-1940* (London: Lothian Foundation Press, 1992), 139.
29 Coudenhove-Kalergi, *Europe Must Unite*, 131.

immediately followed this statement with a qualification. "We must reject the barbaric and totalitarian notion of collective guilt and collective punishment", he insisted. "We all must learn more tolerance, more generosity, more mercy."[30]

One of the British delegates on the Congress's Cultural Committee was David Maxwell Fyfe, former deputy chief prosecutor at the International Military Tribunal in Nuremberg. Alongside Churchill, Maxwell Fyfe would be one of the most influential British Conservatives in the early stages of the European human rights project. Maxwell Fyfe was the first to make a forceful intervention against attempts by other delegates to omit references to a charter and court of human rights in the Congress's Cultural Resolution. Citing his work at the Nuremberg trials, Maxwell Fyfe stated he felt it his "individual responsibility" to fight for the establishment of international human rights safeguards.[31] He claimed that the Nuremberg trials had posed the fundamental question, "What is the duty of a good European?" The trials were necessary for "the establishment of a sounder and saner Europe", reaffirming the principles of international law and offering Germans the opportunity to enter "back into the European stream of thought and development".[32] Reflecting on Nuremberg in retrospect, he observed, "I am certain that the Nazi leaders felt and resented most keenly that they were considered by those who watched the trial to have poisoned the great stream of western European civilization. Again and again they displayed almost what the Romans termed 'desiderium' and the Greeks 'pothos' – a vain longing to be recognized as part of the European family."[33] Subsequently, in July 1948, Maxwell Fyfe would contribute an article to the review *Round Table*,

---

30 Congress of Europe, Vol. 1., Plenary Sessions, 14.
31 Congress of Europe, The Hague, Cultural Committee, Saturday, May 8th 1948, 10.15 a.m., 11, European Movement papers 502, Historical Archives of the European Union, Florence (hereafter: HAEU).
32 David Maxwell Fyfe, Prelude to European Unity: Notes for a Speech at the Literary Luncheon given by W. & G. Foyle Ltd. at the Dorchester Hotel on Friday, February 21, 1947, 5, Papers of Lord Kilmuir [David Maxwell Fyfe], (hereafter: Kilmuir Papers), CAC, dossier 7/2.
33 David Maxwell Fyfe, Notes for a Speech at Brussels made on Saturday 20th December 1947 at 4 p.m. to the Union Belgo-Britannique, Kilmuir Papers, CAC, 7/2.

writing that the resolutions of the Congress of Europe "indicate the importance of the condition of 'membership of the club' being the acceptance of a Charter of Human Rights with its implementation assured by a Supreme Court".[34] The question of which nations would qualify as members of the Council of Europe was a subject of great concern within the European Movement, which began increasingly to employ the new idiom of international human rights norms as a means of facilitating the entry of Germany into this 'club' while excluding the participation of the states in the communist bloc.

THE GERMAN QUESTION AT THE 1949 BRUSSELS CONFERENCE OF THE EUROPEAN MOVEMENT

The organizers of the Congress of Europe could claim much success in the year that followed the conclusion of that event. In July 1948, French foreign minister Georges Bidault asked the Brussels Pact countries to support the creation of a European Assembly. British foreign minister Ernest Bevin initially resisted the idea but relented in January 1949 after Bidault's successor, Robert Schuman, informed him that France would proceed without Britain, if necessary. On May 5, 1949, representatives of ten countries – Belgium, Britain, Denmark, France, Ireland, Italy, Luxembourg, the Netherlands, Norway and Sweden – concluded the drafting of a statute forming a Council of Europe composed of a Committee of Ministers and a Consultative Assembly. The first session of the Council of Europe was scheduled to take place in August and September 1949. Here was a set of state-sponsored initiatives often driven by ulterior strategic considerations, but directed to giving form to a vision of European peace through unity.[35]

---

34 David Maxwell Fyfe, Next Step for 'United Europe' (orig. manuscript for publication in *Round Table*, edition of 21 July 1948), Kilmuir Papers, CAC, 7/3, 3.
35 For national studies of the origins of the Council of Europe, see Marie-Thérèse Bitsch, Le rôle de la France dans la naissance du Conseil de l'Europe, in: *Histoire des débuts de la construction européenne (Mars 1948-Mai 1950) / Origins of European Integration (March 1948-May 1950)*, ed. Raymond Podevin (Bruxelles: Bruylant, 1986), 165-198; Marie-Anne Engelbel, La Belgique et les débuts du Conseil de l'Europe, in: *Jalons pour une histoire du Conseil de*

During this period, the Joint International Committee of the Movements for European Unity renamed itself the European Movement and assumed responsibility for developing recommendations to governments concerning future steps towards juridical, economic, cultural and political unification. It did so through a series of conferences, the first of which took place in Brussels from February 25 to 28, 1949. This conference was dedicated to drafting a proposal for a binding European Convention and Court of Human Rights. It was also responsible for issuing a more general resolution entitled "Principles of a European Policy".

Meanwhile, the U.N. General Assembly had adopted the Universal Declaration of Human Rights on December 10, 1948. The 30 articles of this nonbinding resolution enumerated a broad spectrum of civil, political, economic, social, and cultural rights. Its content, although drawing on a diverse array of philosophical traditions, Western and non-Western, reflected primarily the emergence of social democracy as the fulcrum of political consensus among anti-fascist forces during the course of the Second World War. Despite the disagreements and machinations that characterized the negotiations over the document, as well as the abstention of the Soviet bloc on the final vote, the Universal Declaration was premised on the illusory hope that a common statement of social democratic principles could bridge the ideological divide between Western democracies and communist states.

Some of the leaflets dispersed at the open-air meeting of the European Movement at the Brussels Bourse stated, "United Europe is letting in the former Nazis but keeping out the victors of Stalingrad", and asked, "What are ex-Nazis doing on the platform of the European Movement?" "Dirty German!" cried the protestors when Churchill mounted the stage. The communists were incensed at the suggestion that the Western zones of Germany join a Council of Europe and that Germans participate in the

---

l'Europe: Actes du colloque de Strasbourg (8-10 juin 1995), ed. Marie-Thérèse Bitsch (Bern: P. Lang, 1997), 53-75; Rinaldo Merlone, Faire du Conseil de l'Europe 'l'Union européenne': le projet e Carlo Sforza, in: *Jalons pour une histoire du Conseil de l'Europe*, 77-98; Roland Marx, Enjeux intérieurs et choix internationaux en Grande-Bretagne (1948-1949), in: *Jalons pour une histoire du Conseil de l'Europe*, 39-51. See also John W. Young, *Britain, France and the Unity of Europe, 1945-1951* (Leicester: Leicester University Press, 1984), 108-117.

Brussels Conference on the same terms as the other delegates.[36] Germans had maintained a low profile at the Congress of Europe, keeping largely to themselves, intervening only sporadically in the discussions and having difficulty making their mother tongue understood.[37] At the Brussels Conference, by contrast, they played a more active role.

At the Brussels Conference, the Belgian communist daily *Le Drapeau Rouge* denounced Karl Arnold, the head of the German delegation and Catholic Christian democrat (CDU) minister-president of the land Northrhine-Westfalia, for hindering the denazification of German industry.[38] Arnold did not hesitate to advocate a policy of leniency towards the Germans on the part of the occupying forces and to stress the need to integrate West Germany into Western European regional organizations. He asked his fellow delegates after the rally to consider that "probably every European people has experienced turbulent times in which its duty towards the European community has been disregarded". The misery that Hitler had visited

---

36 For descriptions of the European Movement's open-air meeting at the Bourse, see: M. Léon Jouhaux élu president du Conseil international, *L'Aube*, 28 February 1949; Churchill Beats Booing Reds, *Daily Express*, 28 February 1949; 60 arrests at Churchill meeting, *Daily Graphic*, 28 February 1949; Winston Talks, 60 arrested, *Daily Herald*, 28 February 1949; Churchill defeats Reds – in French, *Daily Mail*, 28 February 1949; Mr. Churchill: Half Europe is in Prison, *Daily Telegraph and Morning Post*, 28 February 1949; Churchill Booed in Brussels, *Daily Worker*, 28 February 1949; Charles d'Ydewalle, Sous les sarcasmes de M. Spaak les communists belges sont mis en déroute, *Le Figaro*, 28 February 1949; Churchill Speech Quietens the Communists, *Manchester Guardian*, 28 February 1949; William J. Humphreys, Churchill Calls Union to Prevent War, *New York Herald Tribune* (European edition), 28 February 1949; Léon Jouhaux élu president du Conseil international du Mouvement européen, *Le Populaire*, 28 February 1949.
37 Bremen to London, Impressions of a German delegate to the Congress of Europe at The Hague, 28 May 1948, British National Archives, Kew, PRO 371/73905.
38 Voilà les homes du 'Mouvement' contre l'Europe, *Le Drapeau Rouge*, 25 February 1949.

upon the German people had allowed them to undergo a process of "spiritual purification", he argued.[39]

Arnold was on the left-wing of the CDU and was co-founder of the *Deutscher Gewerkschaftsbund* trade union.[40] Like the majority of the German delegation at the Brussels Conference, Arnold had been persecuted by the Nazis for his political activities and been imprisoned during the war in a German *Lager*. In his view, these terrible hardships made the Germans uniquely suited to advancing the objectives of the European Movement. "Who is better qualified to lead the way to a better future than those who have learnt wisdom through suffering?" he asked.[41] Arnold was an early and adamant supporter of the economic integration of France and Germany as a means of advancing a rapprochement between the two countries.[42] His words at the Brussels Conference echoed those that Churchill had uttered in the House of Commons on December 10, 1948, the same day that the U.N. General Assembly adopted the Universal Declaration of Human Rights. At that time, Churchill had stated:

"The recent elections in Berlin have been a proof of the resurrection of the German spirit and a beacon casting its light on the minds of a mighty race without whose effective aid the glory of Europe cannot be revived. I hope nothing will be done by the Government – or, so far as we can avoid it, by our allies – to chill or check this important evolution of German sentiment. It is for this reason that I look forward to the day when all these [sic] hateful process of denazification and even the trials of leaders and prominent servants of the Hitler regime may be brought to an end."[43]

Churchill then had stressed the importance of Franco-German reconciliation, once again asking the French to "take the lead in bringing the German

---

39 Speech by Herr Karl Arnold, 28 February 1949, European Movement papers 544, HAEU.
40 Wolfram Kaiser, *Christian Democracy and the Origins of European Union* (Cambridge: Cambridge University Press, 2007), 187.
41 Speech by Herr Karl Arnold, 28 February 1949, European Movement papers 544, HAEU.
42 Kaiser, *Christian Democracy and the Origins of European Union*, 187.
43 Great Britain and Israel, *Manchester Guardian*, 11 December 1948.

people back into the European family. In this way alone can they revive their own fame and regain their place in the world."[44]

The Political Resolution of the Congress of Europe had affirmed that "the integration of Germany in a United or Federated Europe alone provides a solution to both the economic and political aspects of the German problem."[45] The French delegation, however, had stymied efforts to press for the immediate inclusion of Germany in a United Europe. German federalists had responded that West Germany should be admitted without delay because it respected human rights and this was the only legitimate criterion for entry into that body.[46] At the Brussels Conference, in contrast, the initiative to invite Germany to join a Council of Europe came from the French delegation. This reflected a broader shift in French policy towards Germany. As a French foreign ministry memorandum explained, Germans would be more amenable to satisfying French security needs if France were to appeal to the strong "European" sentiment in that country. Without embedding Germany in a Council of Europe, Germans would either dream of Hitler's Europe or succumb to Stalin's Europe.[47]

The French Christian Democrat Robert Bichet secured votes for a motion in favor of the immediate entry of Germany into a Council of Europe, arguing that delegates should not even wait until Germany adopted a federal constitution.[48] He was president of the *Nouvelles Équipes Internationales*, a pan-European organization dedicated to supporting progressive Catholic causes and coordinating the activities of Christian Democrats across the continent. One of its primary objectives was the incorporation of Germany into a United Europe and its second meeting, which took place in Luxembourg in early 1948, had been the first postwar international con-

---

44 Ibid.
45 Resolutions – Congress of Europe – The Hague – May 1948, European Movement papers 1122, 6, HAEU.
46 Baden-Baden to Paris, "Allemagne et Union Européenne", 23 December 1948, Archives Diplomatiques, Paris (hereafter: ADP), Europe (1945-60), Généralités, Box 9.
47 Memorandum: L'Allemagne et l'Union Européenne, 5 January 1949, ADP, Europe (1945-60), Généralités, Box 9.
48 Séance plénière du lundi matin 28 février 1949, European Movement papers 543, 11/1, HAEU.

gress in which an official German delegation, including future German chancellor Konrad Adenauer, had participated.[49] The final recommendations issued by the Brussels Conference stated, "Henceforth, West Germany, and all of Germany when it will be possible, must be invited to integrate itself in this new community, in which all peoples will have the same rights and the same responsibilities."[50]

GOOD GERMANS AT THE COUNCIL OF EUROPE

The inaugural session of the Council of Europe was held in the summer of 1949 in Strasbourg. The choice of Strasbourg as the site of these meetings was a daring move. The most prominent international institutions of the interwar period had been located on neutral ground, with the League of Nations headquartered in Geneva and the Permanent Court of International Justice situated in The Hague. Strasbourg, by contrast, had been at the epicenter of international conflicts for over two centuries. It had changed hands four times during the past eighty years alone, annexed by Germany after the Franco-Prussian War, restored to France at the conclusion of the First World War, seized by the Germans again during the Second World War and now once more finding itself on French soil.

The founders of the Council of Europe had calculated that their choice of locale would transform Strasbourg from a site of Franco-German antagonism into a symbol of a new age of peace through unity. Yet, scars ran deep. A great number of Alsatian youth had been conscripted to fight with the Germans on the Russian front, many never to return. For some, talk of European unity invoked Hitler's plans for a "New Order". Although no Germans would participate in the proceedings of the Council of Europe that summer, some of the residents of Strasbourg worried that the formation of a

---

49 Heribert Gisch, The 'Nouvelles Équipes Internationales' (NEI) of the Christian Democrats, in: *Documents on the History of European Integration*, Vol. 4, ed. Walter Lipgens and Wilfried Loth (Berlin: Walter de Gruyter, 1991), 477-540, here: 480.

50 Conclusions et Recommandations adoptées à la Session Inaugurale du Conseil International du Mouvement Européen, Bruxelles, 25-28 Février 1949, European Movement papers 107, HAEU.

United Europe would facilitate the return of German hegemony in the name of greater "European" ideals.[51] With the West German general election scheduled to occur six days after the start of the Committee of Ministers' first session, there was much trepidation that the Germans would once again opt for nationalism over reconciliation. This time, the Alsatians feared, revanchism might take a more insidious form.

On the same day that Churchill sponsored a proposal to add human rights to the agenda of the Council of Europe's Consultative Assembly, the British opposition leader proclaimed at a European Movement rally that "[t]he life of free Europe depends on association with Germany".[52] German elections took place on August 14, 1949, paving the way for a center-right coalition government. On August 17, in a speech calling for the creation of a European court of human rights, Churchill became the first delegate to argue in the Consultative Assembly for the admission of Germany into the Council of Europe. He asked his fellow delegates to adopt a resolution in favor of an extraordinary session of the Consultative Assembly in December 1949 or January 1950 that would welcome a German delegation in its midst.[53] Konrad Adenauer understood that Germany's path to redemption in the eyes of the world lay through joining the Council of Europe. A week after Churchill's speech, he announced, "As things stand at present, Germany in my opinion would not be eligible to join the Atlantic pact. First we must be a member of the Council of Europe. Then we must quietly await further developments."[54] "It is completely obvious", *Pravda* subsequently observed, "that the European Council is one of the organs of the North Atlantic bloc system – a particular sort of servants' entrance into this system".[55]

---

51 Strasbourg deviendra-t-il le siège des organismes permanents de l'Union Européenne?, *Journal d'Alsace et de Lorraine*, 13-14 February 1949.
52 Strasbourg Rally Hails Churchill, *New York Herald Tribune*, 13 August 1949.
53 First Session, Reports, Part I, 286, Council of Europe Archives, Strasbourg (hereafter: COEA).
54 Adenauer Says Europe Council is 1st Objective, *New York Herald Tribune*, 25 August 1949.
55 Quoted in: Pravda' Sniffs More U.S. Plots at Strasbourg, *New York Herald Tribune*, 31 August 1949.

The bicentennial of Goethe's birth coincided with the first session of the Consultative Assembly, providing an opportunity to cast Germans as fundamentally Good Europeans that had lost their way through succumbing to the temptations of militant nationalism during the past century. Officials from the Council of Europe laid a wreath at a statute of Goethe in Strasbourg University. In Mainz, André Poncet, the French High Commissioner, called Goethe "the great European".[56] Sandro Volta argued in *Il Corriere della Sera* Germans should not consider Goethe as part of their "national glories" but rather as a "citizen of Europe".[57] Alfio Russo, writing in the same newspaper, had already remarked on the "paradox of a Europe that includes Asiatic Ankara and, instead, excludes Frankfurt".[58]

At least one Goethe retrospective argued that the German author's humanism represented a point of synergy between Germanic and Latin understandings of human rights. Pierre Corval wrote in *L'Aube* that the bicentennial should remind Europeans that Goethe's understanding of the European spirit was based on a respect for the dignity of the human person, which was the foundation of the European Movement's human rights proposals. Europe would continue to be a "fiction" until Goethe and the European Movement's vision of "European man" prevailed over the slavery of Soviet totalitarianism.[59]

Churchill's efforts to secure a resolution in favor of an extraordinary session of the Consultative Assembly that would include German delegates were unsuccessful, due primarily to the opposition of British Labourites and the French delegates. Anxieties over the possibility of a rearmed and resurgent Germany were still too great. Yet, for those in the European Movement advocating the creation of a European court of human rights, the means to prevent the revival of antidemocratic forces in Germany had already been defined in its Draft Convention. They hoped that its eventual adoption by Germany would reassure skeptics that Germany was prepared to be a Good European.

---

56 Goethe – The Great 4-Zone European, *Daily Mail*, 29 August 1949.
57 Sandro Volta, La Celebrazione a Francoforte, *Il Corriere della Sera*, 28 August 1949.
58 Alfio Russo, La necessità di legare la Germania all'Occidente, *Il Corriere della Sera*, 17 August 1949.
59 Pierre Corval, L'Homme d'abord, *L'Aube*, 27 August 1949.

Even after Churchill's gambit failed, the leadership of the European Movement would not be deterred from its advocacy of immediate German entry. On September 7, 1949, Sandys called a press conference, declaring, "The European Movement will do all it can to facilitate her admission".[60] On September 8, Layton announced in the Consultative Assembly,

"This list [of rights] which we are proposing, coupled with the right of intervention in some form or another – in the first place by protest, negotiation, and so on, and ultimately in terms of enforcement – constitutes the club rules for this Council. We are therefore drawing up the terms which will decide the admission of any future applicant or country which may be admitted here. We are drawing up conditions which Spain or Germany – to be perfectly frank – or any other country must fulfil, both as regards the items in the list, and as regards accepting the right of intervention, before they can become Members of this Council of Europe."[61]

As Raymond Millet explained in *Le Monde*, the European human rights project was intended to "render possible the admission of other states, that is, Germany. Because, they tell us, suppose that participating nation one day flouts the principles of the Council of Europe. Would it be necessary to exclude it? That would exacerbate its nationalism. By contrast, a decision from the Supreme Court of Human Rights would set it back on the right path without a confrontation."[62]

The European Movement was successful in presenting a European convention of human rights as a means of ensuring the peaceful integration of Germany into the Council of Europe. The Greek and Turkish representatives in the Consultative Assembly's Committee on Legal and Administrative Questions, for example, had initially objected to the drafting of a binding human rights convention but dropped their opposition after it was made clear to them that a convention on human rights was necessary to admit Germany into the "European community".[63] On November 10, 1949, Paul-

---

60 Join Us, Says Sandys to W. Germany, *Daily Worker*, 8 September 1949.
61 First Session, Reports, Part IV, 1186, COEA.
62 Raymond Millet, L'Assemblée Européenne hésite entre la hardiesse et la prudence, *Le Monde*, 9 September 1949, 1.
63 Strasbourg to Paris, 31 August 1949, ADP, Europe (1945-1960), Conseil de l'Europe, 1949-1955, Box 26.

Henri Spaak, the president of the Consultative Assembly and an honorary president of the European Movement, would write to Gustav Rasmussen, president of the Committee of Ministers, to express his dismay that the Committee of Ministers had not yet acted upon the human rights resolution approved by the Consultative Assembly. It was imperative that the Council of Europe act quickly, Spaak argued, because its objective was to reinforce reciprocal confidence in the democratic institutions of "present and future members". Spaak was clearly signaling that it was vital to conclude a human rights convention before the admission of Germany.[64]

If members of the European Movement deployed their human rights project as a mechanism for the inclusion of Germany, they also used it as a means to justify the exclusion of communist regimes from the Council of Europe. As Maxwell Fyfe told the Assembly on August 19,

"I realise that when we lay down tests, those who fail to pass the tests must be excluded. Therefore I appeal to those nations who belong to and revere the great family of Western Europe and Christian civilisation. I make no reflection on those who do not, but I turn to the problem as it exists. Will they not adapt their Governments so as to conform to opinions which are so redolent of that tradition and of that spirit? We seek only to delimit the conditions in which alone the dignity of the human spirit will stand, free, firm and unassailed. May this test which we have propounded become not an exclusion but a passport to our midst."[65]

Just as Churchill had done in his speech at the Albert Hall in May 1947, Maxwell Fyfe did not state outright that countries in the Soviet sphere of influence would be forever ineligible to join a united Europe. Yet, his metaphor of the human rights "passport" implicitly created a two-tier system, whereby states that were members of "the great family of Western Europe and Christian civilisation" had priority over those that were not. Under this logic, there was little doubt that a Germany governed by a coalition of CDU/CSU and FDP under Adenauer would soon be welcomed into the European club.

---

64 Paul-Henri Spaak to Gustav Rasmussen, 10 November 1949, ADP, Europe (1945-1960), Conseil de l'Europe, 1949-1955, Box 26.
65 First Session, Reports, Part II, 452, COEA.

On the first day of the first session of the Committee of Ministers, Derek Kartun of the *Daily Worker* had called the Council of Europe a "massive stunt". "Figuring large in the great stream of United Europe propaganda is the insistent plea that Germany must be brought back into the fold and that the existence of this new body will in some undefined – and indeed undefinable – way guard against a revival of aggressive Nazism", he wrote.[66] Kartun had not anticipated that the drafting of a binding European convention on human rights would provide those advocating German entry with a potent argument for constructing a united Europe whose frontiers would extend east of the Rhine but – with the inconvenient exception of Turkey – not beyond the pale of Christendom.

The question of German participation in common European institutions thrust the language of international human rights norms into mainstream British political discourse. The 1950 general election manifesto of the Conservative Party, issued in January, stated, "Hand in hand with France and other friendly powers we shall pursue the aim of closer unity in Europe. The admission of the Government of Western Germany into the Council of Europe will be supported on the understanding that she accepts freely and fully the Western democratic conception of human rights."[67] The use of the phrase 'human rights' was in marked contrast with the appeal to 'our ancient liberties' in the Conservative Party's previous general election manifesto. International human rights norms were presented as a means of safely reintegrating Germany into the 'West'. On 6 September 1946, US Secretary of State James Byrnes had stated that "it never was the intention of the American Government to deny to the German people the right to manage their own internal affairs as soon as they were able to do so in a democratic way, with genuine respect for human rights and fundamental freedoms".[68]

---

66 Derek Kartun, Council of capitalist Europe, *Daily Worker*, 8 August 1949.
67 Conservative Party General Election Manifesto 1950, in: *Conservative Party General Election Manifestos, 1900-1997*, ed. Iain Dale (London: Routledge, 2000), 88.
68 Stuttgart address by Secretary of State Byrnes, in: *Documents on Germany, 1944-1959: background documents on Germany, 1944-1959, and a chronology of political developments affecting Berlin, 1945-1956*, ed. US Department of State Historical Office (Washington, DC: US Government Printing Office, 1959), 39.

The official title of the European Convention on Human Rights signed in Rome on 4 November 1950 was the Convention for the Protection of Human Rights and Fundamental Freedoms.

West German newspapers would describe the Federal German Republic's signing of the European Convention in November 1950 as a signal diplomatic achievement, for it was the first time that it had entered into an international accord on an equal basis with other states.[69] After West Germany became a full member of the Council of Europe in May 1951, Adenauer gave a speech to the Consultative Assembly in December of that year in which he described adherence to the European Convention as part of the German people's commitment to "European values", for "[a] bitter and very dangerous experience has taught our people that it is necessary to expend all one's energies to maintain, develop and defend the culture of the West, if it is to survive".[70] The West German government's declaration of 27 September 1951 stressing the measures that it had taken to effectuate reconciliation between Germans and Jews stated,

"The attitude of the Federal Republic of Germany to its Jewish citizens is clearly defined through the Basic Law [...]. These legal norms are the law of the land and oblige every German citizen, and especially every state official, to reject any form of racial discrimination. In the same spirit, the German government has also signed the Human Rights Convention adopted by the Council of Europe and has pledged itself to the realization of the legal concepts laid down in this Convention."[71]

---

69 Hallstein unterzeichnet für Deutschland. Die Charta der Menschenrechte vom Ministerausschuß in Rom gebilligt, *Frankfurter Allgemeine Zeitung*, 6 November 1950; Ministerausschuß des Europarats billigt Konvention der Menschenrechte, *Frankfurter Rundschau*, 6 November 1950.

70 Konrad Adenauer, Discours prononcé à l'Assemblée Consultative du Conseil de l'Europe, 10 December 1951, Italian Diplomatic Archives, Rome, Segretaria De Gasperi (1944-52), Box 27.

71 Translation found in: Statement by Chancellor Adenauer to the Bundestag Concerning the Attitude of the Federal Republic towards the Jews, 27 September 1951, in: *Politics and Government in Germany: 1944-1994: Basic Documents*, ed. Carl-Christoph Schweitzer et al. (Providence: Berghahn Book, 1995), 122.

Conclusion

The West German government's statement marked an important initial step in the process of reconciliation between, not only Germans and the Jewish people, but Germany and a wider European civilization. The use of the language of European human rights law in this document was an outcome of both the broader revolution in international human rights norms of the 1940s and the particular transnational civil society initiatives that had emerged from the Congress of Europe. On the surface nothing could have been more different than the *fin-de-siècle* vision of a common European civilization in which culture trumped ideology as the basis of the community of international law and the vision of European civilization expressed by the postwar European unity movements in which the basis of a united Europe rested on the respect for human rights and democracy. Moreover, the postwar European unity movement challenged the Westphalian principle of absolute state sovereignty rather than accommodate it.

Even so, there were also striking continuities between the rights-based reconciliation initiatives of the European unity movements after the Second World War and the *fin-de-siècle* mantra of 'peace through justice'. The imagined community that was the end goal of international reconciliation continued to be framed by a backward-looking and elitist worldview. It is important to keep in mind the retrospective as well as prospective nature of visions of reconciliation after the Second World War. These were visions that looked back not to the fractured Europe of the age of total war but to an imagined Christian and liberal Europe of an earlier era. While the creation of European human rights law was a new means of bringing Germany "back" into the "European family", the civilizational discourse that framed rights-based reconciliation was not novel. It is these continuities that we must keep in mind when telling the story of both postwar reconciliation and the postwar genesis of European human rights law.

Reconciliation in the Aftermath of World War II

Franco-German Rapprochement and Reconciliation in the Ecclesial Domain
The Meeting of Bishops in Bühl (1949) and the Congress of Speyer (1950)[1]

ULRIKE SCHRÖBER

The Franco-German friendship is largely regarded as a prime example of the successful rapprochement of two hostile nations. Through nearly a century filled with resentments, conflicts, and wars, the so-called hereditary enmity of Germany and France developed. Rapprochement efforts, such as attempts by the politicians Gustav Stresemann and Aristide Briand,[2] or of the Catholic Marc Sangnier,[3] in the interwar period ended with the emergence of National Socialism and at the latest with the outbreak of the Second World War. Incorporated into the process of European integration and partly following previous endeavours, the remarkable history of the Franco-German friendship began after this war. The new togetherness of the "coup-

---

1   All quotations originally in German and French were translated into English by the author.
2   Jacques Bariéty, *Les relations franco-allemandes après la première guerre mondiale* (Paris: Pedane, 1977).
3   Denis Lefèvre and Marc Sangnier, *L'aventure du catholicisme social* (Paris: Mame, 2008).

le franco-allemand"[4] became visible particularly through great symbols and in emotional gestures exhibited in the political realm. The signing of the Treaty of Friendship by Konrad Adenauer and Charles de Gaulle in 1963[5] or the handshake between Helmut Kohl and François Mitterrand in 1984[6] serve as examples of this alliance.

Right from the start, this political-diplomatic sphere was in the focus of historical research on Franco-German relations in the post-war period.[7] However, actual efforts by French and German politicians to form an understanding with their neighbours began relatively late.[8] In contrast, many initiatives for rapprochement from civil society started already immediately after World War II, and since the 1990s, these efforts attracted increased research interest.[9] Institutions and organisations such as the *Deutsch-Fran-*

---

4 *Le couple franco-allemand en Europe*, ed. Henri Ménudier (Asnières: Inst. Allemande d'Asnières, 1993).

5 *Der Elysée-Vertrag und die deutsch-französischen Beziehungen 1945-1963-2003*, ed. Corine Defrance and Ulrich Pfeil (München: Oldenbourg, 2005).

6 Matti Münch, *Verdun. Mythos und Alltag einer Schlacht* (München: M-Press, 2006), 499-500.

7 Gilbert Ziebura, *Die deutsch-französischen Beziehungen seit 1945. Mythen und Realitäten* (Stuttgart: Neske, 1997); Ulrich Lappenküper, *Die deutsch-französischen Beziehungen 1949-1963. Von der 'Erbfeindschaft' zur 'Entente élémentaire'* (München: Oldenbourg, 2001).

8 Renate Fritsch-Bournazel, Die Wende in der französischen Nachkriegspolitik 1945-1949: Die 'deutsche Gefahr' verliert die Priorität, in: *Die französische Deutschlandpolitik zwischen 1945 und 1949*, ed. Institut Français de Stuttgart (Tübingen: Attempto, 1987), 7-25; Corina Schukraft, Die Anfänge der deutschen Europapolitik in den 50er und 60er Jahren: Weichenstellungen unter Konrad Adenauer und Bewahrung des Status quo unter seinen Nachfolgern Ludwig Erhard und Kurt Georg Kiesinger, in: *Deutsche Europapolitik. Von Adenauer bis Merkel*, 2nd ed., ed. Gisela Müller-Brandeck-Bocquet et al. (Wiesbaden: VS, 2010), 13-66, here: 18.

9 The anthology of Corine Defrance et al. is a recent published example clarifying the extent of the efforts of civil society on Franco-German rapprochement: *Wege der Verständigung zwischen Deutschen und Franzosen nach 1945. Zivilgesellschaftliche Annäherungen*, ed. Corine Defrance et al. (Tübingen: Attempto,

zösisches Institut (Franco-German Institute) in Ludwigsburg[10] or the *Comité francais d'échanges avec l'Allemagne nouvelle* (French Committee for Exchange with the New Germany)[11] were established at the end of the 1940s. Moreover, since then numerous town twinnings[12] and countless youth meetings[13] took place to bring French and German people into a closer understanding of each other. Franco-German journal projects[14] or the role of prisoners of war and of former soldiers[15] also played an essential role in the Franco-German rapprochement. All these initiatives began significantly prior to political efforts and served politicians as starting bases and points of contact.[16]

2010); Defrance, Société civile et relations franco-allemandes, in: *Wege der Verständigung*, 17-31, here: 17.

10 *Projekt deutsch-französische Verständigung. Die Rolle der Zivilgesellschaft am Beispiel des Deutsch-Französischen Instituts in Ludwigsburg*, ed. Hans Manfred Bock (Opladen: Leske + Budrich, 1998).

11 Carla Albrecht, Das Comité français d'échanges avec l'Allemagne nouvelle als Wegbereiter des Deutsch-Französischen Jugendwerks, *Lendemains* 27 (2002), 177-189.

12 Manfred Bock, Europa von unten. Zu den Ursprüngen und Anfängen der deutsch-französischen Gemeindepartnerschaften, in: *Gemeindepartnerschaften im Umbruch Europas*, ed. Annette Jünemann et al. (Frankfurt a.M.: P. Lang, 1994), 13-35; Corine Defrance, Les premiers jumelages franco-allemands, 1950-1963, *Lendemains* 21 (1996), 83-95.

13 Kirsten Hoyer, Deutsche Jugendorganisationen und deutsch-französische Jugendkontakte in der Nachkriegszeit 1945-1955 – ein Überblick, *Lendemains* 21 (1996), 110-125.

14 René Wintzen, Private und persönliche Initiativen in der französischen Besatzungszone. Die Zeitschriften Documents und Dokumente, Vent debout und Verger, in: *Französische Kulturpolitik in Deutschland 1945-1949. Berichte und Dokumente*, ed. Jérôme Vaillant (Konstanz: UVK, 1984), 143-151.

15 Francois Cochet, Le rôle des anciens prisonniers et des anciens déportés français dans le rapprochement franco-allemand, in: *Le rôle des guerres dans la mémoire des Européens*, ed. Antoine Fleury and Robert Frank (Neuchâtel: P. Lang, 1997), 123-135.

16 Defrance, Société civile, 24; Albrecht, Comité français.

Although there is now substantial research about many actors and groups favouring the Franco-German friendship, the churches and church-related groups remained largely unexplored.[17] This lack of attention is astonishing because the churches played a crucial role in the German situation after 1945. After the war, they were the only functioning organisations and the only institutions that were not regarded as politically compromised. They were engaged in societal and political tasks, were dialogue partners of the allies, and were advocates and benefactors to the German population.[18] At the same time, varied initiatives for the Franco-German rapprochement came from the ecclesial sphere on both sides of the Rhine, as Joseph Zouame-Bizeme concludes:

---

[17] One volume of the journal *Kirchliche Zeitgeschichte* (KZG 14, 2001/2) deals with the relations between German and French Protestants and Catholics in the 19th and 20th century. Further examples are: Martin Greschat, Widerstand und Versöhnung. Der Beitrag des europäischen Protestantismus zur Annäherung der Völker, in: *Christliches Ethos und der Widerstand gegen den Nationalsozialismus in Europa*, ed. Anselm Doering-Manteuffel and Joachim Mehlhausen (Stuttgart: Kohlhammer, 1995), 139-144; Frédéric Hartweg and Daniela Heimerl, Der französische Protestantismus und die "Deutsche Frage" 1945-1955, part 1 and 2, *KZG* 3, 1 (1990), 386-412, *KZG* 4, 1 (1991), 202-235; Michael Kißener, Ein "ragendes Denkmal" des christlichen Abendlandes. Der Bau der Friedenskirche in Speyer 1953/4, *Jahrbuch für Europäische Geschichte* 9 (2008), 93-106; Michael Kißener, Boten eines versöhnten Europa? Deutsche Bischöfe, Versöhnung der Völker und Europaidee nach dem Zweiten Weltkrieg, in: *Die europäische Integration und die Kirchen. Akteure und Rezipienten*, ed. Heinz Duchhardt and Malgorzata Morawiec (Göttingen: Vandenhoeck & Ruprecht, 2010), 53-72; Michael Kißener, Der Katholizismus und die deutsch-französische Annäherung in den 1950er Jahren, in: *Wege der Verständigung*, 89-98; Joseph Zouame-Bizeme, *Aspects des relations réligieuses franco-allemandes de 1945 à 1955* (Strasbourg: Presses universitaires de Strasbourg, 1990).

[18] Michael Strobel, *Kirchen und Besatzungsmächte in der deutschen Nachkriegsgeschichte 1945-1949* (Tübingen: Universität Tübingen, 1992), 1, 76, 146; Martin Greschat, *Protestanten in der Zeit. Kirche und Gesellschaft in Deutschland vom Kaiserreich bis zur Gegenwart* (Stuttgart: Kohlhammer, 1994), 180-183.

"The churches of France and Germany were the avant-garde of the policy of German reconstruction. In doing so, they undertook different projects of the Franco-German reconciliation and different efforts to create peace in the world."[19]

Individuals such as the Jesuit, Jean du Rivau,[20] who set up the *Bureau International de Liaison et de Documentation* (International Office for Liaison and Documentation), or the pastor Georges Casalis[21] in Berlin worked towards reconciliation between the French and the Germans. Face to face with them on the German side stood Lothar Kreyssig, the founder of *Aktion Sühnezeichen* (Action Reconciliation),[22] or Bishop Isidor Emmanuel,[23] who took an active part in the building of the *Friedenskirche St. Bernhard* (St. Bernhard Peace Church) between 1953 and 1954 in Speyer.

In the middle and in contact with these individuals were Robert Picard de la Vacquerie and Marcel Sturm,[24] the French chief military chaplains in both Germany and Austria.[25] Picard de la Vacquerie (1893-1969) was or-

---

19 Zouame-Bizeme, *Aspects*, 372.
20 René Wintzen, L'influence de personnalités, d'institutions et d'initiatives privées sur la politique culturelle française en Allemagne après 1945, in: *Frankreichs Kulturpolitik in Deutschland, 1945-1950*, ed. Franz Knipping and Jacques Le Rider (Tübingen: Attempto, 1987), 335-348; Emmanuelle Picard, Le rôle des Catholiques français dans le rapprochement franco-allemand après la Seconde Guerre Mondiale, *KZG* 14, 2 (2001), 513-532.
21 Kurt Anschütz, "Der ökumenische Glaube ist primär...". Georges Casalis in Berlin 1946-1950 – Einblicke in seine Korrespondenz, *Evangelische Theologie* 54 (1994), 79-101.
22 See the contribution by Christiane Wienand in this volume.
23 Kißener, Ein ragendes Denkmal, 93-106.
24 Marcel Sturm and Robert Picard de la Vacquerie are the focus of my dissertation in process. One aspect of the dissertation is presented in this article.
25 There is no study on Robert Picard de la Vacquerie and there are only some articles about Marcel Sturm. Jörg Thierfelder and Michael Losch, Der evangelische "Feldbischof" Marcel Sturm – ein "Brückenbauer" zwischen den evangelischen Christen Deutschlands und Frankreichs, *Blätter für württembergische Kirchengeschichte* 99 (1999), 208-251; Martin Greschat, Marcel Sturm: l'église évangélique en Allemagne depuis mai 1945, *Revue d'Allemagne et des pays de langue allemande* 21, 4 (1989), 567-575; Christophe Baginski, Zuerst Christ, dann

dained as a Catholic priest in 1921, after which he held various clerical offices in several Parisian parishes. He was also interested in international exchanges. In 1944 he was arrested by the Gestapo for his critical sermons but was later liberated by the allies. Between 1946 and 1951 he was stationed in Germany. In 1951, the Pope enthroned him as bishop of Orléans where he died in 1969.[26] Sturm (1905-1950) was a protestant reformed pastor in South-Alsace from 1929 to 1939 and was affiliated with the ecumenical movement. In World War II, he was injured and captured by the Germans, but was able to escape to North Africa. In 1945, he began his duties in Germany where he died five years later.[27]

As chief military chaplains in the French occupied zones of Germany and Austria,[28] Robert Picard de la Vacquerie and Marcel Sturm were responsible to their respective church leadership and to General Pierre Koenig, the French supreme commander in Germany and director of the military government. Their engagement in Germany branched out in four directions that were interrelated to each other: First, Picard de la Vacquerie and Sturm had to attend to the pastoral care of the French in Germany and the Germans in French war captivity.[29] Second, they acted as special consultants in religious questions for General Koenig. In this respect, they had a certain influence on the French church policy.[30] For example they handled matters

---

Franzose. "Militärbischof" Sturm setzt sich für die Versöhnung ein, *Evangelischer Kirchenbote. Sonntagsblatt für die Pfalz* 36 (1995). However, there is no broad analysis of his engagement in Germany and his efforts on rapprochement.

26 Xavier Boniface, Picard de la Vacquerie (Robert), in: *Dictionnaire des évêques de France au XXe siècle*, ed. Dominique-Marie Dauzet and Frédéric Le Moigne (Paris: Cerf, 2010), 528-529.

27 Thierfelder and Losch, Feldbischof, 210-214.

28 In 1949 the authority of both *aumôniers inspecteurs* was expanded to Austria and the Saarland. Xavier Boniface, *L'aumônerie militaire française (1914-1962)* (Paris: Cerf, 2001), 427.

29 Martin Greschat, Die Kirchenpolitik der französischen Besatzungsmacht in Rheinland-Pfalz, in: *Beati qui custodiunt. Festschrift für Ekkehard Kätsch zum 65. Geburtstag*, ed. Holger Bogs et al. (Darmstadt: Verlag der Hessischen Kirchengeschichtlichen Vereinigung, 2001), 175-188, here: 179.

30 Jörg Thierfelder, Die Besatzungsmacht Frankreich und die evangelischen Kirchen in der französischen Zone. Fälle und Konflikte, *Revue d'Allemagne et des*

of education policy[31] or the discharge of the Germans as prisoners of war[32]. Therefore, they often became "intermediaries" between the military government and the local churches, in which they actively engaged themselves on the behalf of the Germans.[33] Within these activities, the two chaplains were thirdly representatives of their churches and tried to realize the interests of those in Germany.[34] Last but not least they were engaged in favour of the rapprochement between the French and the Germans.

Picard de la Vacquerie and Sturm had a special impact on Franco-German reconciliation in the ecclesial domain after the Second World War. Contemporary witnesses thanked them, deeming them "bridge builders" of the international understanding.[35] Their approaches were diverse and partly connected with other initiatives.[36] Both military chaplains looked for personal contact with their German counterpart, and were important contact persons for the French and the Germans. They endorsed the concerns of the German churches towards the French authorities, and moderated between both interests. Their pioneering work[37] also included the organisation of reconciliation-motivated get-togethers of the French and the Germans.

---

pays de langue allemande 21, 4 (1989), 557-566, here: 560; Jörg Thierfelder, Die Kirchenpolitik der Besatzungsmacht Frankreich und die Situation der evangelischen Kirche in der französischen Zone, *KZG* 2, 1 (1989), 221-238, here: 227.

31 Zouame-Bizeme, *Aspects*, 215-216, 329; Greschat, Kirchenpolitik, 185.
32 Thierfelder and Losch, Feldbischof, 236; Christophe Baginski, *Frankreichs Kirchenpolitik im besetzten Deutschland 1945-1949* (Mainz: Gesellschaft für Mittelrheinische Kirchengeschichte, 2001), 51.
33 Boniface, *L'aumônerie militaire*, 430-431.
34 Thierfelder and Losch, Feldbischof, 214; Zouame-Bizeme, *Aspects*, 328.
35 Evangelisches Kirchenblatt, Nachruf Bender, 114, Zentralarchiv der Evangelischen Kirche der Pfalz (hereafter: ZAPf), Abt. 150.47, Nr. 814, Blatt 60; Rauch to Picard de la Vacquerie, 25 October 1951, Erzbischöfliches Archiv Freiburg (hereafter: EAF), Nb 9/8 Vol. III.
36 For example, Picard de la Vacquerie assisted Jean du Rivau with his center in Offenburg; Boniface, *L'aumônerie militaire*, 431. Georges Casalis reported to Sturm in Baden-Baden; Anschütz, Der ökumenische Glaube, 82.
37 Boniface, *L'aumônerie militaire*, 433.

Two of these gatherings are particularly noteworthy as examples of how actors of the ecclesial domain engaged in favour of Franco-German rapprochement – the Meeting of Bishops in Bühl in 1949 and the Congress of Speyer in 1950. Due to the constant commitments of Robert Picard de la Vacquerie and Marcel Sturm, French and German catholic bishops and Protestants from both countries were brought together to become acquainted and to gain a mutual understanding of each other's missions and thoughts. In the following I will describe and analyse these two meetings in detail. While in a first step both meetings will be presented separately, they are compared in a second step to point out the similarities as well as the differences between these Catholic and Protestant approaches. I will ask for the outcomes and impacts of these meetings, and whether these meetings were successful. Special attention will be given to the specific meaning of rapprochement and reconciliation in the ecclesial context and therefore to the question what these concepts actually meant in these cases.

THE MEETING OF FRENCH AND GERMAN BISHOPS IN BÜHL (1949)

The meeting in Bühl had its forerunners in the successful pastoral congresses of French, Austrian, and German priests in 1947 and 1948.[38] At the end of 1948, Robert Picard de la Vacquerie saw the moment to address a higher ecclesiastical level. He asked archbishop Wendelin Rauch from Freiburg to provide assistance with a meeting between French and German bishops.[39] Rauch who agreed to his colleague's idea believed his church committed to such initiatives:

"Certainly, the Catholic Church might be the first power that allows for the idea of the entity of peoples across borders and the respective actual situation to become visible and put it effectively in the world. And this out of her inmost nature. Through

---

38 Rapport de Picard sur la Rencontre Episcopale Franco-Allemande de Buhl (Bade), Archives de l'Évêché d'Orléans (hereafter: EO), 3 Z 58.
39 Picard to Rauch, 20 December 1948, EAF, Nb 9/70, Vol. I.

her proper supernatural charge, she has most important forces to bring in and to provide for understanding, for unity, and for peace."[40]

The meeting received the agreement and mercy of Pope Pius XII and the benevolent consent of the French government and of the occupying authorities.[41] Despite facilitations from the French agencies,[42] the meeting should be independent of the occupation, free and not imposed upon by any side.[43]

In Bühl, it was to be a "private meeting" "for the understanding of both peoples" at which the participants mainly became acquainted with each other.[44] From 24 to 26 September 1949 fourteen bishops from the French zone of occupation in Germany and from several parts of France came together, amongst them the archbishops of Besancon and Freiburg, Maurice Dubourg and Wendelin Rauch.[45] They started with lunch at the house of Picard de la Vacquerie in Baden-Baden. Towards the evening, the conference was opened by a blessing meditation and speeches at the convent of Maria Hilf (Bühl). During the next days, lectures were given on church-related and religious questions and on theological tasks.[46] Jean-Julien Weber[47] and Joseph Wendel[48] spoke about previous and new developments of the formation of the clergy in both countries. Maurice Dubourg[49] and Karl-Joseph Leiprecht[50] reported the social movements of the Catholic Church in France

---

40 Rauch to Picard, 24 March 1949, EAF, Nb 9/6, Vol. I.
41 Montini to Picard, 22 January 1949, EO, 3 Z 58; Rauch and Dubourg to Pope Pius XII, EO, 3 Z 58.
42 Picard to Schuman, 10 November 1949, EO, 3 Z 60.
43 Rapport de Picard sur la Rencontre Episcopale Franco-Allemande; Montini to Picard, 22 January 1949, both in: EO, 3 Z 58.
44 Rauch to Rusch, 28 April 1949, EO, 3 Z 58.
45 See for participants: Teilnehmerliste, Erzbischöfliches Archiv München Freising (hereafter: EAMFr), 220, 21/1950.
46 Wendel to Muench, 31 January 1950, EAMFr, 220, 21/1950.
47 Les études ecclésiastiques et la formation des clercs dans les Séminaire de France, EAF, Nb 9/6, Vol. I.
48 Le recrutement des nos séminaires – nos soucis nos espoirs, EO, 3 Z 58.
49 Die französische katholische Aktion und ihre spezialisierten Bewegungen, EAF, Nb 9/6, Vol. I.
50 La jeunesse catholique et son organisation en Allemagne, EO, 3 Z 59.

and Germany in retrospect and in relation to the actual situation. The content of the lecture by Albert Stohr was the liturgical commission of the bishop conference of Fulda.[51] Léon-Albert Terrier showed the development of theological work in the last ten to fifteen years in France.[52] Finally, Wilhelm Kempf spoke about the problem of the German refugees with respect to the consequential religious effects at his diocese.[53] The congress ended with a final meditation. For between times there were occasions for discussion and prayers.[54]

The topics that were covered in Bühl had no political content. Thus, the bishops could circumvent any possible difficulties and would not produce much furor. By remaining in the pure ecclesiastic-religious domain they dealt with issues, which were interesting to both sides. The several topics were not covered systematically, but rather the lectures answered the purpose to inform the assembled church leadership about the present conditions in both countries. In this way, they could recognise the situations they were in and the problems each of them had, which were in parts similar. They learned new insights, bringing about enrichment for all.[55] At the end of the meeting, there were no resolutions or common guidelines for further procedures and acts. The reason for this was, as bishop Wendel explained, that "no conference of bishops took part, but rather a personal encounter and exchange. In fact it was also a real and brotherly gathering in the entity of our holy Church."[56] Mainly, the encounter should serve the bishops to become acquainted with each other. In the foreground of this congress was the goal to learn more about the practices in the other country, and to exchange ideas. Here it was possible for former strangers to create trust, and

---

51 Das Liturgische Referat der Fuldaer Bischofskonferenz, EO, 3 Z 59.
52 Die gegenwärtige theologische Arbeit in Frankreich, EAF, Nb 9/6, Vol. I.
53 Problèmes Actuels de la Misère Allemande, EO, 3 Z 59.
54 Konferenz deutscher und französischer Bischöfe im Kloster 'Maria Hilf', Bühl, vom 24. bis 26. Oktober 1949, in: Das Kloster Maria Hilf, ed. Wilhelm Freischlag (Bühl: Discher, 1959), 25-28; Programme de la Rencontre franco-allemande des Evêques, Dom- und Diözesanarchiv Mainz (hereafter: DDAMz), Bestand 45, 1, Nr. 10; Bericht, EO, 3 Z 58.
55 Wendel to Muench, 31 January 1950, EAMFr, 220, 21/1950; Presse-Kommuniqué, EO, 3 Z 58.
56 Wendel to Muench, 31 January 1950, EAMFr, 220, 21/1950.

in so doing, they could establish a solid basis for further steps. With respect to these actions in particular, Michael Kißener, who analyses in his research the role of Catholics on the Franco-German rapprochement, deemed the congress successful.[57] The common bond created by the Christian faith was also important for this meeting. It set the foundation for the good relationship, and helped with facilitating understanding and rapprochement. Thus, the unity of the church, the fraternal gathering of French and Germans, and the very Christian idea of reconciliation were accentuated by the bishops and were experienced at the meeting. Rauch stressed to his colleague, Dubourg, that all had felt in Bühl that "the Holy Spirit, the spirit of love and understanding, is the best interpreter".[58] In a report on the meeting Picard de la Vacquerie explicated further:

"It is even to underline that the principal charm of the meeting consists in the honest openness, in the effort to understand each other, in the cordial simplicity of the liaison between all participants. Nothing separated the bishops, not even the language."[59]

According to the bishops, the meeting would also have positive effects on further sectors. The relations established in Bühl had, as Picard de la Vacquerie noted, a real benefit for Germany, France, and the Catholic Church.[60] On the one hand they could "serve the policy of rapprochement of our two countries"[61] and on the other hand, as Bishop Dubourg believed, they could strengthen the connections of Catholicism "that might unify us in Christ. It is also an effective contribution to the establishment of a peace that might be not only human, but primarily Christian [...]."[62] Such meetings as in Bühl were understood as essential ways of Franco-German reconciliation and the task of the church was to support the basic idea of the togetherness of the peoples in the world.

---

57 Kißener, Boten eines versöhnten Europa, 64-65.
58 Rauch to Dubourg, 29 November 1950, EAF, Nb 9/8, Vol. III.
59 Rapport de Picard sur la Rencontre Episcopale Franco-Allemande, EO, 3 Z 58.
60 Picard to Rauch, 5 November 1949, EAF, Nb 9/6, Vol. I.
61 Picard to Robert Schuman, 10 November 1949, EO, 3 Z 60.
62 Dubourg to Rauch, 7 November 1950, EAF, Nb 9/7, Vol. II.

According to the opinion of all participants, the basis for a long-term relationship was now built with the meeting of Bühl. For example, Picard de la Vacquerie wrote to Rauch: "You may be convinced that the mental bridges that are now tied up on the stable foundation of Christian love will not break down at any time."[63]

How far the bridges that were built between the French and Germans actually persist in the aftermath of this meeting is difficult to evaluate. Nevertheless, further meetings were contemplated and requested by both sides.[64] However, in the sources little or no evidence can be found. Some exceptions are the letters of condolence by the bishops Weber and Dubourg on the occasion of the death of Heinrich Metzroth who had also participated at the meeting in Bühl. The letters suggest that at least some participants stayed in contact also after the meeting.[65] In addition, the effect of this first encounter between French and German bishops should not be limited to solely the church leadership. Bishop Dubourg and Rauch would lobby for a Franco-German rapprochement also towards their priests and believers. Furthermore, there was an exchange created between seminarians of Besancon and Trier in 1950.[66] Thus, the success of the meeting was mainly in the contacts of the bishops there. Except for the affiliated of Dubourg[67] there was little measurable effect beyond the conference.

---

63 Rauch to Picard, 25 October 1951, EAF, Nb 9/8, Vol. III.
64 Rapport de Picard sur la Rencontre Episcopale Franco-Allemande; Picard to Francois-Poncet, 3 November 1949, both in: EO, 3 Z 58; Wendel to Muench, 31 January 1950, EAMFr, 220, 21/1950.
65 Weber to Bornewasser, 22 January 1951; Dubourg to Bornewasser, 24 January 1951, both in: Bistumsarchiv Trier (hereafter: BAT), 84, 907.
66 Dubourg to Rauch, 7 November 1950, EAF, Nb 9/7, Vol. II; Rapport de Picard sur la Rencontre Episcopale Franco-Allemande, EO, 3 Z 58.
67 He also launched an exhibition on the Catholic Germany, which depicted the attitude of the German church during the Third Reich and described the German church and political life. Dubourg to Rauch, 7 November 1950, annex: L'Allemagne catholique, EAF, Nb 9/7, Vol. II.

THE CONGRESS OF FRENCH AND GERMAN PROTESTANTS IN SPEYER (1950)

The Congress of Speyer[68] had its origins in prior contacts between the French and German Protestants.[69] It traced back to the initiative of Marcel Sturm who received assistance mainly from the German side.[70] The first discussions about the gathering took place at a meeting in June 1948 at which Marc Boegner, the president of the *Fédération Protestante de France* (Protestant Federation of France), and Sturm came together with German representatives of the church.[71] According to the French, the content of the Speyer meeting should have a clear political appearance and an actual vision.[72] They thought about involving laymen as much as possible[73] and wished to associate with people who had been in active opposition to National Socialism.[74] Because of several setbacks, the congress could take

---

68 Several Aspects of the Speyer meeting are also discussed in: Martin Greschat, Bemühungen um Verständigung und Versöhnung. Der Beitrag des französisch-deutschen Bruderrates, in: *Revue d'Allemagne et des pays de langue allemande* 36, 2 (2004), 155-174

69 Une rencontre protestante franco-allemande à Spire (17 au 19 mars 1950), *Foi et Vie* 48 (1950), 293-294, here: 293; Zouame-Bizeme, *Aspects*, 252.

70 Assistance came mainly from Martin Niemöller, the president of the *Evangelische Kirche von Hessen und Nassau* (Protestant Church in Hesse and Nassau) and head of the foreign office of the *Evangelische Kirche in Deutschland* (Protestant Church in Germany), and Paul Graf Yorck von Wartenburg, the director of the *Evangelisches Hilfswerk* (Protestant Aid Organization) in the French zone of occupation. Yorck to Bender, 30 July 1948, ZAPf, Abt. 150, 47, Nr. 767; Dr. Federer to Dr. Klaus Mehnert, 10 July 1948, Archiv des Diakonischen Werkes der EKD (hereafter: ADW), Bestand ZB, Nr. 840; Bender to Niemöller, 4 August 1948, Landeskirchliches Archiv der Evangelischen Kirche in Baden (hereafter: LKAB), Bestand GA, 5880.

71 Hartweg and Heimerl, Der französische Protestantismus, 405.

72 Yorck to Gerstenmaier, 26 June 1948, ADW, ZB, 840.

73 Französisch-deutsche Kirchentagung, September 1949, Speyer, ADW, ZB, 840.

74 Yorck to Bender, 30 July 1948, ZAPf, Abt. 150, 47, Nr. 767. This obsession with the Confessing Church provoked critics on the German side. Especially the chairman of the church in Baden Julius Bender was aware of a danger for the

place not until March 1950.[75] They met on a private and unofficial level without the participation of state authorities and the nomination of official church representatives. An "ecclesial meeting between the French and the Confessing Churches" should be reached at the conference and a "programme of a common function for the pacification of the occidental peoples" should be developed.[76]

From 17 to 19 March 1950 approximately 50 people from both countries met in Speyer. They were actors of the church on all levels, theologians, and laymen. The majority of the group was connected to the church in some way, but personalities of society, economy, and politics were also present. The German participants not only came from the French zone of occupation but also from all over Germany. They were nearly exclusively associated with the *Bekennende Kirche* (Confessing Church). The majority of the French had been members of the *résistance*.[77]

At the conference they discussed the political responsibility of the church and the possibilities of a Franco-German rapprochement. For this purpose Heinrich Vogel, professor of theology in Berlin, Charles Westphal, director of the Protestant journal *Foi et Vie*, Hans Iwand from the Protestant Department at Göttingen University, and René Courtin from the Department of Law in Paris gave lectures. Vogel supposed that the church was responsible for the human community, especially for disenfranchised people. In doing so, she will act by proclaiming the truth of the Word of God. Westphal referred to the responsibility of the church for all human activities. By preaching the Gospel the church must uphold the respect for the divine sovereignty and thus the respect of the human person. Furthermore,

---

union of the Protestant Church in Germany. For more see: Bender to Niemöller, 4 August 1948, LKAB, GA, 5880; Aktennotiz über Besprechung in Bad Gleisweiler, 8 December 1949, Archiv der Evangelischen Kirche im Rheinland, Archivstelle Düsseldorf (hereafter: AEKiR-D), Handakten Präses Held 6 HA 004, Heft 352.

75 Aktennotiz über Besprechung in Bad Gleisweiler, 8 December 1949, AEKiR-D, Held 6 HA 004, 352.

76 Presse-Communiqué zur Speyrer Tagung; Yorck to Stempel, 20 January 1950, both in: ZAPf, Abt. 150, 47, Nr. 767.

77 See for participants: Teilnehmerliste für Speyrer Tagung I + II, ZAPf, Abt. 150, 47, Nr. 767.

the church should act as ambassador for the reconciliation of nations and peoples. Iwand spoke about the present danger of the restoration in Europe. To stand against this danger and for peace among peoples, one had to look on Jesus Christ and his message of reconciliation. In order to reach better mutual comprehension, the particularities of peoples that were conserved in the nations should be explored. Courtin explained that nowadays the focus should no longer be on Franco-German antagonism, but rather on the existence of the whole of Europe. Today the message of the brotherhood of all human beings could be successful. The most important task of the churches would be to facilitate mutual meetings between the Germans and the French.[78] Although these topics had a deep reference to the Christian message, they also related to the more 'secular' tasks of the church. If the lectures remained relatively theoretical and abstract, behavior guidelines for the churches allowed for the deduction of political questions and international understanding. They assigned a political responsibility for the actual events in the world to the church. The churches should especially be committed to the rapprochement of Germany and France. To this end, Courtin and Iwand made proposals that were partially included in the adopted common declaration.

The lectures were discussed by the plenum and the "most delicate political questions" were debated "without reserves". Thus, they talked about the question of the Saar, the division of Germany, issues of war criminals, and the reconstruction of Europe. In accordance with the press release, the discussions were handled "in absolute openness"; divisive questions were solved in spiritual liberty and based on the common faith. Disagreement was "less between the two partners as within the respective delegations". The influence of Marcel Sturm on the success of the congress was also highly accentuated.[79]

---

78 See the following articles in *Foi et Vie*, 48 (1950): Une rencontre protestante franco-allemande à Spire (17 au 19 mars 1950), 293-294; Heinrich Vogel, La responsabilité politique actuelle de l'église, 317-326; Charles Westphal, Responsabilité politique de l'église, 327-338; Hans Iwand, Que peuvent faire les églises pour le rapprochement franco-allemand?, 339-358; René Courtin, Sur la contribution des églises à la compréhension franco-allemande, 359-369.

79 Une rencontre protestante franco-allemande à Spire, 294; Presse-Communiqué zur Speyrer Tagung, ZAPf, Abt. 150, 47, Nr. 767; Report Wehr for Sturm, Ar-

Through the time spent together and through the intense discussions in Speyer, both sides had a chance to become acquainted with each other on an equal level, to understand each other's points of view and to revise any existing prejudices. Together they worked out a program for the formation of a common future. At the end it was published in the Declaration of Speyer with concrete proposals for the collaboration of the churches with respect to the Franco-German rapprochement. In this official declaration, they stated, that they met "in the spirit of the ecumenical movement". The aim was to recognize "together the political responsibility" of the churches and to contribute to the "mutual rapprochement" of Germany and France. The Christian faith was mentioned as an essential starting point and condition of rapprochement and finally reconciliation of both peoples:

"In the belief in Jesus Christ, they find their unity and the reconciliation which God keeps ready for all humans and all peoples. Such an obedience in faith let them relate the validity of the divine promise also to the understanding and reconciliation of peoples."[80]

From the outset, the faith formed a common and cross-border bond; it stood over secular disputes and acted as an intermediary. Thus, Protestants from both countries where brought together. They acted jointly, cultivated solidarity, and contributed significantly to the comprehension and, specifically in the Christian sense, to their reconciliation. Moreover, they invoked overcoming nationalism and the discussion of actual changes in the world. The aim was to clarify how to bring to "all people work, bread, and justice".[81] On the last day, a common service was arranged to which state authorities and the public were invited.[82] Gustav Heinemann, one of the participants, German home secretary and chairman of the synod of the Protestant Church in Germany, denoted the congress of Speyer as "the first and promising al-

---

chiv der Evangelischen Kirche im Rheinland, Archivstelle Boppard (hereafter: AEKiR-B), 72: 06-6/3-3.

80 Speyrer Erklärung, *Blätter für pfälzische Landesgeschichte und religiöse Volkskunde* 64 (1997), 281-282, here: 281.
81 Ibid.
82 Sturm to Stempel, 20 February 1950, ZAPf, Abt. 150, 47, Nr. 767.

liance between both our churches". There they also learnt to meet "as brothers of the common Lord Jesus Christ from now on".[83]

"Concrete resolutions" were published alongside the declaration. A provisional commission of seven members per country should appoint a permanent *Bruderrat* (Council of Brothers)[84] to serve as a constant liaison committee of German and French Protestants and to embody "the organic entity of the church". The role of this transnational committee was an "approach to a necessary overcoming of national churchdom".[85] Until 1964 the Franco-German Council of Brothers met twice a year and discussed several subjects such as the German rearmament or the European question.[86] The significance of the Franco-German Council of Brothers was noted in a letter to the German members by Hans Stempel, the president of the *Evangelische Kirche der Pfalz* (Protestant Church of Palatinate) and after the death of Sturm in 1950 an important facilitator for the continuity of the institution:[87]

"[…] the Council of Brothers was engaged to open a new relationship in a very difficult respect. […] There remain souvenirs of theological discussions, of the common listening to the Word, of the community of prayer, and of the deep solidarity on the table of the Lord. This is all not only a souvenir. It is also something gained for us, something is provided for our entire next life. […] Again and again it was attested

---

83 Ansprache Heinemann vor Nationalsynode der Reformierten Kirche Frankreichs in Nîmes, 4 June 1950, Archiv der sozialen Demokratie der Friedrich-Ebert-Stiftung (hereafter: AsD), Abt. 1, Mappe 123, Blatt 59/60.
84 Speyrer Erklärung, 281.
85 Yorck to Evangelisches Hilfswerk, 23 April 1950, ADW, ZB, 355.
86 Zentralarchiv der Evangelischen Kirche in Hessen und Nassau (hereafter: ZAEKHN), 62/1036b; Daniela Heimerl, Der deutsch-französische Bruderrat. Annäherung – Verständigung – Versöhnung, *KZG* 14, 2 (2001), 470-486, here: 482-483, 485.
87 Christophe Baginski, Aus der Isolation zum Neubeginn. Die Evangelische Kirche der Pfalz nach dem Zweiten Weltkrieg, in: *Die Pfalz in der Nachkriegszeit. Wiederaufbau und demokratischer Neubeginn (1945-1954)*, ed. Gerhard Nestler and Hannes Ziegler (Kaiserslautern: Institut für Pfälzische Geschichte und Volkskunde, 2004), 243-261, here: 261.

quietly to us how the engagement of the Council of Brothers has assisted to reduce misunderstandings, to overcome alienation, to create real reconciliation."[88]

Through the Council of Brothers, they came to a new perception in Christ, to a "new retention from the conciliatory power that he gives to all".[89] In fact, the Council of Brothers built an important element of connection and provided a transnational forum for discussions between French and German Protestants. It was a "new sort of working group"[90] notably also for non-church related topics. The break down in the 1960s did not diminish the success of the Council of Brothers.[91] On the contrary, the institution that had emerged from the ecclesial domain created an essential basis for exchange and understanding between the French and Germans, especially in the phase in which "reconciliation" had not yet been obtained politically and within society. Community and solidarity in the faith could be exercised in the council and the unity of the church could be clarified across national borders.

In addition to this important element of connection, the participants of the Speyer meeting promoted the creation of a public discourse. The interest of the official church institutions should be awakened and the churches should be represented at the respective synods. The official and private exchange was to be facilitated and the ideas were to be publicized in the media. A student exchange program was already planned in May 1950 and an exchange of pastors was arranged in the summer of 1950. In the following years, there were a number of reciprocal invitations to synods and church conferences, to enthronements, and church dedications. Additional projects

---

88 Stempel to German members of the Council of Brothers, 9 February 1966, ZAEKHN, 62/0714.
89 Ibid.
90 Martin Greschat, Das Hilfswerk der EKD und die Entstehung des deutsch-französischen Bruderrates, in: *Soziale Arbeit in historischer Perspektive. Zum geschichtlichen Ort der Diakonie in Deutschland. Festschrift für Helmut Talazko zum 65. Geburtstag*, ed. Jochen-Christoph Kaiser (Stuttgart: Kohlhammer, 1998), 135-188, here: 143.
91 The French side limited the necessity of the council to the period following the war. Later, the problems with the colonies and the challenges from an ecumenical world became more relevant.

were contemplated in Speyer, e.g. the journey of a French commission to study the German problems regarding refugees in the German Democratic Republic. This study trip was scheduled between August and September 1950. One Sunday of the year was to be devoted to international understanding and in the planning was the founding of a Franco-German boarding school. Raymond Schmittlein, the competent French chief executive of the Department of Cultural Affairs, soon gave his consent for this binational school. In the aftermath of the Speyer meeting, official church authorities and individual persons came together. Exchanges took place on various levels and their effects were felt beyond the directly church-based level. Parishes, believers, and the youth were all addressed.[92]

CONCLUSION

To conclude, the Catholic and Protestant efforts at rapprochement between France and Germany will be briefly contrasted to explore the particularities of these approaches in civil society.

The analysis of the two meetings, the Bishop Meeting in Bühl and the Congress of Speyer, has revealed, firstly, that individuals had a certain significance in this processes. The chief military chaplains were the initiators of the meetings on both sides.[93] Robert Picard de la Vacquerie and Marcel Sturm were integrated in a broad network of church and policy formation. Both could count on the support of their church leadership and of General Koenig, who organizationally and individually had encouraged their efforts on rapprochement. In addition, they had socialized and communicated with numerous clergymen through their activities in Germany. This had been a starting point for the organization of the meetings. Thus, the two Frenchmen were in turn assisted by individuals on the German side.

Secondly, both meetings had in common that the French and Germans met on an equal level to work and to pray together. However, there were

---

92 Speyrer Erklärung; Protokoll der Sitzung des letzten deutsch-französischen Bruderrates, ADW, ZB, 355; Zouame-Bizeme, *Aspects*, 254-255; Yorck to Evangelisches Hilfswerk, 23 April 1950, ADW, ZB, 355.
93 It was also the personal commitment of Marcel Sturm at the meeting of Speyer that was stressed as the cause of its success.

differences when it came to the respective circle of participants. At the Catholic congress, it was only bishops that met. Primarily, their congress was about direct contacts and exchanges within the church itself. At the Protestant meeting, actors of the church on all levels as well as theologians and laymen were involved. The debaters came from all public domains, including the political sphere and community in general. Right from the beginning, the Protestant congress should have significance beyond church-internal affairs.

Thirdly, while on both sides encounters and discussions were important ways for the understanding between the French and Germans, there was a difference in questions and issues discussed at the respective meetings. The Catholic bishops came together to talk about church developments in both countries. Thus, they created trust through the meeting and the exchange and, in so doing, this trust formed a foundation for further steps. While political issues had thus been avoided at the Catholic gathering in Bühl, the Protestants in Speyer also discussed actual political questions. Concrete approaches on how to confront these questions were envisaged. With the publication of the program, it was hoped to reach the public and to produce a positive effect.

Fourthly, both sides regarded their religion as the basis of rapprochement. The Christian faith could act as a shared starting point and a connecting bond. The brotherly love and the specific idea of 'reconciliation' which both were deeply anchored in the Christian faith, enabled rapprochement and understanding, reconciliation and peace. For this it is important to clarify what 'reconciliation' for the Christian socialized participants of Bühl and Speyer meant. In the Christian sense, reconciliation is the re-constitution of the community with God that was destroyed by the sin and guilt of the human being. Reconciliation is the impact of the life, death, and resurrection of Jesus Christ and in this it is deeply based on the faith. It caused the re-creation of the person before God.[94] Thus, reconciliation is primarily related to the relationship between God and mankind. It cannot be obtained by human acting but it is confirmed by the acting of God in Jesus for all times.

---

94 Dorothee Schlenke, Versöhnung / VI. Dogmatisch, in: *Religion in Geschichte und Gegenwart. Handwörterbuch für Theologie und Religionswissenschaft*, vol. 8, ed. Hans Dieter Betz (Tübingen: Mohr Siebeck, 2005), 1059-1061, here: 1059.

Reconciliation became true in faith and formed a new person. As reconciliation is central to the motivation, identity and objective of Christian action, there is at the same time a new relationship among humans. The human being is also responsible to his fellowmen. The individual has to assume guilt to create the condition for community.[95] 'Reconciliation' – such it is thought in Bühl and in Speyer – stood explicitly in this Christian context. For their international understanding, they adopted a theological concept that was different from the societal and political processes of rapprochement. Differences amongst them could not exist because they were eliminated by the reconciliation in the faith. Their community was created by the faith in the one Lord and by the entity of the church.

It is, fifthly, worth mentioning that questions of guilt and responsibility for the past were hardly discussed at both meetings. One can assume that this absence was related to the Christian understanding of reconciliation described above. Christian people at first and at last depend on the absolution of God and not of men, also if acceptance of guilt and forgiveness are necessary within human communities.[96] However, the Protestants discussed topics that were related to the past such as the question of the Saar, the division of Germany or issues of war criminals. Yet, they did not speak about guilt. One can assume that this was caused by the fact that the Germans who met in Speyer were members of the Confessing Church. Furthermore, there was the *Stuttgarter Erklärung* (Stuttgart Declaration of Guilt) in 1945 in which the Protestant church leadership confessed the German guilt and the joint responsibility of the church. This declaration caused the reopening of international relations for the German Protestants and was concretized in the *Darmstädter Wort* (Darmstadt Declaration) in 1947 by former circles of the Confessing Church.[97] Thus, the participants might have assumed that

---

95 Dorothee Schlenke, Versöhnung / VII. Ethisch, in: *Religion in Geschichte und Gegenwart*, 1061-1062; Lothar Ullrich, Versöhnung, in: *Lexikon der katholischen Dogmatik*, ed. Wolfgang Beinert (Freiburg: Herder, 1991), 536-540, here: 539.

96 Ibid.; Hans-Richard Reuter, Versöhnung / IV. Ethisch, in: *Theologische Realenzyklopädie*, vol. 35, ed. Gerhard Krause et al. (Berlin: de Gruyter, 2003), 40-43, here: 41.

97 *Wie Christen ihre Schuld bekennen. Die Stuttgarter Erklärung 1945*, ed. Gerhard Besier and Gerhard Sauter (Göttingen: Vandenhoeck & Ruprecht, 1985);

the German Protestants had already dealt with their past. On the Catholic side there was the *Fuldaer Hirtenbrief* (1945 Fulda Pastoral Letter) in 1945 in which the German bishops noted the responsibility of Catholics during the Third Reich. However, in accordance with the Pope they denied a responsibility of the German people as a whole.[98] Primarily they did not speak about the war and the Nazi period in Bühl because it was a meeting only concerning ecclesiastical matters in which political issues were avoided.

Finally, coming back to the question of success and impact of these two conferences, it is reasonable to assume that both the Bishop Meeting in Bühl and the Congress of Speyer had been successful. Both sides imposed on their churches the obligation to promote the rapprochement of people and peace in the world. Such encounters as in Bühl and in Speyer had been important milestones in furthering the rapprochement. It is therefore not surprising that the meetings also had broad effects such as the Franco-German exchange projects or the outstanding Council of Brothers. For the significance of the efforts on the Protestant and Catholic side it must also be emphasized that the meetings took place at a time at which the society still had objections to such attempts. In the ecclesial domain, rapprochement between the peoples had begun quite early, even before political efforts had been resumed. Nevertheless, the consent of the French authorities to the meetings already signaled the change of French policy towards Germany.[99]

The meetings of Bühl and Speyer are two prime examples of individuals and societal groups to bring about rapprochement immediately after World War II. The eclectic efforts of both chief military chaplains explain

---

Martin Greschat, Zwischen Aufbruch und Beharrung. Die evangelische Kirche nach dem Zweiten Weltkrieg, in: *Die Zeit nach 1945 als Thema kirchlicher Zeitgeschichte*, ed. Victor Conzemius et al. (Göttingen: Vandenhoeck & Ruprecht, 1988), 115-177; Karl Herbert, *Kirche zwischen Aufbruch und Tradition. Entscheidungsjahre nach 1945* (Stuttgart: Radius, 1989), 61-106.

98 Konrad Repgen, Die Erfahrungen des Dritten Reiches und das Selbstverständnis der deutschen Katholiken nach 1945, in: *Die Zeit nach 1945*, 127-179; Vera Bücker, *Die Schulddiskussion im deutschen Katholizismus nach 1945* (Bochum: Brockmeyer, 1989).

99 Fritsch-Bournazel, Wende in der französischen Nachkriegspolitik.

the special and successful approach of the reconciliation through civil society. Individuals from the Catholic and Protestant church have contributed simultaneously and at a very early stage to the rapprochement of France and Germany not only in the ecclesial domain but also in a broader public. They realized independent from each other, in a similar manner, but incorporating different approaches, the reconciliation on a religious and Christian basis. The entity of the church and the Christian idea of reconciliation served as starting points, triggering further initiatives of rapprochement. Thus, after the end of the Second World War, civil society – and therein religious people – had already started to work toward Franco-German rapprochement thereby creating an essential basis for the later incipient political rapprochement of both countries.

A Right to Irreconcilability?
Oradour-sur-Glane, German-French Relations and the Limits of Reconciliation after World War II

ANDREA ERKENBRECHER

In September 2009, Pierre Lellouche, the French State Secretary for European Relations, visited Verdun for the 25th anniversary of the meeting between the French President François Mitterrand and the German Chancellor Helmut Kohl. The picture of these two men shaking hands on the grounds of the battlefield of Verdun has become a symbol of Franco-German reconciliation. Lellouche remembered 25 years later:

"Neither the German Chancellor Kohl nor the French President Mitterrand knew on 22 September 1984 with any certainty that the Cold War would end five years later [...], but they were fully aware that in some ways they closed the chapter of the mass graves of [19]14-18 and the chapter Oradour-sur-Glane; the chapter of the three major German-French wars [...]."[1]

On June 10, 1944, a unit of the *Waffen-SS* had completely destroyed the French village of Oradour-sur-Glane. 642 men, women, and children were killed in this massacre and the village was burnt down to a landscape of ruins. For the French, Oradour became a symbol of their suffering under Ger-

---

1   Speech delivered by Pierre Lellouche at Verdun on 22 November 2009, http://www.france-allemagne.fr/Rede-von-Pierre-Lellouche-in,4741.html, accessed 5 November 2011. All translations from French and German by the author.

man occupation during World War II.² With the words of Pierre Lellouche, with the gesture at Verdun, the Second World War symbolized by Oradour, should have been a closed chapter. Indeed, this seems to hold true not only for official relations and symbolic politics, but also for transnational relations on the level of society. Today the new village of Oradour has ties with Germany by way of a partnership between the elementary school and the German *Theo Schoeller Grundschule* in Nürnberg. The school in Oradour has even included German into its curriculum. Moreover, with Gerda Hasselfeldt, the former vice-president of the German *Bundestag*, an important political personality is committed to an exchange between Germany and the village.³

However, if we take a closer look, this picture falls apart: Most of the relations with Germany are new and controversial; time and time again, there is resistance from members of the National Association of the Families of the Martyrs of Oradour-sur-Glane (ANFM) against closer ties with Germany. For example, there were emotional discussions in 2004 when it became known that a German delegation of young people and former members of the French *résistance* would attend the commemorative ceremony on June 10, following an invitation by the local mayor.⁴ Even a reconciliation concert given by a German choir 63 years after the crime, was contro-

---

2 Standard works on Oradour include: Jean-Jacques Fouché, *Oradour* (Paris: Liana Levi, 2001); Sarah Farmer, *10 juin 1944, Oradour: Arrêt sur mémoire* (Paris: Perrin, 2007).

3 Henning Meyer, *Der Wandel der französischen 'Erinnerungskultur' des Zweiten Weltkriegs am Beispiel dreier 'Erinnerungsorte': Bordeaux, Caen und Oradour-sur-Glane* (PhD diss., Universität Augsburg, 2006), http://opus.bibliothek.uni-augsburg.de/volltexte/2008/760/pdf/H_Meyer_Erinnerungskultur.pdf, 430-435, accessed 30 May 2011. Concerning the pupils learning German in Oradour: http://www.theo-schoeller-grundschule.de/Unsere_Schule/Partnerschule/partnerschule.html, accessed 30 May 2011. Concerning Gerda Hasselfeldt's commitment: Caroline Ischinger, Den Blick gemeinsam nach vorne richten, *Dachauer SZ*, 25 May 2010.

4 Thomas Schober, *Oradour – eine Warnung an die Menschheit*, http://drafd.org/drafd_2001_09/htdocs/start40_3.html, accessed 23 November 2010; Béatrice Jérôme, Les élus alsaciens participeront aux ceremonies, *Le Monde*, 9 June 2004.

versial.⁵ A town partnership with a German city is still unthinkable to the current day.⁶ Whereas on the level of symbolic politics – in the words of Pierre Lellouche – Oradour belongs to the past, the situation is much more complex when considering Oradour as a reality – an actually existing community. What can reconciliation possibly mean after a particularly brutal crime like the massacre of Oradour? How did those who survived react to efforts of reconciliation from the Germans? How do the descendants of those who were killed deal with such reconciliation attempts today? Moreover, are the Oradour citizens actually reconciled with Germany today?

This article will endeavor to answer these questions. It is a case study that will measure the scope and the success of initiatives from within civil society aiming at reconciliation at a place that was heavily struck and marked by World War II and its aftermath.⁷ In the next section, reconciliation will be defined in order to develop a framework for this analysis. Several factors and conditions of relevance in the processes of reconciliation are identified and applied to the Oradour case. Section 3 will provide an overview of gestures of reconciliation in the context of Oradour as well as a discussion of its successes and failures, problems, and limits. Section 4 contains an analysis of 'Oradour' in its different meanings in order to identify the addressees of the reconciliation gestures as well as the various actors involved in the reconciliation process. Furthermore, this analysis will focus on persons and collectives included in and excluded from the process of

---

5   Andreas Sichelstiel, Europahymne Höhepunkt, *Pegnitz-Zeitung*, 21 May 2007.
6   In 1990 the mayor of Oradour, Robert Lapuelle, said in an interview with Jacqueline Deloffre from the German newspaper *Die Zeit*, that it was still too early for a town partnership, http://images.zeit.de/text/1990/40/Manche-Haende-zittern-noch, accessed 24 April 2008. In an interview with Caroline Ischinger, the new mayor of Oradour, Raymond Frugier, was confident that a closer relationship between Dachau and Oradour would emerge, but didn't speak about a town partnership. Was bedeutet Ihr Besuch in Dachau?, *Dachauer SZ*, 25 May 2010.
7   The following results are based on the research done for my PhD thesis, which deals with "Oradour and the Germans. Dealing with a war crime and its memory: Criminal prosecution, indemnification, revisionism and gestures of reconciliation in the FRG and GDR, 1949-2011". In this article, I will limit myself to the relations between Oradour and the FRG.

reconciliation. Concluding, I will discuss the question of the right to irreconcilability in the case of Oradour.

Reconciliation with Oradour: Determining Factors

In 2009, Veit Straßner criticized the lack of discussion in the social sciences on the concept of "reconciliation" and recommended a definition that will serve as the basis of our reflections:

"Reconciliation is the state of being reconciled as well as the process that aims at this state. The fundamental condition of reconciliation is a burdened past, with which one shall come to terms in order to achieve a state that is defined by the beginning or resumption of trustworthy and cooperative relationships. In this state of reconciliation, peaceful coexistence and cooperation are possible (again). Reconciliation in the double sense of the word takes place on the individual level between perpetrators and victims as well as on the collective level. Reconciliation processes are highly complex internal processes that cannot be demanded, but can be supported or obstructed by external factors."[8]

In looking more closely at some factors of Straßner's definition and applying it to the Oradour case, we find several unfavorable conditions for the process of reconciliation. Firstly, the *burdened past,* which forms the prerequisite of every need for reconciliation, is in this case extremely cruel. In fact, the majority of the victims were women and children who were locked up in the village church. Those who were not killed by gas, shells, or gunshots were burnt alive. Only 52 out of 642 corpses could be identified and buried in individual graves.[9] Such circumstances surrounding death constitute great problems in the process of mourning, since the uncertainties of

---

8   Veit Straßner, Versöhnung und Vergangenheitsaufarbeitung – Ein Vorschlag zur Begriffsbestimmung und Konzeptionalisierung, in: *Amnesie, Amnestie oder Aufarbeitung? Zum Umgang mit autoritären Vergangenheiten und Menschenrechtsverletzungen*, ed. Siegmar Schmidt et al. (Wiesbaden: VS, 2009), 23-36, here: 29.

9   Fouché, *Oradour*, 149-154, 159-166, 180-182.

the victims' death often haunt the surviving family and friends for a lifetime.[10] Furthermore, many of the schoolchildren, who had been the victims in this massacre, came from hamlets outside the village. Their death often left families behind who had lost more than one child or even all of their children on June 10.[11] Jean-Jacques Fouché, philosopher and an expert on the Oradour case, goes so far as to say that "the dimensions of the massacre, especially the fact that most of the victims were women and children, creates irreconcilability".[12]

The second unfavorable starting point for reconciliation concerns the *beginning or resumption of trustworthy and cooperative relationships* after the conflict. The prefix "re-" in "reconciliation" refers to a state prior to the conflict, and in this sense, the term means the re-establishment of the former community.[13] In the Oradour case there was no initial point to go back to. On the one hand, it is doubtful that there are ways back to a former community after a crime like this. On the other hand, no relations had existed between the village and Germany or Germans before the massacre, thus nothing could be revived there. On the contrary, there was an "anti-Boche" culture in the Limousin region and Oradour was no exception in this matter.[14] Therefore, resumption was not at stake here. In fact, the very

---

10 Albert Valade, who lost his sister in the massacre, for example explains that his mother lived for a certain time with the hope that her daughter would come back. Albert Valade, *La page de catéchisme. Oradour-sur-Glane. Les villages sans enfants*, 2nd ed. (Neuvic Entier: Editions de la Veytizou S.A.R.L., 2004), 94. Aline Perney describes that until today the question of how her brother and father died is haunting her. *Tulle et Oradour*, Table ronde, France 3 Limousin, 2004, Archive of the Centre de la mémoire d'Oradour-sur-Glane (hereafter: ACMO), V4.5.2/03.

11 Concerning the situation in the hamlets: Valade, *Page*. Considering the loss of several children also: Farmer, *Oradour*, 212-213.

12 Jean-Jacques Fouché, *Oradour. La politique et la justice* (Saint-Paul: Souny, 2004), 18.

13 Sebastian Friese, *Politik der gesellschaftlichen Versöhnung. Eine theologisch-ethische Untersuchung am Beispiel der Gacaca-Gerichte in Ruanda* (Stuttgart: Kohlhammer, 2010), 8.

14 Fouché, *Oradour*, 92. *Boches* is a derogatory term for Germans.

beginning of the 'relations' between the village and the Germans was marked by a horrible crime.

Thirdly, *external factors* have created an unfavorable context for reconciliation in Oradour, specifically the actions of the French and German state. The French state has played a leading role in Oradour after the massacre. Under General de Gaulle, Oradour became the national symbol of the French suffering at the hands of the Germans during the Second World War. The ruins became public property and were declared historical monuments. High representatives of the French state attended the annual commemoration ceremonies, and the French state financially supported the construction of the new Oradour. A new village was built next to the ruins.[15] According to Straßner, generally external factors like public recognition of the crime and financial support for the victims should actually support a reconciliation process.[16] However, the new village was not even finished when the close relationship between the French state and Oradour ruptured in 1953. As the Oradour trial in Bordeaux made known to the public, Frenchmen from Alsace who were nearly all forced into the SS had participated in the massacre. The question of their criminal prosecution turned into a national crisis. Oradour demanded a prosecution of the French perpetrators together with the Germans whereas the Alsace region insisted that these forced recruited men were only victims. Finally, the French National Assembly granted an amnesty to the already condemned Frenchmen.[17] In Oradour this was felt like a second martyrdom[18] and the consequences were dramatic: the village disassociated itself from the state and retreated into isolation and mourning for years. Feasts and ceremonies were either prohibited or strictly regimented. The streets were left without names, the houses without colour. Over the years, there were no trees or flowers in the village. In the 1960s, the ice covering Oradour started to melt very slowly. But even in the early 1990s, the houses still remained grey and without any

---

15 Farmer, *Oradour*, 79-120.
16 Straßner, Versöhnung, 28.
17 Only the man who had engaged voluntarily in the SS was not granted amnesty. Several studies deal with the trial. The most detailed are Fouché, *Politique*, and Guillaume Javerliat, *Bordeaux 1953: le deuxième drame d'Oradour. Entre histoire, mémoire et politique* (Limoges: Pulim, 2009).
18 Farmer, *Oradour*, 194.

decorations. At that time, the streets were still empty and public events were forbidden in June.[19] The amnesty created a national conflict and henceforth the need for reconciliation with the French state and the Alsace region. The isolation and bitterness that resulted from the Bordeaux process and characterized the double conflict within France is one of the external factors that inhibited the process of reconciliation in Oradour. The tensions between Oradour and the French state have weakened since the 1980s; and in the 1990s reconciliation initiatives followed between Oradour and Alsace.[20]

At a first look, on the part of the Federal Republic of Germany (FRG) two factors were given that theoretically intended to promote reconciliation: criminal prosecution and compensation. Altogether twelve preliminary proceedings were opened by the German public prosecutor's offices regarding the German crime in Oradour.[21] In 1960, a French-German agreement of compensation for the crimes committed by the Nazis made it possible for most of those affected by the massacre to receive indemnification payments from the German state.[22] However, looking at the issue more closely, it is doubtful whether these measures had a positive impact on the reconciliation process. Legally justified or not, the preliminary hearings never led to a tri-

---

19 Farmer, *Oradour*, 204-217; Fouché, *Politique*, 467-476; Meyer, *Wandel*, 403-410.
20 Meyer, *Wandel*, 408-410, 415-418.
21 As there is no study including all the preliminary proceedings in the FRG, I have to refer to the files that have been collected by the public prosecutor's office in Stuttgart. When preliminary proceedings on the Oradour case were initiated in 1995, the office received nearly all the former writs of prohibition. Stadtarchiv Ludwigsburg, Js 48144/89, Roter Band II. Four preliminary proceedings don't appear however and can be found in: Staatsarchiv Nürnberg, 1 AR 29/53; Staatsarchiv Bremen, 20 Js 50/81; Landesarchiv Münster, 45 Js 53/89; Claudia Moisel, *Frankreich und die deutschen Kriegsverbrecher. Politik und Praxis der Strafverfolgung nach dem Zweiten Weltkrieg* (Göttingen: Wallstein, 2004), 187-188.
22 Claudia Moisel, Pragmatischer Formelkompromiss: Das deutsch-französische Globalabkommen von 1960, in: *Grenzen der Wiedergutmachung. Die Entschädigung für NS-Verfolgte in West- und Osteuropa 1945-2000*, ed. Hans Günter Hockerts et al. (Göttingen: Wallstein, 2006), 242-284, here: 275-276.

al in the FRG. Thus, not a single man was ever condemned there.[23] Besides, the West German government was active on behalf of German soldiers who had been condemned in Bordeaux in 1953 and finally achieved their early release.[24] Regarding the compensation, we know that the majority of those entitled to receive payments did accept.[25] Nevertheless, we know nearly nothing on how the agreement was perceived. What is certain is that the early release of the Germans convicted in Bordeaux as well as the fact that the General of the SS-Division *Das Reich* could live a normal life in Germany are mentioned in the book about the massacre and its aftermath sold by the ANFM. However, the book totally ignores the compensation payment.[26]

Regarding the official recognition of the crime as another element supposed to support reconciliation, it was not until the year 2000 that with Gerhard Schröder a German chancellor officially recognized the massacre. He repeated this recognition four years later, but there was no apology for the crime, as some had expected.[27] The long lasting silence of the German chancellors had a particularly negative effect because for several decades, former SS men and revisionists denied in their publications to have been guilty of having committed the massacre. While the French state censored

---

23 In 1983, the former officer Heinz Barth was condemned in the German Democratic Republic (GDR) for having participated in the Oradour massacre. Henry Leide, *NS-Verbrecher und Staatssicherheit. Die geheime Vergangenheitspolitik der DDR* (Göttingen: Vandenhoeck & Ruprecht, 2005), 131-142. Andrea Erkenbrecher, *Der Prozess gegen Heinz Barth 1983. Eine Fallstudie zur politischen Instrumentalisierung von Kriegsverbrecherprozessen in der DDR* (M.A. thesis, Ludwig-Maximilians-Universität München, 2006).
24 Moisel, *Frankreich*, 183-188; Fouché, *Oradour*, 268.
25 This is the result of an evaluation I made of the so-called "fiches de côntrole", index cards that were established for every person who received compensation following the Franco-German agreement. Those cards are archived in the Archive du monde combattant, Caen.
26 Guy Pauchou and Pierre Masfrand, *Oradour sur Glane. Vision d'epouvante* (Limoges: Melting Phot, 2003), 138-139.
27 Meyer, *Wandel*, 433-434; Lucas Delattre, A Oradour, dernière étape de la réconciliation franco-allemand, *Le Monde*, 30 May 2000.

several of those books, the German government did not.[28] This revisionism offended the survivors and the relatives of the victims, which for some is Oradour's third trauma.[29] In conclusion, it can be stated that concerning the actions of the French and the West German state since the end of World War II, the events that obstructed a process of reconciliation outweighed those that supported it.

RECONCILIATION INITIATIVES FROM WITHIN CIVIL SOCIETY

Reconciliation between Oradour and Germany has not been a subject in academic research so far. Nevertheless, the topic is *en passant* mentioned in a few studies, especially the following two aspects: The missing official apology from the German state and the question of Oradour's readiness for reconciliation with Germany.[30] Research on civil society's gestures of reconciliation towards Oradour is just at its beginning.[31] This research desideratum is remarkable because numerous such gestures can be evidenced. Germans have offered help for the reconstruction of the village, they have raised money, they have laid wreaths, have brought their sympathy, memorial plates, and gifts of atonement. They have celebrated church services of atonement and concerts of reconciliation in the new local church of Oradour. When examining civil society's involvement in the reconciliation process, three aspects are particularly remarkable: Firstly, gestures aimed at reconciliation date back to 1947. Secondly, it can be evidenced that the ac-

---

28 Meyer, *Wandel*, 340-344; Jean-Jacques Fouché, *Le négationnisme et le symbole Oradour* (2002), http://www.cerclegramsci.org/rubs/tribune10.htm, accessed 31 May 2011.

29 In his documentary film, *Oradour, le rétour à la vie*, 2009, Marc Desoutter speaks of the "three great traumas", whereas Robert Hébras, one of the men to survive the massacre, uses the expression "injuries".

30 Notably: Fouché, *Oradour*, 241, 244; Jean-Jacques Fouché, Le Centre de la mémoire d'Oradour, *Vingtième siècle. Revue d'histoire* 73 (2002), 125-137; Henning Meyer, *Oradour-sur-Glane und sein Rang in der französischen 'Erinnerungskultur'* (M.A. thesis, Universität Augsburg, 2003), 109-113.

31 Meyer, *Oradour-sur-Glane*, 109-113; Meyer, *Wandel*, 433-434.

tors and the chosen forms of reconciliation efforts are heterogeneous and it further can be established that within this heterogeneity Christian motivations and corresponding symbols have been dominant for quite some time. Thirdly, different phases and turning points can be observed. During the ten years following the massacre, the rejection of such gestures prevailed and the offers aimed at reconciliation remained unanswered. This was the case when in 1947 the German youth magazine *Benjamin* campaigned for young volunteers to support the construction of the new Oradour village. The appeal received a positive response but the offer was vehemently rejected by the ANFM.[32] Moreover, a goblet of atonement from the German branch of *Pax Christi,* a non-governmental Catholic peace movement, offered in 1955 was not accepted.[33] In 1953, a donation from a school in Castrop-Rauxel offered to pay for the planting of a tree in Oradour may have been used for the intended purpose, but there was still no direct contact with Oradour. Not the villagers, but the French High Commissioner André François Poncet signed the letter of appreciation.[34] For the 10th commemoration day of the massacre a delegation of the descendants of the victims of Penzberg and the Rombergpark brought an insignia.[35] As far as we know, this insignia was

---

32 Alfons Erb, Oradour gestern und heute, *Dokumente. Zeitschrift für den deutsch-französischen Dialog* 4, 2 (1948), 86-93.

33 Hedwig Groß, Das Geheimnis der Versöhnung heißt Erinnerung. Vor 50 Jahren verübte eine SS-Division das Massaker von Oradour-sur-Glane, in: *Begegnungsfahrt. 50 Jahre deutsch-französische Geschichte, 50 Jahre Pax Christi Frankreich, 25. April bis 4. Mai 1994*, Bischöfliches Diözesanarchiv Aachen (hereafter: BDA), Ala Pax Christi, vol. 35.

34 H.M., Laßt Bäume darüber wachsen, *Die 7 Tage*, 8 May 1953; Ulrich Brochhagen, *Nach Nürnberg. Vergangenheitsbewältigung in der Ära Adenauer* (Berlin: Ullstein, 1999), 162.

35 The Rombergpark is a park in the German town of Dortmund where in spring 1945 several hundred people, Germans as well as foreigners, were executed by National Socialists. Ulrich Sander, *Mord im Rombergpark. Tatsachenbericht* (Dortmund: Grafit Verlag, 1993). Concerning Penzberg, on 28 April 1945, units of the *Wehrmacht* and a group of *Werwolf* members killed 16 persons. Some of them had tried to save the local mine from being blasted by the National Socialists and therefore had taken over the local power. Among the victims were also persons who haven't been involved in this action at all. *Die tödliche Utopie.*

never posted and the delegation's invitation to people in Oradour to participate in the commemoration of the crimes of Penzberg and the Rombergpark was never answered.[36] "Trustworthy and cooperative relationships" were not established in this phase, a time heavily marked by the crime itself and the so-called second martyrdom of the Bordeaux judgement and the amnesty which followed.

The first turning point in the relationship between Germans and the Oradour citizens took place in 1976 as the result of Vinzenz Kremp's commitment to the village. Born in 1915, Kremp participated in the Second World War as a soldier in the *Wehrmacht*. After the end of the war, he became a member of the *Volksbund Deutsche Kriegsgräberfürsorge* (VDK), engaging in the maintenance of war graves.[37] He committed himself to reconciliation out of his wartime experience, where he might or might not have been involved in a possible war crime.[38] During a church service in Oradour in 1976, he donated, together with a youth group, a candelabra as a reconciliation gift. From this gesture emerged his long-lasting contact with the village and his deep friendship with the local priest, Henri Boudet. Kremp traveled regularly to Oradour and also welcomed Boudet and young people from Oradour to his home in Baden.[39]

However, the election of Raymond Frugier as Oradour's new mayor in 1995 is the most important turning point. Since his inauguration, Frugier has been practicing an active reconciliation policy, first towards Alsace and

---

Bilder, Texte, Dokumente, Daten zum Dritten Reich, fourth ed., ed. Horst Möller et al. (München and Berlin: Selbstverlag Institut für Zeitgeschichte, 2003), 285, 314. Both executions were part of the so-called *Kriegsendphasenverbrechen*.

36 Feierliche Ehrung der Märtyrer von Oradour, *Die Tat*, 19 June 1954; Man muß ihnen das Handwerk legen!, *Die Tat*, 19 June 1954.

37 Joseph Spinner, Vinzenz Kremp (1915-1996), http://www.umkirch.de/ceasy/modules/cms/main.php5?cPageId=166, accessed 31 May 2011.

38 Vinzenz Kremp, *Oradour-sur-Glane*, 2, manuscript, given to the author by Wolfram Kremp. Wolfgang Kremp, Interview with the author, 19 February 2010.

39 Correspondence between Vinzenz Kremp and Henri Boudet, 1976-1986, given to the author by Henri Boudet; Henri Boudet, interview with the author, 9 May 2008.

later on towards Germany.⁴⁰ Whereas Vinzenz Kremp's contacts with Oradour remained unofficial and progressed notably with the local parish, the contacts now shifted to another level. Not only did Frugier officially welcome German delegations but he also welcomed increasingly more people of higher political standing. In retrospect, many innovations took place during his seventeen years in office: In 1997, he officially welcomed for the first time a German mayor in Oradour.⁴¹ In 2000, he officially received Reinhold Bocklet, a high-ranking official in the Bavarian state chancellery.⁴² Then, in 2004, for the first time, he invited a German delegation of young people and former members of the French *résistance* to attend the commemoration ceremony for the 60th anniversary of the massacre.⁴³ Later, in 2007, a German choir was invited to give a concert in Oradour.⁴⁴ The same year and two years later, there was a visit from Gerda Hasselfeldt, the vice president of the German *Bundestag*.⁴⁵ Most of these initiatives grew out of already existing relations or they led to long-lasting associations, which qualifies them as "trustworthy and cooperative relationships". For instance, the visit of Gerda Hasselfeldt led to a return visit in 2010, when, for the first time, a large official delegation of Oradour traveled to Germany that included the mayor, members of the local council, a survivor of the massacre as well as one of the victims' relatives, and the local soccer team. They were warmly welcomed in Dachau by Gerda Hasselfeldt and Peter Bürgel, the local mayor.⁴⁶ Peter Bürgel then was the first German (local)

---

40 Meyer, *Wandel*, 415-418, 430-431.
41 Meyer, *Oradour-sur-Glane*, 110.
42 Gerd Kröncke, Stille in Oradour-sur-Glane, *Süddeutsche Zeitung*, 29 May 2000.
43 Meyer, *Wandel*, 434; Flyer *Einladung zu einer Bildungsfahrt nach Oradour*, http://www.drafd.de/files/flyer_oradour.pdf, accessed 31 May 2011; *Deutsche auf dem Weg nach Oradour*, Auswahl aus einer Ausstellung von Alexandra C. Schmidt, http://www.authentic-beauties.de/pdf/Oradour_Broschuere.pdf, accessed 31 May 2011.
44 Musik kontra Massaker, *Pegnitz-Zeitung*, 26-28 May 2007.
45 *Besuch in Gedenkstätte in Oradour*, http://www.hasselfeldt.de/de/detailles_2,737.htm, accessed 15 September 2007. Press release Bundestagsvizepräsidentin Hasselfeldt reist mit Dachauer OB Bürgel nach Oradour, http://www.hansjoerg-christmann.de/htm/pm2009Juni17.html, accessed 31 May 2011.
46 Laurent Borderie, Foot et émotion pour l'USO, *Le Populaire*, 2 July 2010.

politician to have been officially invited to attend the commemoration ceremony on June 10, 2011 – the last substantial welcoming gesture put forth by Raymond Frugier for the time being.[47]

Looked at from this point of view, reconciliation between Oradour and Germany was a long and difficult process but it became a success story after all. Although, there is no doubt about the constant progress of these relations considering their official character, there are open questions concerning the people who are not involved in this process, the problems this process provoked and its boundaries.

Successes and failures: Vinzenz Kremp and Pax Christi (1955-1994)

The Catholic peace movement *Pax Christi* was founded in France in 1945 with the aim of reconciliation with Germany. In 1948, the German section was founded.[48] German delegations of *Pax Christi* visited Oradour several times. In 1955, Manfred Hörhammer, first secretary of the German branch[49], and son of a German father and a French mother, visited Oradour for the first time, but he came *incognito*. Depressed, as he was to witness the ruins and what had happened there, he did not dare to reveal his identity to the local guide. After the visit, he described his experience in his public diary published in a Catholic magazine. As a result, a reader donated her family jewels to have them transformed into a goblet for the parish of Oradour.[50] The gift was not directly handed over to Oradour but rather the president of the German branch presented it to the Bishop of Lourdes, Pierre-Marie Théas, who was the founder of *Pax Christi* and its president in

---

47 Benoît Sadry, e-mails to the author, 27 April 2011 and 3 June 2011.
48 Michael Kißener, Der Katholizismus und die deutsch-französische Annäherung in den 1950er Jahren, in: *Wege der Verständigung zwischen Deutschen und Franzosen nach 1945. Zivilgesellschaftliche Annäherungen*, ed. Corine Defrance et al. (Tübingen: Narr, 2010), 89-98, here: 90-91.
49 Ibid., 93.
50 Manfred Hörhammer, Aus meinem Tagebuch, *Pax-Christi-Zeitschrift* 2 (1955); Heinz Theo Risse, Oradour beginnt überall. Reflexionen über einige Beispiele christlicher Friedensarbeit, in: *Versöhnung: Gestalten, Zeiten, Modelle*, ed. Heinrich Fries and Ulrich Valeska (Frankfurt a.M.: Knecht, 1975), 133-144.

France. Théas passed the goblet over to the bishop of Limoges, Rastouil, who was, in turn, to pass it on to the parish of Oradour, which, in the end, rejected the object.[51]

In the following decades, the sentiments of the people in Oradour softened, but Manfred Hörhammers' hope, that one day German priests would come to the town, accompanied by a bishop, German women and mothers, and "ask Mother Rouffange [sic] to lead us to the graves and to the graveyard", never came true.[52] Indeed, German delegations came in 1963, 1988 and 1994. They visited the ruins, celebrated church services for reconciliation, brought additional gifts of atonement, and laid down flowers. Actually, the town of Oradour opened up when, in 1988, the parish accepted the once rejected goblet and some French women attended the service. A few years later, in 1994, the pilgrims were warmly welcomed by the local priest, Jean Robert, with whom they celebrated a moving church service and who gave them absolution. In the same year, the deputy mayor welcomed the pilgrims for the first time in the church. However, the reception was short and he told the pilgrims that anger no longer existed in Oradour; nevertheless, there were still resentments. Thus, the group of pilgrims had to conclude: "The way to reconciliation wasn't easy in Oradour, and if we're honest, hasn't been reached yet. We prepared a church service, in which we wanted to ask for forgiveness [...] but our secret wish for inhabitants of the village to share the Eucharist with us did not come true."[53] The outcome of their commitment was far from "trustworthy and cooperative relationships", as Straßner would put it. But why did all efforts fail?

To answer this question it is helpful to compare the commitment of *Pax Christi* to that of Vincenz Kremp, as both of them initiated reconciliation in nearly the same setting. As we recall, working with a youth group in Limoges in 1976 to take care of German war graves, Kremp decided to make a gesture of reconciliation towards Oradour by giving a candelabra as a present to the local parish. As had done *Pax Christi*, he established contact

---

51 Risse, Oradour; Groß, Geheimnis.
52 Hörhammer, Tagebuch. Marguerite Rouffanche was the only woman to survive the massacre in the church.
53 Pax Christi in Oradour. 'Wir wöllen versuchen, uns christlich dem Grauen zu stellen', *Pax Christi* 9/10 (1963); Alice Rapp, Sonntag, 10. Juli 1988, BDA, Ala Pax Christi, vol. 33. Quotation: Groß, Versöhnung.

with the bishop of Limoges first to assess the situation. The bishop consulted the local priest and the ANFM, who both gave the all clear for the deposit of the candelabra in the new church; nonetheless, on the condition that "this deposit is done in a discreet way". Kremp was asked to contact the local priest, Henri Boudet, for more details.[54] They agreed that the gift should be handed over during a Sunday morning church service. That the contact on that Sunday did not end with the church service was due to a coincidence and Henri Boudet. As Boudet had to baptise a child after the church service, he could not welcome the Germans himself. Instead of sending them alone to the ruins of the city, he had organized a meeting in the presbytery and had asked some young people of the parish to welcome the guests. Furthermore, the president of the ANFM and some other people attended the reception. When Boudet finally joined the group, contact had already been made between the young people. The young French invited the German group to come back in the afternoon to visit an exhibition in the local town hall.[55]

From that day on, Kremp kept up the freshly established contact. He invited Boudet and young people from Oradour to an event of the VDK and to his home in Baden. He also traveled regularly to Oradour.[56] In Germany, Kremp's commitment to the village not only resounded in the press, but it also initiated more gestures of reconciliation. The first gesture came from the Freiburg criminal investigation department that donated money to the church of Oradour. Then, the Catholic parish of Umkirch signed a charter to "forever" pay for the church's candles. Several of Kremp's friends came along with him to Oradour in the following years.[57] Aside from these gestures, in the early eighties Kremp contributed in another way to the reconciliation with Oradour. As the revisionist publications on the massacre became increasingly more aggressive in Germany, Kremp, who had some experience in historical research, started working on the events surrounding

---

54 Letter Bishop of Limoges to Archbishop of Freiburg, 1 July 1976, given to the author by Henri Boudet.
55 Henri Boudet, interview with the author, 9 May 2008.
56 Correspondence Kremp-Boudet.
57 Freiburger Kriminalbeamte sammelten für die neue Kirche von Oradour, *Kriegsgräberfürsorge* 4, 11 (1977), 234; Isolde Doelfs, Die Versöhnung vertiefen, *Konradsblatt* 38, 23 September 1979; Correspondence Kremp-Boudet.

the war crimes committed on June 10 in Oradour, and rectified the lies written by former SS men.[58] He thereby advocated for something that Straßner qualifies as an *external factor* to further the process of reconciliation mostly carried out by the state: "an earnest process of coping with the past wrongs as well as solid research into these past wrongs".[59]

Reading the German newspapers reporting on Kremp's commitment to Oradour, one gains the impression that a true "fairytale of reconciliation" had taken place at that time.[60] However, while also other sources prove that on the German side increasingly more people were interested and became involved in Kremp's project, it is difficult to estimate its effect on Oradour. We know that at the time Vinzenz Kremp was well known in the village and, to some extent, he became integrated in the parish. When he came to Oradour, for example, he sometimes read the lesson during the church services. We also know that he was in contact with various other people in Oradour. Among them was the deputy mayor, but above all people of the parish.[61] However, we do not know how strong the bond grew between Kremp and the citizens of Oradour and what this bond meant for the people of Oradour. What is certain is that Kremp's closest friend was Henri Boudet. Their relationship was not only "trustworthy and cooperative", but it had grown into a close friendship. A highlight in this long-lasting friendship was the day in 1986, when Henri Boudet received the *Bundesverdienstkreuz* (Order of Merit of the Federal Republic of Germany) for his commitment to the reconciliation of Oradour and Germany.[62]

It should be noted in this respect that this deep friendship grew with a man who himself was not affected by the massacre. Although, as the priest of the village, Henri Boudet in a way "married" the population,[63] but – to stay with the metaphor – he was not born into the family. It is likely that

---

58 Correspondence Kremp-Boudet; Kremp, Oradour-sur-Glane.
59 Straßner, Versöhnung, 28.
60 For example: Karl-Heinz Darweger, Die Messe von Oradour, given to the author by Henri Boudet.
61 Correspondence Kremp-Boudet; Henri Boudet, Interview with the author, 9 May 2008.
62 Ludwig Wien, Kommt! Wir wollen es wagen!, *Evangelische Kirchenzeitung* 6 (1986).
63 Henri Boudet, Interview with the author, 9 May 2008.

this position enabled Boudet to become some kind of mediator between Kremp and the population.[64] How hard it can be for people, who suffered through the massacre to engage in "trustworthy and cooperative relationships" with Germans, is illustrated by the following scenario. Vinzenz Kremp was for several years in touch with the Cordeau family in Oradour. They were part of the parish and very close to Henri Boudet. During the events of June 10, 1944, the Cordeaus had lost their only daughter, Bernadette. Fourty years after the massacre, their apartment still looked like a museum commemorating their beloved child. One day in the 1980s, Kremp was visiting them with his son and his son's family. Vinzenz Kremp's son had brought with him his just several months old son but Mrs. Cordeau refused to touch the baby since to her it was a "German male".[65]

Coming back to the comparison with *Pax Christi*, we recall that Vinzenz Kremp found in Henri Boudet not only a person with whom he sympathized, but also a mediator to the local population. Contrary to the pilgrims of *Pax Christi*, who had visited Oradour in more or less long intervals, Kremp came back mostly once a year since the contact had first been established. When Henri Boudet left Oradour in 1985, the contact between the two men and between Kremp and different people from Oradour continued. Both factors were responsible for Kremp's contacts to Oradour not to break off after Henri Boudet left the village in 1985.[66] How close these contacts were actually related to the two men is shown by the fact that after Kremp's death all relationships to Oradour stopped. Kremp's children maintained the contact to Boudet, who was visited almost yearly by part of the family until his death in 2011. But their contact with other people from Oradour ended long ago.[67] Even if Kremp had created more solid ties to Oradour than *Pax Christi*, ultimately he did not succeed to establish the kinds of „trustworthy and cooperative relationships" between the inhabit-

---

64 There are a lot of indications in the correspondence between the two men pointing to this role.
65 Wolfram Kremp, Interview with the author, 19 February 2010; Henri Boudet, Interview with the author, 9 May 2008.
66 Correspondence Kremp-Boudet.
67 Wolfram Kremp, Interview with the author, 19 February 2010; Wolfram Kremp, e-mail to the author, 21 February 2010.

ants of Oradour and the Germans that would have outlasted his own engagement and his own death.

The commitment of *Pax Christi* and Vinzenz Kremp took place in what can be considered a period during which Oradour had been increasingly open to such gestures of reconciliation. However, these gestures might not have been approved by all inhabitants of the village. In fact, the church services aimed at reconciliation celebrated by *Pax Christi*, met no response. This lack of involvement showed that the people of the French village were not that enthusiastic about reconciliation efforts. Nevertheless, all these initiatives were tolerated. This tolerance seems to be rooted in the fact that these actions were part of civil society and that the German actors had never asked for an official response. Shortly after the 50th anniversary of the massacre in 1994, the local mayor, Robert Lapuelle, stated in an interview that until this day there were "nuances" in Oradour's dealing with Germans. As could be gathered from his remarks, there were mainly two criteria that decided between acceptable and problematic contacts: The age of the Germans and the nature of the exchange. While there would be no problems on the level of private exchange, it would be difficult once mayors, ambassadors or Members of Parliament were involved. Lapuelle reported that people trampled with rage on wreaths that had been laid down regularly by the *Sozialistische Einheitspartei Deutschlands* (SED), the state party of the former German Democratic Republic (GDR) and that they were just thrown away later. If the German ambassador had asked to lay a wreath during the commemoration ceremony on the occasion of the 50th anniversary of the massacre, he would have had to send him away because the ANFM would not have accepted him. The mayor assured that this was not an act of hostility, but the disposition of the surviving families that would have to be respected.[68] A year later, Raymond Frugier followed Lapuelle in office and in spite of the "disposition of the families", the new mayor abandoned the policy of "non-official relations".

---

68 Stefan Endel, Tröste meine Trauer!, http://www.endell.de/infos/philosophie/index.html, accessed 31 May 2011.

Official relations between Oradour and Germany since 1995 and the role of civil society

We have already mentioned all the new contacts with Germany that had been accepted and to some extend had been accelerated by Raymond Frugier as mayor of Oradour. Analyzing them from the view of civil society, we can see two developments: Firstly, civil society continued playing an important role. Indeed, the first German delegation to have been invited officially to attend the commemorative ceremony on June 10, 2004 in the French village consisted of civil societal actors. Frugier made an interesting choice in inviting German former members of the French *résistance* and youth groups. Because of their role during the war and their age, both were far from sharing any guilt with the perpetrators of the massacre. The head of the delegation was Gerhard Leo, one of the founding members of the *Verband Deutscher in der Résistance, in den Streitkräften der Antihitlerkoalition und der Bewegung 'Freies Deutschland'* (Association of Germans in the French Resistance, DRAFD). Together with different trade unions, DRAFD had looked for young people to join the delegation.[69] Civil society played also an important role as far as the visits of the mayor of Bad Windsheim, Eckhardt, in 1997, and the Bavarian minister Bocklet in 2000 are concerned. Both visits emerged in the context of Franco-German town and regional partnerships. While Eckhardt visited the twin town of Bad Windsheim, located one hour away from Oradour, Bocklet stayed in Limousin to attend to events of regional partnerships between Bavaria and some French regions.[70] Even if Oradour refused to engage in a partnership with a German city, the civil society network of Franco-German town twinnings and regional partnerships had an impact on Oradour's relations with Germany after all.

Secondly, the new relations between Oradour and Germany are excellent examples of the constant interaction between civil society, the private sphere, and the state. To illustrate with two examples: The concert of rec-

---

69 Flyer *Einladung*; Schober, *Oradour*.
70 Ansprache des Ersten Bürgermeisters der Stadt Bad Windsheim, Diplom-Ingenieur (univ.) Wolfgang Eckhardt anläßlich des Besuchs der Gedenkstätte Oradour-sur-Glane mit Kranzniederlegung am 04.10.1997, given to the author by Wolfgang Eckhardt; Kröncke, Stille.

onciliation, given by the choir of Schwaig in 2007, was the highlight of an already long term relationship that had involved actors on a private level as well as on the level of civil society and the state. In 1985, one of the survivors of the massacre, Robert Hébras, was invited to the peace talk organised by the Social Democratic Party of Germany (SPD). He was seated next to Willy Brandt and therefore spent the whole day with the former German chancellor.[71] On this occasion, Hébras met Fritz Körber, member of the SPD and of the *Bezirkstag Mittelfranken* (District Council of Central Franconia). Körber was member of the commission for partnership and international understanding in the *Bezirkstag Mittelfranken* and also the political commissioner for this field since 1982. He had started traveling to Limousin with youth groups from the local *Arbeiterwohlfahrt* (Workers Welfare Association, AWO) one year before.[72] Since he planned to visit Oradour again just a few weeks later, he asked Hébras if he could give the youth group a guided tour through the ruins. Hébras accepted and from that day on, they became friends.[73] When Körber later became mayor of Schwaig, he organised an exhibition on Oradour in his hometown and invited Hébras and Frugier.[74] Körber left his position as mayor in 2006 but the contacts continued on the political and on the private level. In 2007, Körber was at the head of the invited group, including the choir of Schwaig and the chamber orchestra of Fürth. In this gesture of reconciliation even representatives at a higher state level became involved with the German Consul General sending representatives to Oradour to attend the concert.[75] This example draws our attention to the continuous and complex interconnection between the private, the public, and the state in processes of reconciliation.

The second example demonstrates that the politically highest-ranking contact between Oradour and Germany has its origins in private contacts

---

71 Robert Hébras, interviews with the author, 7 May 2008 and 14 May 2008.
72 Fritz Körber, e-mail to the author, 31 October 2011.
73 Fritz Körber, interviews with the author, 31 May 2010 and 2 June 2010.
74 Rede von Bürgermeister Körber zur Eröffnung der Fotoausstellung 'Oradour-sur-Glane – Ruinen als Mahnmal' am 18.10.2005; Begrüßung von Bürgermeister Körber zum Abend der Vorträge mit Bürgermeister Raymond Frugier und Robert Hébras aus dem Limousin am 21.10.2005 im Schwaiger Schloss, both given to the author by Fritz Körber.
75 Andreas Sichelstiel, Europahymne Höhepunkt, *Pegnitz-Zeitung*, 21 May 2007.

and in activities by actors from civil society. Florian Förster worked as a volunteer for the Protestant organization *Aktion Sühnezeichen* (Action Reconciliation, ASF) in the *Centre de la mémoire d'Oradour-sur-Glane* (CMO), which officially opened in 1999. In the light of this experience, he suggested to the vice-president of the German Bundestag Gerda Hasselfeldt to officially visit Oradour. Förster and Hasselfeldt had met before on several occasions. The director of the CMO agreed upon inviting Hasselfeldt and, she then became the first representative of the German state to officially visit the village.[76] Here again different levels of society and state became involved. Hasselfeldt advocated that Oradour be one of the destinations of the youth exchange organized by the German Bundestag on the Day of remembrance of the victims of National Socialism in 2009. During her second visit to Oradour with the mayor of Dachau, Peter Bürgel, in 2009,[77] a friendly match between the Oradour and Dachau soccer teams had been organised.[78] A year later, it was Hasselfeldt's and Bürgel's turn to welcome a delegation from Oradour for a rematch in Dachau.[79] When Peter Bürgel was the first local German politician to officially attend the commemorative ceremony on June 10, official political and private contacts played an important role again. Peter Bürgel had accepted a private invitation to spend a few days with Raymond Frugier at his seaside house after the commemoration.[80]

By welcoming the different delegations and politicians in an official manner, Frugier, as head of the village, spoke in the name of Oradour. In this sense and by applying the criterion of "trustworthy and cooperative relationships", it could be argued that Oradour had reached the decisive stage of reconciliation with Germany. It is here that we reach a crucial point in

---

76 Gerda Hasselfeldt, interview with the author, June 2008.
77 Besides her position as vice president of the *Bundestag*, Hasselfeldt is representing the constituency of Dachau-Fürstenfeldbruck at the German Parliament for a long time. Therefore she is closely linked with the Bavarian town of Dachau. Concerning her constituency: http://www.hasselfeldt.de/de/main/im_wahlkreis_2.htm, accessed 31 May 2011.
78 Press release *Bundestagsvizepräsidentin Hasselfeldt*.
79 Laurent Borderie, Foot et émotion pour l'USO, *Le Populaire*, 2 July 2010.
80 Benoît Sadry, e-mail to the author, 27 April 2010 and 3 June 2010.

the analysis: What is actually meant when we are talking about reconciliation with 'Oradour'?

"ORADOUR, THAT'S COMPLEX...": DIMENSIONS OF 'ORADOUR'

"Oradour, that's complex... ", is the title of one chapter of Jean-Jacques Fouché's book about the *martyred village*.[81] The statement accurately captures the complexity involved when trying to define the meaning of 'Oradour' in the context of reconciliation processes. "Reconciliation", Straßner writes, "takes place on the individual level between perpetrators and victims as well as on the collective level".[82] As far as the German actors are concerned, none of them were men who had participated in the massacre. The actors were part of a collective, which Straßner describes as "the environment concerned by the effects or affects [of the past wrongs], or the society as such".[83] As far as 'Oradour' is concerned, the name takes on several meanings. Oradour represents two *places*, the ruins of the previously existing town as well as the new village nearby. On a *symbolic level*, Oradour can be understood as a *lieux de mémoire* (Pierre Nora). Additionally, it became a "common term" "designating the massacre of a civil population without being able to defend itself by a military force".[84] Oradour as the addressee of gestures of reconciliation could be representative of the *victims who died* in the massacre and who were addressed with gestures like laying down commemorative wreaths in the destroyed village or the local cemetery. However, the commitments for reconciliation with Oradour were foremost directed to the *survivors* of the massacre, e.g., *people living there and having been touched by the atrocities*.[85] At this point, additional as-

---

81 Fouché, *Oradour*, 16. Fouché quoted the mayor of Saint-Junien and General Council of the canton to which Oradour belongs. What the mayor wanted to say exactly wasn't clear.
82 Straßner, Versöhnung, 29.
83 Ibid., 27.
84 Fouché, *Oradour*, 8.
85 Fritz Körber for example, said in an interview that he had tried for years to establish contacts with the inhabitants of Oradour; Sichelstiel, Europahymne. An-

pects need to be considered. The people living in Oradour today can be seen either as individuals or as part of different collectives. On the individual level, there are the survivors of the massacre, the victims' relatives, their descendants, and those who moved to Oradour after the massacre and who are without any connection to the crime. On the collective level, we can distinguish between different groups. Firstly, there is the municipality that includes all the individuals mentioned above. Secondly, as we have seen, the parish seems to be, or seems to have been at a time, a relevant collective as well. In addition, there is the ANFM whose active members were personally affected by the massacre or were related to a victim.[86] Taking into account that only opponents themselves can reconcile[87] one has to reconsider the question about who was involved in the reconciliation processes and who was excluded. This question is of great significance, especially with regard to Frugier's active policy of reconciliation initiated in 1995: Is mere symbolic politics as initiated by mayor Frugier at stake here, is this initiative supported by people other than the mayor, and, above all, who are the people involved?

As has been pointed out, mayor Frugier was the engine and protagonist of most of the initiatives aimed at reconciliation from 1995 onwards. His role as an actor is ambivalent since on the one hand he is the representative of a town in which today the people having been touched by the crime are in the minority.[88] On the other hand, Frugier was himself – in contrast to his

---

other example is the already cited disappointment of the pilgrims of *Pax Christi* contained in their statement that their "secret wish for inhabitants of the village to share the Eucharist with us did not come true". I include here those affected by the massacre, who moved away from Oradour but remained active in the ANFM or the local environment, as did for example Robert Hébras.

86 The conditions for the kindredship have been expanded since 2001. Benoît Sadry, e-mail to the author, 17 October 2011. The different statutes of the association from 1944, 1988 and 2001 can be found in ACMO, 5FP1. The statutes from 1944 have been given to the author by Benoît Sadry. Besides from the ANFM I will elide here different other associations in Oradour.

87 Friese, *Politik*, 89.

88 Meyer, *Wandel*, 374-375. The number of inhabitants grew from 1,145 in 1946 to 2,060 in 2000. Most of the new inhabitants haven't been touched by the massacre.

predessor in office – affected by the massacre. When the German troops arrived in Oradour on June 10, 1944, Frugier's father took his wife and children and fled to the forest. From their hideout, a provisory built cabana in which they stayed for about two weeks, the then four-year-old Frugier saw the church of Oradour burning. Although, the family survived, Frugier feels that the crime left its marks on him.[89] But in public Frugier rarely speaks about his personal experience, although it would extend his policy of reconciliation and his actor role for the dimension of the personally affected. This reluctance may have been nourished from a certain respect for those who more narrowly escaped death than he himself. His reluctance may, however also be seen against the background that he is barred from active membership in the ANFM to this day because no member of his immediate family was murdered and the house of the family escaped the destruction.[90] Therefore, because Frugier operates his reconciliation policy – at least officially – in the role of mayor, Robert Hébras' support of Frugier's policy plays an important role, particularly since Hébras is one of the five men who survived the shootings and managed to escape.[91] Those five men as well as Marguerite Rouffanche, the only women to escape the massacre in the church, had been named *"miraculeux"*, which means "miracles".[92] After the death of Madame Rouffanche in 1988, Robert Hébras became the "incarnation of Oradour".[93] For years now, he is a much or even the most sought-after interlocutor for journalists, mostly neglecting those who sur-

---

89 Raymond Frugier, interview with the author, 23 July 2011.
90 Frugier lost distant relatives in the massacre, the place where the family lived, however, was not destroyed. After the modification of the statutes of the ANFM in 2001, Frugier became some sort of honorary member of the association, but he is still excluded from active membership. Benoît Sadry, e-mail to the author, 15 June 2011, 15 June 2012.
91 Robert Hébras, *Oradour-sur-Glane. The tragedy. Hour by hour* (Montreuil-Bellay: Editions C.M.D., 1994).
92 Farmer, *Oradour*, 129-130, 138.
93 Oradour-sur-Glane. Profession rescapé, *Libération*, 29 September 2011, http://www.liberation.fr/societe/01012362613-oradour-sur-glane-profession-rescape, accessed 16 December 2011.

vived because they flew in time or managed to hide without being discovered by the SS.[94]

Robert Hébras' way to reconciliation with Germany was a long one. In 2003, he explained in a discussion that soon after the massacre he had felt a lot of hate. He concluded that not all people should pay for a massacre they were responsible for just gradually. In retrospect, he saw a turning point in the invitation he received to attend the SPD peace talk by Willy Brandt.[95] Looking at the life of Robert Hébras, one can find several examples of "trustworthy and cooperative relationships" with Germans and his commitment to reconciliation takes on different forms. He has been conducting guided tours through the ruins of Oradour for French and German schoolchildren or other delegations. He has also been working with the *Centre de la mémoire d'Oradour-sur-Glane* where he is constantly available to talk to young people about his experiences, and he has traveled to Germany several times to talk to young people here.[96] Finally, yet importantly, he has played an important role in the policy of reconciliation developed by Raymond Frugier since 1995. The two men form some kind of dual spearhead of the reconciliation process. They often traveled together to Germany or Robert Hébras guided the invited delegations through the ruins of his hometown.[97] His warm-hearted attitude and his openness made a strong

---

94 Referring to the problems between different groups of survivors for example: Fax Jérôme Durix, Directeur départemental, [Ministère des] anciens combattants, 9 October 2000, ACMO, 1ETUD13.

95 Zeitzeugengespräch mit anschließender Fragerunde Robert Hébras, Überlebender des Massakers der SS 1944 in Oradour, in: *Pädagogik wider das Vergessen. Dokumentation. Aus der Vergangenheit für die Zukunft lernen?! Eine Fachtagung zur Bedeutung der Internationalen Jugendarbeit im Kontext von Gedenkstätten und Dokumentationszentren zur NS-Vergangenheit vom 29.05.-1.06. 2003*, ed. Bezirksjugendring Mittelfranken, 10-13.

96 Robert Hébras, interviews with the author, 7 May 2008 and 14 May 2008. Meyer, *Wandel*, 394-395, 431.

97 Meyer, *Wandel*, 394-395, 431; Bundestagsvizepräsidentin Hasselfeldt in Oradour, *Dachauer SZ*, 5 September 2007, 1. Erfahrungsbericht zur 4. Truppenwehrübung des Pionierbrückenbataillon 704 (GerEinh) vom 3.-9.09.2006 in Frankreich mit offiziellem Besuch der Gedenkstätte "Centre de la mémoire d'Oradour", 29, given to the author by Wolfgang Eckhardt.

impression on his guests.[98] But is he representative of all those who have been touched by the massacre? This question gains strength if one considers that Hébras had to leave the presidency of the ANFM in the 1990s. Among other reasons, he was criticized for being to open towards Germany.[99] We know that Hébras is not the only person who was affected by the massacre and who openly favored reconciliation,[100] but after all, the hesitation of the ANFM when it comes to Germany is remarkable.

The standpoint of the ANFM since 1995 vis-à-vis Frugier's policy of reconciliation has been indistinct.[101] When the Bavarian minister Bocklet was welcomed by Frugier in 2000, the ANFM stayed away and told the press that they were not in favor of such an initiative. The president of the association, Claude Milord, added, that there had not been a German apology for the massacre yet and that this was taken badly.[102] Even if the expected apology did not come,[103] one year later the President of the ANFM stressed the need of the Association for more openness – also towards Germany: "Our association has more than ever to accept its responsibilities, maintain its presence and its role when it comes to [...] relations and exchanges with German associations in the name of memory and of Oradour."[104] This new policy found its expression in 2004, when Claude Milord supported the invitation of a German delegation to attend the annual commemoration ceremony in June. However, not all the members of the associ-

---

98 Bundestagsvizepräsidentin Hasselfeldt in Oradour; *Erfahrungsbericht*, 44-45.
99 Meyer, *Wandel*, 366.
100 Camille Senon, interviews with the author, 6 and 12 May 2008; Albert Valade, interviews with the author, 17 and 18 October 2007, 10 May 2008; Marcel Darthout, interviews with the author, 15 October 2007 and 5 May 2008.
101 Meyer, *Wandel*, 431-435.
102 Lucas Delattre, A Oradour, dernière étape de la réconciliation franco-allemand, *Le Monde*, 30 May 2000.
103 In fact the Bavarian minister Bocklet apologized for the massacre but apparently this was not the apology expected, as one of the survivors explained. In his speech on 8 May 2000, the German Chancelor Schröder recognized the massacre but this recognition did not become known in Oradour before June 2001. Meyer, *Wandel*, 433.
104 Claude Milord, réélu président de l'Association des familles de martyrs, *L'Echo*, 8 April 2002, quoted in Meyer, *Wandel*, 364.

ation shared his position as could be read in the press and seen in a local television show.[105] In 2007, the question of inviting a German choir to give a concert of reconciliation met with resistance, obviously from some members of the ANFM. However, toward the German press its president tried to dispel this impression.[106] In 2007, the president of the ANFM did not attend Gerda Hasselfeldt's reception whereas he did attend it two years later. However, he did not send a representative to Dachau in 2010.[107] Once more in 2011 when the mayor of Dachau attended the commemorations of June 10 in Oradour the critical voices came from within the ANFM.[108] To sum it up, although, the president of the ANFM is increasingly more present at the receptions organized by the mayor, the Association still remains passive. On behalf of the ANFM he tolerated such gatherings, and supports them sometimes. The ANFM itself does not, however, act as the initiator of such relations with Germany. Even if the association has also shown itself increasingly more open toward Germany, this new openness has to date not led to "trustworthy and cooperative relationships" to use Straßner's words.

The most intricate question is what underlies this hesitation. Officially the president of the ANFM is repeating how difficult and delicate relations or efforts of reconciliation are when it comes to Germany. Here he refers particularly to those families who never integrated[109] the loss of their beloved ones, and to mothers who lost their children in the massacre. Fur-

---

105 Meyer, *Wandel*, 434; Oradour 2004 – Erinnerung von André, http://drafd.org/?Oradour_04_Andre, accessed 23 April 2011.
106 Sichelstiel, Europahymne; Andreas Sichelstiel, Versöhnung mit Feingefühl, *Pegnitz-Zeitung*, 26-28 May 2007, 11.
107 Concerning 2007 and 2009: Information given to the author by Elisabeth Wohland, member of Gerda Hasselfeldt's staff; concerning 2010: Speech delivered by Raymond Frugier, Visite à Dachau, 22-23 mai 2010 d'une Délégation d'Oradour-sur-Glane, given to the author by Raymond Frugier.
108 Marianne Buisso, 67ème anniversaire du massacre d'Oradour-sur-Glane, 11 June 2001, http://limousin.france3.fr/info/67eme-anniversaire-du-massacre-d-oradour-sur-glane-69163509.html, accessed 15 December 2011.
109 Milord used the French expression "n'ont jamais fait leur deuil". Using the term "integration" I refer to Hansjörg Znoj, *Komplizierte Trauer* (Göttingen: Hogrefe, 2004), 35, who states: "Mourning is understood as the active integration of loss."

thermore, he indicates inter-generational discussions within the associations but is anxious to assure that the ANFM does not put today's Germany on a par with Nazi-Germany.[110] Apart from that, not much is known about the critical voices from within the association – names are never given, details are never referred to. Most of the members of the ANFM remain in the background and do not raise their voice in public.[111] Critical voices in public are rare as was the statement in 2004 of a survivor whose sister was murdered in the church: "I won't go to the commemoration. The mayor has invited Germans!"[112] Thus, vital questions concerning those opposed to reconciliation within the ANFM stay in suspense: Are those who oppose numerous? What actually disturbs them and for what reasons?

The most significant source we can refer to is a discussion on the eve of the massacre's 60th anniversary, organized and broadcasted by the local television. Apart from mayor Frugier, the ANFM-President and the last two *miraculeux* still alive, Robert Hébras and Jean-Marcel Darthout, several women affected by the massacre had also been invited.[113] In some of their statements it has not only become obvious that the trauma of the massacre still has an extremely emotional impact on them, but also the limits of reconciliation and particularly the conflict between cognition and emotion have become visible for some of them. Renée Maneus for example survived as a child while being hidden with her mother and sisters but lost other members of her family. She reported that in theory she of course knew that kind Germans exist and in fact, she personally knew at least one. Nevertheless, it took a long time for her to accept Germans. What Renée Maneus describes here can be seen as an example for the limits of the *will* to reconcile. Reconciliation is not something that can rationally be decided upon. Some

---

110 Questions a ..., ANFM, *Bulletin d'information*, January 2003, ACMO, 5FP6; L'avenir: Avec l'Allemagne?, *Le Populaire*, 11 June 2004; Sichelstiel, Versöhnung.
111 Meyer, *Wandel*, 366.
112 Béatrice Jérôme, Les élus alsaciens participeront aux ceremonies, *Le Monde*, 9 June 2004.
113 The following statements are taken from: Tulle et Oradour, Table ronde, France 3 Limousin, 2004, ACMO, V4.5.2/03.

people *cannot* reconcile even if they would like to.[114] Aline Perney, who lost her four-year-old child and other family members on June 10, 1944, stated that even if she would be a religious person, it would be impossible for her to forgive those who killed her beloved ones. Nevertheless, whereas others would agree with her when it comes to the perpetrators,[115] she is able to describe the impossibility to respond positively to those Germans who had not been involved in the crime:

"I went to Germany, believe me, when I met them I knew that they weren't those who committed the massacre. They apologized but it was stronger than me, it gave me goose flesh, I turned my back on them, I couldn't. I can't, it's impossible."

Not only forgiving, even *accepting* a German delegation in Oradour was impossible for her. The point of conflict is not how to deal with the perpetrators of the massacre among the different actors in Oradour but how to deal with the other Germans. Jean-Marcel Darthout, one of the *miraculeux*, is one of those persons who cannot understand why some people cannot make a difference:

"Sixty years ago, I know it well, me too I lost people in Oradour! Me too, I have mourned the loss of a wife! Me too, I have mourned the loss of a mother! Me too, I suffered! However, the Germans who come to Oradour today are not those who killed my mother and killed my wife, thus I can receive them. *Voilà*, [that is] my position."

---

114 Thomas Hoppe, Erinnerung, Gerechtigkeit und Versöhnung. Zur Aufgabe eines angemessenen Umgangs mit belasteter Vergangenheit – eine sozialethische Perspektive, in: *Versöhnung, Strafe und Gerechtigkeit. Das schwere Erbe von Unrechts-Staaten*, ed. Michael Bongardt and Ralf K. Wüstenberg (Göttingen: Edition Ruprecht 2010), 29-53, here: 45; Straßner, Versöhnung, 2.

115 This is even the case for Robert Hébras as he explained during an interview in December 2011. Un procès des suspects allemands 'improbable', 8 December 2011, video *Réaction de Robert Hébras, rescapé d'Oradour*, http://limousin.france3.fr/info/un-proces-des-suspects-allemands-improbable-71548619.html?onglet=videos, accessed 17 December 2011.

Demeanor and statements made by the President of the ANFM during the local television discussion in 2004 revealed his difficult position: What looks like an unclear policy of the ANFM since 1995 seems to be the result of the difficulty to integrate various opinions.[116] Compared with the policy of the mayor this policy takes more account of those who are more hesitant. As the Association is going ahead slower than the mayor, those members of the ANFM who support an active reconciliation policy find a leader in Raymond Frugier rather than in the president of their association. As both collectives overlap, members of the ANFM can, depending on the subject area, switch to another collective relevant to them. When in 2010, the mayor traveled to Dachau, the ANFM did not send a representative. Nevertheless, several of those accompanying the mayor were members of the ANFM.[117] Since several participants of the delegation have been affected by the massacre personally or are members of victims' families, we can conclude that the reconciliation policy of mayor Frugier today is more than a symbolic gesture. However, as long as the ANFM does not engage in "trustworthy and cooperative relationships" a crucial part of 'Oradour' has not yet reached the state of reconciliation with Germany.

Conclusions: A Right to Irreconcilability?

In 1948, Alfons Erb, an advocate of the Franco-German reconciliation and the founder of the *Maximilian Kolbe-Werk*, a relief organization for the survivors of concentration camps and ghettos, made an interesting observation. When Oradour refused the aid of the youth groups to rebuild their hometown, he criticized the German offer:

"Anyone who reads the above documents, will, profoundly moved, have the burning desire to contribute with all his or her might to make amends, especially with Oradour. It is therefore more so understandable that 'Benjamin' chose Oradour. However, this might have not been a lucky choice. Admittedly, everything that Germans

---

116 Meyer, *Wandel*, 434-435, comes to the same conclusion.
117 This is the case for Robert Hébras and Albert Valade. Valade lost *inter alia* his sister in the massacre. It is also the case for Benoît Sadry, who is both district council in Oradour and deputy secretary of the ANFM.

can contribute by the suggested actions with regard to outwardly visible reparation, is in no proportion to what Germany and the Germans have done (it can all just be a humble contribution to reparation as well as to reconciliation). But this disproportion would have to emerge in the case of Oradour particularly blunt."[118]

Erb pointed out the gap between a crime like the massacre in Oradour and every attempt to make up for it. Considering the hesitation of the ANFM and especially the difficulties of some of the surviving dependents when it comes to Germany, it has to be concluded that Erb's analysis proved right until today. In spite of the multitude of gestures from within civil society, the stage of reconciliation the actors aimed at is not fully reached today. In this respect, we may consider that the greatest possible commitment does not necessarily lead to the greatest possible reconciliation, especially when a great deal of suffering lies beneath.

Different conclusions can be drawn from this result. One could be tempted to argue that against the background of such a horrible crime "trustworthy and cooperative relationships" are ambitious objectives and that a more minimal understanding of reconciliation seems reasonable. Indeed, in his reflections, Straßner refers inter alia to Tuomas Forsberg, who pleads for removing the idea of "mutual harmony or a togetherness of souls" from the concept of reconciliation. Instead, he simply refers to the "degree of tolerance or absence of severe disputes, between the antagonists". This "can be concretely defined in terms of behavioral criteria such as lack of offensive conduct".[119] Nevertheless, in the case of Oradour it seems that this operation would mean to neglect the important outcome that "trustworthy and cooperative relationships" are impossible and undesirable for some of the survivors or surviving dependants. Therefore, the conclusion to be drawn here is a plea for a right to irreconcilability.

Giving reasons for their commitment or policy, different German actors in the Oradour case as well as mayor Frugier stress the link between reconciliation and peace for the future.[120] According to Straßner, the possibility

---

118 Alfons Erb, Oradour gestern und heute, Dokumente und Erwägungen, *Dokumente*, 4, 2 (1948), 86-93, here: 92.
119 Straßner, Versöhnung, 27.
120 For example Fritz Körber in Sichelstiel, Europahymne, and Wolfgang Eckhardt in *Erfahrungsbericht*. Raymond Frugier doesn't use the word reconcilia-

to reconcile plays a "central role, to make a peaceful living together possible".[121] Thus, the notion of reconciliation is highly normative. This "moral surplus"[122] of reconciliation is accompanied by the negative connotation of irreconcilability. The necessity of a plea for a right to irreconcilability is however closely linked to one specific aspect of reconciliation. As Straßner explains, reconciliation processes are "highly complex internal processes that cannot be demanded". Reconciliation, he says, "is always voluntary".[123] This voluntary nature has to be emphasized as the victims had been robbed of their self-determination by the perpetrators during the massacre. Their freedom of decision-making is therefore an essential part of regaining this self-determination.[124] This is why it is regrettable that the president of the ANFM is apparently giving less or little voice in public to those who do not agree with the policy of mayor Frugier.

A further argument for the right to irreconcilability becomes apparent if, after having studied Oradour, we put the individual case back into the national and international context of Franco-German reconciliation. As we have seen in the beginning, Pierre Lellouche used Oradour to symbolize the Second World War as a chapter that had been closed by the Franco-German reconciliation. Because today the Franco-German friendship can be considered solid and robust, relevant actors should be able to accept the refusal of "trustworthy and cooperative relationships" from those who suffered and

---

tion but means what Straßner defines as such. For example: Raymond Frugier, Le mot du maire, in: *Oradour-sur-Glane. Bulletin Municipal, Le Radounaud*, December 2005, Archive of the municipality of Oradour-sur-Glane.

121 Straßner, Versöhnung, 23.
122 Ibid., 33.
123 Ibid., 28-29.
124 My thanks go to Prof. Hans Günter Hockerts who drew my attention to this important aspect. The American psychiatrist Judith Herman is stressing a similar point concerning the process of recovery after endured traumas: "The trauma evokes in the victim a sense of powerlessness and loss of control. For the recovery it is therefore essential that the patient regains his/her strength and the control about him or herself and his life." Judith Herman, *Die Narben der Gewalt. Traumatische Erfahrungen verstehen und überwinden* (Paderborn: Junfermann, 2006), 221.

are just not in the position to reconcile. In other words, the French-German reconciliation does not need to be crowned by a totally reconciled Oradour.

Furthermore, concerning the national level it has to be emphasized once more that while actors from within civil society committed themselves to reconciliation with Oradour, the contribution of the German State was limited. It is here that signs and gestures are still missing. Last autumn the legal authorities of Germany reopened preliminary proceedings in the Oradour case 67 years after the crime. Despite of the great dedication of the public prosecutor in charge, it is likely that these preliminary proceedings will be abandoned, as were the twelve others before.[125] At least the crime of Oradour gained once more attention and perhaps thoroughly carried out investigations are in some way a compensation for some of the survivors and the surviving dependants. Apart from that, the German State has not exhausted its possibilities to support reconciliation yet. As the generation of the contemporary witnesses is nearly gone, there is almost no time left.

---

125 Razzia bei mutmaßlichen SS-Kriegsverbrechern, 5 December 2011, http://www1.wdr.de/themen/panorama/massakeroradour100.html, accessed 18 February 2011; Karen Krüger, Oradour, *Frankfurter Allgemeine Zeitung*, 7 January 2012.

From Atonement to Peace?

Aktion Sühnezeichen, German-Israeli Relations and the Role of Youth in Reconciliation Discourse and Practice

CHRISTIANE WIENAND

In 1958, Protestant church functionary Lothar Kreyssig (1898-1986) founded *Aktion Sühnezeichen* (ASF, literally: Action Sign of Atonement) as an organization that was meant to atone for the National Socialist past. Throughout the 1960s, the organization established itself in the Federal Republic as a valued civil society actor.[1] In the founding appeal with the title *Wir bitten um Frieden* (We ask for Peace), Kreyssig sets the conceptual framework for ASF's reconciliation efforts, which is characterized by the ideas of peace, reconciliation, atonement, and forgiveness. The starting

---

1 In the following decades, the organization received awards for its civil society commitment, such as the Theodor Heuss Prize in 1965 and the *Buber-Rosenzweig-Medaille* in 1993. For comprehensive studies about ASF, see Gabriele Kammerer, *Aktion Sühnezeichen Friedensdienste. Aber man kann es einfach tun* (Göttingen: Lamuv-Verlag, 2008) and Anton Legerer, *Tatort: Versöhnung. Aktion Sühnezeichen in der BRD und in der DDR und Gedenkdienste in Österreich* (Leipzig: Evangelische Verlagsanstalt, 2011). I would like to thank *Aktion Sühnezeichen/Friedensdienste e.V.*, which kindly granted permission to explore its archival material in the Evangelisches Zentralarchiv Berlin (hereafter: EZA) and its Berlin headquarters.

point in Kreyssig's appeal was the acceptance of guilt for the crimes committed during the years of the National Socialist regime.[2] Therefore, the appeal was specifically directed towards those countries, which, according to Kreyssig, had suffered the most from German crimes: Israel, Poland, and Russia. They were asked to allow Germans "to do something good for them in their own country, with our hands and our means […] as a sign of atonement".[3]

Kreyssig had initially intended to call the organization *Aktion Versöhnungszeichen* (sign of reconciliation), yet became convinced that *Sühnezeichen* (sign of atonement) would be a more fitting term: atonement is offered by or on behalf of the one who has become guilty, whereas reconciliation already describes the next step of a mutual agreement between two sides.[4] However, the terms "atonement" (*Sühne*) and "reconciliation" (*Versöhnung*) were not kept strictly separate, but rather appeared to be synonymous in many texts by ASF functionaries, and also in the reflections of ASF volunteers.[5]

---

2   According to Legerer, *Tatort Versöhnung,* 37, a first draft of Kreyssig's appeal written in 1954 did not contain the reference to the extermination of the Jews. Legerer further argues that the intrinsic motivation of an acknowledgment of guilt sets ASF apart from other German and international Christian reconciliation and peace services. Legerer, *Tatort Versöhnung,* 16.

3   Lothar Kreyssig, *Gründungsaufruf der "Aktion Versöhnungszeichen"*, recited by Kreyssig in Berlin on 30 April 1958, quoted according to Martin Huhn et al., *Abstand vom bürgerlichen Leben: eine empirische Untersuchung über Freiwillige im Friedensdienst am Beispiel der Aktion Sühnezeichen / Friedensdienste* (Heidelberg: Wissenschaftlich-Theologisches Seminar der Universität, 1977), 20. All German quotes were translated by the author.

4   He became convinced by his friend Erich Müller-Gangloff, director of the Protestant Academy in Berlin. Kammerer, *Aktion Sühnezeichen,* 14.

5   See my explorations below; see also the fact that *Aktion Sühnezeichen* in English would be Action Sign of Atonement, yet the organization officially calls itself Action Reconciliation; see furthermore Christine Gundermann, Leiden ohne Täter? Deutsch-niederländische Kommunikation über die nationalsozialistischen Verbrechen, in: *Diktaturüberwindung in Europa. Neue nationale und transnationale Perspektiven,* ed. Birgit Hoffmann et al. (Heidelberg: Winter, 2010), 132-

The founding appeal contains a further aspect that was also to become a recurring narrative of ASF's self-conception and the self-perception of its volunteers: the practical reconciliation work was not meant as a form of *Wiedergutmachung*, the official German term for compensation and restitution payments. For one ASF activist, *Wiedergutmachung* represented a "*Wiedergutmachungshandel*",[6] a compensation bargain. ASF therefore explicitly distanced itself and its work from the post-war international politics of Chancellor Konrad Adenauer who used the compensation payments for Israel to support West Germany's efforts of reintegration into the Western community of states.[7] ASF activists also explicitly supported the establishment of official diplomatic relations with Israel years before the Federal Republic would finally consent to it in 1965.[8]

It is noteworthy that Kreyssig, himself a judge in Nazi Germany who was imprisoned due to his protest against the so-called "Euthanasia" program, explicitly included his generation, even those who had opposed the

---

150, here: 144-145, who observes this with respect to the activities of ASF in Rotterdam.

6 Abschrift Generationengespräch, EZA 97/63. For a critical stance see also the report of volunteer Matthias K., Report 10/72, EZA 97/39.

7 About the practice of *Wiedergutmachung* see *Die Praxis der Wiedergutmachung. Geschichte, Erfahrung und Wirkung in Deutschland und Israel*, ed. Norbert Frei et al. (Göttingen: Wallstein, 2005).

8 See paper by the volunteer group Israel IV, EZA 97/45; Legerer, *Tatort Versöhnung*, 211-212, mentions that also the executive board of ASF published a declaration in favour of taking up diplomatic relations. The Federal Republic refrained from establishing official diplomatic relations with Israel for several years in an attempt to avoid antagonising neighbouring Middle Eastern states. This strategy was intended to reduce the risk of an Arab diplomatic recognition of the German Democratic Republic, which in turn would have further reduced the chances of reuniting the divided Germany. Hannfried von Hindenburg, *Demonstrating Reconciliation. State and Society in West German Foreign Policy Toward Israel, 1952-1965* (New York: Berghahn Books, 2007). In this context, the West German Chancellor Konrad Adenauer and his government did not wish to establish official diplomatic relations with Israel, but nevertheless supported the establishment of unofficial contacts through West German civil society actors.

Nazi regime, in his statement of guilt.[9] He followed the tradition of the 1945 Stuttgart Declaration of Guilt by the Protestant Church,[10] which constituted one example among various attempts in the immediate post-war period to reflect on and to acknowledge German guilt, such as the famous university lecture by Karl Jaspers *Die Schuldfrage* (The Question of Guilt).[11] Yet Kreyssig went an important step further by turning rhetoric on guilt and reconciliation into his plea for active, hands-on reconciliation work. Through this practical work, ASF functionaries[12] and the volunteers themselves[13] sought to ask those who had bitterly suffered under the National Socialist regime for forgiveness.

In his founding appeal, Kreyssig did not specifically call upon young Germans to be involved in ASF. Yet de facto, in particular young Germans from their late teens to their early thirties followed the appeal to spend several months working with ASF. While the ASF functionaries, at least in the early years, mainly belonged to the war generation, the actual activists of atonement and reconciliation in Israel were to a large degree young Germans, who had not themselves (or only as children) experienced or supported the National Socialist regime. Thus, the reconciliation activity of

---

9 Apart from this statement, the former perpetrators did not play a role in the reconciliation activities of ASF. The organization's functionaries in the post-war years represented a sub-group of German society, as they had mainly belonged to the milieu of the *Bekennende Kirche* (Confessing Church).

10 See Legerer, *Tatort Versöhnung,* 28-29, for further references to the Stuttgart Declaration of Guilt as background of ASF.

11 Jaspers differentiates four categories of guilt, of which the metaphorical guilt concerns all, not only those who have actually become guilty in a judicial, political or moral sense. Karl Jaspers, *Die Schuldfrage* (Heidelberg: Schneider, 1946), 31-32, 63-65. With his concept of metaphysical guilt and his plea for active purification of guilt, he does not explicitly extend guilt upon the young and the following generations. However, given the context of his lecture to students at the University of Heidelberg, it can be assumed that he also referred to them.

12 See the text *Probleme der Aktion Sühnezeichen,* written by Franz von Hammerstein in 1964 or 1965, EZA 93/692; and the text by Otto Schenk, leader of an Israel volunteer group in the early 1960s, for New Year 1964, EZA 97/693.

13 See report by Klaus K. who explained the idea of his reconciliation activity to a fellow Kibbuznik in 1971, EZA 97/391.

ASF was understood as a representative form of atonement and reconciliation that addressed young Germans, but did not involve the former perpetrators in its active reconciliation practice.[14] The young Germans were not only the object of various debates about the role of the young generation for reconciliation between Germany and Israel; they also exerted an impact on the ways in which reconciliation was discursively perceived and practically implemented.

This chapter explores the role the young generation played in reconciliation practice and in discourse about reconciliation in West Germany and Israel in the 1960s and 1970s. It demonstrates that the inclusion of young Germans was one of the crucial characteristics of the representative, hands-on reconciliation approach of ASF and that this inclusion led towards various and controversial debates about the young Germans as reconciliation activists. The chapter further argues that this integration of young people in reconciliation work created a dynamics due to which the reconciliation activities of ASF in Israel oscillated between the ideas of atonement and peace. In the 1970s, the idea of peace became more and more important, yet this shift towards peace never resulted in giving up the idea of atonement either.

In order to develop the arguments, the chapter provides an empirical chronological analysis of the activities of ASF in Israel starting in 1961, when the first volunteers entered the country and the Eichmann trial took place. It further focuses on the 1970s during which the political situation in Israel had changed to an extent that the need for peace in the Israeli-Arab conflict had become too obvious to be overlooked. The exploration of these activities is placed within the wider context of German-Israeli relations from the 1950s onwards, and within the various accompanying debates in Germany and Israel about ASF activities in particular and about issues of reconciliation and guilt in general. The chapter thereby outlines the charac-

---

14 This representative form of atonement and reconciliation was based on the underlying theological concept of ASF. Referring to the New Testament (particularly to 2 Corinthians 5), founding father Lothar Kreyssig highlighted the analogy of the death of Jesus Christ as a representative act of atonement for the sins of mankind with the activities of Sühnezeichen volunteers for the sins of their fathers. Legerer, *Tatort Versöhnung*, 62.

teristics as well as the problematic and controversial aspects of the reconciliation activities of ASF in Israel.

CALLING THE YOUNG GENERATION IN THE 1950S

Before ASF was founded in 1958, various civil society actors had launched initiatives in the post-war years in order to create a better understanding between Germans and (Israeli) Jews. Already in the late 1940s, Societies for Christian-Jewish Cooperation were founded, which since 1952 organize a so-called *Woche der Brüderlichkeit* (Week of Fraternalism) in the Federal Republic. At the end of the 1950s, German-Israeli study groups (*Deutsch-Israelische Studiengruppen,* DIS) were initiated at several West German universities. By 1962, DIS groups existed at nine West German universities with about 300 members in total.[15] Some of them were linked to the Protestant background, such as the one at the *Freie Universität* Berlin, whose foundation was supported by Protestant theologian Helmut Gollwitzer. In an article about the German-Israeli study groups, Dieter Fleck explicitly placed the activity of the study groups in the context of reconciliation[16] and he emphasized the role of youth on both sides for overcoming prejudices, which, according to him, were "almost not bridgeable"[17] for the older generation.

Young Germans were fascinated by the Holy Land and by the lifestyle of Israeli Kibbutzim and travelled there for shorter work stays and visits during the late 1950s and early 1960s.[18] These groups connected their quest

---

15 Dieter Fleck, Deutsch-Israelische Studentenbeziehungen, *Israel-Forum. Zeitschrift für israelisch-deutsche Beziehungen* 4 (1962), 26-28, here: 26.
16 Ibid., 27
17 Ibid.
18 See the report by ten German students in *Israel-Forum. Zeitschrift für israelisch-deutsche Beziehungen* 6/7 (1959), 3-4. See also Rudolf Weckerling, *Le Chaim – Zum Leben. Reise nach Israel* (Berlin: Käthe Vogt Verlag, 1962) about a work and travel stay of students in Israel. For journeys of young Germans in the early 1950s, see also Martin Kloke, *Israel und die deutsche Linke. Zur Geschichte eines schwierigen Verhältnisses* (Frankfurt a.M.: Haag und Herchen,

for dealing with the Nazi past with reconciliation activities directed towards Israel and Israeli Jews. Young Germans were to play an important role within these activities – repeatedly called upon, for instance, by the Protestant theologian provost Heinrich Grüber (1891-1975),[19] who was one of the founding fathers of the Society for Christian-Jewish Cooperation in Berlin and of the group *Pro Israel*, which supported the establishment of diplomatic relations between Germany and Israel during the 1950s.[20] Grüber asked the youth to "build a bridge between Israel and Germany, between Christians and Jews [...], as they are not as burdened by the past as the elderly".[21] According to Grüber, the young generation's personal non-involvement in the past constituted the main factor that qualified them for reconciliation activity. As we will see below, the fact that the youth has not been personally involved, responsible, or guilty for the past, yet was nevertheless asked to atone and to reconcile for it, also caused irritation.

Young Germans were not only called upon by members of the war generation, such as Heinrich Grüber and Lothar Kreyssig, but also became active themselves, for instance in 1957 when a Hamburg student proposed a gesture of reconciliation towards the Israeli youth on the occasion of a remembrance celebration for Anne Frank in Bergen-Belsen. In her talk, the Hamburg student explicitly referred to the future, and to the responsibility of the young generations to build a joint future by means of reconciliation. She furthermore asked the Israeli youth not to reject the hand offered by young Germans.[22] The Bergen-Belsen meetings were set within a framework of atonement, as the introduction of an atonement mass (*Sühne-Messe*) in 1960 demonstrates. According to the newspaper *The Jewish Way*,

---

1994), 78, and Inge Deutschkron, *Israel und die Deutschen. Zwischen Sentiment und Ratio* (Köln: Verlag Wissenschaft und Politik, 1970), 176-177.

19   In 1961 Grüber was the only witness for the prosecution from Germany who testified against Adolf Eichmann in the Jerusalem trial; in 1964 he was named a Righteous among the Nations by Yad Vashem.
20   For more information on *Pro Israel*: http://www.deutsch-israelische-gesellsch aft.de/dig_information/der_schwierige_begin.htm, accessed 18 December 2011.
21   *Geleitwort* by Heinrich Grüber in Weckerling, *Le Chaim*, 5.
22   Kloke, *Israel und die deutsche Linke*, 81.

this event brought together 70,000 young people and "united [them] to atonement and contemplation".[23]

The importance of the youth for German-Israeli understanding can also be found on the Israeli side. For Israeli Prime-Minister David Ben-Gurion references to the German youth constituted part of his aim to propagate the Federal Republic under Konrad Adenauer to the Israelis as the "new", the "different" or the "other Germany".[24] Ben-Gurion needed this construction in order to legitimize and support his policy of accepting compensation payments by the Federal Republic, which were highly controversial among Israelis.[25] Soon after the end of the war, Ben-Gurion's policy towards West Germany was dominated by his wish to consolidate the Israeli state by integrating it into the evolving West European community and by receiving financial aid from the Federal Republic. In May 1960, Ben-Gurion and Adenauer met at the hotel Waldorf Astoria in New York City where they discussed further financial support for Israel. On this occasion, Ben-Gurion emphasized his belief that the young Germans, once they would learn about the crimes committed under the National Socialist regime, would feel "sorrow and disgrace"[26] for them. Even if Ben-Gurion's emphasis on the new Germany was part of his political calculations – aimed at both sides, his Israeli voters as well as his German political counterparts – he was an important, though controversial voice in the Israeli public that set the tone creating an atmosphere of belief in the existence of a new Germany in which also other voices would join in.

THE IMPACT OF THE EICHMANN TRIAL

On April 11, 1961, the trial against former Nazi functionary *SS-Obersturmbannführer* Adolf Eichmann began before the Jerusalem District Court. The Eichmann trial can be regarded as a turning point in Israel and the Federal

---

23 *The Jewish Way*, Nov./Dec. 1961, 2.
24 For corresponding descriptions of the Federal Republic see for instance Tom Segev, *The Seventh Million. The Israelis and the Holocaust* (New York: Holt Paperbacks, 1991), 191.
25 Segev, *Seventh Million*, 190, 206.
26 Quoted according to Segev, *Seventh Million*, 319-320.

Republic in terms of their ways of dealing with the past,[27] as in both countries, the first 15 years after the end of the Second World War were largely characterized by a silence about the victims of the Holocaust.[28] The media reception of the trial strongly affected the public discourse on the Holocaust in West Germany and Israel, and about the youth in Israel and Germany and their relationship to the National Socialist past.

For many young Israelis the broadcasting of the trial was the first occasion to directly encounter the history and the atrocities of the Holocaust.[29] As Israeli scholars Tom Segev and Idit Zertal have shown, the Eichmann trial in 1961 was intended by Prime Minister David Ben-Gurion and the governing Mapai party as a historical lesson to educate the Israeli youth.[30] Within the West German media, the question to what extent the trial would help to historically educate the German youth was controversially debated, as shown by Peter Krause. While several journalists and publishers opted for providing the youth with the unadorned historical facts, others – most prominently Henri Nannen, the publisher of the *Stern* magazine – feared

---

27 For the public reception of the trial in the German media see Peter Krause, *Der Eichmann-Prozess in der deutschen Presse* (Frankfurt a.M.: Campus, 2002).

28 A developing intellectual discourse of guilt in the immediate post-war years soon faded away. In the Federal Republic from the late 1940s onwards stories about the "German victims" were much more publically present than those about the "victims of the Germans". Robert Moeller, *War Stories. The Search for a Useable Past in the Federal Republic of Germany* (Berkeley: University of California Press, 2003). In Israel, the victims of the Holocaust were publically pushed aside in order to foster the idea of Jewish resistance against the Holocaust. Memorials and memories of Jewish heroes, for instance the resistance fighters during the Warsaw Ghetto uprising dominated the public narrative in the 1950s, such as the Ghetto Fighters House museum *Beit Lohamei Haghetaot*, founded in 1949, and *Yad Vashem – The Martyrs' and Heroes' Remembrance Authority*, founded in 1953. In the early 1950s, the Holocaust was primarily understood as an individual fate and not as a collective experience. Segev, *Seventh Million*, 226.

29 Idit Zertal, *Israel's Holocaust and the Politics of Nationhood* (Cambridge: Cambridge University Press, 2005), 92.

30 Zertal, *Israel's Holocaust*, 97; Segev, *Seventh Million*, 338, 351, 353.

that a confrontation of the German youth with these facts would overburden the young generation with feelings of guilt and shame.[31]

In the context of the Eichmann trial Jewish philosopher Hannah Arendt also reflected on the German youth and its relationship to the past. In her controversial *Report on the Banality of Evil* (1963), Arendt referred to Martin Buber's claim that Eichmann's execution might "serve to expiate the guilt felt by many young persons in Germany".[32] Arendt continued with a statement about the German youth in which she vehemently rejected public expressions of emotions of guilt by the young generation in Germany. Within German society, she distinguishes two groups: young Germans who *feel* guilty and those former functionaries who are again in high positions, who *are* guilty but *do not feel* guilty. Yet she does not appreciate emotions of guilt expressed by young Germans, but rather delivers a negative judgement:

"Those young German men and women who every once in a while [...] treat us to hysterical outbreaks of guilt feelings are not staggering under the burden of the past, their fathers' guilt; rather, they are trying to escape from the pressure of the very present and actual problems into a cheap sentimentality."[33]

In Arendt's perspective, feelings of guilt of the young generation are not the same as admittance of real guilt and repentance for this guilt. She suggested that an involvement with the past by expressing feelings of guilt only results in ignoring the problems of the present. Indeed, there are accounts in which young Germans referred to sentiments of guilt, which also even might have resulted in a motivation to become engaged in reconciliation activity in Israel.[34] However, the example of ASF volunteers contradicts Arendt's assumption, since their activities were not only shaped by a wish to

---

31 Krause, *Eichmann-Prozess*, 265-277.
32 Hannah Arendt, *Eichmann in Jerusalem. A Report on the Banality of Evil* (New York: Penguin, 2006), 251.
33 Ibid.
34 In the course of an essay competition of the journal *Israel-Forum*, young Germans Sybille von Foelkersamb and Helga Leonhardt answered the question "Why am I interested in Israel" by referring to feelings of guilt. *Israel-Forum. Zeitschrift für israelisch-deutsche Beziehungen*, 11 (1962), 23, and 2 (1963), 25.

deal with the past, but also by direct confrontation with the present political situation both in Germany and in Israel.

The Eichmann trial not only had an impact on larger debates about the National Socialist past and on the ways in which young people in Israel and Germany should be involved in this reflection of the past. The trial also affected reconciliation efforts by young Germans in Israel both in discursive and practical terms. During the time of the trial, Protestant student pastor Rudolf Weckerling from West Berlin travelled to Israel with a group of young German students and young professionals.[35] In the light of the trial, the fact that the group mainly consisted of young Germans was used as an argument both for and against such a trip. Before the group had left Germany, people in Germany and in Israel had advised the group to postpone their stay to the time after the trial; one argument was that young people could be overburdened by such a trip, as it would require consciousness of the past and a willingness to take over responsibility for the past. Other Israelis, however, supported the journey of the young Germans and differentiated the Germans in young people looking for ways to reach the Israeli people, and in those who were personally guilty.[36]

While Weckerling's group was allowed to pursue its two-month journey through Israel which also included some work activity in a Kibbutz, the trial against Eichmann had postponed the work stay of the first group of ASF volunteers in Israel for several months until fall 1961. In January 1961 the Israeli mission in Germany had declared that it would not support visits of German groups because of the trial.[37] Another problem was to find an in-

---

35 The trip was organized by the *Deutsche Arbeitsgemeinschaft Christlicher Aufbaulager* (Weckerling, *Le Chaim*, 9) and supported by ASF (Legerer, *Tatort Versöhnung*, 188). Apart from Weckerling himself (born in 1911) and a secretary (born in 1923), the group consisted of young Germans born between 1929 and 1940, thus the participants were between 32 and 21 years old at the time. See the list of participants in Weckerling, *Le Chaim*, 176. Like Lothar Kreyssig and Heinrich Grüber, Weckerling was also former member of the Confessing Church. About Weckerling see *100 Jahre Rudolf Weckerling. Festschrift*, ed. Freyja Eberding et al. (Berlin: Aktion Sühnezeichen Friedensdienste e.V., 2011).

36 Weckerling, *Le Chaim*, 10.

37 Legerer, *Tatort Versöhnung*, 202.

stitution or a Kibbutz that would host the ASF group for a period of several months. Yet thanks to a combination of individual initiatives and institutional requests ASF volunteers were finally allowed into the country by invitation of the Kibbutz Urim in the Negev desert.[38] This first work stay was preceded by finally unsuccessful plans of the ASF headquarters together with the Catholic Una Sancta Movement and Catholic Church functionaries to build a triconfessional atonement monastery (*trikonfessionelles Sühnekloster*) in Jerusalem, which was meant to bring together Jews, Catholics, and Protestants.[39] While the *Sühnekloster* would have emphasized the spiritual aspect of atonement and reconciliation, the work stays stood for the practical reconciliation concept of ASF.

In early October 1961 the first eleven volunteers finally entered Israel to conduct social work in the Kibbutz Urim in the Negev desert. More volunteers followed in the next years, and by 1968, twelve ASF groups, each consisting of around 15 volunteers – mostly young professionals, but also university and school students – had worked in various other Kibbutzim and in social institutions.[40] For ASF volunteers, their practical work and the opportunity to live with Israelis for several months was a means to demonstrate their reconciliation efforts.[41] This hands-on approach of reconciliation activity and the fact that the volunteers did not complain about, and partly even volunteered for hard work was also valued by people who became to know the volunteers as working colleagues.[42] Yet, the developing images of

---

38 For a description of the preceding negotiations between various ASF functionaries and Israeli institutions and individuals in order to set up the start of the first volunteer group see Legerer, *Tatort Versöhnung*, 200-205; Ansgar Skriver, *Aktion Sühnezeichen. Brücken über Blut und Asche* (Stuttgart: Kreuz-Verlag, 1962), 120-130; Kammerer, *Aktion Sühnezeichen*, 78-79.
39 Legerer, *Tatort Versöhnung*, 189-199.
40 Legerer, *Tatort Versöhnung*, 490, provides an overview over the projects of the twelve groups up to 1968. Most of the activities were of a social nature, while at three sites, a home for the blind in Jerusalem, a children's home in Alyn and in Kibbutz Bachan, ASF volunteers were involved in building activities.
41 Report 32/71, Dieter H., August 1971, EZA 97/391; Report 23/71, Klaus K., July 1971, EZA 97/391.
42 See the encounter between Christel Eckern and her Kibbutz colleague Ada, recounted in Christel Eckern, *Die Straße nach Jerusalem. Ein Mitglied der "Akti-*

German volunteers also depended on the circumstances in which they worked and on the people they met. Members of the ASF working group in Kibbutz Nir Eliahu in 1962 realized there was no interest among their Kibbutz chaverim – among them many young Israelis who had only heard of the Nazi crimes in the context of the Eichmann trial – to talk about German guilt or about the specific atonement task of the ASF group.[43] According to one observer the young Israelis lived for the future and for a new society,[44] and therefore much less in the past.

Even if the ASF volunteers were not the first Germans working in Israel,[45] their presence provoked public interest within the Israeli media reaching beyond the walls of the Kibbutzim in which the volunteers worked. In his article in the newspaper *Jerusalem Post*, the journalist Ben-Adi explained the main goals of the organization to his readers, by also pointing

---

on Sühnezeichen" berichtet über Leben und Arbeit in Israel (Essen: Ludgerus-Verlag, 1962), 68-69. See also the letter of the director of the Ahava Home for Children and Youth in Haifa who appreciated the work of the ASF volunteers in her institution. Ullmann to von Hammerstein and Schenk, 14 August 1964, EZA 97/693. See also letter by Jehuda Riemer to the editor of the *New York Times* about the participation of Sühnezeichen volunteers in the work and social life in Kibbutz Urim, 1 December1962, quoted according to *Geschichte(n) erleben. Aktion Sühnezeichen Friedensdienste in Israel 1961-2011*, ed. Aktion Sühnezeichen (Berlin: Aktion Sühnezeichen Friedensdienste e.V., 2011), 24, and the article *Some do repent!* by Jehuda Riemer, *Jewish Frontier*, 17 July 1962.

43 Diary entry, 23 June 1962, EZA 97/395.

44 Diary entry, 1 July 1962, EZA 97/395. As the number of Kibbutzim that would allow Germans to stay and work with remained limited – according to a report from 1965 only 7 out of around 240 Kibbutzim accepted German youth groups – it even happened that once the young people from Germany arrived, the Kibbutz members had already lost interest in them, as there had been so many other youth groups before them. This frustrating experience was reported by a youth group from the Bonn Society for Christian-Jewish Cooperation. Bericht über eine Begegnungs- und Studienreise nach Israel, 54, Politisches Archiv des Auswärtigen Amts (hereafter: PA-AA) B36/193.

45 Apart from those already mentioned, Legerer, *Tatort Versöhnung*, 202, refers to groups of the *Christlicher Friedensdienst* and of the *Herz-Jesu-Orden* who helped building streets.

out it was young Germans who sought to take over collective responsibility for the German people and for the past by providing symbolic acts of atonement.[46]

AFTER THE ARRIVAL: GERMAN AND ISRAELI DEBATES ON THE ROLE OF YOUTH FOR RECONCILIATION

The young German reconciliation activists operated within various realms of political and societal tensions in Germany and Israel, tensions that evolved out of diverging assessments of the past and the present. Throughout the 1960s, discourses about German youth continued in Germany and Israel, now often explicitly linked to the presence and the activities of ASF volunteers in Israel Kibbutzim, social institutions, and at Yad Vashem. Both the term atonement and the idea of reconciliation connected with the fact that the young generation was to pursue atonement and reconciliation on behalf of their fathers raised debate in both countries and among various social groups, producing positions that ranged from consent to objection.

Even if the young Germans provoked public attention, this did not mean that Israelis who commented on their presence would easily regard them as protagonists of the "new Germany", as propagated by Ben-Gurion. The Israeli journalist Michael Schaschar from the newspaper *Haaretz*, for instance, remained reluctant in his evaluation of the young Germans. He had visited the ASF group in Kibbutz Hasolelim in July 1964 and engaged the volunteers in a talk about their worldviews, about their parents, and their knowledge of the past. He particularly remarked that the relaxed and open atmosphere of the talk changed when he asked the young Germans about their own parents, which only lead to vague answers. According to Schaschar, the young Germans acknowledged the past crimes, but they referred to the perpetrators as to an anonymous part of the population. The journalist remained critical and refrained from praising the reconciliation activity of the volunteers. He also wanted to know whether the young Germans believed that a new Hitler could rise in today's Germany. The answers did not

---

46 Germans work in the Negev, *Jerusalem Post*, 9 January 1962; see also Skriver, *Aktion Sühnezeichen*, 135, who refers to an article in the Hungarian newspaper *Nj-Kelet* published in fall 1961.

satisfy Schaschar and he even concluded his article with the remark that a large part of the German population still did not express moral regret for the past.[47]

While many German and Israeli politicians regarded the exchange of ambassadors between Germany and Israel in summer 1965 as an important step for the bilateral relations between the two countries, sentiments among the Israeli population were not that unanimous. The German magazine *Der Spiegel*, for instance, reported in July 1965 that many Israelis feared that the Germans would see the exchange as a "final act of reconciliation", while for them "the atonement of the sons is not yet finished".[48] An open rejection of everything connected with Germany was particularly common amongst the conservative and orthodox milieu in Israel.[49] Politicians such as the founder of the conservative Herut party Menachem Begin, whose parents had been murdered during the Holocaust, counteracted German-Israeli relations for decades, also on the level of cultural exchange.[50] Yet one particular German of the young generation also earned Begin's respect. This was the "Nazi hunter" Beate Klarsfeld (*1939). In a recent interview, Klarsfeld explained her good relationship with Menachem Begin: she argues that Begin was impressed by the fact that young Germans like her demonstrated their responsibility for the crimes committed under the National Socialist past.[51]

Negative or sometimes even hostile attitudes towards the German reconciliation activities were not limited to elderly people or Holocaust survivors. Young Israelis had their problems with the presence of Germans seek-

---

47 Michael Schaschar, Sie kamen, die Verbrechen ihrer Väter zu sühnen, *Haaretz*, 24 July 1964, German translation in EZA 97/45.
48 *Der Spiegel*, 28 July 1965, 50.
49 Report by German ambassador von Puttkamer, 13 April 1972, 3, PA-AA, AV Neues Amt 2.357.
50 Segev, *Seventh Million*, 382-383, argues that the closer the relations between Germany and Israel became on the diplomatic, political and economic level, the more those who were against reconciliation with Germany concentrated on agitating on the cultural level.
51 Interview Klarsfeld with Esther Schapira, Hessischer Rundfunk, *Sonntagsgespräch*, 30 January 2011.

ing reconciliation, too.[52] In November 1966, German ambassador Rolf Pauls reported on a demonstration of Israeli students belonging to the conservative Herut party in front of the German embassy in Tel Aviv. The students showed banners reading, "There is no other Germany" or "No friendship with the murderers of six million Jews".[53] Yet these open rejections did not remain uncommented among Israeli politicians. Knesset member David Hacohen, for instance, criticized the young Israeli's unwillingness to support the Germans in their efforts to overcome the National Socialist past.[54]

Within the West German society of the 1960s, the reconciliation activities of ASF and other organizations provoked ambivalent attitudes, reaching from support to indifference[55] and open rejection; this ambivalence documents the existence of a highly fragmented West German society with respect to the issue of how to deal with the Nazi past in the present. Hostile antipathy towards ASF was expressed from notoriously known revisionist right-wing circles in their newspapers and in anonymous hate letters that reached the ASF headquarters.[56] Even though ASF evolved from a Pro-

---

52 At the occasion of the Eichmann Trial, for instance, German observers reported back to Germany that many young Israelis were reluctant towards Germany and the Germans. Report by Gerhard von Preuschen, 13, PA-AA, B36/541.
53 Report German Embassy to Foreign Office, PA-AA, AV Neues Amt 2.357. German ambassador Pauls – a former decorated *Wehrmacht* officer – was, at least at the beginning of his service in Israel, a controversial person for many Israelis. Eckart Conze, Norbert Frei, Peter Hayes and Moshe Zimmermann, *Das Amt und die Vergangenheit. Deutsche Diplomaten im Dritten Reich und in der Bundesrepublik* (München: Karl Blessing Verlag, 2010), 500-502.
54 See the German translation of Hacohen's statement in PA-AA, AV Neues Amt 2.357.
55 In October 1963, for instance, four ASF functionaries traveled through Lower Saxony, Hamburg and Bremen in order to give lectures about the organization's work. As newspaper articles document, there was only little interest in these events. Kein Interesse für die Sühne, *Hamburger Echo*, 5 October 1963; Nur fünf kamen zum "Sühnezeichen", *Landeszeitung für die Lüneburger Heide*, 21 October 1963.
56 Deutschland muss sühnen – sühnen – sühnen, *Deutsche National Zeitung*, 10 May 1963; letters to the editors of *Schlesische Rundschau* and *Deutsche Natio-*

testant background – which means that Protestant church functionaries and pastors had not only signed Kreyssig's founding appeal, but also subsequently supported the organization idealistically and financially – ASF and its work in Israel were by no means equally praised in all parts of the Protestant church circles. In his *Report from the Biblical Land* in the *Evangelisches Gemeindeblatt München* (Protestant Church Newspaper Munich) journalist Helmut Winter wrote in November 1966 about his experiences in Israel and the reception of the work done by ASF. He raised doubts whether the activities of the young Germans in Israel were at all worthwhile. According to Winter, the Israelis were much more interested in receiving German weapons, and to see former Nazis punished than to acknowledge and approve of the reconciliation work done by the ASF volunteers. He even concluded that Jews would lack understanding for the Christian ideas of reconciliation and forgiveness.[57]

A critical stance towards reconciliation activities in Israel in general and those of ASF in particular was not limited to the right-wing background or to critical Protestant circles that raised doubts whether Christians and Jews could really speak the same language when it comes to reconciliation. Critique also arose from other parts of West German society. It was the connection of youth, guilt, and atonement that caused problems of understanding, particularly among young Germans. In a letter to the editor an anonymous reader of the *Neue Illustrierte Köln* from 1964 declared:

"Recently, I was asked to participate in an 'atonement trip' to Israel. I refused. I have nothing against the Jews. But I also never did them any harm. Thus, what should I atone for? [...] What do we have to do with the sins of our fathers? I am fed up with this talk about our guilt! I am not aware of being guilty of anything. [...] Why should we atone when the real perpetrators of the Third Reich lead a rather happy life as judges, politicians, and globetrotters!"[58]

---

nal Zeitung, both in EZA 97/983. The anonymous writer of a postcard that reached ASF in den mid-1960s, calls the ASF functionaries "*Volksverräter*" and one anonymous hate letter was even written on grey toilet paper. See collection in EZA 97/582.

57 Helmut Winter, Bericht aus biblischem Land III, *Evangelisches Gemeindeblatt München*, 27 November 1966, 8.

58 *Neue Illustrierte Köln*, 43, 1964.

The author of the letter refused to be held responsible for "the sins of our fathers", particularly when the perpetrators were still alive, and thereby pointed at a generational conflict. Linked with a dissent against the West German politics towards Israel, this attitude was also widespread among the young Left in Germany, which becomes apparent in a statement by trainee lawyer Eberhard Sommer who wrote to author Günter Grass in June 1967. In his letter, Sommer explicitly rejected the idea that the older generation would transfer their guilt to the young Germans.[59] These critical attitudes towards an involvement of young Germans in activities of reconciliation in and for Israel, centred on the same issues also young German reconciliation activists in Israel – those working for ASF as well as others – dealt with: the question of why the young generation should be involved in overcoming the past by means of reconciliation activities as representatives for those who had actually committed crimes in the past and had actually become guilty?

When in April and May 1965 a group of young Germans organized by the *Gesellschaft für christlich-jüdische Zusammenarbeit* in Bonn travelled to Israel, the young people aimed at building personal contacts with Israelis and also expressed their hope to contribute towards reaching mutual understanding.[60] During their trip, various occasions occurred during which the young Germans were not only faced with the German past, but at which they came to discuss about this past and their own relationship to it. The discursive framework in which these discussions took place was grounded in talks of the young Germans with Israelis about the German politics of *Wiedergutmachung* payments and about the diplomatic recognition of the state of Israel through the Federal Republic. These talks apparently triggered various and controversial debates about the West German policy towards Israel and about the role the German youth should play in the German-Israeli relations. Did young Germans have a specific responsibility resulting from the annihilation of the Jews and did this responsibility necessarily result in a particular political attitude towards Israel? Discussions reached a point at which the leaders of the study group proposed a model for further discussion according to which the youth was regarded responsi-

---

59 Letter in Kloke, *Israel und die deutsche Linke*, 119.
60 The group wrote a lengthy report about their *Begegnungs- und Studienreise*, which can be found in PA-AA, B36/193.

ble, not based on an individual guilt, but through the "concrete, historically imposed obligation of all Germans to publically rehabilitate the German name".[61] Yet this model was not accepted by all discussants and remained a point of open debate, as some regarded the answer as being too obvious, too often expressed in a society that was not open about the past.

A constant debate about these questions can also be found among the volunteers and functionaries of ASF. As already mentioned above, texts written by ASF functionaries suggest that the personal non-involvement of the ASF volunteers in the Nazi regime was understood as a representative form of atonement. Yet as Anton Legerer explored, the concepts of atonement and reconciliation in the programmatic texts were not clearly defined.[62] This might have been one reason for a constant debate about these terms among young ASF volunteers. Particularly the question of how to bring together the threefoldness of guilt, atonement, and youth was at the core of ongoing debate and reflection. This question was also closely connected with the practical reconciliation work of the volunteers. In October 1964, a group of volunteers working in Kibbutz Hasolelim visited the ghetto exhibition in Lochamei Haghetaot, which they described in their group diary as an intense experience that made them feel ashamed and sorry for the past. In this situation, the group that until then had several encounters with Israelis who all had expressed their appreciation for the young Germans, started to doubt whether they could at all atone for the past.[63] Asked by an Israeli student magazine to comment on the motivation for his reconciliation activity, a member of the same volunteer group explained that he/she as a German felt affected by what the German people had done during the National Socialist regime. In this context, the volunteer connected the guilt of the Germans with the practical reconciliation activity of ASF and explained: "I have to take over the guilt of the fathers [...]. Guilt demands atonement and I have to go to the people and tell them how sorry I am about what has happened".[64] The volunteer furthermore explicitly re-

---

61 Ibid., 31.
62 Legerer, *Tatort Versöhnung*, 54.
63 Diary entry of the group Israel IV, 23 October 1964, EZA 97/396.
64 Diary entry of the group Israel IV, 2 February 1965, EZA 97/396.

ferred to his activities in Israel as a representative activity for the parents' generation.[65]

ASF volunteers also connected their reflections about their role as reconciliation activists in Israel with political aspects. In July 1966, the volunteer group criticized that the West German ASF functionaries did not comment upon current political developments in the German-Israeli relations in their regular newsletters. According to the volunteers, these newsletters contained "only pious words" and were "only about the past".[66] The volunteers argued that the lessons from the past were useless if they were not applied to the present situation: "Should we not see the past in its connection with the present and the future?"[67] The fact that the idea of atonement and the integration of young people for pursuing atonement was and remained problematic in the understanding of the reconciliation activity of ASF not only was a repeatedly discussed topic among volunteers, but can also be seen in statements by those functionaries and supporters of the organization who through their theoretical reflections sought to set a framework for the reconciliation work of the volunteers.[68]

---

65 This issue of representative reconciliation activity was also repeatedly reconsidered by ASF functionary and author Volker von Törne (1934-1980), for whom the question of generational responsibility and guilt also played a personal role. Von Törne was the son of an SS soldier, a fact he also reflected upon in his writings and his poetry. See his texts and poems as well as the speeches delivered on the occasion of his funeral in Volker von Törne, *Zwischen Geschichte und Zukunft. Aufsätze – Reden – Gedichte* (Berlin: Aktion Sühnezeichen / Friedensdienste e.V., 1981), which document the strong feelings of guilt that constituted a central topic for him.
66 Diary of the group Israel VII, 22 July 1966, EZA 97/399.
67 Ibid.
68 See the text *Was heißt Sühnezeichen?* about atonement and guilt by the director of the West German ASF branch Franz von Hammerstein, in EZA 97/10. While Hammerstein wanted to adhere to the idea of atonement, theologian and ASF supporter Helmut Gollwitzer declared in a letter from August 1966 that one cannot urge the young people to always solidarize with the guilt of their fathers, but that they have a natural desire for looking more towards the future. Gollwitzer concluded that the work of the organization must therefore be extended. Gollwitzer to K. Scharf, August 1966, EZA 97/10.

A critical (self-) evaluation of the connection of reconciliation and the youth is largely missing in 1960s diplomatic and political rhetoric of German-Israeli relations, in which a focus on youth and the young generation was also much prevalent.[69] There, the young generation was addressed as an important actor for German-Israeli cooperation, but without reflections about why young people should take up this role, and without a critical assessment of the inherent problematic aspects. In the context of establishing a German-Israeli commission that coordinated German-Israeli youth exchange, the German Minister for Youth, Family and Health Käte Strobel wrote to her Israeli counterpart Zalman Aran in 1969,

"I very much hope that we can achieve a partnership between the young generations of our countries. We would like to attract the young people to become engaged with reconciliation and peace by having a clear knowledge about guilt and the past."[70]

To highlight the importance of the young generation for further developing German-Israeli relations and for reconciliation became a common theme in the diplomatic exchange between German and Israeli politicians. When German ambassador Jesco von Puttkamer presented his credentials in Jerusalem to Israeli president Zalman Sbazar in May 1971, they both put special emphasis on the continuation of the German-Israeli youth exchange. Sbazar made explicit that he shared Puttkamer's aspiration that through the young generation in Germany "the good-will to open new pages in the rela-

---

69 This also resulted in practical political consequences in the sense that there were various efforts on the German and the Israeli sides to establish and institutionalize a German-Israeli youth exchange, which was established already in the mid-1950s through visits of student groups, but became more institutionalized only after official diplomatic relations were established in 1965. For the history of the German-Israeli youth exchange see for instance Irma Haase, Deutsch-Israelischer Jugendaustausch, in: *20 Jahre Deutsch-Israelische Beziehungen*, ed. Deutsch-Israelischer Arbeitskreis für Frieden im Nahen Osten e.V. (Berlin: Deutsch-Israelischer Arbeitskreis für Frieden im Nahen Osten e.V., 1985), 85-135; *Der deutsch-israelische Dialog*. Teil III: Kultur, Vol. 8, ed. Rolf Vogel (München: K.G. Saur, 1990), 244-374.

70 Strobel to Aran, 4 December 1969, PA-AA, AV Neues Amt 2.232.

tions between the two peoples may be promoted".[71] The political function of young German reconciliation activists in Israel became also apparent already before the official establishment of the German embassy in Tel Aviv in 1965. The ASF building *Haus Pax* in Jerusalem had already previously served as a meeting point for non-accredited diplomats and ASF members.[72] Moreover, after Rolf Pauls was officially appointed German ambassador in Israel, he met there with ASF volunteer groups in order to discuss the German-Israeli relations and his plans as ambassador.[73]

This positive attitude towards young Germans who traveled to and worked in Israel can also be found within the discourse in Israel. In the early 1960s, a volunteer group of ASF met David Ben-Gurion personally, who had retired in the meantime, and who called the young volunteers "ambassadors for Israel in Germany".[74] Ben-Gurion's perspective signifies the political impact that he attached to the ASF volunteers, as in his eyes they should help to support Israel and the Israeli case back home in Germany. In addition, other ASF supporters in Israel – such as the religious philosopher Martin Buber – argued that the main task of the ASF volunteers was not situated in Israel, but at home in Germany. When Otto Schenk, the leader of a volunteer group, visited Buber in his Jerusalem home in November 1963, he asked him what the young German volunteer could do once returned to Germany. Buber's stance on this issue was that reconciliation with the people of Israel was not a question of German-Jewish relations but a mere German issue. For him, the young Germans were responsible for bringing about reconciliation among Germans, not between Germans and Jews.[75] Buber therefore rejected the idea of atonement and reconciliation of the young generation with Israelis or Jews, but he emphasized the need that the young generation was able to do something for the inner reconciliation

---

71 Inaugural speech von Puttkamer and reply by the President of Israel, PA-AA, AV Neues Amt 2.353.
72 Legerer, *Tatort Versöhnung*, 21.
73 For instance, diary of the group Israel VIII, 19-25 November 1966, EZA 97/399; Dietrich P., Kritische Stellungnahme zum Einsatz der Sühnezeichengruppe Israel IX, 25 October 1967, EZA 97/710.
74 Otto Schenk, Als Deutscher in Jerusalem, EZA 97/693.
75 Abschrift Protokoll von Otto Schenk über das Gespräch mit Martin Buber, November 1963, EZA 97/692.

within German society.⁷⁶ Buber and Ben-Gurion were not the only Israelis whom the young Germans encountered and who emphasized that the main task for their reconciliation activities was not in Israel, but in Germany.⁷⁷ The idea that young Germans who had visited or lived in Israel could exert a positive impact on German society was not limited to the young volunteers of ASF as an article in the German-speaking Israeli newspaper *Jedioth Chadashoth* from April 1964 demonstrates, highlighting the role of German visitors to Israel for fighting against antisemitism in Germany.⁷⁸

Young Germans in general and ASF volunteers in particular had also other prominent supporters in Israel. One of them was the author and journalist Schalom Ben-Chorin (born in Munich in 1913 as Fritz Rosenthal), who placed the German youth at the centre of one of his articles in *Jedioth Chadashoth* in June 1964. In his article, Ben-Chorin recounted an interview with Gideon Hausner, the attorney general and chief prosecutor in the Eichmann trial. The starting point for the interview was a public statement by Hausner in which he negated Ben-Gurion's claim that there is an "other Germany". Ben-Chorin did not consent with Hausner in this point and engaged him in a discussion about the German youth as a representative of this new Germany. In the end Ben-Chorin found a consensus with Hausner and both agreed that the efforts of German youth for a new Germany are to be acknowledged and supported.⁷⁹

---

76 This aspect was also emphasized by Helmut Gollwitzer. In 1978, he stressed the special responsibility of young Germans – who deliver those signs of atonements their parents were not able to perform – for securing a positive development of Germany in present and future times. Helmut Gollwitzer, Die Aktualität der Aktion Sühnezeichen – einige theologische Anmerkungen, *zeichen,* September 1978, 5.

77 See reports about conversations between volunteers and Israelis in the diary of group Israel IV, 2 June 1964, EZA 97/396.

78 Die Motive des neu-deutschen Antisemitismus, *Jedioth Chadashoth*, 10 April 1964.

79 Gibt es kein anderes Deutschland?, *Jedioth Chadashoth*, 19 June 1964. Ben-Chorin and his wife Avital backed the activities for Jewish-Christian understanding by Protestant church circles in various ways; they were among the Israeli friends of ASF, and Ben-Chorin used his publicity to campaign for the

Even the Israeli parliament Knesset discussed about the issue of German youth activities.[80] In a Knesset discussion in March 1966, Knesset member David Hacohen took a positive stance towards young Germans. He showed himself convinced that many young Germans were ashamed of the crimes of the parent generation. He also made clear that these crimes could not count as a valuable reason to reject activities of young Germans in Israel. For Hacohen, the fact that the German youth showed emotions of disgust and shame regarding the deeds of their fathers laid the ground to accept their presence in Israel and their wish to become friends of Israel by compensating for the past.[81]

Asher Ben Nathan, the first Israeli ambassador in the Federal Republic, also belonged to those Israeli politicians to whom it was important to address and to make contacts with the youth.[82] While serving as an ambassador in Bonn, Ben Nathan frequently met with young Germans and toured through various West German universities, giving talks and participating in discussions.[83] He also supported German-Israeli youth exchange, advertising this idea in the Israeli public, for instance in an interview with the Israeli newspaper *Jedioth Achronoth* in April 1966. In fact, for Ben Nathan the exchange between young Germans and Israelis was much more desirable

---

German youth and its good intentions in Israel. Ablehnung auf sich nehmen, *Frankfurter Allgemeine Zeitung*, 8 March 2011.

80 ASF volunteer Albrecht E. mentions a poll in the Knesset about his ASF group in a letter to his mother from 2 May 1963, EZA 97/712. Inge Deutschkron refers to a Knesset debate in January 1962 after Protestant pastor Dieckmann had visited Israel; Dieckmann had used this occasion to discuss with Israeli school students and their parents the Jewish-German relations and had then asked the young Israelis to establish an exchange of letters with young Germans. Deutschkron, *Israel und die Deutschen*, 185.

81 German translation of Hacohen's statement, PA-AA, AN Neues Amt 2.357.

82 Asher Ben Nathan, Herausforderungen im Schatten der Geschichte, in: *Israel und Deutschland. Dorniger Weg zur Partnerschaft. Die Botschafter berichten über vier Jahrzehnte diplomatische Beziehungen (1965-2005)*, ed. Asher Ben Natan et al. (Köln: Böhlau, 2005), 24-41, here: 31.

83 Ibid., 36-38. At the time of the student revolts in the Federal Republic, Ben Nathan was frequently met by students in tumultous situations in which he was accused as the ambassador of the aggressive state of Israel.

than, for instance, partnerships between German and Israeli towns as they would, he claimed, interfere with the sentiments of Holocaust survivors in Israel.[84] Young Germans, in contrast, would not harm these survivors due to their presence. Once back in Israel, Ben Nathan continued to support activities of young Germans in Israel and he sought understanding for their good intentions among Israelis, particularly among young Israelis.

However, it is noteworthy that even those Israelis who emphasized the positive character of the German youth and its role for German-Israeli relations, such as Ben Nathan, did so without explicitly referring to the activities of the young Germans as acts of "reconciliation". Ben Nathan once wrote, "instead of reconciliation I was talking about understanding".[85] This also was the case among decided supporters of the activities of ASF. In November 1962 the American magazine *Time* had published an article about German ASF volunteers in Israel. In response to this publication, Jehuda Riemer, leader of Kibbutz Urim in which ASF volunteers had worked, wrote to the editors of *Time* magazine: "The dreadful memories of the Hitler period and the successful survival of undiscovered Nazis in present-day Germany (both East and West) prevent a reconciliation of the German and Jewish Peoples."[86] Nevertheless, Riemer explicitly appreciated and supported personal efforts of young Germans to help bridging the gap the past had opened between the older generations.

IN THE AFTERMATH OF THE SIX-DAYS-WAR

With the Six-Days-War in 1967, the debates surrounding guilt, responsibility, reconciliation, and atonement continued, yet were supplemented with intensifying discourses about the notion of peace. Within West German society, the Six-Days-War constituted a turning point with respect to the overall attitude towards Israel. On the one side, there were increasingly radicalized left-wing students to whom Israel constituted the oppressive occupier, while the Palestinians were regarded as the suppressed or the "victims of

---

84 Interview Asher Ben Nathan with *Jedioth Acharonoth*, 15 April 1966, German translation in PA-AA, AV Neues Amt 2.357.
85 Ben Nathan, Herausforderungen, 30.
86 Riemer to Time Magazine, 1 December 1962, EZA 97/708.

the victims".[87] On the other side, there was an increasing support for Israel and for its military successes among conservative Germans. This support was publically articulated through the West German *Springer* publishing house, owned by Axel Springer who regarded reconciliation with Israel a moral duty.[88]

Functionaries and Israel volunteers of ASF took a position between these extreme poles. Reports demonstrate that the volunteers' stance on Israel spanned from Israel-romanticism, pro-Israeli attitudes and a strong identification with Israel's politics throughout the 1960s, to emerging ambivalence and criticism in the late 1960s and early 1970s.[89] The conflict between Israel and its Arab neighbours, and the need for peace in the Middle East region were felt by ASF volunteers in their practical daily work in Kibbutzim and social institutions,[90] and in their every-day experiences.[91]

---

87 For this complex relationship between the German Left and Israel see Kloke, *Israel und die deutsche Linke*.

88 *Unternehmensgrundsätze* of the Axel Springer publishing house, http://www.axelspringer.de/artikel/Grundsaetze-und-Leitlinien_40218.html, accessed 20 May 2011. Springer's personal engagement in reconciliation between Germans and Israeli Jews still raises ambivalent evaluation, as the conference *Axel Springer. Juden, Deutsche und Israelis* (Frankfurt a.M., 27-28 March 2011) demonstrated.

89 A romantic view on Israel can particularly be found among the first Israel volunteers in the early 1960s, for instance in Eckern, *Straße nach Jerusalem*; Legerer, *Tatort Versöhnung*, 215-219. Those volunteers who had experienced the Six-Days-War in Israel even shared the enthusiasm for Israel's military success when they enthusiastically wrote on 28 June 1967 about the war as a new struggle of existence of the Jews in Israel who mainly belonged to the survivors of the Holocaust. Sühnezeichen, *Geschichte(n) erleben*, 26.

90 The diary of the volunteer group Israel VI provides a detailed account about a struggle between a group of Arab farmers and the Kibbutzniks of Kibbutz Bachan about the use of land. Diary entry of the group Israel VI, 21-23 July 1965, EZA 97/398. See also diary entry of group Israel II, 9 February 1962, EZA 97/737. See furthermore the report by Klaus K., EZA 97/391, who mentions that his Israeli counterparts were not much interested in his wish to atone for the past, as the present conflict was much more important to them.

91 This reached a critical peak in April 1978 when two ASF volunteers were killed and several injured through a bombing attack of a Palestinian terrorist. This

For several volunteers, it became more and more difficult to differentiate between the "Jewish victims" to whom they offered their signs of atonement, and the "Israeli perpetrators" whose behaviour they regarded as worthwhile criticizing. This situation was particularly problematic for those who went to Israel with ASF from the late 1960s onwards as *Kriegsdienstverweigerer* (conscientious objectors) who had opted against military service in the Federal Republic for pacifist reasons.[92] Volunteers told in their reports that they encountered barriers, when they wanted to discuss the Arab-Israeli conflict with Israelis, particularly elderly ones.[93] Among the volunteers were some who were very cautious whether they as young Germans were at all in a position to criticize the political situation in Israel,[94] whereas other volunteers exposed themselves and their criticism openly and identified with the Palestinians.[95]

It is not astonishing that the presence of German conscientious objectors was regarded as a problem in parts of the Israeli public, for which the Israeli wars and the Palestinian conflict meant to secure the threatened existence of the state of Israel. Even supporters and friends of ASF in Israel felt increasingly at unease with the organization and with some of its volunteers,[96] the more the ASF volunteers began to question or to criticize Israeli politics towards Palestinians and the more the aspect of peace became important to the practical work. In the late 1960s and throughout the 1970s the

---

event intensified an already ongoing debate about the role of the organization in Israel and within this conflict.

92 In 1969, ASF was officially appointed to offer Peace Service (*Friedensdienst*) for those young male Germans who rejected military service. In the 1970s, two-third to three-fourth of all ASF activists in all countries were conscientious objectors. Lilach Marom, 'On Guilt and Atonement'. Aktion Sühnezeichen Friedensdienste and Its Activity in Israel, *Yad Vashem Studies* 35 (2007), 187-220, here: 200.

93 Rolf T., Report 22/71, EZA 97/391.

94 Ibid.

95 See the book by ASF volunteers Jan Metzger, Martin Orth and Christian Sterzing, *Das ist unser Land – Westbank und Gaza-Streifen unter israelischer Besatzung* (Bornheim-Merten: Lamuv, 1980). About the book and the discussions within ASF about the book see Legerer, *Tatort Versöhnung*, 225-226.

96 Marom, On Guilt and Atonement, 201.

ASF programs in Israel were complemented by projects with Arabs, and activities to foster peace between Israelis and Palestinians.[97]

The emphasis on the aspect of peace in the everyday work of ASF in Israel, but also elsewhere, even led to a change of the organization's name. In 1968, the name was extended to become *Aktion Sühnezeichen Friedensdienste* (the official English name from then onwards is Action Reconciliation Service for Peace). At that time, many ASF volunteers and functionaries required the organization to also look forward towards peace instead of only looking backwards to atonement. Nevertheless, even the change in the organization's name did not stop discourses about the name and the future contents of the ASF activities. In spring 1970, the term atonement was once again highly debated within the organization.[98] In an official letter to members and friends of the organization, the organization argued that to abandon the term atonement would mean a trivialization of the work; furthermore, the letter explained that atonement and peace well belonged together as atonement is meant to lead towards peace.[99]

Reports by ASF volunteers and conscientious objectors from the early 1970s suggest that the aspect of reconciliation and the importance to deal with the Nazi past remained crucial to the activists in Israel, which they also took as a starting point for their engagement for peace.[100] ASF volunteers in Israel in the early 1970s found different, partly diverging answers

---

97 For instance through work in *Neve Schalom* (Oasis of Peace), which sought to provide an interconfessional meeting space for Christians, Jews and Muslims. Report Edeltraud M. and Gottfried R., February 1973, EZA 97/392.

98 See the documents in preparation of the general meeting on April 10 and 11 1970, EZA 97/10.

99 Letter, 19 March 1970, EZA 97/10.

100 In 1974, a group of conscientious objectors wrote a joint report about their self-understanding as pacifists working in Israel. The reason why they chose ASF as organization for their peace service was, according to their report, their belief in the necessity of an active dealing with the past as precondition for reconciliaton. As post-war generation they did not regard the question of guilt as central, but their active engagement for reconciliation between Jews and Christians, Jews and Germans as well as Arabs and Jews. This should be accompanied by a critical solidarity to both Israelis and Palestinians. Report by Michael D. and Hans-Volker K., March 1974, 7-8, EZA 97/392.

to the question of how to link the idea of atonement to their work in Israel and to their presence there as young Germans. Volunteer Hans-Joachim M., who worked in the Kibbutz Shaar Haamakim, reflected about his work with ASF in April 1972. He considered how he, born in 1947 – "two years after the liberation of the Concentration Camps" – and other young Germans of his age, could contribute towards atoning for the "misdeeds of the Nazi time".[101] In his account, the crimes committed in the past are depersonalized, as he does not refer directly to his parents or his parents' generation. For Hans-Joachim M. the caritative work with elderly Jews in his Kibbutz constituted the way in which he as a young person actively contributed to bringing forward the idea of atonement and understanding between the German and the Jewish people.[102] He thereby emphasized the character of the hands-on reconciliation approach by ASF, which he favored over a mere rhetoric of reconciliation. Other volunteers thought along similar lines by claiming that the personal contacts with people in Israel would contribute to improving the image of the German youth.[103]

But there were also generational discrepancies among the young German volunteers in Israel, discrepancies that led towards a diverging understanding of the issues of guilt and atonement. After Barbara G., a 22-year-old ASF volunteer in Israel in 1970/71 returned to her hometown Fulda, she gave an interview to a regional newspaper. She claimed that she and her 14 co-volunteers had not gone to Israel in order to atone; with their service they "did not want to nor could they atone for something for which they as young Germans did not feel responsible".[104] This provoked vehement criticism of another volunteer, Lutz M., born in 1940, who was still in Israel at the time, and who expressed his unease with Barbara G.'s rejection of the young generation's responsibility and the impossibility of atonement. Lutz M. referred to the representative understanding of atonement and reconciliation by young people who felt responsible for the guilt committed by the older generation. For him it was clear that "the age of the volunteers does not release them from the responsibility for Auschwitz, as it continues to

---

101 Report Hans-Joachim M., April 1972, EZA 97/392.
102 Ibid.
103 Report Elfie G.-H., February 1971, EZA 97/391.
104 Quoted according to report Lutz M., 13/72, EZA 97/391.

exist in another form even in our present – and as long as we live we are also affected by it".[105]

The idea of atonement not only remained a debated term among activists themselves, but also for their Israeli supporters[106] and particularly for those at which the reconciliation activities were directed to. Even Israelis who did not in principle object to establishing contacts with the volunteers of ASF expressed their doubts about the name *Sühnezeichen* and the practical implementation of atonement by young Germans. In April 1968 *Jedioth Chadashoth* published a letter to the newspaper's editor, written by a reader who had been in contact with some volunteers, in which we can read the following:

"The name *Sühnezeichen* again has something to do with German fanaticism. How can the children of those who have become guilty wish to atone for something which they were not even part of? Their attitude is therefore unnatural right from the start."[107]

The writer of the letter questioned whether the young German volunteers could fulfill the claim for atonement at all. The letter continued to criticize the attitude of the young German volunteers with respect to the Israeli-Palestinian conflict, which in the author's opinion resulted in anti-Israeli sentiments that were also expressed by the German reconciliation activists. It concluded that "we should not have accepted this gesture of sacrifice, as this gesture resulted from a completely wrong view".[108]

Another term that caused unease among Israeli Jews was the underlying idea that atonement and reconciliation are connected to the notion of forgiveness, a term that played an important role in the reconciliation concepts of the Christian churches and among reconciliation activists, such as

---

105 Ibid.
106 See the texts by Israeli ASF supporters in EZA 97/785 about a discussion taking place in 1974.
107 *Jedioth Chadashoth*, 11 April 1968, 3, quoted in Legerer, *Tatort Versöhnung*, 215-216.
108 Ibid.

ASF.[109] The aspect of asking for forgiveness constituted a problematic issue for some of the recipients of reconciliation activities in Israel. Pinhas Rosen, Israeli Minister of Justice from 1949 to 1961, and member of the Knesseth until 1968, stated to the Israeli newspaper *Maariv* in December 1968 that he was far from hating all Germans and that he welcomed visitors from Germany in Israel. However, he continued to say that he was neither able to forget nor to forgive.[110] His statement points at a crucial issue in reconciliation matters. What if the one to whom reconciliation is offered cannot forgive and therefore does not fulfill a prerequisite for reconciliation according to the Christian conception of reconciliation; a conception that is present within the conceptual framework of reconciliation and atonement of Protestant German groups active in Israel, such as ASF? Additionally, according to Jewish moral law, it is not possible for Jews to grant forgiveness in the name of others.[111] It has also been argued that in the aftermath of the Holocaust reconciliation could only be possible between the murderers and the murdered.[112]

Even if the idea of peace became more central to debates about the young Germans for their reconciliation activities in Israel during the late 1960s and early 1970s, also the idea of atonement, as problematic as it was for many volunteers, remained important for the self-understanding of the activists (if not in a positive sense than at least as a term that was constantly

---

109 See also Gundermann, Leiden ohne Täter, 144, who emphasizes this aspect of asking for forgiveness in her study about the activities of ASF in the Netherlands.

110 See German translation of the interview in letter German Embassy Tel Aviv to the Foreign Office Bonn, 23 December 1968, PA-AA, B36/458.

111 For the diverging Christian and Jewish conceptions of repentance, forgiveness and reconciliation see Peter J. Haas, Forgiveness, Reconciliation and Jewish Memory after Auschwitz, in: *After-Words. Post-Holocaust Struggles with Forgiveness, Reconciliation, Justice*, ed. David Patterson and John K. Roth (Seattle and London: University of Washington Press, 2004), 5-16.

112 See the argument by Theodor W. Adorno, refered to by Susan Neiman, *Das Böse denken. Eine andere Geschichte der Philosophie* (Frankfurt a.M.: Suhrkamp, 2006), 384. Such an understanding has to reject reconciliation efforts by ASF activists.

discussed) and for the debates taking place about their work and their presence in Israel.

In the course of these debates, functionaries, volunteers and friends of ASF claimed that an "outward reconciliation" (*Versöhnung nach außen*) must be followed by an "internal change" (*Wandlung im Innern*).[113] This intensified an argument that ASF supporters in Israel had brought forward: that the main reconciliation task of the *Sühnezeichen* volunteers was not situated in Israel, but at home in Germany. In fact, already in the early 1960s, the returning Israel volunteers were invited by city majors, local schools, and church groups to tell about their experiences.[114] In the late 1960s, these programs intensified, and it became common practice for many volunteers to continue with their engagement for ASF by giving lectures to school classes and youth groups about their experiences as volunteers after their return home. At these occasions, the returned volunteers were met by other young Germans with interest, yet again with questions and partly criticism about the connection of atonement, guilt and the task of the young generation in offering atonement, in acknowledging guilt and in pursuing reconciliation.[115]

CONCLUSION

Based on the Christian idea of representative atonement for a guilt committed by others, the reconciliation practice of ASF was shaped by the engagement of young Germans as reconciliation actors. Through the inclusion of young Germans the organization and its members showed that they regarded atonement and reconciliation as an ongoing task pursued by the future generations who did not simply draw a *Schlusstrich* under the past. In this

---

113 Kammerer, *Aktion Sühnezeichen*, 114.
114 Diary entries of Israel groups III, VII and VIII, 18 March 1964, EZA 97/396; 21-24 September 1966 and 15-18 March 1967, both EZA 97/399.
115 Reports by Joachim R. about a four-week information tour through Württemberg in February/March 1973 and by Martin B., Vincent B. and Marion R. about their information week in Cologne in March 1973, both EZA 97/392; see also report by Susanne P. who held an information week in Stuttgart schools and congregations in July 1972, EZA 97/391.

way the young generation became the central reconciliation activists who committed practical reconciliation work as representatives of those who had actually lived through the National Socialist regime. The young Germans reflected about their experiences as reconciliation activists in Israel in various ways. They also attracted attention from those Israelis they met during their practical work, Israeli politicians, and the Israeli media. The integration of the young generation in reconciliation activities from the 1950s onwards provoked debates in West Germany and Israel, which centered on the issues of guilt, atonement, and peace, and which discussed the role the young generation was to play in reconciliation discourse and practice.

As demonstrated in this chapter, discourses on reconciliation and practical experiences of young Germans as reconciliation activists in Israel between 1961 and the 1970s oscillated between underlying ideas of atonement, resulting from the past, and ideas of peace, directed towards the future. While more and more importance was laid upon the idea of peace from the late 1960s onwards, the idea of atonement has not simply been displaced by the idea of peace, as both ideas were present in the ASF activities and concepts from the beginning, but were attached with different weight and importance at different times.[116] The integration of young Germans in reconciliation efforts between Germany and Israel – in the discourse about the role of the young generation for reconciliation and in practical reconciliation activity – impacted on and accompanied this shift. The more every-day life in Israel became dominated by the problems among Israelis and Palestinians and by the Middle East conflict, and the more young Germans tried to contribute towards achieving peace among Israelis and Arabs, the more these contemporary political issues became part of the young people's considerations about the past and about their role as activists for reconciliation.

The analyzed discourses on the role of the young generation for reconciliation also contribute to further developing a differentiated understanding on how guilt and atonement were transferred in the post-war decades. In her study about the transfer of guilt and atonement to the following generations, theologian Katharina von Kellenbach argued that a combination of

---

116 In contrast to my understanding, Legerer, *Tatort Versöhnung*, 220, implies that the integration of the peace movement and the inclusion of conscientious confessors has led to a "dilution of the original mission".

rather unspecified confessions of guilt – for instance the guilt confessions by the Protestant and Catholic Churches after the Second World War – together with a general amnesia within West German society in the early post-war period has led to a transfer of the moral obligation to deal with the Nazi past to the second and third generations.[117] Given the results of this chapter, it should be added to von Kellenbach's argument that the transfer of guilt was not only – as she claims – rooted in an "unconscious participation in a solidarity community of guilt".[118] As demonstrated above, this transfer of guilt was also consciously promoted by the various political and personal discourses on the role of German youth as reconciliation activists, discourses that developed parallel to the silence on the crimes of the past in the post-war years and went, as could be shown, further right into the 1960s and 1970s.

Looking beyond the timeframe discussed in this chapter, reports of ASF volunteers and other accounts of young people engaged in German-Israeli dialogue suggest that the debates about the role of youth in reconciliation discourse and in reconciliation practice did not cease, but continue to exist.[119] Each "young generation" working in Israel tried and tries anew to negotiate its own position and its responsibility with respect to the past. And each young generation is anew an object of debate concerning the role of youth for reconciliation.[120] These negotiations are influenced by contempo-

---

117 Katharina von Kellenbach, Theologische Rede von Schuld und Vergebung, in: *Von Gott reden im Land der Täter. Theologische Stimmen der dritten Generation seit der Shoa*, ed. Katharina von Kellenbach et al. (Darmstadt: Wissenschaftliche Buchgesellschaft, 2001), 46-67, here: 63.

118 Ibid.

119 Sühnezeichen Friedensdienste Forum. Rundbrief für die Mitglieder und den Freundeskreis, 35 (1986); Protokoll 2/86, EZA 97/68. For more recent standpoints see the accounts of young Germans and Israelis in *Dissonant Memories. Fragmented Present. Exchanging Young Discourses between Israel and Germany*, ed. Charlotte Misselwitz and Cornelia Siebeck (Bielefeld: transcript, 2009).

120 See, for instance, the report about German-Israeli relations on *Kol Jisrael* radio station, 28 January 1984, and the weekend insert of *Haaretz*, 7 November 1986, both EZA 97/814. And most recently the former German President Christian Wulff who was accompanied by a delegation of young Germans on

rary developments such as the intensifying Israeli-Palestinian conflict, contemporary media debates about victims and perpetrators or own experiences as volunteers. At the core of these discourses about reconciliation there remain attempts to deal with issues of guilt and responsibility, atonement and peace.

---

his state visit to Israel in November 2010, and who explained his idea of the youth delegation by explicitly referring to the concept of a generational responsibility for the past and the future. Interview with *Jedioth Aharonot*, 28 November 2010.

Reconciliation in Postcolonial Settings

Apologising for Colonial Violence
The Documentary Film *Regresso a Wiriyamu*, Transitional Justice, and Portuguese-Mozambican Decolonisation

ROBERT STOCK

When Aníbal Cavaco Silva, President of Portugal, went for a state visit to the Mozambican capital Maputo in March 2008, he was asked by a journalist if he would apologise for the 'colonial war', namely for the massacre of Wiriyamu where about 400 people were killed by Portuguese special forces. He responded:

"People make history every day, with all its defects and virtues. Regarding history, I try to identify the positive facts, because, if we keep looking back at the past, we will lose the future."[1]

Cavaco Silva avoided a direct answer and instead tried to contextualise the violence committed by Portuguese troops during the war of decolonisation, as a seemingly 'normal' element of a universal history of humanity. The newspaper *Jornal de Notícias* also reports that Cavaco Silva emphasised

---

1 Quoted in Luís Andrade de Sá, Pr/Moçambique, Cavaco contorna Guerra Colonial propondo o 'Lado positivo da História', *Jornal de Notícias*, 24 March 2008. This and the following citations from Portuguese sources are translations by the author. This paper forms part my PhD thesis on decolonisation and documentary films from Mozambique and Portugal at the International Graduate Center for the Study of Culture (University of Gießen).

some of his positive recollections relating to previous stays in Mozambique back in the days of colonialism. This rather conservative and nostalgic point of view causes astonishment. However, it could also be assumed that perhaps the context of a press conference was not the proper place for speaking about such an issue since it did not provide the right setting and preparation for the demanded apology. Was the response by Cavaco Silva then appropriate? Did it not ignore the experience of the victims of this or other violent excesses, and the violence of the 'colonial situation' in general?[2]

About ten years before, the documentary film *Return to Wiriyamu* directed by Felícia Cabrita and Paulo Camacho proposed a different perspective on the subject eschewed by Cavaco Silva.[3] This Portuguese film production deals with the massacre of Wiriyamu (northern Mozambique, Province of Tête) conducted by Portuguese troops on December 16, 1972 and brings together one of the perpetrators and some of the survivors.[4] As this paper will show, this film and its background provide the opportunity to reflect and think about the complexity and ambiguity of postcolonial and apologetic contexts.

The two situations mentioned allude to a broader context, where the discussion of the colonial past and connected experiences of violence has become an important issue in most societies of the former European colonial powers. These debates are not restricted to academic discourse but also

---

2   For a different attitude see the speech of Mário Soares, former President of Portugal, that he gave in Maputo on 23 June 2005. There, he refers to his encounter with Samora Machel in 1974, when he was Foreign Minister and involved in the Lusaka Accord, where the transfer of power to the *Frente da Libertação de Moçambique* (Frelimo, Mozambican Liberation Front) was negotiated. He, too, speaks about his exile in France before 1974 and his participation in demonstrations against Marcello Caetano in London in 1973. Mário Soares, *Conferência de Mário Soares na Universidade Eduardo Mondlane in Maputo* (Lisboa: Arquivo & Biblioteca Fundação Mário Soares, 23 June 2005).

3   Felícia Cabrita and Paulo Camacho, *Regresso a Wiriyamu* (SIC 1998, Portugal).

4   It was broadcasted on 19 November 1998 as part of the series *Grande Reportagem* (Great Report) on the private television channel *Sociedade Independente de Comunicação* (SIC, Independent Communication Society). Marina C. Ramos, Regresso a Wiriyamu, *Público*, 19 November 1998, 44.

reach a wider public and influence political decisions.[5] In France, the year 2000 marked a turning point for the discussion of the Algerian War of Independence (1954-1962). In fact, just one year before, the conflict in Algeria had been recognized as a 'war' by the French parliament. A public debate discussed the violence during the war,[6] while historians analysed practices of torture utilized by the French Armed Forces.[7] Despite this unsettling chapter of history, French politicians advocated the positive interpretation of colonialism.[8] In the United Kingdom, studies of the decolonisation of Kenya troubled the image of the seemingly civilized British manner of

---

5 Andreas Eckert, Der Kolonialismus im Europäischen Gedächtnis, *Aus Politik und Zeitgeschichte*, 1/2 (2008), 31-38, here: 33.

6 On 20 June 2000, *Le Monde* published an article in which a former member of the Algerian Liberation Front reported on the torture that she had experienced during her imprisonment. Shortly after, General Aussaresses wrote about such violent practices (not showing any sign of regret) that he and others had used against prisoners in the war.

7 Robert Aldrich, Imperial Mise En Valeur and Mise En Scène. Recent Works on French Colonialism, *The Historical Journal* 45, 4 (2002), 917-936, here: 933. A detailed analysis is offered by Joshua Cole, Intimate Acts and Unspeakable Relations. Remembering Torture and the War for Algerian Independence, in: *Memory, Empire and Postcolonialism: Legacies of French Colonialism*, ed. Alex Hargreaves (Lanham: Lexington Books, 2005), 125-141. See also Neil MacMaster, The Torture Controversy (1998-2002). Towards a 'New History' of the Algerian War, *Modern & Contemporary France* 10, 4 (2002), 449-459.

8 Loi no. 2005-158 du 23 février 2005 portant reconnaissance de la Nation et contribution nationale en faveur des Français rapatriés. Article 4 of the law states: "University research programmes [will] accord to the history of the French presence overseas, notably in North Africa, the place that it deserves. School curricula [will] recognise, in particular, the positive role of the French presence overseas, notably in North Africa, and [will] accord the history and the sacrifices of the soldiers of the French Army who came from these territories the eminent place to which they have a right." This law was retracted shortly after its introduction. Quoted in Robert Aldrich, Colonial past, post-colonial present: History wars French-style, *History Australia* 3, 1 (2006), 14.1-14.10, here: 14.8.

withdrawing from its overseas territories.[9] The out-dated permanent exhibition at the *Musée Royal de l'Afrique Central* in Tervuren, near Brussels, still holds a rather colonialist view on the history of the Congo, and hence provoked discussions regarding the mass murder in Belgian Congo that took place around 1900.[10]

In Portugal, discussions about the colonial past can be observed as well even if they are shaped in a specific way.[11] Since the 1990s, mainly veterans of the decolonisation wars have been publishing an increasing number of memoirs and historical accounts. Over the last decade, the growing willingness of veterans to speak about their experience in the wars of decolonisation in the media – which, at the same time, became more open for these debates – has fostered an intensive and ongoing discussion about the colonial past in Portugal. This phenomenon also extends to the film production since there is a continuously increasing number of documentaries and fea-

---

9   Richard Dowden, State of Shame, *Guardian*, 5 February 2005, on the books by David Anderson, *Histories of the Hanged: The Dirty War in Kenya and the End of Empire* (New York: W.W. Norton, 2005) and Caroline Elkins, *Britain's Gulag: The Brutal End of Empire in Kenya* (London: Jonathan Cape, 2005), http://www.guardian.co.uk/books/2005/feb/05/featuresreviews.guardianreview6, accessed 25 May 2011

10 There are already plans for the renovation of the museum building and the whole exhibition. The latter "is taking place in collaboration with external experts and representatives of the African diaspora". Permanent Exhibition. In: Royal Museum for Central Africa, http://www.africamuseum.be/renovation/newexhibition, accessed 28 March 2012. See also Sabine Cornélis, Colonial and Postcolonial Exhibitions, in: *A Historical Companion to Postcolonial Literatures in English*, ed. Prem Poddar and David Johnson (Edinburgh: Edinburgh University Press, 2005), 21-23, here: 22.

11 For a discussion of this issue that does not consider media representations see Isabel dos Santos Lourenco and Alexander Keese, Die blockierte Erinnerung: Portugals koloniales Gedächtnis und das Ausbleiben kritischer Diskurse 1974-2010, *Geschichte und Gesellschaft* 37, 2 (2011), 220-243, here: 221. For a critical perspective regarding the memory of the Portuguese New State see Teresa Pinheiro, Facetten der Erinnerungskultur. Portugals Umgang mit dem Estado Novo, *Neue Politische Literatur* 55, 1 (2010), 7-22.

ture films dedicated to the wars of decolonisation.[12] Many of them can be perceived as interventions in a context, where speaking about the 'colonial war' constitutes a difficult issue and often creates polemical debates.

It is evident that many of the debates and studies mentioned focus on the consequences of colonial history, decolonisation and postcolonial immigration into Europe. At the same time, there is only little reflection on memory politics in the African context,[13] where the colonial past – more than postcolonial excesses of violence committed by the independence movements against political opponents and other parts of the populations[14] – is also an object of public and political discourse.[15] Moreover, if then the examination of African memory politics proves to be a rare topic of academic discourse, the analysis of postcolonial memories situated between Europe and Africa transcending national boundaries, and being appropriated by different and sometimes competing social groups, really turns out to be a future task.[16]

This article contributes to this rather unexplored field. Its focus lies on an apology for past wrongs in the lusophone context, namely Mozambique and Portugal, and its filmic representation. The following case study sheds new light on the postcolonial negotiation of transnational memory; a process that takes place not only in the realm of official bilateral relations, but to which members of civil society such as veterans, survivors and journalists make their contribution. To grasp this complex issue, the article ana-

---

12 João Maria Grilo, *O cinema da não-ilusão: Histórias para o cinema português* (Lisboa: Livros Horizonte, 2006), 91.

13 Richard P. Werbner, *Memory and the Postcolony: African Anthropology and the Critique of Power* (London and New York: Zed Books, 1998).

14 Victor Igreja, Frelimo's Political Ruling through Violence and Memory in Postcolonial Mozambique, *Journal of Southern African Studies* 36, 4 (2010), 781-799; Dalila Cabrita Mateus and Alvaro Mateus, *Purga em Angola: O 27 de Maio de 1977* (Porto: Asa Editores, 2007).

15 Carola Lentz and Jan Budniok, Ghana@50 – celebrating the nation: An eyewitness account from Accra, *zeitgeschichte-online*, December 2010, http://zeitgesc hichte-online.de/Themen-Lentz-Budniok-12-2010, accessed 27 February 2012.

16 See for example one of the few studies in this respect: Andrea L. Smith, *Colonial Memory and Postcolonial Europe: Maltese Settlers in Algeria and France* (Bloomington: Indiana University Press, 2006).

lyses how the violent experience of Mozambican-Portuguese decolonisation is reflected in the documentary film *Return to Wiriyamu*.

The film is a striking example for showing that it is important to consider the procedure and effects of apologies, not only on the macro level of inter-state relations, but also on the micro level of social interactions. On this level, the physical wounds, emotions, and persisting images of the former adversaries that often continue to shape the relationships between perpetrators and victims up to the present, can be re-negotiated. To observe how the moment of the apology emerges in particular situations, and to analyse the specific elements that are constitutive to such interactions, provides knowledge and understanding of apologies for past wrongs and related dynamics along with new insights. For my argument, I am specifically interested in addressing two levels of analysis: the first explores the background of the making of the film drawing on an in-depth interview with the Portuguese journalist Felícia Cabrita; the second level deals with the specific perspective in which the film visualizes the encounter of both perpetrators and victims. In other words, how does the film proceed when translating a process in which people meet that were on opposing sides during the war of decolonisation into moving images? I argue that there is a complex relation between the two levels because seemingly both personal and filmic memory are connected to particular contexts, truths, and related objectives.

My examination starts with a brief overview of the concept of apologies for past wrongs in postcolonial settings. In sketching out some cases, it will become clear that there is still a great lack of approaches researching apologetic contexts at the level of social interactions and in relation to media representations. Subsequently, I outline the process of democratisation in Portugal and explore the attempts of transitional justice that occurred right after the revolution in 1974. This will provide the background for an in-depth analysis of the documentary *Return to Wiriyamu*. The main parts of the paper constitute an analysis of an interview I conducted with Felícia Cabrita in July 2010 and an examination of some of the central scenes of the documentary. To conclude my analysis, I draw on some newspaper articles that point to the reception of the film in Mozambique and Portugal.

APOLOGIES FOR PAST WRONGS ON THE MACRO AND MICRO LEVEL

One astonishing part in the documentary *Return to Wiriyamu* is the sequence, in which one of the perpetrators of the massacre comes back to the crime scene and meets with some of the survivors. In this encounter, the former Portuguese officer apologises for the deeds of the unit that committed the massacre. Even if this particular apology is in some ways unique, it can be related to similar attempts in postcolonial contexts. However, all these apologies are embedded in specific frameworks, as the following brief overview will show. One of the functions of apologies for past wrongs consists of demonstrating that a state, a social group or an individual holds at the time the apology takes place different values than from those held in the past when certain acts were committed. As Robert Weyeneth observes,

"acknowledgment of historical wrongs comes in diverse forms: outright apologies, requests for forgiveness, [...] expressions of regret, and payments of reparations and compensation. Apologies can be communicated in a wide range of ways through verbal statements issued publicly, joint diplomatic declarations, [...] reports, legal judgments, [...] days of observance, reconciliation walks, monuments and memorials, [...]. Both individuals and institutions apologize, for personal transgressions and for collective wrongs."[17]

There are steps that precede and follow the processes mentioned: Remorse and regret are expressed in order to show that a conscience about the performed wrong exists. This can open a possibility for a dialogue where victims and perpetrators speak about their experiences. Within this context, the different perspectives on the crime become evident. Perpetrators have the opportunity to acknowledge what they have done. Furthermore, an apology is able to show the change of attitude of a former adversary, and this could "pave the way for the former victims to forgive, and help construct a new image of the former enemy".[18] Nevertheless, as Nick Smith indicates – in

---

17 Robert R. Weyeneth, The Power of Apology and the Process of Historical Reconciliation, *The Public Historian* 23, 3 (2001), 9-38, here: 20.
18 Jennifer M. Lind, *Sorry States. Apologies in International Politics* (Ithaca: Cornell University Press, 2008), 12.

contrast to the work of Tavuchis[19] –, a "categorical apology" could be difficult to achieve because it involves several interdependent factors.[20] However, if an apology is indeed accepted and perpetrators are forgiven, then a process of reconciliation between two or more actors involved could be initiated. Yet, (attempts of) truth telling, acknowledgment, apology, and forgiveness do not open perspectives for long-term reconciliation in every case.

In the context of international politics, the specific language of apology in postcolonial contexts often emerges due to questions of material compensation. The centenary of the outbreak of the annihilation war against the Herero in German South-West Africa was commemorated in 2004. It provided the reason for Heidemarie Wieczorek Zeul, then Minister for German development cooperation, to visit Namibia. In Okakara, the place where the war against the Herero had started, she gave an official speech that did not include an apology. However, she did add an important sentence: "Everything I said in my speech was an apology for crimes committed by Germany."[21]

Until then, the German government and the Foreign Office had avoided an apology due to claims of reparations that were already in course.[22] Officials stated that Germany already supported Namibia with a great amount of money in development cooperation. The Herero who attended the ceremony in Okakara were satisfied with the words and the contrition expressed

---

19 Nicholas Tavuchis, *Mea Culpa: A Sociology of Apology and Reconciliation* (Stanford: Stanford University Press, 1991).
20 For Smith, a "categorical apology" is constituted by nine elements: corroborated factual record, acceptance of blame, possession of appropriate standing, identification of each harm, identification of the moral principles underlying each harm, shared commitment to moral principles underlying each harm, recognition of victim as moral interlocutor, categorical regret, and performance of the apology. Nick Smith, *I Was Wrong: The Meanings of Apologies* (Cambridge: Cambridge University Press, 2008), 140-142.
21 Quoted in Larissa Förster, Jenseits des juristischen Diskurses. Die Entschuldigung Von Heidemarie Wieczorek-Zeul in Namibia, *afrika süd. zeitschrift zum südlichen afrika* 5 (2004), 8-10, http://www.issa-bonn.org/publikationen/5-04f%F6rster.htm, accessed 25 February 2012.
22 But the Namibian Government did not support the claims by the Herero.

by the minister. Shortly thereafter, rumours circulated that the Herero would eventually drop the charges; however, it turned out, this was not the case.

In postcolonial contexts, one can find other examples in which regret is expressed, but due to fear of material reparation claims, the word "sorry" is usually avoided.[23] This was the case with Tony Blair's statements in 2007 when the bicentenary of the abolition of slavery was commemorated in the UK. It was also the case in 1999, when the Australian Prime Minister John Howard regretted "that indigenous Australians suffered injustices under the practices of past generations" and refused to apologise to Aborigines for the government policy.[24] As Howard-Hassmann and Lombardo observe, the expression of regret with simultaneous refusal of apology – often to avoid claims for material redress – is widespread in the postcolonial political sphere. However, the authors also question the progress that would be made by such gestures:

"It is unclear whether the small, tentative steps to acknowledge and regret the harms perpetrated against Africa by Western powers will have any real impact upon international relations. Nor it is altogether clear that apologies might have any real meaning or impact within Africa, or to African citizens."[25]

The mentioned apologies or the attempts to avoid them are part of complex processes where legal issues condition foreign relations. Nevertheless, for the following case study it is important to examine the different aspects of apologies not only on the level of inter-state relations or relations between governments and pressure groups from civil society, but rather on the micro level of social interactions. This level clearly differs from diplomatic, official declarations or apologies by members of governments, who were not directly involved in historical wrongs. The aim here is to observe a complex situation – seen through the prism of a film – that brings people to-

---

23 Eckert, Der Kolonialismus, 36.
24 Weyeneth, The Power of Apology, 18.
25 Rhoda Howard-Hassman and Anthony P. Lombardo, Words Require Action: African Elite Opinion About Apologies from the West, in: *The Age of Apology: Facing up to the Past*, ed. Mark Gibney (Philadelphia: University of Pennsylvania Press, 2008), 216-228, here: 218.

gether to re-negotiate their roles as victims and perpetrators that result from colonial violence and persist to influence their lives and relations to each other up to the present. One can explore how the moment for the apology emerges in specific settings, analyse the crucial elements constitutive to such interactions and hence shed a new light on apologies for past wrongs and related dynamics. To grasp such social processes, ethnographic approaches have proven to be particularly useful. One example is the methodological framework outlined by Tim Kelsall who acted as an observer of the hearings for the Truth and Reconciliation Commission in the Tonkolili District in Sierra Leone in July 2003. In discussing the specific conditions of this cultural-religious setting and the resulting difficulties in bringing forth the truth, and by highlighting the significance of the closing reconciliation ceremony of the hearings where the perpetrators were forgiven, Kelsall concludes that:

"One must look beyond the notion that after four days of telling the truth, reconciliation would logically follow, the ceremony merely underlining a state of affairs that truth had brought into being. It is more plausible to view the entire five days of the hearings as a ritual building to the climax of the final ceremony, upon which the purpose of the Commission hinged. [...] ritual, at its most effective, has the power to transform perceptions and emotions and therefore situations, and it is for this reason that it ought to be taken seriously by truth commissions."[26]

His analysis of the perspectives of the different parties involved in the hearings – victims, perpetrators, commissioners, and the audience – provides a productive framework through which the apology for the massacre in Wiriyamu can be considered. Kelsall's analysis makes clear that such reconciliation rituals are shaped by a series of factors such as speeches, body gestures and emotional response.

Besides this, other aspects can influence processes of apology and forgiveness. Considering a case described by Marie Breen Smyth, who is very critical regarding forgiveness, one topic, as some observers noted, was of particular importance in the reconciliation process in South Africa. Breen

---

26 Tim Kelsall, Truth, Lies, Ritual: Preliminary Reflections on the Truth and Reconciliation Commission in Sierra Leone, *Human Rights Quarterly* 27, 2 (2005), 361-391, here: 386.

Smyth affirms that "victims and survivors may feel under pressure to grant some form of absolution or forgiveness to perpetrators"[27] by arguing that the media can constrain processes of apology and forgiveness. Her point of reference is the television series *Facing the Truth* produced by BBC in 2006, in which in the presence of Archbishop Desmond Tutu encounters of victims and perpetrators of the conflict in Northern Ireland took place. In one of the three parts, Mrs Sylvia Hackett met Loyalist Michael Stone, the murderer of her husband. Although, at first unwilling, later in the program she was led to shake hands with Stone, but immediately afterwards, she had a breakdown:

"Following the prompts from Tutu, an international figure, and under the glare of television cameras with the question of what millions of viewers would make of a refusal to forgive, the pressure on Mrs Hackett to shake the hand of Michael Stone was almost irresistible. It was almost impossible for her not to shake the hand of the perpetrator."[28]

The gesture of shaking hands thus can be a sensitive issue that at least in this case does not have a clear 'message'. As it turns out, being on television and therefore addressing a wide audience can create tensions and contradictive emotions due to presupposed expectations on the part of oneself, the other participants and the viewers. Furthermore, there are other questions arising: Can such problems to be resolved in public? Is this helpful? Or should these sensitive issues rather be treated in a setting that would respect the privacy of the victims and therefore not pressure them? It is, however, difficult to judge the television program solely from the analysis by Smyth. Donna Hicks, who was one of the participants, describes another issue of the program *Facing the Truth*, which in her view turned out to be successful. Though, she carefully admits:

"Even if one creates the right conditions for healing and reconciliation, not everyone is ready for it. There are steps along the way that are more difficult for some than

---

27 Marie Breen Smyth, *Truth Recovery and Justice after Conflict: Managing Violent Pasts* (New York: Routledge, 2007), 17.
28 Ibid., 18.

others. For some, the reasons were personal and emotional, and for others, it was political."[29]

The examples given above point to the intricate relationships in situations involving former colonial powers and independent states in Africa, and show the complicated processes of apology and forgiveness that are taking place between victims and perpetrators in different social and political contexts. One can draw several connections from the outlined cases to Mozambique and Portugal. First of all, there was no officially pronounced apology of Portugal for the committed violence during the 'colonial war'.[30] There were however moments of fraternization between Portuguese and Mozambican politicians and militaries during the difficult situation in 1974-1975,[31] that became even more complex through the sudden and massive exodus of the Portuguese settler population.[32] Secondly, Mozambique – similar to the case of Namibia and Germany – profits from the Portuguese development cooperation. Additionally, in contrast to the Herero, who managed to form a pressure group, it seems that rural populations in Mozambique, which during the war of independence were targets of attacks, continue to have 'no voice' and remain in a subaltern position.[33] This does not mean that an

---

29 Donna Hicks, Reconciling with Dignity, *European Forum for Restorative Justice*, http://www.euforumrj.org/readingroom/Terrorism/DHicks.pdf, accessed 9 November 2011.
30 Since there is no published work available, I gratefully acknowledge information about this point provided by Dalila Cabrita Mateus (email to author, 21 March 2012).
31 Norrie MacQueen, *The Decolonization of Portuguese Africa: Metropolitan Revolution and the Dissolution of Empire* (London: Longman, 1997), 133-134.
32 Hundreds of thousands of Portuguese settlers left Mozambique in 1974-1975. Private property was mostly nationalized and claims for indemnity were about to be filed. However, this was "an unrealistic objective and the claims were never finalized". Maria Beatriz Rocha-Trindade, The Repatriation of Portuguese from Africa, in: *The Cambridge Survey of World Migration*, ed. Robin Cohen (Cambridge: Cambridge University Press, 1995), 337-341, here: 338.
33 This is not only due to economic factors but also to the general political situation in Mozambique. Although a multiparty system was introduced in the 1990s, it still remains a difficult task to discuss the colonial past or processes of the

attempt to bring some of them together with a perpetrator of colonial violence would bring 'positive' results more easily. On the contrary, it seems that staging an apology for the filming of a documentary also turns out to be a problematic issue. It not only causes potential constraints on the participants imposed through the medium and seemingly forces apologies. It probably also constitutes the non-visibility of some interactions that took place but were either not filmed nor included in the final edition of the film.

TRANSITIONAL JUSTICE IN PORTUGAL'S POST-REVOLUTIONARY PERIOD

Following is a brief overview of the historical circumstances that characterised the post-revolutionary period in Portugal. It will discuss the transition from authoritarian rule to a democratic government as a troubled process where different approaches were chosen in order to achieve a solution that provided the conditions for a long lasting compromise forming the basis for the Portuguese republic. What is of interest here is the issue of "how societies address legacies of past human rights abuses, mass atrocity, or other forms of severe social trauma, including genocide or civil war, in order to build a more democratic, just, or peaceful future".[34] The background information provided here sheds some light on the unfinished process of transitional justice in Portugal that continued to inform the socio-political situation in the 1990s. This too affected to some extend the reception of the documentary film *Return to Wiriyamu* as will be shown below.

The authoritarian regime of António de Oliveira Salazar lasted for about four decades. Since the beginning of the 1960s, several independent movements challenged its power in the African territories because the *Estado*

---

post-revolutionary period. Frelimo is still the most powerful party and tries to exercise control over the narratives of the past, be it colonial or socialist. M. Anne Pitcher, Forgetting from above and Memory from Below: Strategies of Legitimation and Struggle in Postsocialist Mozambique, *Africa: Journal of the International African Institute* 76, 1 (2006), 88-112.

34 Louis Bickford, Transitional Justice, in: *Encyclopedia of Genocide and Crimes against Humanity,* Vol. 3, ed. Dinah Shelton (Detroit: Macmillan Reference, 2004), 1045-1047, here: 1045.

Novo did not accept negotiations with the movements. The *coup d'etat* on April 25, 1974 abolished the regime and ended the war in the colonies. When the revolution took place, there was only a small opposition to the regime; but this was sufficient to create a critical situation of political radicalisation. The resulting political instability characterised the transition to democracy. Whereas the *Movimento das Forças Armadas* (MFA, Movement of the Armed Forces) solely aimed at stopping the war in the colonies, left wing groups demanded immediate decolonisation and the transfer of power.[35]

In the period of transition from 1974 to 1976, one finds attempts to purge the institutions and the people that collaborated with the authoritarian regime.[36] Compromised mayors, civil servants, headmasters of schools and universities were ousted from office; censorship was abolished; agents of the secret police *Polícia Internacional e de Defesa do Estado* (PIDE) were arrested and waited for their judgement in prison. There was also a significant change in the Armed Forces: Generals, officers and other ranks in the Army, Navy and Air Force were purged and a new generation of young militaries entered the institution.[37]

One of the most important reactions to the purge (led mainly by centre/left wing militaries and politicians) was an attempted coup on November 11, 1975 planned by right wing militaries. This incident marked a turning point in domestic politics in Portugal. From this moment on, issues like "reconciliation" and "pacification" were emphasised by the politics of the government. Consequently, agents of the secret police that had been imprisoned after their arrest were not convicted but freed and reintegrated into the society. The militaries that were admittedly removed from their positions were not made responsible war crimes that they had possibly commit-

---

35 Jorge Ribeiro, *Marcas Da Guerra Colonial* (Porto: Campo das Letras, 1999), 272.

36 António Costa Pinto, Purges and Counter-Purges, in: *Transitional Justice. How emerging democracies reckon with former Regimes*, ed. Neil J. Kritz (Washington, DC: US Institute of Peace Press, 1995), 291-295, here: 291.

37 António Costa Pinto, Ajustando Contas com o Passado na Transição para a Democracia em Portugal, in: *Política da Memória, Verdade ou Justiça na Transição para a Democracia*, ed. Alexandra Barahona Brito (Lisboa: Imprensa de Ciências Sociais, 2004), 87-108, here: 93-94.

ted.[38] Among them was also the former Commander-in-Chief of Mozambique, General Kaúlza de Arriaga, a hardliner of the regime.[39] After having returned from Mozambique, where the Wiriyamu massacre happened while he was in a leading position, this general was involved in a failed *coup d'état* in 1973.[40] His attitude and political point of view contributed to his imprisonment in September 1974 because the MFA was concerned that he would perhaps head a movement that potentially could stop the decolonization of Angola and Mozambique.[41]

Therefore, those responsible for crimes like the massacre of Wiriyamu were not sentenced. This strategy to grant amnesty is well known in transitional settings where newly emerging political players are still dependent on actors of the old regime, in this case the armed forces. Still, it caused an unresolved situation, were questions of guilt were suppressed. Like the 'colonial war' in general, soldiers involved in excessive violence were hence not considered a topic for public debate. Particularly in the 1990 public attempts to discuss certain incidents of the colonial past and their complex and ambiguous consequences slowly started to surface. This also extended to economic developments and social questions like the repatriation of Portuguese settlers from Angola and Mozambique after 1975.[42] The documen-

---

38 Pinto, Ajustando Contas com o Passado, 102-103.
39 Kaúlza de Arriaga, *A Luta Em Moçambique, 1970/1973* (Braga: Intervenção, 1977), 75; Malyn Newitt, *History of Mozambique* (Bloomington: Indiana University Press, 1995), 529-532.
40 Hugo Gil Ferreira and Michael W. Marshall, *Portugal's Revolution: Ten Years On* (Cambridge: Cambridge University Press, 1986), 29-30.
41 Since 1977, Arriaga was involved in a lawsuit against the Portuguese state concerning his 'unjustified' detention. The Supreme Court decided about this trial only in 1987 and convicted the Portuguese State to indemnify. Kaúlza de Arriaga, *Novas Sínteses. Politica, a Africa Portuguesa* (Lisboa: Prefácio, 2001), 125-126.
42 Dalila Cabrita Mateus and Álvaro Mateus, *Angola 61. Guerra Colonial: Causas e consequências; 04 de Fevereiro e o 15 de Março* (Alfragide: Texto, 2011), 209-211.

tary film *Return to Wiriyamu* made by Felícia Cabrita and Paulo Camacho is one of them.[43]

THE DOCUMENTARY RETURN TO WIRIYAMU

The decolonisation of the Portuguese territories in Africa was a prolonged and destructive confrontation characterised by violence. In Mozambique, the armed struggle against the colonial rule started 1964 and lasted for 10 years. One of the most violent incidents of these wars that gained enormous public attention at the time was the massacre of Wiriyamu conducted by Portuguese special troops *Comandos* on December 16, 1972 in the village Wiriyamu, where nearly 400 persons were killed.[44] It became known internationally through a report by Father Adrian Hastings published on July 10, 1973 in the *London Times*, shortly before Marcelo Caetano, the successor of António de Oliveira Salazar, arrived in London for a state visit.[45] Hastings received the information about the killing from Spanish Burgos Fathers, who were working near the crime scene and had managed to smuggle their report out of Africa to Spain. After the violent attack, some of the sur-

---

43 The film is thus a specific moment of a far reaching process of the negotiation in postcolonial relationships that here cannot be elaborated on in more detail. On the cultural dimensions of this process see Fernando Arenas, *Lusophone Africa. Beyond Independence* (Minneapolis: University of Minnesota Press, 2011); Carolin Overhoff Ferreira, *Identity and Difference. Postcoloniality and Transnationality in Lusophone Films* (Münster: Lit, 2012).

44 MacQueen, *The Decolonization of Portuguese Africa*, 48-49; Mustafah Dhada, Contesting Terrains over a Massacre: The Case of Wiriyamu, in: *Contested Terrains and Constructed Categories: Contemporary Africa in Focus*, ed. George C. Bond and Nigel Gibson (Boulder: Westview, 2002), 259-276, here: 265.

45 Some Frelimo key leaders even hold the view that the revelations about the massacre and their impact on the image of Portugal did more for the "revolution than decades of fighting in Mozambique". General Hama Tai quoted in Dhada, Contesting Terrains over a Massacre, 274.

vivors had come to the mission station and the fathers had collected their testimonies.[46]

Nearly three decades had passed, when the documentary film *Return to Wiriyamu* was produced in 1998. There were many reasons for its production. Among them was the changed relationship between Mozambique and Portugal. The end of the civil war in 1992, and the consequently new political conditions[47] offered a chance for a new beginning, regarding economic and personal connections between people in both countries that had been nearly stopped since the short period of rapprochement around 1980, and the official visit of the President of Mozambique Samora Machel in Lisbon in 1983.[48]

---

46 Adrian Hastings, *Wiriyamu* (London: Search Press, 1974); Álvaro B. Marques, *Quem Matou Samora Machel?* (Lisboa: Ulmeiro, 1987), 212.

47 After gaining independence in 1975, the young Mozambican state, a socialist regime under the Frelimo, suffered from destabilization policies driven by Apartheid regimes in South Africa and Rhodesia. This led to a violent war between Frelimo and *Resistência Nacional Moçambicana* (Renamo, National Resistance Movement) that only ended in 1992, when Frelimo and Renamo signed the General Peace Agreement. The first democratic elections took place in 1994. Alice Dinerman, *Revolution, Counter-Revolution and Revisionism in Post-Colonial Africa: The Case of Mozambique, 1975-1994* (London and New York: Routledge, 2006), 29-30.

48 MacQueen, *The Decolonization of Portuguese Africa*, 44-50; William Minter, *King Solomon's Mines Revisited: Western Interests and the Burdened History of Southern Africa* (New York: Basic Books, 1986), 329. This process was part of a broader change in foreign politics, particularly regarding cooperation policies in the *Países Africanos de Língua Portuguesa* (PALOP, Portuguese Speaking African Countries). Portugal, who had left the Development Assistance Committee in 1974, rejoined it in 1991, "when it was beginning to assist the important new nation building processes in the PALOPs, involving peace building, democratisation and economic reform"; *Development Co-Operation Review Series. Portugal*, ed. OECD and DAC (Paris: OECD Publishing, 1997), 7. In 1998, Mozambique was on the first place of the recipients of the Portuguese cooperation; OECD and James H. Michel, *Development Cooperation Report, 1998. Efforts and Policies of the Members of the Development Assistance Committee* (Paris: OECD Publishing, 1999), 123.

The Making Of

The Portuguese journalist Felícia Cabrita began working on the massacre of Wiriyamu in 1992 and is thus part of the above mentioned process. In an interview, Cabrita explained her interest in the massacre of Wiriyamu and referred to the way that the Portuguese Army wrote its official history:

"The only thing that exists is the official version, [there exist] some pages that are false. So, we didn't have one single testimony of somebody who participated in that incident. And history, whenever it is possible, is obviously written with living people, and at best with several people. It is clear that in a work like this, we could not limit ourselves to listen only to one witness."[49]

This also holds true in the broader societal context of Portugal where, after 1974, inconvenient episodes of the wars in Africa were often silenced and kept away from the public. Therefore, speaking to the militaries who conducted the massacre and finding the survivors in order to record their testimonies would provide material to contest the way the wars in Mozambique and elsewhere were historicised.[50]

After having investigated information available about the massacre and after meeting some of the Portuguese soldiers involved in it, Cabrita encountered Antonino Melo who had commanded this operation. While others talked about the committed violence without feelings of regret, the reaction of Melo was different:

"Obviously, I had the idea that he was a monster and postponed the interview with him until the end. I thought I would be badly received. […] many years have passed

---

49 Interview with Felícia Cabrita conducted by the author on 26 July 2010 in Lisbon.
50 See for example the volume on the history of the war in Mozambique published by the General Staff of the Portuguese Armed Forces: Comissão para o Estudo das Campanhas de África, *Resenha histórico-militar das Campanhas de África: Dispositivo das nossas forças: Moçambique* (Lisboa: Estado-Maior do Exército, 1989). Recent publications in military history seem also to be characterised mainly by unilateral perspectives. See Santos Lourenco and Keese, Die blockierte Erinnerung, 239-240.

since then, but in contrast to what I had imagined, I met a suffering man who was conscious about what he had done and who was disturbed because of all this."[51]

The emotional state Melo was in, even two decades after the massacre had been committed, pointed to "a sense of remorse, regret, or sorrow that accompanies admission of a wrong".[52] Following the journalist, this constituted an important condition for his later participation in the documentary. Additionally, the recognition of an offense is often a first step in a process leading to a possible apology that can motivate gestures of forgiveness or even a process of reconciliation.

When Cabrita had spoken to the Portuguese soldiers, she decided to go to Mozambique in order to search for the survivors of this extremely violent incident. She succeeded in finding some of them. Her encounters and interviews with the survivors resulted in an article published in the weekly *Expresso*.[53] Cabrita's commitment in 1992 constitutes an important element in the later process of the production of the documentary film; it enabled her to establish relationships with persons in Portugal and Mozambique who had experienced the violence of Wiriyamu.[54] This social interaction was a crucial basis for the making of the film and consequently provided the framework within which the apology of Antonino Melo would take place. It is, however, important to bear in mind that without the decision of the television channel SIC to invest in the film project, hardly anything would have happened.

The project was proposed to SIC as a part of the series *Grande Reportagem* by Felícia Cabrita and Paulo Camacho, when the 25th anniversary of the massacre was approaching.[55] Cabrita asked Antonino Melo to write a

---

51 Interview Cabrita.
52 Howard-Hassman and Lombardo, Words Require Action, 219.
53 Felícia Cabrita, Os Mortos não sofrem, *Expresso. Revista*, 5 December 1992, 12-21.
54 In her articles, Cabrita uses a journalistic style, mainly based on re-narration of the testimonies given by the survivors of the massacre. This proceeding is criticised by Dhada who states that Cabrita leaves the villagers again "mute". Dhada, Contesting Terrains over a Massacre, 271.
55 Simultaneously, Cabrita did work on another article about the massacre for the journal *Expresso*, which was published shortly after the screening of the docu-

diary about his experience in Mozambique, which later served as one of the main sources for the script of the documentary.[56] Thus, Cabrita had to decide which of the former Portuguese soldiers would be the protagonist of the film. She asked Antonino Melo, "because he had shown great regret during the first work [in 1992 and wanted to] [...] apologise".[57] According to Cabrita, Melo almost immediately agreed upon participating in the film although in similar cases "many former combatants [...] are reluctant or unwilling to participate for fear of reprisal, prosecution or the stigma that could follow such disclosures".[58]

As the presence of a non-convicted war crime perpetrator in Mozambique seemed to be a risky undertaking, the film team took some precautionary measures:

"Supposedly, his [Antonino Melo's] name was horrifying in Mozambique. [...] Therefore, I was very cautious and his name was always hidden. We went along with him pretending that he was our cameraman. Because we had two cameramen, one Portuguese and one from Mozambique that was also working for SIC."[59]

This kind of approach is of course highly ambiguous. On the one hand, Antonino Melo belonged to a unit of the *Commandos* involved in a war crime and had never been prosecuted for it. On the other hand, he was the only one of the Portuguese soldiers who had shown regret, was willing to go to Mozambique and to be confronted with the past. However, this obvious and inevitable dilemma has to be seen in the context of the film, where a kind of exculpation of Antonino Melo is proposed, as will be shown below.

---

mentary on television. Felícia Cabrita, Wiriyamu, *Expresso. Revista*, 21 November 1998, 154-171.

56   Interview Cabrita. As Melo was born in Mozambique, he did not only write about his military experience and the massacre but also about his life in Beira and in the capital Lourenço Marques (now Maputo). One can presume that this twofold narrative had a better chance to be accepted by SIC in comparison to a script that would only include the oral reconstruction of the massacre.

57   Interview Cabrita.

58   Breen Smyth, *Truth Recovery*, 10.

59   Interview Cabrita.

In 1998, the film team went to Mozambique and filmed in Maputo, Beira and in Tête, at places connected to the biography of Antonino Melo. This included places such as the school he went to, the hotel where he spent his honeymoon, and the house in Beira where he used to live as a child. Then, in and near Tête, the team split up. While Paulo Camacho, the cameraman Karl de Sousa and Antonino Melo were filming at sites around Cahora Bassa, at the river Mazói, and at other locations, Felícia Cabrita and the other cameraman Paulo Cepa were searching for the survivors:

"[...] we managed to search for the individuals with whom I had talked five years before. The idea was to find the same persons, bring them to Wiriyamu, where a monument exists that contains some of the bones of the victims [...] There, a meeting with Antonino Melo would take place, but on the condition that neither they nor Melo knew the date on which the encounter would be happening."[60]

Cabrita found some of the survivors and interviewed them again on their experience of the massacre. She met again with the people whose families had been destroyed by the excessive violence of the Portuguese *Commandos* and the involved PIDE agents. At the same time, she was trying to get a sense of how the survivors would react in case of meeting one of the perpetrators:

"I would interview them again and pose always a question in the end: If one day, one of those men came back here in order to apologise for what he did, how would they react? [...] After having talked to everybody, I understood that there was no danger. There was one young man, he was a bit nervous, but I thought that [due to the presence of the oldest] [...] a lack of control was impossible. So, I was relatively calm about the situation."[61]

Taking into account the professionalisation of experts in the context of Truth and Reconciliation Commissions nowadays,[62] it is surely doubtful

---

60 Interview Cabrita.
61 Interview Cabrita.
62 See for example Pumla Gobodo-Madikizela, Intersubjectivity and Embodiment: Exploring the Role of the Maternal in the Language of Forgiveness and Reconciliation, *Signs* 36, 3 (2011), 541-551.

whether a journalist has the capacity, the skills and time to prepare people who suffer from traumatic experiences, for an encounter with a perpetrator. Nonetheless, the survivors accepted to speak with her about the massacre; and despite the preliminary work and judging the potential consequences for Antonino Melo, it was all a risky task. Moreover, it was difficult to foresee the consequences for him in such a situation, as this was no "officially promoted truth recovery mechanism"[63] but only a television project without the approval of the Mozambican authorities. At this point, it is important to mention two further aspects: first, Antonino Melo, as other former combatants of the 'colonial war', had already begun a psychological treatment with the well-known psychiatrist Afonso de Albuquerque before the work on the documentary had started.[64] Secondly, regarding the victims and their preparation for the meeting with the perpetrator there is little information accessible. It can be presumed that they drew on the general background of national reconciliation in Mozambique when they were faced with the situation of how to deal with the presence of Antonino Melo and the film team.[65]

---

63 Breen Smyth, *Truth Recovery*, 8.
64 The group around Albuquerque was the first to recognize the long-term consequences of post-traumatic stress disorder in the case of the former combatants of the 'colonial war' in Portugal. Carlos Anunciação, 'Stress Traumático': Fenómeno, etiologia e tratamento, *Revista de Psicologia Militar* 10 (1997), 147-161, here: 150.
65 A public judgment with a subsequent re-integration of the so-called traitors who collaborated with the colonial regime took place around 1980. It is reported that the 'compromised' showed generally gratitude and enthusiasm for the learning process at those staged meetings framed by a regime of a socialist one party system. The long-term effect of this process is difficult to measure due to the 16-year war. A process of national reconciliation and a silence followed the General Peace Agreement in 1992 over the conflict that had stopped immediately. Former adversaries got along apparently without any "rancor over past abuses". Priscilla B. Hayner, *Unspeakable Truths: Transitional Justice and the Challenge of Truth Commissions* (New York: Routledge, 2011), 200; Andrea Bartoli, Forgiveness and Reconciliation in the Mozambique Peace Process, in: *Forgiveness and Reconciliation. Religion, Public Policy & Conflict Transformation*, ed. Raymond G. Helmick and Rodney Lawrence Petersen (Philadelphia: Tem-

When the day of the meeting arrived, the teams made an appointment at the memorial of Wiriyamu. Until that particular moment, the protagonists in the film – the victims and the perpetrator – had only spoken about their experiences separately in the presence of a journalist, the camera, and the cameraman. The encounter was thus a particular situation because it implied a personal face-to-face confrontation between victims and the perpetrator, who had not met before.

When remembering the encounter between the survivors and Melo, Felícia Cabrita foregrounded three aspects. The first is connected to her personal experience and her work as a journalist. At the moment when Melo approached the group standing next to the monument and started to introduce himself as the commander of the troops that had committed the massacre,

"[…] it was somehow one of the most impressing moments in my work as a journalist, and I always do complicated jobs. But I think it was the only time that I got emotionally involved and had to turn around, when Melo started to speak […] I had to turn around, I could not hold it and started to cry."[66]

The second aspect mentioned by Cabrita relates to a reaction of one of the survivors who recognises Melo not primarily as a perpetrator but as the one who had spared some lives in the situation of the mass killing:

"The girl [Augusta Creya] who had told me five years before, when I had done the first work, that a blond man had saved her and her mum in those conditions, gave

---

pleton Foundation Press, 2001), 361-382. For the issue of the "compromised" see the homepage by Colin Darch: The Comprometidos, 1978-1982, Mozambique History Net, http://www.mozambiquehistory.net/comprometidos.html, accessed 27 February 2012. Some information about this is also provided in a personal account of a former colonial soldier who also participated in the massacre of Wiriyamu: Dalila Cabrita Mateus, Valeriano Baúlque. Entrevista, in: *Memórias do Colonialismo e da Guerra*, ed. Dalila Cabrita Mateus (Porto: ASA, 2006), 649-659, here: 657-658.

66 Interview Cabrita.

Melo a hug and thanked him. [...] On the one hand, it is revolting [...] It is difficult. [...] Because they knew that this man had destroyed their families."⁶⁷

In this statement, the ambiguity regarding Melo as a brutal perpetrator becomes evident. The monstrousness of the soldier as a killing machine is humanized. The gesture of embracing described by Cabrita underscores this view. It is however not evident that this is a gesture of forgiveness.⁶⁸ One can presume that her reaction demonstrates mainly how grateful she is for not having been murdered. However, the question whether she forgives Melo for murdering parts of her family, is not explicitly mentioned and therefore remains open.

The third aspect emphasised by Cabrita has to do with the local Chief. After Melo did apologise and after the spontaneous reaction of the girl, it was the Oldest to express his view regarding the apology brought forward by Melo.

"And the answer of the oldest was 'There were a lot of wars after that one, and even worse ones'. [...] That people suffered a lot, not only with our presence but also afterwards continued to suffer. But there exists a capacity of accepting the adversary and accepting the other who comments on his behaviour and [and the deeds committed]."⁶⁹

Here, the excessive violence of December 1972 is contextualized in the postcolonial history of Mozambique. Following independence, the country did not reach peace but entered in another armed conflict due to its geopolitical situation as a neighbour of Apartheid states like South Africa. Another fact mentioned by Cabrita is the virtue of those Mozambicans who are able to accept a perpetrator who explains his deeds done in the past. But in this case, such a reaction could at most be conceived as the starting point

---

67 Interview Cabrita.
68 Gobodo-Madikizela describes a case where women forgive the person that had murdered their sons by expressing their forgiveness verbally and through the gesture of embracing. Both verbal explanation and gesture of the women are preceded by specific emotions that trigger feelings of empathy. Gobodo-Madikizela, Intersubjectivity and Embodiment, 346-347.
69 Interview Cabrita.

for the beginning of a process of dialogue and acknowledgment, because there are no convincing signs and expressions of forgiveness or reconciliation.

In Cabrita's view, the apology of Antonino Melo was well received and accepted by the survivors. Therefore, the journalistic practice, the documentary film work and the interaction with and between the different actors involved in this process apparently had a positive outcome. She remembers that on the day after the encounter Melo was spending time with the survivors on their *machambas* (vegetable garden, small territories for subsistence agriculture), looking at the cattle and having lunch with them. It seems that "he had become a family member from one day to another".[70] This comment suggests a constructive effect of Melo's apology on the survivors who welcomed him and got along with him. It is however necessary to question this perspective, ask for other reactions to the apology of Antonino Melo, and explore if his gesture led to forgiveness or even reconciliation. In order to do this, it will be necessary to analyze not only the making of the film but also the film in its final version as broadcasted on the television channel SIC in November 1998.

The edited version

In order to reconstruct the historical events, the documentary *Return to Wiriyamu* relies mainly on personal accounts of eyewitnesses. The central figures of the film are the officer Antonino Melo who commanded the massacre and the surviving victims of Wiriyamu. The film is structured as follows: In the first part, it focuses on the biography of Melo, in particular on his childhood, youth and early manhood. These stages in his live are connected to places in Maputo and Beira. Furthermore, his military education is highlighted in order to explain the ideological background and cultural context Melo's generation was influenced by. In this section, a considerable amount of footage is used. Towards the second part of the film, the team gets closer and closer to Tête. There, the encounter takes place at Wiriyamu and Melo apologises for his deeds to the survivors of the massacre. Afterwards, the documentary brings together different points of view in order to reconstruct the massacre of Wiriyamu without any reference to archival im-

---

70 Interview Cabrita.

ages. Among the collected voices are the testimonies of survivors, Spanish fathers and sisters of the mission in Tête, former colonial soldiers, and of Antonino Melo. Consequently, within the structure of the film the narrative gains a new dimension: the monologue of Antonino Melo is enriched by northern-Mozambican voices that give a view on the experience of the victims. Through the video interviews, the survivors are able to tell an experience firsthand that until then was just known to the public through the mediation of Spanish missionaries, a few newspaper articles, and scarce historiographical accounts.[71]

The encounter between Antonino Melo and the survivors took place at the memorial for the victims of Wiriyamu. Melo reaches the place by car and after leaving, the camera follows him while approaching the group waiting for him. Here, a deep synthesiser sound is introduced and creates suspense. Melo joins the group and since everyone knows about the purpose of the meeting, he comes straight to the point using the following words:

"Good day. You are the Oldest? Many years ago, I was the commander of the Commandos that came to this village and killed a lot of people, like you remember, at that time we were all young and got orders from our generals to come here and kill the villagers. 25 years later I am here again, I want to honour the dead, those who died that day, and I would like to apologise to the survivors for everything that happened."[72]

In his statement Melo mentions different aspects. First, he chooses to address Baera, the Oldest, whom he thus considers the most important person in this situation. The Oldest here is probably seen as a respected person with authority and decision power. Supposedly, there are hopes by Melo that if Baera would forgive him, the other survivors would follow his way.

---

71 See for example José Amaro, *Massacres Na Guerra Colonial: Documentos Secretos: Tete, Um Exemplo* (Lisboa: Ulmeiro, 1976). The individual meaning of each testimony is modified by their inclusion into the narrative of the documentary film. But in the separate shots, viewers are still confronted with the survivors that tell the stories of their suffering, sometimes looking straight into the camera. Such records have definitely a different impact than a written re-narration of their experience.

72 Cabrita and Camacho, *Regresso a Wiriyamu*, 00:32:38-00:33:20.

A second point consists in acknowledging the mass murder of the villagers in 1972 – an important point, since the Portuguese Armed Forces had officially denied the killing of the 400 people.[73] But Melo does not fully admit his guilt. Instead, he expresses his leading role in the incident using the third person plural to indicate that he was part of a military unit that committed the massacre. Thus, he avoids connecting a specific deed to his very person. Thirdly, he makes a distinction between his identity as a young man and soldier that aims at attributing the guilt to the Commander-in-Chief or other commanders and therefore to factors that he as an individual obviously could not influence because he and the commandos unit were only 'following orders'. Furthermore, he tries to introduce a broader human practice that respects the memory of the dead. This appears to be a universal condition, but in fact one has to be careful here, as perspectives on how the dead are to be honoured might differ in the context of military tradition, religion or in more broader terms of Portuguese and northern Mozambican society and culture.[74] Melo finally states that he returned in order to apologise *to* the survivors. But an apology is not only addressed at a particular individual or group, it also should include a specification of the wrongs committed. Melo dismisses such clarity by declaring "for everything that happened". Considering the reflections of Smith one would have to problematize the status of this statement as an apology, for it does not correspond to what Smith defines as a "categorical apology".[75] It seems that this is a moment of avoiding to take responsibility. However, the way in which Melo articulates his apology can also be seen in relation to the emotions that appear in such situations: Commonly shame, guilt, embarrassment, remorse, and regret emerge.[76] In the view of Cabrita, as Melo speaks, his "voice is faltering"

---

73 But since he comes as a private person embedded in a film project and not as a representative of the army, this acknowledgment has its limits, especially having in mind any kind of material reparations.

74 For apologies in diverse religious and cultural context, see Smith, *I Was Wrong*, 114-125.

75 Among a variety of aspects, identification of harm is central to the categorical apology: "The offender will identify each harm, taking care not to conflate several harms into one general harm or apologize for only a lesser offense or the 'wrong wrong'." Ibid., 141.

76 Ibid., 101.

and he "is ashamed" of the past wrongs.[77] Moreover, it seems that there is another emotion to be considered. Notice that Melo is somewhat aloof as he speaks and that this uneasiness is potentially owed to feelings of prudence and/or fear. Both Felícia Cabrita and the cameraman Karl de Sousa are convinced that Melo was seriously worried about the encounter. He even had an escape plan in case of an attempt of taking revenge. Therefore, the avoidance to designate his particular deeds in the very beginning of the encounter possibly reveals a certain precaution. In this respect, one could also speak of a strategic character that informs the speech of Antonino Melo.

After the apology, Baera, the Oldest, answers him in local language,[78] which is then translated into Portuguese by an interpreter who remains invisible:

"[…] we don't bear you any grudge, because we know very well that war is war, because it wasn't you alone, it was an order to conduct the massacre here. Now it is necessary that we get along well with you."[79]

Baera asserts that there is no danger for Melo and sets the frame for a peaceful interaction without vengeance. He acknowledges the situation of war as well as the conditions mentioned by Melo, and is thus following the provided argument of attributing the guilt to others and not primarily to this specific person. However, what follows neither constitutes an explicit acceptance of Melo's apology nor does it express any kind of forgiveness. Instead, the Oldest just points to a future process of getting closer and establishing a good relationship. In his position as authority he obviously proceeds in a cautious manner.

Besides the verbal exchange, one has to consider another moment at the beginning of the encounter. After having expressed the apology and having received the answer from the Oldest, Melo moves towards him and reaches

---

77 Cabrita, *Massacres em África*, 277.
78 Curiously, while he is speaking, Baera does not appear in a medium close up, as Melo does. Instead, the camera keeps focusing on Melo, in a medium shot/medium close up shot. The voice of Baera is even lowered and an inner monologue by Melo who explains his nervousness is superimposed on the voice that speaks in a local language.
79 Cabrita and Camacho, *Regresso a Wiriyamu*, 00:33:38-00:34:01.

out his hand. The offer for shaking hands is accepted by Baera who also moves towards the other. This physical interaction seemingly closes the scene in front of the camera and suggests that the apology might have a positive effect on the future relation between the former aggressor and the victims. Nevertheless, as I have shown above, such a gesture can have various interpretations. Therefore, one could on the contrary presume that there is little empathy here between the protagonists, as they did not embrace.[80] Shaking hands in this case can also signal a gendered dimension of apology due to forms of masculinity that are connected to cultural and different social settings (e.g. military education). Somehow, as they do not show emotions and as the film does not give any further clues of the recorded moment – at the level of the voice over, for instance – it is difficult to understand whether there were other signs and/or gestures of acceptance or forgiveness.[81]

After Melo's apology, conversations between the victims and the perpetrator took place near the monument where they talked about what had happened on the day of the massacre. The film puts parts of this encounter and parts of the previously recorded interviews with the respective protagonists together in order to reconstruct the massacre. Here, a series of tensions and difficulties become visible.

As Cabrita mentioned, there was one of the survivors who was a bit "nervous".[82] But at least two survivors of the massacre in the film did not seem to welcome the presence of the Portuguese military: António Michone

---

80 Such a physical interaction happened for instance during the Lusaka Meeting in June 1974, where Foreign Minister of Portugal, Mário Soares embraced the future President of Mozambique Samora Machel, "an attempt to fix the talks from the beginning in a non-adversarial context". MacQueen, *The Decolonization of Portuguese Africa*, 133. The gesture of embracing plays also a significant role in other apologetic context as observes Gobodo-Madikizela, Intersubjectivity and Embodiment, 546-547.

81 This view based on the film can be contrasted with Cabrita's perspective. She writes that while Baera answered, the "rest of the group nods with every word of the Oldest. Tenente, the rudest, perhaps motivated by the reaction of the others, alleviates and greets him [Melo]." It is a moment that is not visible in the documentary. Cabrita, *Massacres em África*, 278.

82 Interview Cabrita.

and Vasco Tenente. The case of Vasco Tenente deserves special attention because this specific case allows us to observe how through the use of cinematic montage the different perspectives of the historical event brought forward by each of the participating protagonists come together. Furthermore, Tenente plays a crucial role in complicating the issue of apology that is at stake here. This will also become evident later when analysing the end of the film, where he and Melo appear.

The problematic dimension of the encounter is already visible in the scene of the apology, where the camera focuses not only on the interaction between Baera, the Oldest, and Melo, but also observes the face of one of the survivors, Vasco Tenente. The viewers can see his rather hostile facial expression framed by a close up, which emphasises the expressed emotional state associated to feelings like non-acceptance, anger, or grudge. This reaction of rejection is connected to the fact that he lost his whole family in the massacre. Framed by a medium long shot, Tenente stands in front of Melo and explains: "I am alone, my mother, my brothers died here because of the war. This is the only thing that I can tell you."[83]

In the beginning of this section of the film, Antonino Melo explains that there was an order to 'clean up the zone' which meant murdering everyone present there. In December 1972 the systematic murder started, although violent interrogations conducted by the PIDE agents did not reveal any connections between the locals and the Mozambican Liberation Front Frelimo. Melo acknowledges that due to a lack of ammunition it was not possible to kill all villagers by shooting and that it was he who took the decision to gather people in the huts and kill them by throwing grenades into the huts:

"One began to put the people into the huts, in groups, and the soldiers threw grenades in there, either they died burning or the ones that eventually managed to flee were shot."[84]

Melo's explanations about the massacre given in the shade of a tree can be seen as a late oral confession that breaks with the conventions of military discipline – turning public a war crime as a former member of the armed

---

83 Cabrita and Camacho, *Regresso a Wiriyamu*, 00:34:08-00:34:19.
84 Cabrita and Camacho, *Regresso a Wiriyamu*, 00:39:31-00:39:42.

forces. Interestingly, Melo uses the third person "one" in this instance indicating therefore a collective action. Such a statement can be regarded as problematic in this apologetic context because the "active voice claims responsibility. The passive does not."[85] Only several scenes later in the film he affirms, "I reached the point, where I threw a grenade into a hut". After the explosion, Melo remembers, the roof of the hut blew up. Finally, the huts were burned with the villagers inside.

The survivors confirm this proceeding although with some differences. At the memorial site, Vasco Tenente, whose mother died in the massacre, speaks about his survival: "Then, they put us into the hut of my mother. When we were inside [...] they closed the door and threw in a grenade."[86] He continues:

"When I was with my mother in the hut, [...]. We did hide under the cereal pot. When we were under the cereal pot, the door opened with the explosion. I took that way and escaped."[87]

When Tenente explains how he escaped, images from the second camera show him together with António Melo at the memorial site and thereby make the dialogical structure of the meeting at the memorial visible. As Gobodo-Madikizela observes in the context of Truth and Reconciliation Commissions in South Africa, such a dialogue can allow "victims and survivors to revisit the sites of trauma, [...]. Through dialogue, victims as well as the greater society come to recognize perpetrators as human beings who failed morally."[88]

Another person who appears in the film and who contributes to Tenente's testimony is Baúque, a former colonial soldier of the Special Forces *Commandos*.[89] He already affirmed in an earlier scene that villagers trying

---

85 Smith, *I Was Wrong*, 35.
86 Cabrita and Camacho, *Regresso a Wiriyamu*, 00:40:33-00:40:47.
87 Cabrita and Camacho, *Regresso a Wiriyamu*, 00:40:53-00:41:09.
88 Gobodo-Madikizela, Intersubjectivity and Embodiment, 543.
89 Like most of the former African soldiers that appear in the film, Baúque was interviewed in Maputo and not in Wiriyamu. All these Mozambicans had passed through the process of the *Comprometidos* in the 1970s (see footnote 65). But they had not revealed details about the massacre at that time. Both Felícia Cabri-

to escape were also shot and confirms here that he remembers a child running away during the massacre. As Vasco Tenente says it was not easy to escape from the murdering: "Then, they wanted to kill me and shot at me, I did not count how many times they shot at me."[90] His account is followed again by a statement of the former colonial soldier, who asserts, that he did not try to shoot at a child he saw running away. What remains open in the juxtaposition of these two statements is whether the child Baúque saw was in fact Tenente or another person or whether other soldiers of the *Commandos* had tried to shot Tenente.

In this scene, the perspectives of survivors and perpetrators on the massacre are spliced together in a particular way. The filmic montage of the different testimonies enables to confront the accounts of Vasco Tenente, Melo, and Baúque with each other. But there is no voice off that would explain or guide the viewer's attention to assure the 'truth' of one of the versions. The viewer is left with an impression of uncertainty about whose memories might be right. However, the survivor's testimonies have a strong impact and the film foregrounds, although in a very particular way, the physical marks that the colonial violence had left on their bodies. In this context, their scars provide evidence for the committed acts and authenticate their narratives. Consequently, the film assures that there is no doubt that the Portuguese commandos committed those violent acts. On the other hand, there is an impression that the veterans of the *Commandos* intend to safeguard the image of the colonial armed forces from crimes like killing children or raping women. Various survivors also address such aspects in the film; however, the perpetrators neither confirm nor deny them directly.[91] In such particular scenes of the film, one is confronted with the fact

---

ta and Camilo de Sousa confirm that it was only when Antonino Melo arrived in Maputo for the making of the documentary that they spoke about what happened in December 1972. The reason for this was firstly, that, they were still accepting Melo as their (former) superior. Secondly, they were assured that the documentary was not to be broadcasted on Mozambican television.

90 Cabrita and Camacho, *Regresso a Wiriyamu*, 00:41:09-00:41:39.
91 Melo assumes that the massacre was a *criminal act*. Although in some moments of the documentary he does not fully recognise the violent acts of the massacre described by the survivors (rape for instance). He just affirms that the area of the village was so big that he could not control every move of the soldiers. There-

that this documentary is no formal truth recovery process that can provide "a structure within which irreconcilable accounts can be juxtaposed and compared". On the contrary, it appears, that sometimes "the contest between divergent accounts [...] occur[s] in a piecemeal [...] fashion".[92]

The tension between Vasco Tenente and Antonino Melo is not resolved at the end of the film. Instead, both of them are shown in separate scenes at the memorial of Wiriyamu and this in turn highlights the ambiguous effects of the encounter and the apology. First, Tenente appears:

"Twenty five years passed and we are still collecting the bones. Here, a lot of people died. [...] A lot of people died in the forest and we were still not able to collect all of the bones. When I find some of the bones, I have to store them at the monument."[93]

After this statement, Tenente puts the collected bones into a small repository at the monument. It seems that he, whose family was killed during the massacre, is still struggling with this loss. The images and his account about how he and others relate to this place that constitutes a crucial point in their biographies, suggest that Tenente did not forgive Melo for the things he had done. Like in other cases, "certain kinds of damage and judgments may nevertheless linger indefinitely".[94] This impression is underscored in the film insofar as Tenente is shown alone at the memorial and not together with Melo.

In the next sequence, Antonino Melo visits the memorial. As he approaches the monument the camera follows him and the voice off reflects his thoughts:

"During many years, I tried to forget the hell of that day. I decided to go back in order to resolve this story definitely and find some tranquillity. I even thought that they would kill me. But it turned out worse. Those who I destroyed welcomed me

---

    fore, Melo doubts some of the related acts and states: "I didn't see such things and don't know if they happened." Cabrita and Camacho, *Regresso a Wiriyamu*, 00:30:27-00:31:32.
92 Breen Smyth, *Truth Recovery*, 9.
93 Cabrita and Camacho, *Regresso a Wiriyamu*, 00:57:29-00:58:19.
94 Smith, *I Was Wrong*, 133.

peacefully and without critique. It was hard for me to understand them. What we did, was a criminal act."[95]

The violence at Wiriyamu, it seems, marked also some kind of turning point in the biography of Antonino Melo. His memory of the incident persisted and created feelings of remorse that he wanted to get rid of through the encounter with the survivors. As it turns out, it was he who could not forgive himself whereas some of the villagers showed a reconciliatory attitude.[96] Melo's inner conflict is visualised by the image of the small repository in the memorial with the bones inside and covered by a glass window. There, against the background of the mortal remains, the mirror image of Antonino Melo appears.

The documentary proposes that the apology had limited effects. No embracing, no hand shaking, not even a joint visit to the memorial in the end. These two sides of the story of the massacre of Wiriyamu seem to continue being irreconcilable. But the juxtaposition of solitary rites of mourning and persisting troubling memories suggests a very ambiguous idea, namely that both survivor and perpetrator are haunted by the past. Their present lives are conditioned by what they experienced in 1972. It seems contradictory, but this leads to the effect, that – to a certain extend – the figure of Melo becomes a 'victim' as well, as he 'suffers' from what he has done.[97] Conse-

---

95 Cabrita and Camacho, *Regresso a Wiriyamu*, 00:58:20-00:58:54.
96 Others, of course, did not welcome the initiative of Melo as the example of Vasco Tenente shows. One has to be cautious here. The dramatic aspect created by the documentary film does not necessarily mean that there had been a real tension between Tenente and Melo. Rather, one could think of this also as a filmic relationship that is shaped by conventions of television film making that often try to produce effects of suspense or surprise in order to convince the viewers to stay watching the programme.
97 In an earlier scene, Melo describes how he and his unit went a second time to the crime scene at the beginning of the year 1973 in order to remove the corpses. After 'cleaning up', the *Commandos* got into an ambush. It is suggested that this was an attempt by the Portuguese Armed Forces to kill those soldiers who were not only perpetrators but also eyewitnesses of that massacre. Thus, Melo claims that he was an aim for attack. However, he was only a quasi victim because he eventually managed to dominate the situation.

quently, and despite all the efforts of giving voice to those survivors without a voice, the documentary also constructs a rather ambiguous 'community of victims'[98] that once participated in the same historical event. Here, one can observe a specific victimizing discourse that shapes the figure of the perpetrator; Melo is not only conceived as the confessing soldier, but his characterization in the documentary points to a dimension of a man who was part of a generation of about 800,000 male Portuguese who participated in a mandatory military service in the 'colonial war'.[99] His psychological and filmic victimization corresponds to an often-articulated opinion in Portugal, stating that those young men were sacrificed by the *Estado Novo* while implicitly downplaying their potential agency and responsibility for violent acts committed in the former colonies.[100] This argument is also brought forward by the documentary film: Although Melo admits in the end that the massacre was a crime, he is ultimately not the one to be sentenced to have been guilty of this violence. One could rather, as the film suggests, hold the former Commander-in-Chief of the then colony Mozambique responsible for it. This was, as a caption reads in the closing credits of the film, General Kaúlza de Arriaga.

---

98 This is a term used by Judith Keilbach in order to analyse the specific inclusion and treatment of *Zeitzeugen* in television documentaries. She explains that there is a recent trend to present a community of people that exists due to the common participation in the same historical event. There, one can observe a blurred distinction between victims and perpetrators. Judith Keilbach, Zeugen, Deutsche Opfer und traumatisierte Täter: Zur Inszenierung von Zeitzeugen in bundesdeutschen Fernsehdokumentationen über den Nationalsozialismus, *Tel Aviver Jahrbuch für deutsche Geschichte* 31 (2003), 287-306, here: 300-301.

99 Additionally, as the film tells in its first half, Melo's family belonged to the group of 'returnees' that after the end of colonial rule in Mozambique left the country and lost nearly all their belongings due to the political circumstances at the time.

100 Such a victimizing discourse is for instance provided by the Monument to the Overseas Combatants in Lisbon, which also includes a memorial that honours the approximately 9,000 fallen Portuguese soldiers of the 'War in Overseas'. Teresa Pinheiro, Portugiesische Erinnerungskulturen, http://www.tu-chemnitz. de/phil/europastudien/swandel/erinnerung/kolonialkrieg.htm, accessed 3 November 2011.

Conclusion

The analysis shows that the documentary film by Felícia Cabrita and Paulo Camacho is a complex audiovisual articulation connected to specific socio-historical circumstances of the postcolonial relationships between persons from Mozambique and Portugal. It reflects the sophisticated and ambiguous nature of apologies for past wrongs. Through the critical observation and examination of the micro level of social interaction of this particular apologetic context, the difficulties, ambiguities and emotions connected to this situation were considered. The film and its background exemplify how victimhood and perpetration can be re-negotiated and modified. Simultaneously it also demonstrates how the effects of past wrongs continue to have a persisting impact on relationships between survivors and perpetrators up to the present.

The film provided a specific framework for the apology of Antonino Melo, who, as one of the perpetrators, came back to Mozambique and visited Wiriyamu in order to apologise for his deeds to the survivors. Although a respectable and courageous act, the apology situation captured by the film proves to be ambiguous possibly due to the fact that victims and perpetrators had not spoken directly to each other before. In this context, the apology seems to be a starting point rather than the outcome of a common endeavour.

As this analysis indicates, the structure of the filming process and the final media product differ to a considerable extend. Whereas Felícia Cabrita highlights a rather productive outcome, the film centres on the antagonistic positions of Antonino Melo and Vasco Tenente. The confrontation and filmic juxtaposition of the testimonies of Melo, other former colonial soldiers, and the survivors, does not only reveal difficulties in reconstructing the history of the massacre, but they, too, hint at the problematic filmic construction of a 'community of victims'. The film argues to a certain extend that the issue of the massacre is resolved neither between victims and perpetrators nor in relation to the former responsible leading militaries of the Portuguese Armed Forces.

In Portugal, the latter alludes to unfinished processes of transitional justice and is reflected by the subsequent debate, after the broadcasting of the documentary on television that centred on the figure of the former Commander-in-Chief of Mozambique. Several journalists took up the opportunity to investigate the possibility of convicting General Kaúlza de Arriaga for the massacre committed during his service in Mozambique.[101] However, the Portuguese law determined prescription of such crimes after 15 years and thus did not enable a judgment of General Arriaga. In other words, despite the public discussion, Arriaga was not charged and did not change his attitude regarding the 'allegedly' mass murder. When speaking about Wiriyamu, he continued to communicate the 'official' version stating "that approximately 60 persons died, among them terrorists and non-terrorists".[102] He thereby ignores

"[…] the reality of much of the tragedy of the war. Not only does he deny the significance of the massacres of civilians by the troops under his command, he also denies the disastrous conditions of the war, preferring to see the events of 1974 and the subsequent independence of the colonies as acts of political treason."[103]

This point of view is contradicted by the documentary, despite all ambiguities and problems resulting from the editing and framing of the accounts of the interviewed survivors.[104] In this respect, one cannot underestimate the value of the collected testimonies of the victims included in the film; because they constitute a crucial element in constructing an audiovisual evidence of the violence carried out by the Portuguese Armed Forces during the war of decolonisation in Mozambique. As a journalist wrote, "the television documentary about the massacre of Wiriyamu […] recovered the

---

101 Miguel Carvalho, Amaral quer julgar Kaúlza, *O Independente*, 5.
102 Kaúlza de Arriaga quoted in João Paulo Guerra, *Descolonização Portuguesa: O Regresso das Caravelas* (Lisboa: Oficina dos Livros, 2009), 61.
103 Paulo de Medeiros, Hauntings. Memory, Fiction and the Portuguese Colonial Wars, in: *The Politics of War Memory and Commemoration*, ed. Timothy G. Ashplant (London: Routledge, 2000), 209-210.
104 Here, one could still complicate the picture and point to the linguistic dimension of the audiovisual testimonies. Some are given in broken Portuguese, others in local language, and then translated in subtitles. Does an account given in Portuguese offer the same opportunities for articulation of suffering as the mother tongue? Hence, this alludes to the broad field of postcolonial linguistic politics in the PALOP.

memory of this genocide of 400 Mozambicans – men, women and children".[105]

These brief remarks point to a broader field of postcolonial relationships, in which the complex consequences of the war of decolonisation are discussed. This unfolding panorama of transnational memory practices that in the meantime goes beyond questions of guilt and is thus enabling new and other forms of interaction needs further investigation in order to acquire more detailed and differentiated insights. It appears to be an urgent task because the common future and relationships between people from African and European states may also depend on the negotiation of the colonial past and wrongs connected to this shared history. In this respect, it will be crucial to discuss in a productive manner not only wrongs of the colonial period but the post-revolutionary processes in the countries of both continents as well. Some attempts pointing in this direction are already visible in a series of countries.[106] In the context of globalised media representation, this holds true also for documentary productions. Since *Return to Wiriyamu* a number of documentaries have been produced on the topic of decolonisation in Portugal and other countries as well. By and large, these films aim at the production and transmission of knowledge about decolonisation, by bringing together the actors in these processes.[107] An analysis of these films is yet to be made and can be productive for the understanding of the complex dimensions of decolonisation, the cultural dimensions of memory politics and their negotiation in moving images.

---

105 Comment by Fernando Couto about the film in the weekly *Domingo* on 14 February 1999; Fernando Couto, *Vivências Moçambicanas* (Maputo: Ndjira, 2010), 73.

106 Regarding Portugal: Patrick Chabal, Nós e a África. A Questão do Olhar, *Africana Studia* 1, 1 (1999), 67-84; Pinheiro, Facetten der Erinnerungskultur, 21; Robert Stock, 'Zusammenhalt und Einheit aller Kämpfer'. Die museale Repräsentation des Portugiesischen Kolonialkrieges (1961-1974) in der Gegenwart, *Berliner Debatte Initial* 20, 3 (2009), 117-26.

107 The effects and consequences of these films, such as the series by Joaquim Furtado entitled *The War. The Colonial, The War of Independence, The Overseas War* (RTP/Correio da Manhã 2009) are to be analysed by future investigations.

Facing Postcolonial Entanglement and the Challenge of Responsibility
Actor Constellations between Namibia and Germany[1]

REINHART KÖSSLER

As has been argued persuasively, Germany emerged in 1919 as the first "postcolonial nation in a still-colonial world".[2] Under the Treaty of Versailles, she was stripped of her colonial possessions, which entailed what has been termed "phantom pain"[3] – at least to a point in time when German national identity and indeed, existence had been put to enormously more momentous hazards. The years following World War II were occupied by various efforts to grapple with the grave and violent heritage of the Nazi

---

1   This contribution reflects part of my research carried out within the research and capacity building project "Reconciliation and social conflict in the aftermath of large-scale violence in Southern Africa: The cases of Angola and Namibia", which is based at the Arnold Bergstraesser Institute, Freiburg and funded by the programme "Knowledge for Tomorrow" of the Volkswagen Foundation.
2   Marcia Klotz, The Weimar Republic: A Post-Colonial State in a Still-Colonial World, in: *Germany's Colonial Pasts*, ed. Eric Ames et al. (Lincoln: University of Nebraska Press, 2005), 135-147, here: 141.
3   Leo Kreutzer, Deutsche Heimat und afrikanische Wahlheimat in Hans Grimms Roman "Volk ohne Raum". Zur Dekolonisierung eines "Kolonialismus ohne Kolonien", in: *Erinnern verhandeln: Kolonialismus im kollektiven Gedächtnis Afrikas und Europas*, ed. Steffi Hobuss and Ulrich Lölke (Münster: Westfälisches Dampfboot, 2007), 179-193, here: 179.

war of expansion and the Holocaust. Overall, the colonial past was sidelined in this process in public memory. Such 'colonial amnesia' has been questioned in particular in connection with the genocide perpetrated by the *Schutztruppe* (German colonial army) in 1904-1908 in what was then German Southwest Africa, today independent Namibia.[4] One may speak of partial re-activation of a repressed content of public memory, which at least in its mainstream is linked to a clear re-evaluation, in effect reversing former interpretations. At the same time, this process forms part of a larger, transnational process of remembrance linked to wider post-colonial concerns, focusing here particularly on memory politics going on in Namibia. In this way, we observe a further stage of entangled history between Namibia and Germany that has been initiated during the 19th century, even several decades before formal colonisation took place in 1884. Concurrently, this perspective leads, on several levels to the politics of such post-colonial, transnational remembrance.

Along with a brief rehearsal of the historical record, the following paper addresses a case of transnational and post-colonial politics of apology and reconciliation, which is of considerable current relevance and presents an experience still in the making. Negotiations and conflicts about the past and its meaning have acted on strategies of amnesia and marginalisation on both sides. The over-all process involves a surprising array of actors in a rather complex web that cannot be exhausted here. Still, as will emerge from the exposition, governments and non-state actors have mobilised divergent meanings and understandings of reconciliation. However, all these conceptions relate to one set of historical events, the Namibian War of 1903-1908.

I begin by sketching out the divergent trajectories of remembrance that relate to the genocide, both in Namibia and in Germany. In the former, complexity is added by regional differences while in the latter case the discussion is inserted into the broader issues of post-World War II memory politics. This is followed by a closer look at the mnemoscape in Namibia contrasting memory practices and concerns of German speakers with those of descendants from the victims of genocide. I then recount exemplary memory practices amongst Ovaherero and Nama in Central and Southern Na-

---

4 As is usual in the literature, the term 'Namibia' will pertain to the country even before it was finally officially adopted at the time of independence in 1990. Occasionally, GSWA or SWA will be used.

mibia. These practices testify to communal resilience and contrast starkly with the hegemonic, nationalist master narrative of the ruling party South West Africa People's Organization (SWAPO), which focuses on the experience of the Northern regions. What emerges is a tension-ridden web of concerns and claims, both to spaces and to recognition. With a view particularly to the ongoing negotiation process of historical memory between Namibia and Germany, a closer look at how Namibians of various strands construe 'Germany' then provides further background for an understanding of this process itself, which has evolved in highly conflictual ways since the Namibian independence in 1990. This account then contrasts in particular state and non-state actors, the latter, mainly Namibian victims, represented by traditional leaders, and German advocacy groups. Noting the turning point of the centennial of the genocide in 2004, the process is taken up to the dramatic events surrounding the return of human skulls in Berlin in September 2011. In this way, the difficulties involved in unravelling the complex post-colonial situation are highlighted. Further, light is shed on the ways in which clearly divergent interests and concerns link up with post-colonial memory issues.

THE FIRST GENOCIDE OF THE 20TH CENTURY AND ITS REMEMBRANCE

Most serious scholars concur that the campaigns of the *Schutztruppe* during the Namibian War amounted to the perpetration of genocide.[5] This refers above all to the intent to annihilate not just combatants, but entire ethnic groups by various means. The same goes for the chain of command reaching to the General Staff and the government in Berlin as well as to the emperor. The genocide was perpetrated, in a first stage by sealing off the waterless Omaheke steppe in Eastern Namibia not allowing Ovaherero fugitives to return to areas where they could survive. A second phase, this time also targeting Nama, is marked by concentration camps where men, women, and children were interned and forced to labour under conditions that resulted in exorbitant death rates. This was complemented by deportations,

---

5   Marion Wallace, *A History of Namibia. From the Beginning to 1990* (London: Hurst, 2011), 177-182.

both inside Namibia and to the German colonies of Togo and Cameroon. A third stage refers to the Native Ordinances that stripped groups deemed insurgent of their land and worked towards transforming them into a docile labour resource by means of stiff pass laws, ceilings on settlement strength, and a prohibition to own large stock, which destroyed the symbolic fabric of Herero society.[6] The resultant structure of settlement and land ownership is the hallmark of the landscape and settlement pattern in Central and Southern Namibia still today.

Nevertheless, the survivors did coalesce to reassert the communal nexuses that had been shaken to their foundations. South African rule of 1915 did not bring an end to the tribulations of indigenous Namibians, as many had hoped for. The reserves the new administration introduced were designed as little more than repositories for migrant labour. Still, they afforded opportunities for communal resilience.[7] We shall turn to the form of commemorations that were linked to this resilience in the following section.

In Germany, the response to the war and the genocide it involved was also significant – not only since arguably this was the last victorious war a German army fought during the 20th century. One salient feature is the high public profile of the genocide and other atrocities committed by German troops. The Great General Staff published a lavish two-volume account of the war.[8] A mushrooming array of books of fiction and memoirs extolled the exploits of the German troops and pointedly justified the annihilation of indigenous peoples who supposedly had not put to good use the

---

6   Jürgen Zimmerer, *Deutsche Herrschaft über Afrikaner. Staatlicher Machtanspruch und Wirklichkeit im kolonialen Namibia* (Münster: Lit, 2001), 68-94.

7   Reinhart Kössler, *In search of survival and dignity. Two traditional communities in southern Namibia under South African rule* (Windhoek: Gamsberg Macmillan, 2005), part 1; Wolfgang Werner, *"No one will become rich": Economy and society in the Herero reserves in Namibia, 1915-1946* (Basel: Schlettwein 1998).

8   *Die Kämpfe der deutschen Truppen in Südwestafrika*. Auf Grund amtlichen Materials bearbeitet von der Kriegsgeschichtlichen Abteilung I des Großen Generalstabes. Erster Band: *Der Feldzug gegen die Hereros* (Berlin: Mittler, 1906); *Die Kämpfe der deutschen Truppen in Südwestafrika*. Auf Grund amtlichen Materials bearbeitet von der Kriegsgeschichtlichen Abteilung I des Großen Generalstabes. Zweiter Band: Der *Hottentottenkrieg* (Berlin: Mittler, 1907).

land given by God.⁹ Such literature was included in set readings in school.¹⁰ The fledgling production of post cards took to the theme and conveyed a range of images, which included scenes of emaciated prisoners and executions.¹¹ In addition, the political realignment known as the *Bülow Block* was forged in the 'Hottentot Elections' of 1907, which saw intense campaigning on the issues of the colonial war.¹² Broadly speaking, one may say that these developments coincided with the ascendancy of what Geoff Eley has termed 'radical nationalism' in Germany.¹³

In contradistinction to other genocides of the 20th century,¹⁴ even some of the more gruesome aspects were aggressively exposed to the public. In this way, acts that today would be categorised without question as crimes against humanity found their way into everyday German life. They were banalised and thus became more acceptable. Moreover, adversaries were

---

9 Gustav Frenssen, *Peter Moors Fahrt nach Südwest. Ein Feldzugsbericht* (Windhoek: Benguela Publishers, 2002, 1st ed. 1906); Medardus Brehl, *Vernichtung der Herero. Diskurse der Gewalt in der deutschen Kolonialliteratur* (München: Wilhelm Fink, 2007).

10 Gunther Pakendorf, The Literature of Expropriation: "Peter Moor's Journey to South-West" and the Conquest of Namibia, in: *Namibia in Perspective*, ed. Gerhard Tötemeyer et al. (Windhoek: CCN, 1987), 172-183, here: 176.

11 Felix Axster, "… will try to send you the best views from here": Postcards from the Colonial War in Namibia (1904-1908), in: *German colonialism, visual culture, and modern memory*, ed. Volker M. Langbehn (New York: Routledge, 2010), 55-70.

12 Frank-Oliver Sobich, *'Schwarze Bestien, rote Gefahr': Rassismus und Antisozialismus im deutschen Kaiserreich* (Frankfurt a.M.: Campus, 2006); John Philipp Short, Colonisation, War and the German Working-Class: Popular Mobilisation in the Reichstag Elections 1907 (Paper presented at the conference "1904-2004 – Decontaminating the Namibian Past. A Commemorative Conference", University of Namibia, Windhoek, 17-21 August 2004).

13 Geoff Eley, Reshaping the Right: Radical Nationalism and the German Navy League, 1898-1908, *The Historical Journal* 21, 2 (1978), 327-354.

14 Robert Gellately and Ben Kiernan, *The Spectre of Genocide: Mass Murder in Historical Perspective* (Cambridge: Cambridge University Press, 2003).

pointedly framed in racial terms.[15] All this may be understood as one further strand within a tendency that enabled many Germans three or four decades later to victimise also their immediate neighbours.[16]

Moreover, even after the loss of the colonies, the colonial quest was kept alive and many former agents of colonialism as well as institutions serving it or economic enterprises involved in colonial ventures, turned to the new colonial sphere that was envisaged in Eastern Europe during World War II.[17] In this way, the colonial discourse remained largely unbroken in Germany after the loss of the colonies. This experience could be integrated into the larger picture of unjust humiliation ostensibly inflicted by the victors through the peace terms and thus fed into colonial revisionism. That attitude was taken up and its aims were pursued, with varying intensity by the Nazi regime well into World War II.[18]

After World War II, colonial revisionism was no more an option, and a clear discursive break occurred. In West Germany, nurturing the tradition of the *Schutztruppe* was relegated to rather marginal groups while a majority found themselves preoccupied with seemingly more pressing issues. Moreover, for those who undertook seriously to grapple with Germany's dire past of the first half of the 20th century, the shadow of the Shoah tended to overwhelm all other concerns. At the same time, the early loss of the colonies could now be viewed with a certain 'relief' as not being implicated in the conflicts and dirty wars that accompanied the sustained independence movements of the day.[19] It may be argued that such colonial amnesia is still prevalent, even if on the other hand there is a tendency in popular culture to

---

15 Pascal Grosse, What Does German Colonialism Have to Do with National Socialism? A Conceptual Framework, in: *Germany's Colonial Pasts*, ed. Eric Ames et al. (Lincoln: University of Nebraska Press, 2005), 115-134.
16 Omer Bartov, Defining Enemies, Making Victims: Germans, Jews, and the Holocaust, *The American Historical Review* 103 (1998), 771-816; Reinhart Kössler, From Genocide to Holocaust? Structural parallels, *afrika spectrum* 40 (2005), 309-317.
17 Jürgen Zimmerer, *Von Windhuk nach Auschwitz? Beiträge zum Verhältnis von Kolonialismus und Holocaust* (Berlin: Lit, 2011), chapter 10.
18 Karsten Linne, *Deutschland jenseits des Äquators? NS-Kolonialplanungen für Afrika* (Berlin: Ch. Links, 2008).
19 Kreutzer, Deutsche Heimat, 179.

transpose dramatic and sentimental fiction or film to the erstwhile colonies or generally, to 'Africa' where then decidedly German stories are played out.[20]

However, the centenary of the genocide in 2004 marks a certain shift in memorialisation also in Germany. Enhanced awareness of and debate about the events enforced the interrelated issues of remembrance, apology, reparation, and reconciliation. The interrelationship between these concepts is quite controversial. As will become clear, polar positions are represented by a clamour for silence or denialism along the lines of the otherwise well-known 'final stroke' rhetoric; and on the other hand, the linkage between active memorialisation and reparation based on an official apology by the German government. In this case, reparation denotes more than material compensation, namely an actual process of restoring victims' integrity and dignity through the full acknowledgment of past wrongs and their recognition as equals.[21] These issues can be understood from the vantage point of 2004 and subsequent developments. In each case, actors include governments as well as various strands of civil society. Arguably again, such dynamism as can be discerned in the issue derives from non-state actors. Their array differs starkly on the Namibian and on the German side.

ACTORS, SITES AND EVENTS ON THE NAMIBIAN MNEMOSCAPE

As should emerge from the following, it makes sense to operate with an inclusive notion of a mnemoscape to encompass the entire array of contradictory memory landscapes, actualised and potential memory contents, and actor formations. Especially with reference to a highly variegated historical record and associated differential claims and concerns, it is important to

---

20 Wolfgang Struck, The Persistence of Colonial Fantasies: Colonialism as Melodrama on German Television, in: *German Colonialism and National Identity*, ed. Michael Perraudin and Jürgen Zimmerer (New York: Routledge, 2010), 224-231.
21 *To Repair the Irreparable. Reparation and Reconstruction in South Africa*, ed. Erik Doxtader and Charles Villa-Vicencio (Claremont: David Philip, 2006).

stress the spatial, temporal, as well as social dimensions of mnemoscape.[22] One important dimension of the latter concerns the starkly diverse endowment of actors with resources and power. As a result, actors' chances to make themselves heard are distributed quite unevenly. This forms a crucial aspect of the memory process.

In Namibia, the commemoration of the war and the genocide began quite early. It encompassed two main, structurally opposed strands. On the one hand, the German colonial power started almost immediately after the event the ritual memory of the supposedly victorious Battle of the Waterberg, which according to this reading had sealed the German claim to Namibian soil with German blood. From this stems an annual ritual that was to become a mainstay of identity politics of German speakers in Namibia. It underwent several important changes, in particular reflecting efforts at alliance building after World War II, first with Afrikaners, later also with groups involved in the attempts at internal settlement, notably Ovaherero.[23] This event, which consistently featured the German imperial flag, was finally banned by the president in 2003, thirteen years after independence; there was little activity by German speakers during the centennial year of 2004.[24] Another important and related dimension of the memory politics of German speakers in Namibia concerns colonial buildings, which are represented as central features of national heritage.[25]

Up to 2009, arguably the most important and certainly the most conspicuous site with respect to this, was the ensemble of the *Christuskirche* and the Rider Statue in central Windhoek. Both were built as markers of the German claim to the land after the defeat of primary African resistance. In

---

22 Reinhart Kössler, Facing a Fragmented Past. Memory, Culture and Politics in Namibia, *Journal of Southern African Studies* 33 (2007), 362-382.
23 Larissa Förster, *Postkoloniale Erinnerungslandschaften. Wie Deutsche und Herero in Namibia des Kriegs von 1904 gedenken* (Frankfurt a.M.: Campus, 2010), 185-231.
24 Larissa Förster, The German Cemetery at the Waterberg, in: *Genocide in German South-West Africa. The Colonial War of 1904-1908 and its Aftermath,* ed. Jürgen Zimmerer and Joachim Zeller (Monmouth: Merlin, 2008), 252-258; Förster, *Postkoloniale Erinnerungslandschaften*, 318-329.
25 Andreas Vogt, *National Monuments in Namibia* (Windhoek: Gamsberg Macmillan, 2004).

the words of the German governor in 1912, the Rider Statue was intended as a symbolic statement "to proclaim to the world that we are and will remain masters here"[26] while the church forms part of an array of similar, and evenly named buildings in various German colonies that served the same purpose.[27]

In terms of memory politics, the removal of the Rider Statue some 150 meters away from its original site clearing the ground for a monumental Independence Memorial Museum became a rallying point for German speakers shortly after the turn of the millennium. At the same time, the issue served as one of the rare instances when various communities with stakes in memory politics related to German colonialism communicated amongst each other at least in a minimal way. When plans to move the Rider became first known in public in 2001, the local German language newspaper in a random survey elicited responses such as 'They want to take from Namibians all our history. They only value their own'.[28] Significantly, 'our' and 'their' here referred to rather vague entities, but obviously were constructed to exclude from 'Namibians' the incumbent government, which could boast a massive and uncontested majority. A more elaborate argument against the removal stressed the monument's reference to the fallen *Schutztruppe* soldiers, which from this view motivated the sacralisation of the periodic memory rituals performed at the site, such as the laying of wreaths. The claim of a 'sacrosanct' nature of the statue was linked, in some hazy way with the physical dangers it would face when removed from its pedestal and relocated.[29] Counterarguments pointed to the aggressive form in which the mon-

---

26 Quote in: Joachim Zeller, *Kolonialdenkmäler und Geschichtsbewußtsein. Eine Untersuchung zur kolonialdeutschen Erinnerungskultur* (Frankfurt a.M.: IKO, 2000), 120.

27 Markus Braun, EKD im Schatten des Kolonialismus. Jubiläum von Hundert Jahre Christuskirche, in: *Windhoek transparent* (online) 99 extra, 2011, http://www.transparentonline.de/index.php?option=com_joomdoc&task=doc_details&gid=145&Itemid=77, accessed 14 June 2011.

28 *Allgemeine Zeitung* (Windhoek), 6 June 2001.

29 Andreas Vogt, Status und Zukunft des Reiterdenkmals – eine Denkschrift, *Allgemeine Zeitung*, 20 June 2008.

ument asserts colonial, and German, domination of the country.[30] Subtexts and more subtle discourses should be noted as well. Thus, an Otjiherero speaker pointed out at one occasion that as his father had instructed himself and his brother, the Rider marked the spot where the concentration camp had been located during the Namibian War;[31] prisoners had also been used for constructing the *Christuskirche*. The statue was eventually relocated in front of the *Alte Feste*, the colonial fortress, which has been rededicated as National Museum. Significantly, the painstaking process of carefully hoisting it from its pedestal, disassembling the latter, storing the entire ensemble for several months and re-assembling the complete monument was financed by private donations. This speaks clearly not only to the zeal of a large section of the German speakers in the country to preserve specifically markers of the German colonial past, but also to the material means at their disposal to do so. In this way, the economic power of a rather small but disproportionately privileged group enables them to project quite vigorously their particular vision of the past, which to a considerable extent revolves around the denial of the genocide.[32] The latter dimension became quite clear once again at the rededication ceremony for the Rider. Speeches skirted the realities of the war, while traditionalist associations from both Namibia and Germany, in particular the Association for the Tradition of Former Protection and Overseas Troops – Friends of the Former German Protectorates[33] figured prominently. The trope of reconciliation, which, though rather ill defined, is ubiquitous in post-colonial Namibia, was on this occasion trans-

---

30 Phanuel Kaapama, Memory Politics, the Reiterdenkmal and the De-Colonisation of the Mind, *The Namibian* (Windhoek), 22 August 2008.
31 Luther Zaire, oral statement, Bahnhof Langendreer, Bochum, 17 March 2004; personal communication, 21 June 2004.
32 Reinhart Kößler, Im Schatten des Genozids. Erinnerung in einer extrem ungleichen Gesellschaft, in: *Genozid und Gedenken. Namibisch-deutsche Geschichte und Gegenwart*, ed. Henning Melber (Frankfurt a.M.: Brandes & Apsel, 2005), 49-77; Reinhart Kössler, Entangled history and politics: Negotiating the past between Namibia and Germany, *Journal of Contemporary African Studies* 26, 3 (2008), 313-339, here: 320-328.
33 *Traditionsverband ehemaliger Schutz- und Überseetruppen und der früheren deutschen Schutzgebiete*; see also http://www.traditionsverband.de/.

lated into a claim raised by German speakers for proper respect of their own culture, language and identity.[34]

In many ways, the evolution of specific forms of African memory politics in Namibia took an inverse form in relation to this tradition of asserting colonial and settler dominance. This may be exemplified in particular by annual commemorations. These events took root from the mid 1920s onwards and may be considered as first public expressions of the processes of resilience of communal nexuses mentioned above. At the same time, they contribute importantly to the further reproduction of these nexuses. In various ways, these endeavours in Central and Southern Namibia took their clue and reference from events and personages connected to the Namibian War. Moreover, they involved the symbolic and temporary re-appropriation of salient places and spaces that had been lost to the respective communities as a consequence of that war.[35] However, this took the shape of subaltern practices that were marked by the colonial situation, which the actors had to confront on a daily basis. The systematic subjection implied by this situation was addressed and expressed in various ways at the very outset when these commemorations were first constituted. This becomes evident if we consider the two most important, Herero Day that even today refers to the momentous reburial of Samuel Maharero in Okahandja, the traditional capital of his group, the Red Band in 1923, and Heroes Day in Gibeon, the traditional centre of the //Khowesin or Witbooi.

The reburial of Samuel Maharero in 1923 marked the emergence of Ovaherero as once again a vociferous and rather solid ethnic grouping.[36]

---

34 *Allgemeine Zeitung*, 1 November 2010, 2 November 2010, 3 November 2010, 15 November 2010, 23 November 2010, 3 December 2010.

35 Gesine Krüger, *Kriegsbewältigung und Geschichtsbewußtsein: Realität, Deutung und Verarbeitung des deutschen Kolonialkriegs in Namibia* (Göttingen: Vandenhoek & Ruprecht, 1999), 282-290; Reinhart Kössler, Communal Memory Events and the Heritage of the Victims. The Persistence of the Theme of Genocide in Namibia, in: *German Colonialism and National Identity*, 235-250, here: 243-244; Förster, *Postkoloniale Erinnerungslandschaften*, 256-259.

36 Jan-Bart Gewald, The Funeral of Samuel Maharero and the Reorganisation of the Herero, in: *Genocide in German Southwest Africa. The Colonial War of 1904-1908 and its Aftermath,* ed. Joachim Zeller and Jürgen Zimmerer *(London: Merlin Press 2008)*, 207-216.

One particularly spectacular feature was and still is the "ceremonial occupation of Okahandja" by the formations of the typical *oturupa*, when "the uniformed troops symbolized and demonstrated the vision of a united people, reinforcing their claim to ancestral land".[37] In this, the event stunned contemporaries, and the spatial claim as well as the determination to continue a memory practice in which communal resilience and coherence crystallised with such clarity was underscored by a vow to return each year to the graves in Okahandja.[38] By now, this vow has been kept for nearly 90 years. However, the annual commemoration was also marked by restrictions; thus, in 1923, Samuel Maharero's heir apparent was allowed to remain in Namibia only on a temporary basis. During South African colonial rule, regular submissions to the colonial authorities were required. Consent was conditional on the banning of marching by the Herero *oturupa* – often misunderstood as a kind of mock army or quasi-military organisation. Once the Reverend Michael Scott had emerged as a champion of Herero grievances and of opposition to the proposed incorporation of Namibia into South Africa after World War II, it was decreed that no white person must address the festive crowd.[39] Today, these issues are largely forgotten. What remains is the festive appearance of ritually dressed men and women parading in long columns and visiting the chiefly graves, which are located in central Okahandja. Certainly not least because of its colour and the proximity of the event to the capital of Windhoek, some 80 km to the south, this has also become a tourist attraction. Apart from this more public form of commemoration, Herero Day takes place rather out of public sight at the *Herero Kommando,* which is located in the township a few kilometres away. Here, the recounting of history, as well as for some years claims for reparations from Germany, form the main contents of a long succession of speeches.

---

37 Gesine Krüger and Dag Henrichsen, 'We have been captives long enough. We want to be free': Land, uniforms and politics in the history of the Herero, in: *Namibia under South African rule: Mobility and containment 1915-1946,* ed. Patricia Hayes et al. (Oxford: James Currey, 1998), 149-174, here: 159.
38 Krüger and Henrichsen, We have been captives long enough, 158.
39 Kössler, Communal Memory, 242-247. On Michael Scott see Freda Troup, *In face of fear. Michael Scott's challenge to South Africa* (London: Faber & Faber, 1950).

Again, Heroes Day in Gibeon, still also known by its former name of Witbooi Festival or *Witbooi Fees*, harks back to a humble commemoration at the graveyard to honour the group's prominent dead in 1930. Among these, *Kaptein* Hendrik Witbooi who in his advanced age was killed in action in 1905 during the Nama-German War, stands out as a clairvoyant and militant fighter against colonialism.[40] The communal commemoration of Hendrik Witbooi's death can be traced back to 1930, when a small commemoration was held under the tutelage of the resident missionary and the magistrate.[41] Under the guidance of his evenly named great-grandson, the event has been transformed into a pageant that links a long succession of elements and lasts for three days. Items range from the centrally important church service to historical re-enactment to cultural demonstrations including dances of various ethnic groups in Namibia to pure enjoyment, such as the informal dance in the evening. In this way, spiritual concerns connected to honouring the dead are closely related to educative and political aims: to instruct the youth in history, above all concerning the contribution of Witbooi to anticolonial resistance and the liberation struggle, and by the same token to advance claims in the context of present-day, independent Namibia.[42]

These two rather prominent examples may stand in here for an entire host of commemorations that are held today, mostly on an annual basis, across Central and Southern Namibia. The overwhelming majority of these periodic rituals refer to personages or events linked to the Namibian War.[43]

---

40 See his celebrated *Diary* (Witbooi 1995).
41 Johannes Olpp, Eindrücke einer Reise über die sieben Rh. Missionsstationen des Namalandes (II), *Berichte der Rheinischen Missionsgesellschaft* 87 (1930), 136-145; here: 140-141. For further context see Kössler, *In search of survival*, pt. III.
42 Kössler, *In search of survival*, 249-253; Reinhart Kössler, "A luta continua": Strategic Orientation and the Politics of Remembrance. The Example of the Witbooi "Heroes Day" in Gibeon, in: *Genocide in German South-West Africa*, 217-230; Reinhart Kössler, Political Intervention and the Image of History: Communal Memory Events in Central and Southern Namibia, in: *The Long Aftermath of War: Reconciliation in Namibia*, ed. André Du Pisani et al. (Freiburg: Arnold Bergstraesser Institut, 2010), 371-402, here: 284-393.
43 See also Memory Biwa, Stories of the Patchwork Quilt: an Oral History Project of the Nama-German War in Southern Namibia, in: *The Long Aftermath of War*,

This underscores the fact that for people relating to this region of Namibia – the area under effective colonial control in German times – the events of the Namibian War, the genocide, and the concentration camps still form the central feature of their historic memory. For people relating to the Northern regions on the other hand, different events and in particular, the liberation struggle of the 1970s and 1980s, figure much more prominently.

The commemorations can thus be read as efforts by communities in Southern and Central Namibia to assert their historic role in anti-colonial resistance.[44] Within the overall mnemoscape of Namibia, such endeavour has a two-pronged thrust beside the obvious reproduction of the communal nexus in a festive get-together linked with recounting the common past. On the one hand, the commemorations effectively address the specific national narration that has become hegemonic in post-independent Namibia. This narration pegs the construction of the nation not only to the trajectory of the ruling party SWAPO[45] but also to an overwhelming emphasis on the military aspects of the liberation struggle of the 1970s and 1980s. Significantly, President Hifikepunye Pohamba, when appearing at the Bondelswarts Festival in Warmbad in the southeastern-most corner of the country in October 2008, responded to the rehearsal of the community's exploits during the Nama-German War by confessing not only his utter ignorance but also the incompetence of his speechwriters who had failed to prepare him adequately for the occasion.[46] The relevant information is obviously available, also

---

331-70; Förster, *Postkoloniale Erinnerungslandschaft*, 247-268; Jan-Bart Gewald, Herero Annual Parades: Commemorating to Create, in: *Afrikaner schreiben zurück. Texte und Bilder afrikanischer Ethnographen*, ed. Heike Behrend and Thomas Geider (Köln: Köppe, 1998), 131-152; Kössler, Political intervention and the image of history: Communal memory events in central and southern Namibia, in: *The Long Aftermath of War*, 371-402, here: 379-384, 293-399.

44 Kössler, Facing a fragmented past.
45 André du Pisani, The Discursive Limits of SWAPO's Dominant Discourses of Anti-colonial Nationalism in Postcolonial Namibia – a First Exploration, in: *The Long Aftermath of War*, 1-40.
46 Autor's field notes, 25 October 2008; Kössler, Political intervention, 371-372; for historical background, see Andreas Heinrich Bühler, *Der Namaaufstand gegen die deutsche Kolonialherrschaft in Namibia von 1904-1913* (Frankfurt a.M.: IKO, 2003).

in accounts very close to SWAPO,[47] even though the most extensive official account available arguably downplays the agency of Ovaherero or Nama.[48] The point is that the image of history amongst Namibia's liberation elite virtually excludes these contents. Yet in spite of mostly opposed, polar evaluations in particular by Otjiherero and Nama speakers on the one hand and by German speakers on the other, the events of the Namibian War still form a central and possibly the main historical reference for people referring to Central and Southern Namibia as their home region. The anecdote underscores graphically how this is marginalized in the official version of history, as well as the potential of staged oral accounts and performative events to provide a certain counterweight against the officially received narrative.

THE CONSTRUCTION OF 'GERMANY' AND ITS RESPONSIBILITY

Inevitably, these endeavours are intertwined with various references to 'Germany' and the 'Germans'. They occur in speeches, in claims and in appearances of specific personages at commemorations. This is partly due to one of the poles in the post-colonial relationship. In central and southern Namibia, the vestiges of German rule are obvious – less so in often carefully renovated colonial buildings seen not least as attractions for German tourists. More importantly, the re-ordering of space initiated and first undertaken under German rule in the wake of the genocide[49] – and indeed as one of its integral components – remains a ubiquitous feature of the landscape as well as of everyday life. Prevailing land property relations shape the region as a fairly rigidly ordered countryside, largely devoid of humans and geared to a market-oriented economic endeavour. This entails the right of admission to spots where the graves of ancestors of black Namibians are still remembered, and to areas many still consider as their ancestral land.

---

47 Peter H. Katjavivi, *A history of resistance in Namibia* (London: James Currey, 1988), 10.
48 SWAPO, *To be born a nation: The liberation struggle in Namibia* (London: Zed Press, 1981), 13-14.
49 See also Zimmerer, *Von Windhuk nach Auschwitz*.

Even where this is not complemented by the position of a dependent farm labourer, these features serve as constant reminders of historic loss and trauma, which is transmitted through the oral tradition. The connection appears even more obvious on account of the large number of German speaking commercial farmers and the high profile presence of German speakers at privileged positions in economic life in general. Further, some of this group have played a vociferous part in debates around the evaluation of German colonialism in the country, above all denying the colonial genocide.[50]

On a more personal, even intimate plane, a discourse mainly among Otjiherero speakers refers to their own German ancestry. This is linked to the record of sexual violence during the Namibian War, rape and forced prostitution, but also various forms of concubinage. Reference is made to physical features of the speakers, such as light skin or straight noses. One main issue concerns the difficulty with which children of such fathers are located within the complex dual kinship system. A more immediate concern, however, points to the distinct negligence of most German men who even when parentage was known and in some way acknowledged, on their return to Germany just left their offspring and their mothers to their own devices, cutting all ties and denying belonging or affiliation and above all, responsibility. This discourse was strongly articulated at the centennial commemoration of the fateful Battle of Ohamakari on 14 August 2004, most conspicuously by the wearing of placards showing the names of the German ancestors (sometimes several) of their bearers. This was complemented by individual expressions of concern and distress.[51]

An indispensable component of this discourse addresses German responsibility. This responsibility is couched in a three-pronged identification, which is premised on the overarching idea of kinship that has been forged by the illegitimate relationships in question. Such kinship is construed not only in relation to the families of common forebears, but to 'Germans' and 'Germany' at large, which terms also tend to be construed within a framework of kinship. Further, this identification is extended to German speakers in Namibia, quite regardless of whether they actually claim a Namibian identity. Under the circumstances, this construct clearly

---

50 Kössler, Entangled history and politics, 320-328.
51 Personal observation; Förster, *Postkoloniale Erinnerungslandschaften*, 319-321.

translates into responsibility that has been neglected not only by German progenitors of grandparents and great-grandparents, but also by 'Germany' at large. Neglect of parental duty – unquestionable in the case of the overwhelming majority of German forefathers of living Ovaherero – in this way is transferred to Germany, and Ovaherero at large are seen as its victims.

From a Namibian perspective, 'Germany' forms an integral part of the mnemoscape in question. 'Germans' and 'Germany' therefore are seen as actors, to some extent even as a kind of amalgamated collective actor within this mnemoscape. Arguably, this looks different from a German vantage point, for two reasons. The first, most obvious and possibly also the most intractable one, concerns the clearly smaller amount of attention accorded in Germany to anything that happens in and about Namibia, including Namibian-German relations, as opposed to the much greater attention given to Germany, and in particular to Namibian-German relations, in Namibia. At least on the face of it, this is related to the stark differences that exist between the two countries in population size and economic power, but at least the latter consideration clearly refers back to the colonial connection. Except for a few fleeting moments and also regardless of the ideological consequences of the Namibian War, Namibia was mostly rather marginal to Germany, whereas Germany on the other hand has been of quite central importance to Namibia for some 150 years. As already mentioned, this applied to the violent imposition of a new social and spatial order; German speakers continued to occupy a central and influential position within the settler colonial structure. Regardless of some frictions, they arranged themselves with South African rule and even became a mainstay of the Apartheid regime.[52] They remain an economically powerful and conspicuous grouping in independent Namibia. Moreover, Germany has recognised "a particular relationship" based on a special responsibility on account of colonial rule[53] and consequently, German presence in the development sector is also very conspicuous.

---

52 Martin Eberhardt, *Zwischen Nationalsozialismus und Apartheid. Die deutsche Bevölkerungsgruppe Südwestafrikas 1915-1965* (Berlin: Lit, 2007); Brigitta Schmidt-Lauber, *"Die verkehrte Hautfarbe". Ethnizität deutscher Namibier als Alltagspraxis* (Berlin: Reimer, 1998).

53 Janntje Böhlke-Itzen, *Kolonialschuld und Entschädigung. Der deutsche Völkermord an den Herero 1904-1907* (Frankfurt a.M.: Brandes & Apsel, 2004), 7.

This contrasts starkly to the low significance of Namibia as a foreign relations or trading partner, seen from the perspective of the public sphere in Germany as well as German politics at large. Here, relevant government activity is largely inconspicuous and civil society activity, while present, is limited to special interest circles. Quite a few initiatives exist to provide links with Namibia, such as school partnerships, and a quite active German-Namibian Society along the classic lines of a friendship society promoting general information, economic links, development projects, and in this context also tourism.[54] However, these bodies have and intend to have only limited impact at best on memory politics related to the colonial past. This is left to small pressure groups that work towards a pro-active approach to the colonial past in Germany. Their limited potential is also due to a negligible post-colonial presence, clearly in contradistinction to Germany's neighbour countries like Netherlands, Belgium or France.[55] Still, these small, but active groups can be understood as a rather new phenomenon, in the wake of the decline of the more conventional solidarity movement. They pursue an agenda of awareness rising about colonial issues, largely on a local level. As a result, a network of post-colonial initiatives has developed that actively takes up memory issues.[56]

BETWEEN AMNESIA AND REPARATIONS: NEGOTIATING THE PAST

Up to Namibian independence on 21 March 1990, the country's colonial past under German rule played a rather marginal role, even for (West) German solidarity groups that supported the liberation struggle.[57] On the other

---

54 http://www.dngev.de.
55 *Kolonialismus und Erinnerungskultur. Die Kolonialvergangenheit im kollektiven Gedächtnis der deutschen und niederländischen Einwanderungsgesellschaft*, ed. Helma Lutz and Kathrin Gawarecki (Münster: Waxmann, 2005).
56 As a representative website, http://www.freiburg-postkolonial.de; http://www.freiburg-postkolonial.de/Seiten/Links.htm also gives an overview of similar activities in other German cities.
57 Reinhart Kössler and Henning Melber, The West German solidarity movement with liberation struggles in Southern Africa: A (self-)critical retrospective, in:

hand, black Namibians did not have a chance of raising their voices effectively before independence had been achieved.[58] For such reasons, the independence date can be seen not only as a turning point in the political set-up and fortunes of the country, but also as a point of departure for a novel politics of memory. Given this perspective, it should also be noted that in spite of latter-day triumphalist rhetoric, this was a classical case of pacted transition.[59] The terms had been set to a large extent by prior agreements within the UN system. The process in terms of Security Council Resolution 435 (1978) was set into motion in 1988 by the Tripartite Agreement between the US, South Africa and Angola about the ending of the war situation in that country, which had become closely linked to the Namibian liberation struggle. The constitution was a product of very speedy deliberation by the Assembly that had been elected in late 1989. Here, SWAPO had been denied a two-third majority and depended on reaching an agreement with the opposition.[60] These circumstances as well as the need to avoid social and economic disruption coalesced into an overall policy orientation of "reconciliation", stalling any potential controversies and further struggles. This silencing of public controversy had profound consequences for the dealing with the past.[61] In general, potential controversy was relegated to the realm of academic or more or less private pursuit.

Germany's Africa policy revisited: Interests, images and incrementalism, 2nd ed., ed. Ulf Engel and Robert Kappel (Münster: Lit, 2006), 101-123.

58 Peter Katjavivi, From Colonialism to Bilaterality. Challenges of the Namibian-German Relationship, in: *The Division of the Earth. Tableaux on the Legal Synopses of the Berlin Africa Conference*, ed. Dierk Schmidt (Köln: Verlag der Buchhandlung Walter König, 2010), 91-93.

59 Guillermo O'Donnell and Philippe C. Schmitter, *Transitions from Authoritarian Rule. Tentative Conclusions about Uncertain Democracies* (Baltimore and London: Johns Hopkins University Press, 1986), 37-39.

60 Lionel Cliffe, *The Transition to Independence in Namibia* (Boulder and London: Lynne Rienner, 1994), chap. 9; *The Namibian Peace Process: Implications and lessons for the future*, ed. Heribert Weiland and Matthew Braham (Freiburg: Arnold Bergstraesser-Institut, 1994).

61 Justine Hunter, Dealing with the Past in Namibia: Getting the Balance Right Between Justice and Sustainable Peace?, in: *The Long Aftermath of War*, 403-433;

Nevertheless, independence also meant the possibility for issues to come into the open that had long been nurtured in the relative privacy of oral tradition and personal transmission through the generations. Now was the first chance to move beyond such subaltern practices and link such memory contents to public initiatives. Most important amongst such initiatives were the forays by leading Ovaherero who aimed at reaching some understanding with the German government on the premise of its accession to the guilt incurred by the former Imperial government.

Such forays met a rather stern rebuff on occasion of the state visits of the German Chancellor Helmut Kohl in 1995 and the German President Roman Herzog in 1998, when Herero delegations were either not admitted or met only on an informal level. While Kohl praised specifically the services of the German speakers towards Namibia's development, President Herzog voiced concern about the future of the German language in the country.[62] These experiences exacerbated the sensitivities of "ex-colonial Namibians about representatives of the former colonial power and their successors in the country".[63] Against this backdrop, the Herero People's Reparation Corporation (HPRC) was formed. This body pursues a court case in the USA under the Alien Tort Claims Act (ATCA). The German state and German companies are held liable for reparations on account of the war crimes committed in Namibia under the German colonial regime and for the exploitative conditions that prevailed and from which the companies had profited.[64] This action resonates with cases brought under the same legislation also against the German state and German companies by former forced labourers during World War II, where an out of court settle-

---

Reinhart Kößler, Zweierlei Amnesie und die komplexe postkoloniale Lage Namibias, *Die Friedenswarte* 86 (2011), 73-99.

62 Henning Melber, "We never spoke about reparations". German-Namibian relations between amnesia, aggression and reconciliation, in: *Genocide in German South-West Africa*, 259-273, here: 265-266.

63 Ibid., 265.

64 Jeremy Sarkin, *Colonial Genocide and Reparations Claims in the 21st Century: The Socio-Legal Context of Claims under International Law by the Herero against Germany for Genocide in Namibia, 1904-1908* (Santa Barbara: Praeger, 2008); Böhlke-Itzen, *Kolonialschuld*, 31-32.

ment was reached in 1999.[65] In a whole series of events, the centennial commemoration of the Battle of Ohamakari (Waterberg) on 14 August 2004 stood out.[66] This brought together between 5,000 and 10,000 Ovaherero from all over Southern Africa and beyond. This was an important step in the reproduction and re-constitution of Herero ethnicity. At the same time, quests for alliances amongst different ethnic groups in Namibia as well as of the difficulties in actually forging such alliances were evident. These problems existed above all between the two committees that had formed during the preceding year in order to organise the long commemorative calendar of the centennial that culminated on August 14. The cleavage between the two committees reflected the unresolved juxtaposition of two forms of traditional leadership amongst Ovaherero as well as diverging party political orientations. Moreover, a certain amount of Herero exclusionism found expression in a tendency to claim victim status solely for this group.[67] On the other hand, the Ohamakari event was marked by efforts to underline historical bonds. Thus, the appearance of Ndonga King Kauluma from Northern Namibia, was linked to the successful attack on fort Namutoni by Ndonga warriors during the Herero-German War in 1904. Again, Nama groups from Southern Namibia were clearly underrepresented on the programme, and the only scheduled speech did not materialise.

The central feature, however, was the speech of the German Minister of Economic Cooperation, Heidemarie Wieczorek-Zeul. She surprised many and went against the grain of established government policy when she acknowledged that the crimes of the *Schutztruppe* and its leadership

"would today be called genocide [...]. We Germans accept our historical and moral responsibility and guilt incurred by Germans at that time. And so, in the words of the Lord's Prayer that we share, I ask you to forgive us our trespasses and our guilt.

---

65 http://www.stiftung-evz.de, accessed 25 March 2009.
66 Förster, *Postkoloniale Erinnerungslandschaften*, 278-308.
67 Henning Melber, Namibia's Past in the Present: Colonial Genocide and Liberation Struggle in Commemorative Narratives, *South African Historical Journal* 53 (2005), 98-119, here: 116-117.

Without a conscious process of remembering, without sorrow, without apology, there can be no reconciliation – remembrance is the key to reconciliation."[68]

This wording clearly referred to the prevailing idea in Germany that remembrance forms the basic legitimate approach towards dealing with a cruel past and mass crimes involved in it, and that this will engender reconciliation. It did not quite work this way on this occasion. After the Otjihereo version of the Minister's speech had been read out, there was a loud interjection: "Where's the apology?" Only when the Minister had come back and had stressed that she thought she had given one, the audience seemed to be satisfied. This speaks to the importance of ritual wording in adequate dealing with the past in this context. At the same time, the inherent problems and contradictions of this carefully worded speech in terms of a viable reconciliation process were to be revealed through subsequent developments. These developments revolved around the interlinked issues of reparation, which the speech had skirted, and of acknowledgment of the victims (in their descendants) as partners in dialogue.

Wieczorek-Zeul's speech clearly digressed from the line taken at that time by the German cabinet. Only a few weeks before, the *Bundestag* had passed a motion that carefully avoided the word 'genocide' and on that account, caused considerable irritation and stir in Namibia.[69] The Minister's speech therefore attested her personal courage, but it proved also an important limitation to her apology. Even though given by a Cabinet member, it still did not emanate from a Cabinet decision, but precisely the opposite, from the Minister's personal resolve. Much less was the apology rendered by a representative of the German people as the sovereign body in question, such as the President or the *Bundestag*.

Further, it soon became clear that this courage was not matched by a political strategy to reach a form of reconciliation that would be acceptable

---

68 http://www.inwent.org/E+Z/content/archive-eng/10-2004/stud_art3.html, accessed 29 June 2011, quoted from Förster, *Postkoloniale Erinnerungslandschaften*, 283, who uses a rendering of the oral delivery.
69 Reinhart Kößler, Berlin weiß nichts vom Völkermord, *afrika süd* 4 (2004), 12; Luther Razemua Zaire, Enttäuschend – Beschämend – Historisch falsch. Offener Brief, *afrika süd* 4 (2004), 13.

to all parties concerned, most of all to those in the victim position.⁷⁰ The months following the Ohamakari event were marked by spurious activities that did not coalesce into such a meaningful dialogue driven by victims' concerns. In particular, the Minister unilaterally announced in May 2005 a reconciliation initiative that would bring 20 million Euro to the regions of Namibia predominantly inhabited by victim communities. Not surprisingly, this announcement was met by objections from Herero spokespersons since there had been no prior consultations and the whole initiative therefore was seen as unilateral. Even in late 2005, on occasion of a visit of President Hifikipunye Pohamba in Berlin, the Namibian delegation refused to sign the necessary agreement.⁷¹ The diplomatic *éclat* could be patched up, but at the time, it underscored a serious difference in approach of how to deal with the challenge to come to terms with a colonial genocide and to reach reconciliation between the heirs of the victims and the perpetrators.

Subsequent developments highlighted these differences. At the same time, the issue was drawn into a labyrinthine web of countervailing interests, including party political concerns on both sides. An interesting realignment concerned the linkage that developed between the German Left Party and the Namibian NUDO party headed by Paramount Chief Kuaima Riruako. Some Left Party deputies started to champion the concerns of the HPRC as well as other issues related to the genocide from 2005 onwards. On the side of the German Left, stalwarts from GDR times were hesitant about such a line up, as long as SWAPO, with whose formerly exiled leadership they shared close bonds, had not pronounced clearly its approval.⁷²

---

70 Since neither survivors nor perpetrators of what happened in 1903-1908 are still alive today, it is appropriate to clearly distinguish between personal experiences and guilt, and between longer term consequences and historic responsibility, such as that of German citizens. These considerations lead to the wordings of "victim position" and "perpetrator position"; but see on victims and perpetrators Don Foster et al., *The theatre of violence. Narratives of protagonists in the South African conflict* (Oxford: James Currey, 2005).

71 Joachim Zeller, Festgefahren. Ratlosigkeit angesichts der vorläufig gescheiterten Versöhnungsinitiative zwischen Namibia und Deutschland, *afrika süd* 6 (2005), 32.

72 Personal observation at the seminar "Deutsche Kolonialverbrechen. Wie kann Wiedergutmachung für die Herero und Nama aussehen?", Rosa Luxemburg

Still, a motion was tabled in the *Bundestag*, and Left MP Hüseyin Aydin, who had also been the main sponsor of that motion appeared as one of the speakers at Herero Day, 2006. He underscored the yet unfulfilled responsibility of the "Federal Republic of Germany as the legal successor of the Imperial Reich [...] towards the surviving victims of the genocide and their posterity".[73] This line of thinking, which focused on the continuity of the German state, differs distinctly from the discourse centring around obligations based on kinship and blood ties as articulated by Ovaherero (*supra*). Still, both coalesced in a common perspective, featuring an intimate connection between apology, reparation and reconciliation.

At the same time, SWAPO departed from its previous stance of not supporting any demand for reparations on the grounds that this might entail the risk of fostering tribalism, favouring one or other ethnic groups over others. In October 2006, the National Assembly carried a motion tabled by Riruako with only one member abstaining.[74] When introducing his motion, the Paramount Chief had reiterated the wish for "the German Government to convene a consultative conference to set up an agenda for dialogue".[75] In the event, the passing of the motion by the National Assembly, which was clearly aimed at furthering such a process, has so far not contributed towards a continued momentum as had emanated from Wieczorek-Zeul's apology. Rather, the halting process of transnational and post-colonial memory politics that had been given a new turn in 2004 has shifted once again. Namibian victim communities have by no means backed down on their demand for reparations. However, at least temporarily, symbolic politics have moved to the foreground. This is interlinked with important realignments in Namibia.

Foundation, Berlin, 13-14 October 2006; see www.freiburg-postkolonial.de/Seiten/Rez-Linke-Seminar-Namibia2006.htm, accessed 4 June 2011.

73 Hüseyin Aydin, MdB, Rede am Herero-Tag in Okahandja (Namibia), 27 August 2006, as disseminated via email to author; see also *New Era* (Windhoek), 31 August 2006; *The Namibian*, 1 September 2006.

74 *The Namibian*, 27 October 2006.

75 *The Namibian*, 20 September 2006.

INTRICACIES OF SYMBOLIC POLITICS AND RECONCILIATION

This new turn, which rounds off this account, involves a fairly extensive range of changes. First, the number and to some extent the structure of civil society actors on the Namibian side has changed significantly. In 2004, the victim position was articulated and occupied largely by Ovaherero, even though split into two competing committees. During the following years, an array of further ethnic groups voiced their demands for recognition of past suffering and of the contribution of their forebears to the anti-colonial struggle, as well as for adequate redress. Thus, early in 2005, the newly formed Damara Cultural and Heritage Forum pointed out that regardless of the marginal role accorded to Damara within accounts of the Namibian War, 17,000 of their people had disappeared during the war. In motivating the intervention, Chief Gaseb stressed a widely inclusive notion of victim groups who all "have a history", thus closely linking victim status and "history".[76] The insistence on the latter by a spokesperson for a group that has been notoriously marginalized both in social terms and in historical accounts once again demonstrates the importance carried by inscription into the national record in this way.

The issue of remembrance and claims connected with such quests also furthered closer cooperation among Nama traditional leaders. In late 2006, nine of them appealed for a "meaningful dialogue" with the German government, while insisting that the Namibian government should attend properly to the identification and further treatment of the human remains that had been found near the southern Namibian port of Lüderitz, and which were attributed to former prisoners at the concentration camp on Shark Island.[77] At this historic site, the commemoration in early 2007 of the centenary of the death of Chief Cornelius Frederick of Bethanië who had perished in the concentration camp marked a galvanizing point.[78] By late 2007, a joint declaration by Ovaherero and Nama traditional leaders was released. The text indicted the German government and the *Bundestag* as well as the Namibian government for denying direct negotiations between the repre-

---

76 *The Namibian*, 26 January 2005.
77 *The Namibian*, 19 October 2006.
78 *New Era*, 19 February 2007.

sentatives of the victimised groups and the German government. The declaration listed a series of measures to improve the lives of these groups based on "seeking redress for the wrongs of the past in order for the wounds to heal and for resultant genuine reconciliation and peaceful co-existence amongst the Nama/Ovaherero and the German people in our country and for a lasting friendly bilateral relations [sic] between the two countries".[79] The conflations contained in this appeal are characteristic for the complex situation it addressed: The principle addressees are the two governments, but at the same time, the German state is seen as closely connected to the ethnic group of German speaking Namibians, and the aim is defined by the hope to reach friendly relations between the two countries, Germany and Namibia. This phrase, only seemingly ill construed, contains in a nutshell central difficulties that are involved in coming to terms with the postcolonial relationship that exists between Namibia and Germany.

These difficulties may be conceptualised precisely in problems involved in the identification, and indeed, in the construction of the relevant collective actors and protagonists. This concerns obviously the central issue of who should be held responsible on the one hand and who shall be entitled to claims for recognition and eventually, reparation on the other. This question does not merely concern what may appear as a mere confusion between 'Germany', 'Germans' and 'German speakers'. It also concerns the definition and constitution of 'Namibia', as well as that of the victim groups.

These problems of definition and identity formation are bound up with the process of colonisation and subsequent transformations, right up to Namibia's independence as a sovereign state. The act of colonisation did not only entail the definition of boundaries, as occurred with the formation of *any* form of modern statehood, but it also set into motion a process whereby the sovereign rights of indigenous groups or their leaders were progressively reneged. In Namibia, this process came to an abrupt and decisive conclusion through the genocide of 1904-1908. For most African groups within

---

79 Joint Position Paper from the Nama and the Ovaherero People on the Issue of Genocide and Reparation, 14 December 2007, signed by Ovaherero Paramount Chief Kuaima Riruako and Chief David Frederick (Bethanië); http://ovahererog enocideassociationusa.org/images/Document%20pdfs/New%20pdfs%202_20_0 8/Ovaherero_NamaPosition%20Paper.pdf, accessed 10 July 2011.

the Police Zone, this event decisively terminated any chance for autonomy or for the exercise of sovereign rights, which at least according to some readings had still been implied by the protection treaties concluded with the fledgling German colonial power in the 1880s.[80] While the difficulties encountered in asserting claims that emanate from this mass crime today can be related to the eurocentric bias of international law,[81] the heritage of colonisation and spatial reorganisation also entails that today the sovereign power claiming to legitimately speak for *all* Namibians is the national government. This makes it quite difficult to arrange meaningful relations, let alone negotiations, between representatives specifically of victim groups and the German government. As can be observed, the Namibian government is constantly mindful that such a process might be seen to subvert its own hard won sovereignty. The chagrin of representatives of victim groups who refuse to "accept that we have initially raised the issue and now it should be *about us* and yet *without us*"[82] refers precisely to such structural underpinnings.

At the same time, the quest to bring together relevant stakeholders in Namibia along the lines of civil society actors also runs into problems, which can be related to memories of past conflicts between ethnic groups, but more often, to current rivalries. Arguably, the most important issue here divides Ovaherero over the issue of legitimacy of traditional leadership, pitting Paramount Chief Riruako, who claims popular election for lifetime, against the heads of the Five Royal Houses who rely on genealogical legitimacy. This cleavage is reinforced by opposing party political alignments. Similarly, Damara are divided over claims made by traditional leaders for legitimacy and jurisdiction, and again this is reinforced by opposing party loyalties.

---

80 Malte Jaguttis, Paths to a Hearing of the Herero Case under International Law. Beyond the Patterns of Colonial Self-Description?, in: *The Division of the Earth*, 76-84; Jörn Axel Kämmerer, The Persecution of the Herero from the Perspective of Public International Law, in: *The Division of the Earth*, 85-90.

81 M.N. Kaapanda-Girnus, A Third World perspective on the History of International Law. The Herero Genocide as the Perfect Crime?, in: *The Division of the Earth*, 94-98.

82 Joint Position Paper.

Such divisions have made it difficult to constitute a joint body for action. Still, during the 2000s an Association of Nama Traditional Authorities was formed, and this has worked as a core to assemble a broad coalition to work for reparations and reconciliation with reference to the genocide, which encompasses Ovaherero, Damara, San, and Basters. Yet, such an alignment turned out not to be all-inclusive, leaving out larger or smaller sections of most ethnic groups.

Thus, there is a multiplicity of actors on the Namibian side, while it is only at first sight that the respondent to claims is easily identified to be the German state. As already mentioned, within the Namibian debate, this encompasses German speakers who live in Namibia as citizens, as well as descendents of *Schutztruppe* soldiers, in particular with reference to the concerns of their black descendants in Namibia. Such aspects make it quite clear how symbolic issues and concerns for recognition are in fact inextricably intertwined with the demand for reparations that has occupied centre stage for some time but again cannot be construed exclusively as a demand for material benefits.

It is against this backdrop that the dynamics around the restitution of human remains taken to Germany during its colonial rule in Namibia evolved. The fate of severed heads, in particular those taken from fallen leaders during the war, had been a concern since a long time,[83] but it had not been a public affair of particular note. This began to change with the discovery of human bones near Lüderitz in October 2006 and their obvious connection with the concentration camps, which had existed in this southern port town during the Namibian War.[84] The issue gained further momentum through the centennial commemoration for Cornelius Frederick in February 2007 as mentioned above. Here, one main grievance articulated concerned Cornelius Frederick's head. According to oral tradition, this head had been severed from the dead body and sent to Germany. This account has been contested by historians as not being factual;[85] however, the more important social fact is the belief that in such a case spurs actors on. Here, it gave rise to the de-

---

83 E.g., informal talk with *Kaptein* Petrus Koper of the Red Nation, Berseba, 3 June 1995.
84 *New Era*, 16 October 2006.
85 *New Era*, 19 February 2007; Casper Erichsen, email to author, 20 February 2007.

mand for the return of human remains from Germany. The Shark Island event proved an important stage in the process that at the end of 2007 brought together Nama and Ovaherero traditional leaders in a joint effort to make claims towards the governments and parliaments of both states, demanding recognition above all by being included within any process of negotiation and reconciliation.[86] Remarkably, this statement now treats the genocide perpetrated against both Ovaherero and Nama on an equal footing. It thus overcomes former tendencies towards victim competition and Ovaherero exclusionism. For nearly four years, subsequent efforts centred increasingly around the quest for returning human skulls taken from Namibia to Germany during colonial times and housed in various research institutions in Germany.

The story of the restitution and of the efforts bringing it into the range of possibility and even likelihood by the end of 2011 shall not be recounted here in full. Suffice it to say that beginning with some TV features in mid-2008, there developed a certain heightened sensitivity for the issue in parts of the German public.[87] In October 2008, the Namibian government formally requested repatriation, under the understanding that the skulls would be given a heroes' burial at Heroes Acre outside Windhoek.[88] However, the coalition of Ovaherero and Nama traditional leaders objected to this and insisted the skulls should be placed into the proposed Independence Museum as a constant reminder of the great and often undervalued contribution Namibians in the South and Centre of the country had made to anticolonial resistance.[89]

The negotiations about restitution of the skulls evolved haltingly over more than two years, precisely since the formal process also had to reflect the complex constellation of historical facts, of remembrance and of current agendas. Nama and Ovaherero traditional leaders took more than a year to

---

86 Joint Position Paper.
87 For documentation on this process, see http://www.freiburg-postkolonial.de/Seiten/anthropologische-schaedelsammlungen.htm, accessed 10 July 2011; http://www.africavenir.org/de/projektkooperationen/restitution-namibian-skulls/datum/2008/02/26.html, accessed 10 July 2011.
88 *The Namibian*, 21 October 2008.
89 *Allgemeine Zeitung*, 2 October 2009; personal communication with Ida Hofmann, Windhoek, 25 October 2008, 5 May 2011.

hammer out their positions vis-à-vis the Namibian government. They finally petitioned formally to act on the matter through diplomatic channels late in 2009.[90] At the same time, consensus was reached that the skulls, once returned, should be housed in a museum. In the words of Paramount Chief Riruako, "our history cannot be buried, they were beheaded in public, and thus we have to retain them in public". At the same time, 28 May 2010 was announced as the date when representatives of the communities concerned would proceed to Berlin to receive the skulls and perform apposite rituals before bringing them to Namibia. The date was meant to commemorate the day in 1908 when the concentration camps were closed. A further demand concerned proper documentation about the fate of the skulls, including the research that had been undertaken on them.[91]

In the event, negotiations between the various parties concerned dragged on for more than another year. This involved also negotiations on the level of the two embassies in Windhoek and Berlin with their various counterparts. Only late in March 2011, the Namibian government felt they were in a position to set the procedure into motion for actual repatriation of the skulls. One reason had been the time taken up by scientific work at the University hospital *Charité* in Berlin and at the University Archives in Freiburg, where skulls had been located which had to be identified first as actually coming from Namibia. At this occasion, it was stressed by Utjiua Muinjangue speaking for the 1904 Herero Genocide committee that "in our African culture, we believe in ancestral spirits. When those skulls come home, I am sure the spirits of our ancestors will rest in peace." On the other hand, the ultimate aim of reparations from Germany remained on the agenda.[92]

Ensuing developments once again underscored the fallacies implied by the actor constellation in the repatriation and reparation issue.[93] The envisaged date of 28 May 2011 eventually did not materialise on account of conflicts that surfaced around the composition of the delegation that was to

---

90 *The Namibian*, 1 and 2 October 2009; *Allgemeine Zeitung*, 2 October 2009.
91 *New Era*, 2 October 2009.
92 *New Era*, 25 February 2011.
93 For the following see detailed documentation on http://www.freiburg-postkoloni al.de/Seiten/anthropologische-schaedelsammlungen.htm; besides, I rely on participant observation in Namibia during May 2011 and in Berlin in late September 2011, as well as press documentation and email correspondence.

travel from Namibia to Berlin. Ostensibly, these conflicts revolved around the composition of the 54 proposed delegates. There was a contest between a coalition of two committees, bringing together Ovaherero and Nama on the one hand and another committee formed by Ovaherero and closely related Ovambanderu. The dispute also had party political dimensions, given the diverse allegiances of the two Ovaherero groups concerned, and it articulated the pervasive leadership bifurcation amongst Ovaherero pitting Paramount Chief Riruako against the Royal Houses. In this way, the issue of how the delegation would be composed mobilised deep and central conflicts that were exacerbated by further competition to be included as a kind of recognition of an individual's as well as their community's importance and standing. Difficulties could not be resolved in time, and the entire event was called off. Subsequently, it was rescheduled twice, and a delegation of altogether more than 70 people finally arrived in Berlin, late in September 2011.

In the view of many, what followed was a communication disaster on the side of the German government. It became clear that official pronouncements painstakingly avoided the term 'genocide'. A press statement by the foreign office took official occlusion to the point of speaking merely of "skulls of deceased members of the population groups of Herero and Nama brought to Germany during colonial times".[94] In addition, the government was less than forthcoming in acknowledging the delegation or in engaging them into exchanges. They did not receive the cabinet minister who was at the head of the Namibian delegation and they were not represented at important side events. This concerned in particular the memorial service conducted by the venerable Namibian Bishop Zephania Kameeta at the *Matthäuskirche* (Berlin-Tiergarten), where the seats reserved for German VIPs remained empty, safe for the presence of Wieczorek-Zeul. At a panel discussion, organised by civil society groups at the central *Haus der Kulturen der Welt*, representatives of the government or of the coalition parties were also absent. Added disappointment and resentment were

---

94 Pressemitteilung: Übergabe und Rückführung von Schädeln verstorbener Angehöriger der Volksgruppen Herero und Nama aus Namibia, 27 September 2011, http://www.auswaertiges-amt.de/sid_599AF8AB5706903D8C42417691EF7B18/DE/Infoservice/Presse/Meldungen/2011/110928-%C3%9Cbergabe-Sch%C3%A4del-Herero-Nama.html, accessed 13 October 2011.

caused by the announcement that contrary to expectations, the restitution document would not be signed at the core ceremony, by the Namibian minister of culture and by a German minister, but rather by a representative of the *Charité*, on the German side. This was motivated by considerations of German cultural federalism.[95] The unease and chagrin that had been building up within the Namibian delegation coalesced with similar feelings among parts of German civil society who had worked for publicity and side events, in particular for the panel discussion. In particular, groups of Afro-Germans organised a protest at the actual hand over ceremony at the *Charité*. When Minister of State in the Foreign Office, Cornelia Pieper, once again evaded the term genocide in her speech and merely asked for "reconciliation" without stating clearly the reasons why she considered that necessary, she was met with noisy demonstrations of displeasure and boos. The Minister then left the occasion without taking proper leave of the Namibian dignitaries. Regardless of the circumstances, this was seen as deeply disrespectful on the Namibian side, and in line with the German government's previous behaviour, while they welcomed the protests.[96]

This dissonance must also be related to the great symbolic importance of the delegation's actions at various occasions.[97] Take only the whole group entering the *Charité* for their first encounter with the skulls, announcing their coming with solemn prayer, hymns and battle cries, or similar features at the church service and at the handover ceremony. Similar observations apply to seeing off and welcoming ceremonies in Windhoek. At the airport there, a crowd of a few thousand who broke the ranks met the delegation and the skulls. There were extensive ceremonies on subsequent days in Parliament Gardens and Heroes Acre, which also underscored the emphatic meaning attached to the "repatriation"[98] in Namibia. At the same time, the incongruence with the approach of the German government ap-

---

95 Cornelia Pieper MdB, Staatsministerin im Auswärtigen Amt to Yvonne Ploetz MdB, Schriftliche Fragen für den Monat Oktober 2011, Fragen Nr. 10-14-16, 12 October 2011.
96 Interviews, Windhoek, March 2012.
97 The following remains strictly impressionistic, pending more in-depth study underway.
98 Alexactus T. Kaure, On Repatriation, Reparation, Restitution and Reconciliation, *The Namibian*, 7 October 2011.

peared obvious. In part, this may also explain the enormous and certainly unforeseen media echo on the occasion of the handover and Pieper's walkout. By insisting on formal niceties and legal considerations, above all to avoid by any means to utter words that might possibly be used in a legal case for reparations, German officials completely missed what moved their Namibian counterparts – quite regardless of the inference that such painstaking care actually attested implicitly to an awareness that there was really a cause also for material reparations. Pieper's speech was a clear expression of this dilemma when she asked for reconciliation on account of circumstances she had not bothered or dared to spell out. Amnesia was replaced, in this way, by what appears as a half-official ban on a word or even on a factual statement.

However, also on the Namibian side not everything was monolithic and harmonious. The skull issue and attendant events brought dormant, festering issues into the open. Obviously, this applies to the greatly divergent regional experiences such as regional differences in historical trajectories that entail regionally tinted hegemonic narratives.[99] This is further exacerbated by complaints about neglect by the SWAPO government for concerns of the communities affected by the genocide, ranging from advancing claims for reparations from Germany right to a more vigorous and equitably land reform.[100] It may have been such considerations, besides obvious chagrin about high-handed German official behaviour that prompted Prime Minister Nahas Angula a week later to come out with a strong demand that Germany respond to an official submission about reparations the Namibian government had made some while ago.[101]

---

99 Kössler, Facing a fragmented past.
100 Alfredo Tjiurimo Hengari, The Republic Must Show Solidarity With The History Of Genocide, *The Namibian*, 7 October 2011.
101 *New Era*, 13 October 2011.

Outstanding Dialogue, Persistent Post-Colonial Situation

This episode, then, focused once again the issues that shape post-colonial conflict and negotiation between Namibia and Germany. Even though the skull issue itself is by no means concluded as the repatriation of further skulls has been envisaged for 2012, the event can be seen as setting a provisional and temporary end to a trajectory of transnational memory politics set into motion at the Ohamakari commemoration in 2004. This trajectory revolves around the modalities and consequences of the recognition of genocide perpetrated under the authority of the German state, and the apology offered by the Minister. As has become clear in pronouncements, also from the delegation in Berlin, their quest for a dialogue with 'Germany' remains on the agenda. For them, such dialogue and the recognition it implies are prerequisite to the reconciliation they offer and strive for. Given the stance taken once again by the German government, a process with its potential consequences of making claims for reparations effective seems unlikely for the near future. Yet even moves in the realm of symbolic politics, while more feasible, seem to run into the difficulties that follow from the refusal to openly address and name facts that had been acknowledged already by Wieczorek-Zeul, albeit not in the capacity of a representative of the German nation. With a pointer, one might say that with the partial exception of Wieczorek-Zeul's departure, the official German attitude implies a quest for silent reconciliation and thereby, at best limited recognition of the other. As long as the Namibian counterparts are not prepared to play along, this strategy may work on the advantage of a privileged power position, but will hardly be able to silence protest on the Namibian side or indeed from active parts of German civil society.[102] One may therefore argue that the communication disaster around the return of the skulls was due in part to diplomatic misunderstandings and possibly incomplete negotiating during the run-up to the event. However, such contingent aspects do not exhaust the matter. The events underscore the complexity of the post-colonial situation and the quest for reconciliation.

---

102 For an account of a similar reconciliation strategy on the part of the Namibian government with respect to the liberation war of 1966-1989, see Kössler, Zweierlei Amnesie.

This complexity involves constellations of state and non-state actors in both Namibia and Germany and their at times difficult means and forms of communication. One main difficulty refers to the position of both governments who are styled as the main actors on the diplomatic level, but have demonstrated only limited potential in filling these roles. In Namibia, victim groups and affected communities continue to clamour for direct negotiation and dialogue with 'Germany', focusing clearly on the German government. Conversely, the German government has relied on arguments relating to cultural federalism and the niceties of the administration of cultural goods to fend off an official role for itself at the handover ceremony that before had seemed obvious to most observers. The government therefore is mediating between their Namibian counterparts in government and various instances, such as scholarly institutions, in Germany in contradictory ways. Again, civil society actors in Germany have been to some extent in longer contact with affected communities and their leaders or linked up readily with members of the delegation in Berlin in September 2011. It remains to be seen whether these contacts will bring a new quality to transnational civil society relationships between the two countries. So far, these did exist e.g. in the form of some school partnerships and close contacts between church bodies, but these have rarely addressed memory issues on a public scale.

In this way, not only does the image of the past remain a contested terrain both in Namibia and in Germany, but so remain the conclusions that are drawn even from widespread consensus about certain issues, such as the perpetration of genocide in 1904-1908. Namibia stands out, even among German ex-colonies, for the urgency with which this colonial past is addressed, and even though interest within Germany has arguably increased in recent years, there remains a huge hiatus between the levels of public interest in both countries. Again, this reciprocates, at least to some extent, the asymmetrical colonial and post-colonial situation and thus for those concerned remains an issue to reflect as well as to act upon. The post-colonial situation is here to stay for a foreseeable future and its acknowledgement remains a political challenge. Moreover, the experience of September 2011 may be read as an emphatic assertion precisely of the post-colonial quality of the relationship that has been the subject of this paper – a relationship marked not only by highly unequal means of those involved to make themselves heard, but also by highly unequal needs actually to listen. This can be considered as a hegemonic relationship in the sense of quite differential possibilities of agenda setting. It remains to be seen to what measure recent events have aroused further awareness in Germany about the country's post-colonial dimensions and how existent and new actors both in Namibia and in Germany will be able to work together in possibly also changing this hegemonic relationship.

Instruments of Reconciliation: Commissions in European and Global Perspective

Political Reconciliation in Northern Ireland and the Bloody Sunday Inquiry

MELINDA SUTTON

On 29 January 1998, Tony Blair announced the establishment of a new judicial inquiry chaired by Lord Saville of Newdigate into the killings of thirteen unarmed civil rights demonstrators in Derry on 30 January 1972, claiming that

"Our concern now is simply to establish the truth, and to close this painful chapter once and for all [...] I believe that it is in everyone's interests that the truth be established and told. That is also the way forward to the necessary reconciliation that will be such an important part of building a secure future for the people of Northern Ireland."[1]

Establishing the truth was not the only motive for re-opening the inquiry into Bloody Sunday; the announcement came at a pivotal point in the negotiations leading to the Belfast Agreement in April 1998, and played a key role in easing Anglo-Irish relations and relations with the Nationalist community and their political representatives in Northern Ireland. However, the apparent belief that establishing the truth of what had happened twenty six years earlier would lead to reconciliation in Northern Ireland is one which requires some examination, as it raises questions about the nature and interpretations of the conflict in Northern Ireland (thus the nature of reconcilia-

---

1 Tony Blair, House of Commons, *Hansard*, 29 January 1998, Vol. 305, Col. 502.

tion there), the impact of the past on contemporary politics and society, and how this legacy can be dealt with in a way that promotes reconciliation rather than recrimination. This chapter assesses the state and nature of reconciliation in Northern Ireland, before examining the problem of dealing with the legacy of conflict and the initiatives which have aimed to address this issue. Finally, a case study of the Bloody Sunday Inquiry is employed to examine the use of public inquiries as a means of dealing with the past. The Bloody Sunday Inquiry was not the sole government initiative to address the past; Ken Bloomfield produced a report on the issue in April 1998, while the Consultative Group on the Past, chaired by Robin Eames and Denis Bradley, issued its recommendations in January 2009. Neither was it the only initiative aimed at addressing nationalist grievances; the government introduced a series of measures, including parading legislation, and policing and justice reforms. Although the Bloody Sunday Inquiry was not operating in a vacuum, and cannot therefore be used as the only marker of reconciliation, it does highlight the problems posed by the past for reconciliation, and the difficulties involved in addressing the legacy of the Troubles.

THE STATE AND NATURE OF RECONCILIATION IN NORTHERN IRELAND

In some ways, the Northern Ireland peace process itself can be understood as a process of reconciliation. Republicans reconciled their aspiration for a united Ireland to the fact that a majority of the population of Northern Ireland supported the union with Great Britain, and decided to pursue constitutional, rather than violent, means of achieving Irish unity, with the exception of a small minority of dissidents. For their part, the majority of Unionists agreed to share power with Republicans, and formerly implacable political opponents began to work together in a power-sharing executive at Stormont. Diplomatic relations between the United Kingdom and the Republic of Ireland have been largely normalised, epitomised by the first state visit of a British monarch to the Republic of Ireland for one hundred years in May 2011. Of Bloomfield's four peace processes – the peace process, the political process, the international process, and the community process –

three appear near completion.² However, the fourth process, the community process, provides the

"greatest grounds for continuing concern [...] Sectarian segregation is still deeply entrenched; physical separation between hostile communities remains inevitable in too many areas; contentious marches and parades heighten tension and reinforce animosity".³

The number of peace walls constructed after the paramilitary ceasefires in 1994 provided a stark visual and physical reminder of the continuing divisions between the two communities in Northern Ireland.⁴ In 2010, the Northern Ireland Life and Times survey reported that fifty five per cent of respondents lived in areas where the majority of their neighbours were of the same religion, while sixty-one per cent said that all or most of their friends were of the same religion as them.⁵ One could even interpret the existence of the power-sharing executive led by the Democratic Unionist Party (DUP) and Sinn Féin as representative of this failure of social reconciliation, as the presence of two sectarian blocs forced to share power with each other.

Connolly suggests that reconciliation has three main elements: "a lack of bitterness in political and other public relationships, a dialogue between former enemies based on the present rather than the past, and a single, uni-

---

2   Kenneth Bloomfield, *A Tragedy of Errors: The Government and Misgovernment of Northern Ireland* (Liverpool: Liverpool University Press, 2007), 3. Bloomfield was the head of the Northern Ireland Civil Service from 1984 to 1991, was appointed Victims Commissioner for Northern Ireland in 1997 and was also a member of the Independent Commission for the Location of Victims' Remains.
3   Ibid.
4   BBC News, The walls that don't come down, 2011, http://news.bbc.co.uk/1/hi/northern_ireland/8121362.stm, accessed 20 May.
5   http://www.ark.ac.uk/nilt/2010/Community_Relations/SRELNGH.html, http://www.ark.ac.uk/nilt/2010/Community_Relations/SRELFRND.html, accessed 28 November 2011.

fied version of past events".[6] Using this definition, it is clear that reconciliation in Northern Ireland is incomplete. The comments of Tom Elliott, then leader of the Ulster Unionist Party, after the 2011 Northern Ireland Assembly elections, when he described Sinn Féin supporters as "scum" and said that he "would not forget" the past, reveal both bitterness and a failure to engage with his former enemies "based on the present rather than the past".[7] Powell has made the point that the two communities have their own "internally consistent and mutually exclusive" histories of Northern Ireland, indicating the absence of a "single, unified version of past events", which Connolly suggests is a necessary element of reconciliation.[8] Although it is debatable whether this is even possible, given the plurality of histories in any society, the use of these different pasts to legitimise and reinforce division is clearly antithetical to reconciliation. However, if one adopts Porter's argument about the two connotations of reconciliation, where "the negative connotation highlights our being reconciled *to* some state of affairs – such as one in which the claims of difference can no longer be dismissed or ignored – the positive connotation highlights our being reconciled *with* those who are different from us", perhaps post-conflict Northern Ireland offers an example where the negative connotation of reconciliation is dominant.[9] Unionists and Nationalists are becoming reconciled *to* each other, but not yet *with* each other.

Kelly and Hamber argue that reconciliation can be achieved by pursuing five interrelated strands: developing a shared vision of an interdependent and fair society; acknowledging and dealing with the past; building positive relationships; encouraging significant cultural and attitudinal

---

6   Christopher K. Connolly, Living on the Past: The Role of Truth Commissions in Post-Conflict Societies and the Case Study of Northern Ireland, *Cornell International Law Journal 39* (2006), 401-433, here: 410.
7   BBC News, Tom Elliott attacks 'Sinn Fein scum', http://www.bbc.co.uk/news/uk-northern-ireland-13323770, accessed 20 May 2011.
8   Jonathan Powell, *Great Hatred, Little Room: Making Peace in Northern Ireland* (London: Bodley Head, 2008), 58. Powell was Tony Blair's Chief of Staff and played a key role in facilitating discussion between the parties from 1997 to 2007.
9   Norman Porter, *The Elusive Quest* (Belfast: Blackstaff Press, 2003), 66. Italics in original.

change; and engaging in substantial social, economic and political change.[10] The British government has been particularly involved in promoting social, economic and political change in Northern Ireland, as part of its engagement in the peace process, through a series of confidence-building measures aimed at addressing the alienation of nationalists from the state. This programme included legislation to deal with contentious parades, the incorporation of the European Convention on Human Rights into UK law, the encouragement of a Bill of Rights for Northern Ireland, policing reform, prison reform, de-escalation of military operations in Northern Ireland in accordance with the levels of violence, a review of emergency powers legislation, and action on employment equality.[11] Barton and McCully point out that the existence of two parallel and separate educational systems in Northern Ireland is often blamed for the perpetuation of community divisions, and therefore initiatives in educational policy aimed at overcoming those divisions, such as the mandated cross-curricular themes of Education for Mutual Understanding and Cultural Heritage, introduced in the 1989 Education Reform (Northern Ireland) Order, are "regularly promoted as important contributors to peace and reconciliation".[12] These initiatives were intended to play an important role in encouraging changes in attitudes, the construction of positive relationships with those from different traditions and in the development of a shared vision of an interdependent and fair society.

The failure of the various parties to the conflict to engage wholeheartedly in addressing the legacy of the past has nevertheless meant that reconciliation remains an elusive goal. This is partly linked to the existence of two competing narratives of the conflict in Northern Ireland, which present the conflict either as an internal conflict between Nationalists and Union-

---

10 Gráinne Kelly and Brandon Hamber, *Reconciliation: a working definition* (Belfast: Democratic Dialogue, 2004).
11 Colin Knox and Pádraic Quirk, *Peace Building in Northern Ireland, Israel and South Africa: Transition, Transformation and Reconciliation* (Basingstoke: Macmillan, 2000), 46.
12 Keith C. Barton and Alan McCully, History Teaching and the Perpetuation of Memories: The Northern Ireland Experience, in: *The Role of Memory in Ethnic Conflict*, ed. Ed Cairns and Mícheál D. Roe (Basingstoke: Palgrave Macmillan, 2003), 107-124, here: 107-108.

ists, or as one in which external actors and forces, particularly the British state and British imperialism, played a significant role.[13] These competing narratives have an impact on understandings of who is to be reconciled in Northern Ireland. In an internal conflict analysis, reconciliation is primarily between Nationalists and Unionists within Northern Ireland, whereas in an analysis, which highlights, for example, the role of British imperialism, reconciliation must include British state actors. Connolly argues that the failure to address the legacies of the conflict means that "Northern Ireland has yet to establish 'truth' in the form of a broadly-acceptable narrative of the Troubles upon which peace and reconciliation may be built".[14] This suggests that in the absence of a shared interpretation of the past (or at least interpretations which are not diametrically opposed to one another), a post-conflict society cannot move towards a shared future. It also has an effect on some of the other strands of reconciliation outlined by Kelly and Hamber. Building positive relationships based on trust and tolerance, and changing cultures and attitudes are difficult where suspicion, prejudice and intolerance remain due to the legacy of past conflict. Cairns and Roe argue that unless the past, and memories of the past, are addressed,

"groups are often left with a sense of 'victimhood' that stems from unacknowledged and unreconciled historic losses. These in turn present a powerful barrier to traditional methods of peacemaking and diplomacy and create new senses of wrong and injustice thus creating the potential for future conflict."[15]

Where loss and suffering is unacknowledged, groups and individuals remain alienated from the post-conflict society.

Although there have been initiatives dealing with discrete aspects of the past, for example, the Bloody Sunday Inquiry, there has been no initiative introduced to deal comprehensively, with the participation of all parties to the conflict, with the legacy of the past. This is partly due to the absence of

---

13 Bill Rolston, Assembling the jigsaw: truth, justice and transition in the North of Ireland, *Race and Class* 44, 1 (2002), 87-105, here: 88.
14 Connolly, Living on the Past, 414.
15 Ed Cairns and Mícheál D. Roe, Introduction: Why Memories in Conflict?, in: *The Role of Memory in Ethnic Conflict*, ed. Ed Cairns and Mícheál D. Roe (Basingstoke: Palgrave Macmillan, 2003), 3-8, here: 4-5.

consensus on who constitute the victims of the conflict. Although the draft Bill of Rights for Northern Ireland suggests that "the loss and suffering of *all* victims of that conflict and the responsibility of *State and non-State participants* are appropriately and independently established and/or acknowledged",[16] Hamber refers to the notion of a hierarchy of victims in Northern Ireland where some groups refer to themselves as 'innocent' victims, which implies that 'guilty' victims also exist.[17] He also argues that "[M]any victims of paramilitary violence feel that their suffering is seen as less important in light of the concessions to political (largely Republican) prisoners";[18] in this way, concessions and measures such as prisoner releases have had a negative impact on the way in which the past is perceived and addressed.

The perception of ignored victimhood also exists for victims of state violence, who "feel they have always been secondary victims because the hegemony of the British state remains".[19] This is also linked to the issue of the two discourses about the Northern Ireland conflict; where the internal conflict narrative is dominant, the role of state violence in the problem of the past is ignored, and victims of state violence marginalised. In addition, there is reluctance amongst the parties to the conflict to engage in questions of truth recovery, particularly Sinn Féin and the British state.[20] The combined effect is that the past has been exploited for political advantage; as Marie Breen Smyth argues, "the uses to which suffering has been put in

---

16 Making a Bill of Rights for Northern Ireland: A Consultation by the Northern Ireland Human Rights Commission (Belfast: Northern Ireland Human Rights Commission, 2001), Cl. 8 (a) 1. Emphasis added.

17 Brandon Hamber, Dealing with the Past: Rights and Reasons: Challenges for Truth Recovery in South Africa and Northern Ireland, *Fordham International Law Journal* 26 (2002-2003), 1074-1094, here: 1090.

18 Ibid.

19 Ibid.

20 Christine Bell, Dealing with the Past in Northern Ireland, *Fordham International Law Journal* 26 (2002-2003), 1095-1147, here: 1107. In contrast, Lawther suggests that it is, in fact, Unionists and Loyalists who are opposed to the introduction of formal truth recovery processes; Cheryl Lawther, Unionism, Truth Recovery and the Fearful Past, *Irish Political Studies* 26, 3 (2011), 361-382, here: 362.

Northern Ireland have often served an agenda more preoccupied with political advantage than with healing or reconciliation".[21] For example, in March 2011, Martin McGuinness and the DUP's Gregory Campbell clashed in an Assembly debate on the past when Campbell asked McGuinness to make an "unambiguous statement of his involvement" in the Troubles; in response, McGuinness accused Campbell of being "embedded in the past".[22]

DEALING WITH THE LEGACY OF THE PAST IN NORTHERN IRELAND

Despite reluctance to examine the past comprehensively, there have been several initiatives examining aspects of the past in Northern Ireland. Within civil society, these have frequently taken the form of community storytelling and oral history groups, such as the Dúchas Oral History Group which recorded testimonies about experiences of the conflict in nationalist West Belfast,[23] and the Ardoyne Commemoration Project, which collected stories from the friends and relatives of all those from Ardoyne in North Belfast who died during the conflict.[24] Although these are often based within specific communities, such as that of nationalist West Belfast, and have therefore developed "specifically to address the historical experience of particular communities", Graham Dawson suggests that this form of truth recovery need not necessarily be divisive, as it creates opportunities for "encountering other perspectives and narratives".[25]

---

21 Marie Breen Smyth, *Truth Recovery and Justice After Conflict: Managing Violent Pasts* (London: Routledge, 2007), 85.

22 Martin McGuinness and Gregory Campbell clash, http://www.belfasttelegraph.co.uk/news/politics/martin-mcguinness-and-gregory-campbell-clash-15106734.html, accessed 28 November 2011.

23 http://www.rascal.ac.uk/index.php?CollectionID=205&navOp=locID&navVar=39, accessed 18 May 2011.

24 Ardoyne Commemoration Project, *Ardoyne: The Untold Truth* (Belfast: Beyond The Pale, 2001), http://cain.ulst.ac.uk/issues/victims/ardoyne/ardoyne02a.htm, accessed 25 May 2011.

25 Graham Dawson, *Making peace with the past: Memory, trauma and the Irish Troubles* (Manchester: Manchester University Press, 2007), 25.

Alternatively, there are groups which campaign on behalf of specific groups of victims, such as Relatives for Justice (RFJ), campaigning for the recognition of victims of state violence,[26] and Families Acting for Innocent Relatives (FAIR), who call for the recognition of the suffering of Unionists in South Armagh.[27] However, Eilish McCabe of RFJ has pointed out that Unionist victims' groups often refuse to cooperate with groups who have connections to Republican paramilitaries; Dawson argues that "this attitude demonizes not only the Republican paramilitaries, but nationalist families and whole communities [...] In doing so, it reconstitutes traditional sectarian divisions and hampers any possibility of cross-community reconciliation."[28] Tonge highlights a similar problem for civil society groups engaged in conflict resolution; such groups need to develop "sufficient cross-community contacts to make the group appear non-sectarian and afford [them] a genuine prospect of ameliorating the conflict from below".[29] Where civil society groups are drawn solely from one community, particularly when addressing the problem of the past, the danger is that the group will focus on the experience of their own community to the exclusion of other communities, and thus precludes the development of the "single, unified version of past events" which Connolly argues is necessary for reconciliation.

The past has also been examined through state-sponsored initiatives, from apologies for specific events to commissions on the past and inquiries into particularly controversial deaths. In October 1997, Kenneth Bloomfield was appointed as Victims' Commissioner and asked "to look at possible ways to recognise the pain and suffering felt by victims of violence arising from the troubles of the last thirty years, including those who have died or been injured in the service of the community".[30] Bloomfield reported in

---

26 Rolston, Assembling the jigsaw, 95.
27 http://victims.org.uk/s08zhk/index.php?option=com_content&task=view&id=1&Itemid=2, accessed 25 May 2011.
28 Dawson, *Making peace with the past*, 285.
29 Jonathan Tonge, *The New Northern Irish Politics?* (Basingstoke: Palgrave Macmillan, 2005), 215.
30 We Will Remember Them: Report of the Northern Ireland Victims' Commissioner, http://cain.ulst.ac.uk/issues/victims/docs/bloomfield98.pdf, accessed 25 May 2011.

April 1998, but was heavily criticised for reinforcing the notion of the hierarchy of victims; Lundy and McGovern suggest that this approach "sowed anew the old seeds of ostracism" by implying that there were more deserving victims, and therefore less deserving victims.[31] The Consultative Group on the Past, established in June 2007 to examine the legacy of the past in Northern Ireland, sought to move away from the hierarchy of victims perception, demonstrated by the recommendation of a £12,000 recognition payment to the relatives of all those killed during the conflict.[32] However, this particular recommendation proved highly controversial, as Unionist leaders vehemently criticised the suggestion that the families of dead paramilitaries should be treated the same as the families of civilians killed by paramilitary actions.[33]

As various recommendations for dealing with the legacy of the past in a comprehensive manner failed to meet with sufficient cross-community consensus, the past has instead been dealt with through examining discrete events, for example, the inquiries into Bloody Sunday, Billy Wright, Rosemary Nelson and Robert Hamill, as well as commissions dealing with specific groups of victims, such as the Independent Commission for the Locations of Victims' Remains (ICLVR), focusing on the Disappeared.[34] Bell suggests that this approach to dealing with the past was part of the confidence-building strategy of the British government in relation to the peace process, that it amounts to little more than a "balancing of Unionist and Nationalist demands" and therefore has done little to discourage the politicisa-

---

31 Patricia Lundy and Mark McGovern, The Politics of Memory in Post-Conflict Northern Ireland, *Peace Review* 13, 1 (2001), 27-33, here: 29.

32 Report of the Consultative Group on the Past: Executive Summary, http://cain.ulst.ac.uk/victims/docs/consultative_group/cgp_230109_report_sum.pdf, accessed 25 May 2011.

33 For example, Nigel Dodds of the DUP, who argued that "[T]here can be no moral equivalence between the people who were murdered in the Shankill Road bombing and the criminal Thomas Begley who murdered them", BBC News, Reaction to Eames/Bradley Report, http://news.bbc.co.uk/1/hi/northern_ireland/7856590.stm, accessed 25 May 2011.

34 The term *Disappeared* refers to "those killed and buried in secret by proscribed organisations prior to 10 April 1998 as a result of the Northern Ireland conflict", http://www.iclvr.ie/, accessed 25 May 2011.

tion of the past.[35] The only initiative which sought to examine comprehensively and systematically every death relating to the Troubles was the Historical Enquiries Team of the Police Service of Northern Ireland; however, the team's objective was to establish the circumstances of each death, rather than to promote reconciliation.[36]

CASE STUDY: THE BLOODY SUNDAY INQUIRY

On 30 January 1972, members of the First Battalion of the British Army Parachute Regiment opened fire on an anti-internment march organised by the Northern Ireland Civil Rights Association (NICRA) after a small group of protesters were involved in low-level rioting and stone-throwing. Thirteen unarmed men were shot dead and a further fifteen people were wounded, one of whom later died of his injuries. The next day, the Home Secretary, Reginald Maudling, announced that an independent inquiry would be established to examine the "circumstances of the march and the incidents leading up to the casualties which resulted".[37] This inquiry was established under the chairmanship of the Lord Chief Justice, John Widgery, but could hardly be described as independent. In a meeting with Widgery, the Prime Minister, Edward Heath, instructed him to remember during his inquiry that "we were in Northern Ireland fighting not only a military war but a propaganda war".[38] Central to this propaganda war was the internal conflict narrative that Britain was a "neutral umpire between two warring tribes" in Northern Ireland.[39] Accordingly, the Widgery Report exonerated the soldiers, claiming that "[T]here is no reason to suppose that the soldiers would

---

35 Bell, Dealing with the Past in Northern Ireland, 1101.
36 Introduction from the Chief Constable, http://www.psni.police.uk/historical-enq uiries-team, accessed 27 May 2011.
37 Reginald Maudling, House of Commons, *Hansard*, 31 January 1972, Vol. 830, Col. 33.
38 Edward Heath, 1 February 1972, quoted in Dermot P.J. Walsh, *Bloody Sunday and the Rule of Law in Northern Ireland* (Basingstoke: Macmillan, 2000), 63.
39 Rolston, Assembling the jigsaw, 88.

have opened fire if they had not been fired upon first".[40] Instead, Widgery concluded that "[t]here would have been no deaths in Londonderry on 30 January if those who organised the illegal march had not thereby created a highly dangerous situation in which a clash between demonstrators and the security forces was almost inevitable".[41] Thus the organisers and the marchers were condemned for engineering the situation, while the soldiers, though occasionally criticised for firing which "bordered on the reckless", were cleared of responsibility for the deaths and injuries sustained on Bloody Sunday.[42]

The combination of Bloody Sunday and the Widgery Report had profound consequences for the relationship between the Nationalist community in Northern Ireland and the British state. It demonstrated that

"the rule of law had been completely abandoned by Britain in its attempt to shore up unionist power in the State and that consequently, a state of war existed. For some, the killings on Bloody Sunday justified the use of violence against the State. For others, they indicated that peaceful protest was impossible and eventually the nonviolent street protest of the civil rights movement withered away."[43]

In doing so, it cemented the alienation of Nationalists from the British state, and increased doubts that they would ever be treated fairly within the United Kingdom. Furthermore, it had implications for the relationship between Nationalists and Unionists, as many Unionists adopted the official version of Bloody Sunday, as instituted in the Widgery Report, and blamed the protesters for the events of that day.[44] Dawson points out that although "there have always been some Protestants and Unionists sympathetic to the suffer-

---

40 Lord Widgery, Report of the Tribunal appointed to inquire into the events on Sunday, 30th January 1972, which led to loss of life in connection with the procession in Londonderry on that day (London: Her Majesty's Stationery Office, 1972), http://cain.ulst.ac.uk/hmso/widgery.htm, accessed 25 May 2011.
41 Ibid.
42 Ibid.
43 Angela Hegarty, The Government of Memory: Public Inquiries and the Limits of Justice in Northern Ireland, *Fordham International Law Journal* 26 (2002-2003), 1148-1192, here: 1167.
44 Dawson, *Making peace with the past*, 90.

ing and injustice endured on and after Bloody Sunday, for many years this was given no effective public voice. Recognition of the atrocity was at best grudging."[45] This presents another example of the difficulty of reconciliation "when a section of the population can continue to deny that the state ever acted wrongly whilst another section feels their suffering has never been acknowledged".[46] With the British state denying its culpability in the events of Bloody Sunday and the majority of Unionists supporting this denial, the families of those killed on Bloody Sunday and the wider Nationalist community felt that their suffering had been denied and marginalised.

The sense of injustice engendered by Bloody Sunday and the Widgery Report meant that the families and the Nationalist community adopted "alternative ways to remember it and to tell its version of the truth".[47] Annual commemorative marches were organised in Derry, initially by NICRA and then by Sinn Féin, from 1973 to 1989. The strong association of the Bloody Sunday campaign with Sinn Féin during a period when Sinn Féin was unrepentantly supportive of the IRA and armed struggle meant that the campaign did not attract much support or sympathy outside militant Nationalism. However, there was no specific organisation campaigning on behalf of the Bloody Sunday victims "as a cause in itself" until 1987, when the Bloody Sunday Initiative (BSI) was established.[48] The BSI realised that "if the campaign was to succeed it would have to be made accessible to individuals and interest groups outside Republicanism" and therefore took over the organisation of the annual commemoration in 1989 and began to lead the campaign for the institution of a new public inquiry into Bloody Sunday.[49] McCann suggests that this was "symbolic of a shift back from outright rejection of the legal and constitutional system, and tentatively towards the pursuit of remedies within the system".[50]

---

45 Ibid., 121.
46 Lundy and McGovern, The Politics of Memory, 30.
47 Hegarty, The Government of Memory, 1170.
48 *The Bloody Sunday Inquiry: The Families Speak Out*, ed. Eamonn McCann (London: Pluto Press, 2006), 8. McCann was one of the organisers of the civil rights march on 30 January 1972 and was a prominent campaigner for a new inquiry into Bloody Sunday.
49 Ibid., 7.
50 Ibid., 8.

In parallel with the shift towards searching for remedies within the framework of the UK state and legal system and with the efforts to broaden the campaign's support base, the Bloody Sunday campaign attracted increasing support within Northern Ireland, in the Republic of Ireland and in Britain. In 1992, former Northern Ireland minister Peter Bottomley asked whether there would be a re-examining of the conclusions of the Widgery Tribunal.[51] This request was echoed by his fellow chair of the cross-party New Consensus group, Harry Barnes, who wrote to the Prime Minister, John Major.[52] In the same year, the leader of the Social Democratic and Labour Party (SDLP), John Hume, wrote to Major to request a new inquiry; although the request was denied, Major acknowledged that all those killed on Bloody Sunday should be regarded as innocent of the allegations that they had been handling explosives and firearms.[53] The Irish Government also pursued the call for a new inquiry through diplomatic channels, and submitted a report of all the new evidence about Bloody Sunday to the British government in June 1997. The report concluded that Widgery "must be replaced by a clear and truthful account of events on that day, so that its poisonous legacy can be set aside and the wounds left by it can begin to be healed".[54]

While the expectation of the two governments in Dublin and London was that granting a new inquiry would aid reconciliation, the Bloody Sunday campaigners had different expectations. Hegarty points out that "it is sometimes the case that people call for public inquiries because they believe that *they* know the essential truth about a situation and simply want the state to 'own up'. Long campaigns for 'the truth' or for new public inquiries to be set up also heighten this expectation."[55] The Bloody Sunday

---

51 Peter Bottomley, House of Commons, *Hansard*, 7 February 1992, Vol. 203, Col. 325W.
52 Michael Mates, House of Commons, *Hansard*, 15 June 1992, Vol. 289, Col. 383W.
53 McCann, *The Bloody Sunday Inquiry*, 11. McCann suggests that Major thought that this acknowledgement would bring the matter to a close.
54 Department of the Taoiseach, *Bloody Sunday and the Report of the Widgery Tribunal: The Irish Government's Assessment of the New Material* (Dublin: Department of the Taoiseach, 1997).
55 Hegarty, The Government of Memory, 1158. Italics in original.

families had been campaigning for twenty-six years by the time Blair announced the Bloody Sunday Inquiry in January 1998. Hegarty argued in a later article that the families also expected the new inquiry to "operate much more as a truth commission than an orthodox public inquiry and that there would be less investigation of the events and rather more exposition of the local version".[56] This is echoed by McCann, who argued that "[C]ampaigners in Derry hadn't demanded a new inquiry because they wanted to be told the truth. They didn't need a report from Lord Saville to find out what happened, but to find out whether the state would acknowledge what happened."[57] The expectation was that the narrative that the campaigners had maintained since 1972, in opposition to the official state version of Bloody Sunday, would finally be officially recognised and acknowledged as the truth.

Despite not coinciding with the reasoning of the Bloody Sunday families and campaigners, the Bloody Sunday Inquiry also played a significant role in the Northern Ireland peace process. In his covering letter for the report sent to the British government, the Taoiseach Bertie Ahern wrote that "I believe that your approach to this issue can help to remove a source of profound distress not only to the relatives but to the nationalist community generally".[58] This implied that a new public inquiry into Bloody Sunday might conciliate wider Nationalist opinion and increase Nationalist confidence and support for the peace process. Walsh suggested that "[I]f justice is finally done with respect to Bloody Sunday, it is reasonable to suppose that nationalists will be more willing to place their trust in the promise of equal citizenship and the new political, social and cultural environment inherent in the peace agreement."[59] Blair wrote that his motivation for establishing the new inquiry was to "assuage Nationalist opinion", but that "pressure from the Irish" also played a role in his decision.[60] The Irish government announced that their report on the new evidence would be published, and Walsh argues that "[I]t was hardly a coincidence [...] that the

---

56 Angela Hegarty, Truth, Law and Official Denial: The Case of Bloody Sunday, *Criminal Law Forum* 15 (2004), 199-246, here: 225.
57 McCann, *The Bloody Sunday Inquiry*, 7.
58 Ibid., 17.
59 Walsh, *Bloody Sunday and the Rule of Law*, 284.
60 Tony Blair, *A Journey* (London: Hutchinson, 2010), 165.

UK government announced the establishment of a new public judicial inquiry on the eve of the twenty-sixth anniversary, the same day that the Irish government published its report."[61] The fact that the new inquiry was established partly in response to pressure from the Irish government may have contributed to the opposition to the inquiry mounted by anti-agreement Unionists, who encouraged their followers to see it as "part-and-parcel of a wider sell-out of Protestant-Unionist interests" alongside parading legislation, policing reform and prisoner releases.[62]

Another role that the Bloody Sunday Inquiry played in the peace process was to "demonstrate to nationalists and republicans that we were even-handed and that the British government no longer had anything to hide".[63] This acknowledges that the Widgery Report had represented an effort on the part of the British government to obscure what had happened on Bloody Sunday. It is, however, interesting that Powell suggests that the Bloody Sunday Inquiry would demonstrate British neutrality in relation to Unionists and Nationalists in its handling of the peace process; in contrast, Dawson argues that the Bloody Sunday Inquiry "required a major shift in stance, away from the state's ideological self-representation as the honest broker and towards an admission of its role as an active party to the conflict".[64] Powell's description of the Weston Park talks in 2001 is more illuminating regarding his depiction of British even-handedness:

"[The] SDLP had pressed hard for inquiries into murder cases where there was a suspicion of collusion by the security forces, including the case of Patrick Finucane […] We were very reluctant to agree to this. After the continuing Bloody Sunday inquiry, the last thing Northern Ireland needed to do was to spend more of its time

---

61 Walsh, *Bloody Sunday and the Rule of Law*, 296.
62 McCann, *The Bloody Sunday Inquiry*, 18. The Parades Commission was established in 1998 to regulate contentious parades in Northern Ireland; Unionists viewed it as an attack on their culture. The policing reforms recommended by the Patten Commission in 1999 were criticised by Unionists as an insult to the role of the RUC in combating terrorism during the Troubles. The release of Republican prisoners from 2000 onwards was also opposed by Unionists, given the failure of the IRA to commit fully to decommissioning.
63 Powell, *Great Hatred, Little Room*, 45.
64 Dawson, *Making peace with the past*, 81.

looking back rather than preparing for the future. But in the end, in order to get the SDLP to accept the police reforms, we had to support the idea of an international judge looking at whether there were grounds for public inquiries into a series of individual cases. For their part, the Unionists wanted the list of cases to be considered to include Billy Wright, the LVF [Loyalist Volunteer Force] leader murdered in the Maze prison, to balance the otherwise exclusively Catholic bias."[65]

With regards to these inquiries, British even-handedness amounted to little more than trying to balance Nationalist and Unionist demands.

The balancing act approach was evident in other areas of the British government's involvement in the peace process; the former Northern Ireland Secretary, Mo Mowlam, wrote that the role of the British government was "like walking a tightrope, weighing the interests of one side against another and trying not to lose anyone".[66] One of the drawbacks of this approach, however, was that it was difficult to balance the demands of the two sides. Mowlam argued that it was "easier to move on some of the nationalists' issues – because they were often about making N. Ireland a fairer and more equal place to live for everyone – than on unionist demands".[67] Nationalist demands required recognisable change, whereas Unionist demands involved maintaining the status quo; as a result, the level of proposed change was frequently insufficient for Nationalists, but too much for many Unionists. As Porter argues, the balancing act approach can mean that "reconciliation ceases to function as a substantive moral ideal entailing a genuine reaching out to others and the requirements of balancing and inclusion are easily reduced to tactical ploys useful in the game of maximising one's cultural and political advantage".[68] Understanding this point is essential in understanding the differing reception of the Bloody Sunday Inquiry in the two communities in Northern Ireland (and, to a certain extent, amongst the two main political parties in Britain), and the reasons for its failure to fulfil the projected aim of promoting reconciliation.

The differences in reception are particularly evident in the parliamentary debates surrounding the announcement of the Bloody Sunday Inquiry

---

65 Powell, *Great Hatred, Little Room*, 199.
66 Mo Mowlam, *Momentum* (London: Hodder and Staughton, 2003), 164.
67 Ibid., 167.
68 Porter, *The Elusive Quest*, 78.

and the announcement of the report, and in the reactions in Northern Ireland, Britain and the Republic of Ireland. McCann highlighted the spectrum of opinion in the responses to the inquiry in Northern Ireland in his description of the Inquiry as "an achievement in which the Catholic/Nationalist community might rejoice and which Protestants/Unionists might accept, whether grudgingly or in a spirit of generosity, in the interests of the new accord".[69] Given the nature of zero-sum politics in divided societies such as Northern Ireland, the simple fact that the Bloody Sunday Inquiry was welcomed by the Nationalist community was sufficient reason for it to be opposed by sections of the Unionist community, as any gain for one community was interpreted as necessarily entailing a loss for the other.

At the very least, the establishment of the Bloody Sunday Inquiry was interpreted by many Unionists as indifference to the suffering sustained by the families of other victims of the Troubles, particularly those from the security forces. The DUP MP Sammy Wilson asked why it was considered necessary to re-open the inquiry into Bloody Sunday when "it was not considered necessary to hold an inquiry into the deaths of many RUC [Royal Ulster Constabulary] soldiers and innocent civilians who had been killed by terrorists".[70] This opinion is particularly echoed by those victims' groups who represent Protestant and Unionist victims, for example, Leslie Finlay, a representative of the West Tyrone-based victims' group, Voice:

"These big inquiries now that I hear tell about, on Bloody Sunday and Pat Finucane and Rosemary Nelson, all right, then, they can enquire as much as they like, these people, but [...] [there] were no enquiries in Castlederg [...] over twenty murders in the Castlederg area and they couldn't get anybody out to investigate it."[71]

As Dawson argues, "Protestant and Unionist victims also have tended to respond to the success of those campaigns where some public recognition has been secured from the State [...] as a denial and exacerbation of their own communities' memories of trauma, suffering and loss".[72] The perception

---

69 McCann, *The Bloody Sunday Inquiry*, 18.
70 Sammy Wilson, House of Commons, *Hansard*, 3 November 2010, Vol. 517, Col. 967.
71 Leslie Finlay, quoted in Dawson, *Making peace with the past*, 286.
72 Ibid.

that the British government's approach to the past and truth recovery was too heavily focused on addressing the grievances of the Nationalist community was elaborated by Jim Shannon:

"I want truth for the people at Darkley Hall, the people at La Mon, the people who were at Enniskillen on Remembrance Sunday, and the people who were murdered at Ballydugan. I want the truth for all those people. If we are to have truth, we must have it for everyone, not just for selected people. The fact that this process seems to be trying to obtain the truth for selected people is what annoys me."[73]

The dangers of this perception going unaddressed were highlighted by the leader of the Irish Labour Party, Eamon Gilmore:

"I recognise that righting one particular wrong done to one particular group is a sensitive issue when so many wrongs have been done to so many other innocent victims. Some people in the Unionist community have criticised the cost of the Saville inquiry and the extent of the media attention given to the killings on Bloody Sunday. They can point, accurately, to the contrast with so many major atrocities involving paramilitaries, which received much less attention."[74]

This highlights the hazards of an approach to the past, indeed an approach to peace-making and reconciliation, which relies on the balancing of interests.

Another factor in the differing reception of the Bloody Sunday Inquiry was due to its role in building the confidence of the Nationalist community in the peace process. Jeremy Corbyn suggested that the Bloody Sunday Inquiry "will help to give an awful lot of people confidence that the Government are serious about the search for peace in Northern Ireland".[75] Indeed, Corbyn's colleague and former Northern Ireland Secretary, Paul Murphy even proposed that had the Bloody Sunday Inquiry not been established,

---

73 Jim Shannon, House of Commons, *Hansard*, 3 November 2010, Vol. 517, Col. 988.
74 Eamon Gilmore, Dáil Éireann, 30 June 2010, Vol. 714, Number 1, Col. 40.
75 Jeremy Corbyn, House of Commons, *Hansard*, 29 January 1998, Vol. 305, Col. 514.

"there would not have been a successful peace process".[76] Although the Bloody Sunday families felt that the inquiry should not take place solely as a confidence-building measure,[77] they also acknowledged that

"even if the establishment of the Inquiry came about as part of the manoeuvring and quid pro quo of the peace process, and was not simply the results of our own efforts, the fact remains that the British government was willing to take this step towards some sort of resolution, and we in the spirit of reconciliation have to accept that".[78]

However, the role of the Inquiry as a confidence-building measure contributed to its negative reception amongst Unionists. An editorial in the Unionist-leaning *Daily Telegraph* argued that

"The decision to launch the Bloody Sunday Inquiry, the plans for demilitarisation as a bargaining chip with terrorists and the suggestions that there should be a 'day of reconciliation', in which British soldiers are somehow equated with the IRA, are all offensive and all highly political. They show that our security policy is now not shaped by a sense of the national interest and by the need to keep the peace, but an obsession with a process of concession that has no bottom line."[79]

The *News Letter* pointed out that "Bloody Sunday has become so bound up in republican propaganda that unionists find it difficult to sympathise with the plight of relatives who are seeking an official apology from the Government".[80] Rather being seen as "a search for truth and justice, which surely is in the interests of all the people of Northern Ireland, whatever their political or religious beliefs",[81] the Bloody Sunday Inquiry was interpreted by many Unionists as "a one-sided sop to buy nationalist and Republican

---

76 Paul Murphy, House of Commons, *Hansard*, 3 November 2010, Vol. 517, Col. 966.
77 According to Harry Barnes, House of Commons, *Hansard*, 29 January 1998, Vol. 305, Col. 512.
78 Liam Wray, quoted in McCann, *The Bloody Sunday Inquiry*, 157.
79 Editorial: Spineless wonders, *Daily Telegraph*, 15 March 2000.
80 Apology needed for Bloody Sunday, *News Letter*, 3 February 1997.
81 Dennis Canavan, House of Commons, *Hansard*, 29 January 1998, Vol. 305, Col. 510.

support for the peace process".[82] Given the Inquiry's role in building Nationalist confidence in the talks leading to the Belfast Agreement, it is unsurprising that the Inquiry was primarily opposed by anti-Agreement Unionists.

Finally, there was considerable scepticism over whether the Bloody Sunday Inquiry would result in the anticipated outcome of societal healing and reconciliation. Views on this tended to be split along communal lines, with John Hume arguing that the Inquiry would hopefully "be a major part of the healing process in our divided community".[83] By contrast, his Unionist counterpart, David Trimble, suggested that this hope was misplaced, and that "[O]pening old wounds like this is more likely to do more harm than good".[84] This was echoed by Conservative MP John Wilkinson who argued that "reinvestigating these matters will just exacerbate the pain, sorrow and grief, and lead to further alienation of loyal people in Northern Ireland".[85] Although scepticism tended to be located within the Unionist community, Jean Hegarty, one of the Bloody Sunday campaigners, suggested that reconciliation through the Bloody Sunday Inquiry was impossible "because I don't think feelings in Derry towards the army about Bloody Sunday have changed. And the Inquiry has probably alienated the Unionist community even more."[86]

The range of opinion, and often bitter feelings, towards the Bloody Sunday Inquiry is indicative of the difficulties surrounding the achievement of political and social reconciliation in Northern Ireland. It has raised many questions over the use of public inquiries as a method of dealing with the legacy of the past. As Lord Bew, one of the historical advisers to the Bloody Sunday Inquiry, has pointed out,

---

82 Dawson, *Making peace with the past*, 202.
83 John Hume, House of Commons, *Hansard*, 29 January 1998, Vol. 305, Col. 504.
84 David Trimble, House of Commons, *Hansard*, 29 January 1998, Vol. 305, Col. 504.
85 John Wilkinson, House of Commons, *Hansard*, 29 January 1998, Vol. 305, Col. 513.
86 Jean Hegarty, quoted in McCann, *The Bloody Sunday Inquiry*, 154.

"[T]he government has a legacy from the Bloody Sunday Tribunal – not just the heavy financial cost – but also the claims from other victims of the 'Troubles' to have their stories respected by the state. It has unfinished business here, and it needs to reflect on the way it has gone about its work thus far."[87]

Breen Smyth has related these issues to the question of reconciliation, and how new approaches might be developed:

"Concern about the scale and costs associated with the Bloody Sunday Inquiry [...] have led some to question the feasibility of judicial, adversarial processes as the way forward in dealing with Northern Ireland's past. Concern about the adversarial approach and its culture which is largely antithetical to negotiation, compromise or resolution have led some towards favouring a restorative over a retributive model. Others favour a more interactive, dialogical approach, where the history is rewritten by participation at all levels of society through a narrative process."[88]

By contrast with public inquiries, the latter model would theoretically lead to the development of a shared history, and thus a shared present and future.

Conclusions

It would be unfair to suggest that there have been no successes in the current approaches to the legacy of the Northern Ireland conflict. The Bloody Sunday families welcomed the Saville Report and the subsequent apology from Prime Minister David Cameron, with the majority finding some degree of closure in the report; Tony Doherty, one of the campaigners, suggested that

"The vast majority of the families felt that what we had brought about, what we had achieved on 15 June, with the Saville Report as an exoneration, with the words of

---

[87] Paul Bew, The Role of the Historical Adviser and the Bloody Sunday Tribunal, *Historical Research* 78, 199 (2005), 113-127, here: 116.

[88] Breen Smyth, *Truth Recovery and Justice*, 179-80.

David Cameron, with apology and accepting political responsibility for the atrocity of Bloody Sunday, that it was now time for us all to consider moving on."[89]

The work of the ICLVR in locating the remains of the Disappeared, and the role of the Historical Enquiries Team (HET), have both been welcomed by the families and friends of those killed as a result of the conflict. The role of the various civil society groups, both single- and cross-community, has been important in supporting families and victims, in raising awareness of the issues involved, and in engaging with state-sponsored initiatives on dealing with the past. The state-sponsored initiatives, such as the Bloomfield Report and the work of the Consultative Group on the Past, have highlighted the issues surrounding the past and the difficulties involved in addressing those issues.

However, the consultations of these initiatives have also revealed the wide disparity in attitudes towards the past and how to deal with the legacy of conflict, and the single-community victims' groups in particular have often played a role in reinforcing the social divide, rather than overcoming it. As Breen Smyth argues, both civil society and state-sponsored initiatives for dealing with the past "have failed to achieve a comprehensive paradigm shift in the wider society, but rather have been configured into the conflict itself, which persists, at least in the minds and rhetoric of the main protagonists and their followers".[90] The past remains an arena of conflict, which reflects the nature of the peace process as a means of transforming the Northern Ireland conflict from violence to politics, rather than resolving said conflict. The lack of consensus over suggested means of examining and dealing with the legacy of the past is an example of the conflict being continued by other means and is reflective of the lack of reconciliation that addressing the past is supposed to engender.

---

89 BBC News, 'Last' Bloody Sunday march takes place in Derry, http://www.bbc.co.uk/news/uk-northern-ireland-12319055, accessed 25 May 2011.
90 Breen Smyth, *Truth Recovery and Justice*, 93.

From Truth to Reconciliation
The Global Diffusion of Truth Commissions

ANNE K. KRÜGER

On April 14 to 15 in 2011, an international conference took place in Tunis under the topic "Addressing the Past, Building the Future: Justice in Times of Transition".[1] This conference was hosted jointly by different non-governmental organizations (NGOs) as the Arab Institute for Human Rights, the International Center for Transitional Justice (ICTJ) and the Tunisian League for Human Rights in cooperation with the United Nations Office of the High Commissioner for Human Rights and with support from the Open Society Foundations. Besides discussions on criminal justice and security sector reforms, truth commissions were a major topic. José Zalaquett, a former member of the Chilean National Truth and Reconciliation Commission, gave insights into the Latin American experiences and mentioned the need for implementing measures such as truth seeking. Priscilla Hayner, founding member of the non-governmental International Center for Transitional Justice and currently a Senior Adviser at the Centre for Humanitarian Dialogue, was invited to talk about the Argentine truth commission. Together with Tawfik Bouderbla, the President of the Tunisian "Committee for Investigating the Truth on the Violations During the Last Events", a commission of inquiry on the human rights violations during the revolution, she discussed the establishment of a truth commission for dealing with the

---

1 See for the conference report http://tjtunis.blogspot.com/, accessed June 2011.

long-lasting dictatorship, highlighting the importance of looking into the broader context of human rights violations.

This recent event demonstrates that truth commissions have obviously become a well-known and widely recognized tool for dealing with past regime crimes after political transitions. With the support from NGOs and even from the United Nations, international experts advise countries in political transition in establishing a truth commission by sharing their experiences with the national political elite and civil society activists.

Yet, truth commissions were firstly recognized as a particular phenomenon in the realm of transitional justice research only a little more than fifteen years ago.[2] With the breakdown of Latin American military dictatorships, the question of how to deal with past regime crimes drew attention of political actors, NGOs, and the academia. It led to the rapid development of transitional justice as both, practice and research. Besides questions of legal prosecution or amnesty, another emphasis was put on the "right to know" and the acknowledgement of committed crimes via truth commissions.

Since the 1980s, about 40 truth commissions[3] have been established worldwide to uncover the truth about past human rights violations in order to bring reconciliation to societies after violent conflict and repression. The definition of a particular practice of dealing with past crimes as a "truth commission" and its establishment in various countries as well as international demands for truth commissions after political transitions demonstrate that truth commissions have become recognized as an adequate solution to national past politics.

In this context, I am addressing truth commissions as a global phenomenon. I will shed light on the question why truth commissions are estab-

---

[2] Priscilla B. Hayner, Fifteen Truth Commissions – 1974 to 1994: A Comparative Study, *Human Rights Quarterly*, 16 (1994), 597-655.

[3] I draw on data collected by Priscilla Hayner, Mark Freeman, Geoff Dancy et al., and the United States Institute of Peace. Priscilla B. Hayner, *Unspeakable Truths: Facing the challenge of truth commissions* (London and New York: Routledge, 2011); Mark Freeman, *Truth Commissions and Procedural Fairness* (New York: Cambridge University Press, 2006); Geoff Dancy, Hunjoon Kim and Eric Wiebelhaus-Brahm, The Turn to Truth: Trends in Truth Commission Experimentation, *Journal of Human Rights* 9, 1 (2010), 45-64; http://www.usip.org/publications-tools/digital-collections, accessed June 2011.

lished across the world *although* in every country the political conflict, the level of violence or the cultural environment differ distinctively from the situation in other countries. I draw attention to the institutionalization and global diffusion of a specific cultural practice of coming to terms with the past, which we can find as an empirical fact in many countries all over the world *independent* of a particular cultural background or political conflict. In other words, I will not attempt to answer why sometimes truth commissions are established and sometimes they are not. Nor do I focus on the specific cultural or political context in which a particular truth commission has been set up. Instead, I ask why have truth commissions become globally accepted as a legitimate standard tool in the transitional justice repertoire? This approach differs from most of the extensive research literature on transitional justice and truth commissions, which has focused mainly on questions of national past politics and its effects on national democratic consolidation. In order to answer this question, I will proceed in four steps. First, I will introduce truth commissions as a transitional justice standard as well as an object of transitional justice research. I will provide some insights into what truth commissions are and what they do. Secondly, I will take a closer look on the history of truth commissions, the process of their institutionalization as a well-known standard of transitional justice and their global diffusion. In a third step, I will highlight the formation of an epistemic community as the promoter of truth commissions. I will conclude by discussing the expectations related to truth commissions and the rationale they provide in the context of their institutionalization as a widely recognized answer to gross human rights violations.

TRUTH COMMISSIONS IN TRANSITIONAL JUSTICE RESEARCH

With the breakdown of Latin American dictatorships, the question how to deal with past regime crimes in the context of democratic consolidation became a prominent issue. In the years of military dictatorships in Latin America, a widespread network of human rights activists developed that collected information in particular about the "disappeared"[4] and worked on drawing public attention to the massive human rights violations.[5] Now, after the collapses of the Latin American autocratic regimes, human rights activists, who had already demanded to stop and investigate *current* human rights violations for many years, turned their claims towards the disclosure of and accountability for *past* regime crimes, which in many cases had been committed already years ago.[6] A new political issue surfaced that became known as transitional justice. With the breakdown of the Soviet Union and its satellite states and, furthermore, with the overcoming of the apartheid regime in South Africa, the geographic scope of transitional justice also expanded beyond Latin America.

Transitional justice comprises a wide range of different practices of dealing with past regime crimes. However, here I will focus on one particular practice of transitional justice that has spread across the world since the 1980s. Along with special courts – such as the International Criminal Tribunal for former Yugoslavia (ICTY) and the International Criminal Tribunal for Rwanda (ICTR)[7] or most prominently the International Criminal Court (ICC) in The Hague[8], truth commissions have become of major interest in the research on transitional justice procedures.[9] According to Hayner and Freeman, truth commissions are officially established by a presidential or royal decree, a parliamentary decision, or a peace agreement, but exist only for a limited time. They consist of several commissioners who range

---

4 The "disappeared" are persons who were kidnapped by the regime without any official notice and then never reappeared.
5 Kathryn Sikkink, Human rights, principled issue-networks, and sovereignty in Latin America, *International Organization* 47, 3 (1993), 411-441.
6 Paige Arthur, How "Transitions" reshaped Human Rights: A Conceptual History of Human Rights, *Human Rights Quarterly* 31, 2 (2009), 321-367.
7 Rachel Kerr and Eirin Mobekk, *Peace and justice: Seeking accountability after war* (Cambridge: Polity Press, 2007).
8 William A. Schabas, *An introduction to the International Criminal Court* (Cambridge: Cambridge University Press, 2001).
9 *Truth v. justice: The morality of truth commissions,* ed. Robert I. Rotberg and Dennis Thompson (Princeton: Princeton University Press, 2000); Freeman, *Truth Commissions*; Hayner, Fifteen Truth Commissions; Hayner, *Unspeakable Truths.*

from politicians to human rights activist or even churchmen. They are supported by a staff providing technical support for the investigations and in some cases even psychological assistance to the victims.[10]

Truth commissions differ significantly from courts. Instead of judicially proving individual responsibility of single perpetrators,[11] truth commissions try to draw as complete a picture as possible of the extent of serious human rights violations and their structural background. By writing up the truth in an end report, truth commissions construct a historical narrative about the past as well as about their own role in overcoming it. This collective narrative shapes the understanding of the past by contributing to the collective remembrance of it.[12] Truth commissions thus take part in the formation of a new collective identity by constructing an "imagined moral community"[13] which is based on a clear normative demarcation from the past.

Courts legitimate their actions by referring to (international) law; truth commissions as non-judicial organizations do not have this kind of legitimation. Regarding the question of legitimacy, the global acceptance of truth commissions as an appropriate means for transitional justice becomes an empirical puzzle. On which grounds are they expected to be a legitimate answer to gross human rights violations besides the courts? To tackle this puzzle, I will sketch out the historical process in which truth commissions emerged and how they became institutionalized as a widely accepted transitional justice standard.

---

10 Priscilla Hayner, Truth Commissions, in: *Encyclopedia of Genocide and Crimes Against Humanity*, vol. 3, ed. Dinah Shelton (Detroit: Thomson Gale, 2004), 1045-1047; Freeman, *Truth Commissions*.

11 Every truth commission has found its own way of dealing with the problem of accountability. While some truth commissions collaborated with the courts, others published the names of perpetrators in their final reports. Some truth commissions were not allowed to attribute individual guilt.

12 Molly Andrews, Grand national narratives and the project of truth commissions: a comparative analysis, *Media, Culture and Society*, 25, 1 (2003), 45-65.

13 Tanya Goodman, Performing a "new" nation: The role of the TRC in South Africa, in: *Social Performance: Symbolic Action, Cultural Pragmatics and Ritual*, ed. Jeffrey C. Alexander et al. (Cambridge: Cambridge University Press, 2006), 169-192, here: 176.

THE GLOBAL DIFFUSION OF TRUTH COMMISSIONS

The first official truth commission was established in Bolivia in 1982. It was inspired by an unofficial commission of inquiry in Brazil that had been established by the archdiocese of Sao Paulo under the military dictatorship in 1979 in order to collect information about the disappearances of civilians. In contrast to the Bolivian truth commission, which never published an end report, the first truth commission that finished its work by handing over a final report to the government was held in Argentina in 1983. Although the *Comisión Nacional sobre la Desaparición de Personas* (National Commission on the Disappeared, CONADEP) was contested to some extent, because it was not allowed to publicly name individual perpetrators,[14] its end report called *Nunca más* (Never again) became a national bestseller and founded the "literary genre of truth reports".[15] In 1985, another Latin American truth commission was established by the Uruguayan parliament. As in the case of its predecessors, it was set up in order to find out the fate of the "disappeared".

The first African truth commission took place in Uganda after the regimes of Idi Amin and Milton Obote in 1986.[16] With the financial support of the Ford Foundation, which sent the Chilean human rights activist José Zalaquett to assist the commission in 1987, this truth commission finally published an end report in 1994.[17] Already before, in 1974, the Ugandan

---

14 But the names leaked through and were published by the media. Ruth Fuchs and Detlef Nolte, Die Aufarbeitung von Regimeverbrechen und der Demokratisierungsprozess in Lateinamerika: Argentinien und Chile in vergleichender Perspektive, in: *Nach Kriegen und Diktaturen – Umgang mit Vergangenheit als internationales Problem: Bilanzen und Perspektiven für das 21. Jahrhundert*, ed. Alfons Kenkmann and Hasko Zimmer (Essen: Klartext, 2005), 29-48.

15 Anika Oettler, Einmal „nunca más!" und nie wieder? Die Dynamik der historischen Aufklärung in Argentinien und Guatemala, in: *Bilder nach dem Sturm: Wahrheitskommissionen und historische Identitätsstiftung zwischen Staat und Zivilgesellschaft*, ed. Christoph Marx (Berlin: Lit, 2007), 36-73, here: 40. All translations in this article were made by the author.

16 Hayner, *Unspeakable Truths*, 239-240.

17 http://www.usip.org/publications/truth-commission-uganda-86, accessed June 2011.

president Idi Amin had established a commission of inquiry into the disappearances of people in Uganda. Some refer to this commission as the first truth commission.[18] But the results were neither published nor did Idi Amin have to face any consequences. He was in power before and after the commission took place. Instead, the members of this commission had to face serious consequences afterwards such as trials or even assaults.[19]

In the literature, the Nepalese Commission of Inquiry to Locate the Persons Disappeared during the Panchayat Period has also been integrated into the collection of truth commissions.[20] Like in the first Latin American and African Commissions, it was set into office in early 1990 to disclose information about the persons who "disappeared" under the Panchayat Regime from 1961 until 1990.

These first cases show that fact-finding about the "disappearances" became a major concern in the political transformation processes of the 1980s. To collect information about this secretly performed practice and to acknowledge its victims became a substantial factor for the credibility of the new political elite. While the consequences of judicial prosecution were discussed controversially, "the right to know" emerged as a widely shared assumption about what should be done about past crimes.[21]

In 1990, another Latin American truth commission, the Chilean *Comisión Nacional de Verdad y Reconciliación* (National Truth and Reconcilia-

---

18 Hayner, Fifteen Truth Commissions; Hayner, *Unspeakable Truths*; Lutz Niethammer, Wahrheitskommissionen im Vergleich, in: *Bilder nach dem Sturm*, 15-35. For critical comments, see Freeman, *Truth Commissions*.
19 Hayner, Fifteen Truth Commissions, 612.
20 http://www.usip.org/resources/commission-inquiry-nepal-90, last accessed June 2011. The United States Institute of Peace (USIP) does not consider the Nepalese commission to be a truth commission but a commission of inquiry. Hayner, *Unspeakable Truths*, Dancy et al., The Turn to Truth, and Freeman, *Truth Commissions*, instead define this commission as a truth commission.
21 Gloria Park, Truth as Justice: Legal and Extralegal Development of the Right to Truth, *Harvard International Review* 31, 4 (2010), http://hir.harvard.edu/bigideas/truth-as-justice?page=0,1. Park talks about the "right to truth". I will use instead the "right to know" because this term has been used by the United Nations in the Joinet-Report on transitional justice. UN document, Economic and Social Council, E/CN.4/Sub.2/1997/20/Rev.1, 2 October 1997.

tion Commission), was set into office by a presidential decree of newly elected president Patricio Alwyn. It was the first truth commission that called for "truth" and "reconciliation" already in its title. Human rights activist José Zalaquett was appointed as a member of this commission that was chaired by the politician Raúl Rettig. When the truth commission was established, the country was still in a tense political situation, because former dictator Augusto Pinochet continued to be the supreme commander of the military forces. To underline its credibility and to foster public as well as political acceptance, President Aylwin distributed the appointment of the commissioners equally among the opponents of the Pinochet regime and its supporters.[22] In contrast to its predecessors, this truth commission's mandate included more than disclosing the truth about the "disappeared". Against this volatile political backdrop, the Chilean truth commission was supposed to reach towards a collectively accepted picture of the past and the origins of the dictatorship.[23]

By signing the UN brokered peace agreement in 1991, the government of El Salvador and the guerilla organization *Frente Farabundo Martí para la Liberación Nacional* (FMLN) agreed to establish a truth commission for El Salvador. Referencing the Argentine and Chilean examples, the end report from El Salvador declared that in order to guarantee the commission's sovereignty only international commissioners should be appointed.[24] Against this backdrop, the UN Secretary-General Boutros Boutros-Ghali announced former Columbian president Belisario Betancur, former president of the Inter-American Court of Human Rights Thomas Buergenthal and former Venezuelan minister of foreign affairs Reinaldo Figueredo Planchart as commissioners of the *Comisión de la Verdad para El Salvador* (Truth Commission for El Salvador).[25] It was the first time that the United

---

22 Guido Klumpp, *Vergangenheitsbewältigung durch Wahrheitskommissionen: Das Beispiel Chile* (Baden-Baden: Nomos, 2001).

23 *Decreto Supremo* No. 355 on the establishment of the *Comisión Nacional de Verdad y Reconciliación*, 25 April 1990.

24 UN Security Council, *From Madness to Hope: the 12-year war in El Salvador: Report of the Commission on the Truth for El Salvador*, S/25500, 1993, Annex, 12.

25 Wolfgang Pasternak, *Wahrheitskommissionen: Dargestellt an den Beispielen von El Salvador, Guatemala und Südafrika* (Aachen: Manz, 2003), 58.

Nations took part in the establishment of a truth commission. Their engagement shows that already in the early 1990s an international awareness of this particular practice of coming to terms with the past had emerged. The references to the Argentine and the Chilean example underline that national transitional justice practices had been recognized as being transferable to other countries in transition to democracy. Truth commissions became thought of as a viable solution to assist peaceful and democratic consolidation.

In 1992, the German parliament established the *Enquête-Kommission zur Aufarbeitung von Geschichte und Folgen der SED-Diktatur in Deutschland* (Enquête Comission for the Inquiry into the History and Consequences of the Socialist Dictatorship in Germany). The parliament drew on a pre-existing instrument for advising the parliament in complex political, economic or social affairs.[26] Germany was the first country to establish a truth commission although trials had already taken place before. However, the results of these trials had caused disappointment especially among former GDR human rights activists.[27] Legal restrictions posed a problem to sanctioning officially committed regime crimes.[28] Markus Meckel and Martin Gutzeit, the co-founders of the GDR social democrats in October 1989, initiated an officially sanctioned *Enquête-Kommission*, which was then estab-

---

26 Christian Heyer and Stephan Liening, *Enquete-Kommissionen des Deutschen Bundestages: Schnittstellen zwischen Politik und Wissenschaft* (Berlin: Deutscher Bundestag, 2004). It is important to note that an *Enquête-Kommission* differs significantly from a commission of inquiry, which is another parliamentarian investigation instrument. It has no judicial powers. Instead, besides politicians, external experts are also members of this commission and serve to provide broad knowledge about a particular issue. Commissions of inquiry instead are designed to focus more specifically on singular events. For a further distinction of truth commissions and commissions of inquiry see http://www.usip.org/publications/truth-commission-digital-collection, accessed June 2011.

27 Petra Bock, Von der Tribunalidee zur Enquete-Kommission. Zur Vorgeschichte der Enquete-Kommission des Bundestages "Aufarbeitung von Geschichte und Folgen der SED-Diktatur in Deutschland", *Deutschland Archiv* 11 (1995), 1171-1182.

28 Klaus Marxen and Gerhard Werle, *Die strafrechtliche Aufarbeitung von DDR-Unrecht: Eine Bilanz* (Berlin: de Gruyter, 1999).

lished unanimously by all parties in the Bundestag. Like in other countries before, it was mandated to disclose the structural circumstances of the socialist dictatorship and the individual suffering of the victims in order to come to a clearer picture of the communist past, to acknowledge its victims and to strengthen a democratic political culture.[29] The establishment of the German Enquête-Kommission thus presents truth commissions not only as an appropriate solution for dealing with the past, but also as an expedient addition to trials.

To date, the South African Truth and Reconciliation Commission (TRC) has been the most prominent truth commission. It was established by the Promotion of Reconciliation and National Unity Act of 26 July 1995 and chaired by Arch Bishop Desmond Tutu. Human rights activist Alex Boraine became the deputy chairperson. Although, the South African concluding report also refers to Argentina and Chile as two examples of truth commissions,[30] the TRC had some unique features. It was the first commission that had the power to grant amnesties in cases of an extensive confession. Yet, the underlying mission of the TRC was even more important. Tutu emphasized "reconciliation" achieved by "forgiveness" as the main goal of the commission in reaching for the "rainbow nation".[31] The public hearings of this commission were therefore not only designed to educate people about the severe and structural human rights violations during the apartheid regime but also as a public arena for the collective catharsis of the South African people.[32]

---

29 Andrew H. Beattie, An Evolutionary Process: Contributions of the Bundestag's Inquiries into East Germany to an Understanding of the Role of Truth Commissions, *International Journal of Transitional Justice*, 3, 2 (2009), 229-249; Anne K. Krüger, "Keine Aussöhnung ohne Wahrheit": Die Enquête-Kommissionen zur "Aufarbeitung" und "Überwindung der SED-Diktatur", in: *Nach Krieg, Gewalt und Repression: Vom schwierigen Umgang mit der Vergangenheit*, ed. Susanne Buckley-Zistel and Thomas Kater (Baden-Baden: Nomos, 2011), 131-149.
30 Truth & Reconciliation Commission of South Africa, *Report*, Vol. 1 (London and New York: MacMillan, 1999), 111-112.
31 Desmond Tutu, *No future without forgiveness* (New York: Doubleday, 1999).
32 Martha Minow, *Between vengeance and forgiveness: Facing history after genocide and mass violence* (Boston: Beacon Press, 1998).

This brief and only partial overview of first truth commissions demonstrates already that – despite different cultural, political, and societal backgrounds – this transitional justice practice has become widely accepted as a legitimate solution to the problem of how, after political transitions, to deal with systematic human rights violations committed by a former regime or during a civil war. In the initial phase in the 1980s, first commissions emerged defining their goals and their means in a similar way. They emanated from the concern, shared across national borders, about the fate of "disappeared" relatives and friends. In a second phase in the early 1990s, this kind of dealing with past human rights crimes was recognized as a possible option for transitional justice. Truth commissions enlarged their focus from individuals towards the structural and historical background; their task developed into drawing an exhaustive picture of the past crimes and their context. Furthermore, truth commissions were installed via peace agreements under the auspices of the United Nations. Moreover, even where trials had already been held before, truth commissions were established in addition. With the establishment of the South African Truth and Reconciliation Commission, the institutionalization of truth commissions as a recognized transitional justice standard had reached its crucial point. The huge national and international public attention to the TRC and its professionally organized outreach made this commission a referential point or even a prototype for future truth commissions. Today, we can find truth commissions all over the world in Asian countries like South Korea or Timor Leste, in Islamic countries such as Morocco, in ex-Yugoslavian Serbia and Montenegro. And also in Latin America and Africa, further truth commissions have been set into office. Thus, truth commissions have developed from a tool to publicly disclose information about the "disappeared" towards a widely applied practice of dealing with past crimes and their structural background in order to account responsibility to the culprits and to acknowledge their victims.

This brief overview of the global diffusion of truth commissions has also shown that in many cases truth commissions have built on the experiences of earlier commissions. In order to better understand these transnational processes, it is necessary to focus on actors and organizations that have contributed to the worldwide spread of truth commissions.

Promoting Truth Commissions

During the military dictatorships in Latin America, relatives and friends of "disappeared" persons organized to gather information on the whereabouts of their loved ones. One of the most prominent examples is the Argentine *Asociación de las Madres de Plaza de Mayo*. After the political transition, they claimed that it was indispensable "to understand the truth, otherwise a shadow of sadness will forever hang over the descendants of this shattered generation".[33] These NGOs pressured the newly elected governments not to ignore the severe human rights violations of the past. They demanded an officially mandated fact-finding about the "disappearances" in order to publicly acknowledge these secretly committed human rights violations as well as to provide assistance to the relatives.[34] Members of these NGOs took part in discussions about the establishment of a truth commission. In Bolivia, Carmen Loyola Guzmán even became the executive secretary of the *Comisión Nacional de Desaparecidos*, representing the Bolivian *Asociación de Familiares de Detenidos Desaparecidos y Mártires por la Libertad Nacional* (ASOFAMD), a NGO committed to finding the whereabouts of the "disappeared".

This NGO was also among the founders of the *Federación Latinoamericana de Asociaciones de Familiares de Detenidos-Desaparecidos* (FEDEFAM). The FEDEFAM was founded in 1982 as a transnational umbrella organization for the investigation on "disappearances" of civilians. In order to exchange information about the kidnappings, these locally founded and then nationally organized groups had started to cooperate with other such groups in neighboring countries already during the military dictatorships. Nowadays, the FEDEFAM has members in many Latin American states, which in most of the cases have also established truth commissions.[35]

First academic discussions entering the human rights activists discourse on transitional justice date from the 1980s. They centered on questions of

---

33 Argentina: Self-Amnesty, *Time*, 3 October 1983, http://www.time.com/time/magazine/article/0,9171,926231,00.html#ixzz1Mb5inDMR, accessed June 2011.

34 Veit Strassner, *Die offenen Wunden Lateinamerikas: Vergangenheitspolitik im postautoritären Argentinien, Uruguay und Chile* (Wiesbaden: VS, 2007).

35 http://www.desaparecidos.org/fedefam/, accessed June 2011.

punishment versus amnesty.[36] The crucial question of the discussions was whether punishing the former elite would jeopardize the political stability of (re)nascent democracies.[37] Transitional justice[38] had to balance the demands for procedural justice on the one hand and the hope for the consolidation and reintegration of society on the other one. Especially the Argentine laws, which stopped the prosecution of perpetrators in 1986, caused major discussions.[39] Yet, besides these debates on legal issues, a new way of granting justice to the victims surfaced. Public knowledge and acknowledgement of the committed crimes became recognized as a new form of justice that could help to build a moral foundation for the consolidating democracies. The "right to know" was seen as a necessary precondition for restoring social trust in political institutions and for reintegrating the victims into society.[40] Nonetheless, disclosing the truth was not regarded to be

---

36 For a profound discussion of legal prosecution and its potential benefits and consequences see the collection of articles from Aryeh Neier, Jaime Malamud-Goti, José Zalaquett, Diane F. Orentlicher and Carlos S. Nino (among others) in *Transitional justice: How emerging democracies reckon with former regimes*, 3 vols., ed. Neil J. Kritz (Washington, DC: United States Inst. of Peace Press, 1995).

37 Diane F. Orentlicher, 'Settling Accounts' Revisited: Reconciling Global Norms with Local Agency, *International Journal of Transitional Justice* 1, 1 (2007), 12-13.

38 The term "transitional justice" itself became prominent in the late 1990s after the publication of the compendium "Transitional justice" in 1995 by Neil Kritz. See Arthur, How transitions shapes Human Rights.

39 See the discussion between the lawyer Diane Orentlicher and Carlos Nino who advised Argentine president Alfonsín in his transitional justice policies in Diane F. Orentlicher, Settling Accounts: The Duty to Prosecute Human Rights Violations of a Prior Regime, *The Yale Law Journal* 100 (1991), 2537-2615; Carlos S. Nino, The Duty to Punish Past Abuses of Human Rights Put into Context: The Case of Argentina, *The Yale Law Journal* 100 (1991), 2619-2640; Diane F. Orentlicher, A Reply to Professor Nino, *The Yale Law Journal* 100 (1991), 2641-2643; Orentlicher, Settling Accounts Revisited.

40 Park, Truth as Justice.

a trade-off for procedural justice.[41] It rather became recognized as an additional component of transitional justice.[42]

These academic discussions about accountability, amnesty, and the "right to know" took place in a number of conferences that were held from the end of the 1980s onwards. One of the most prominent conferences was hosted by the Aspen Institute in 1988 under the title "State Crimes: Punishment or Pardon?" against the backdrop of the resurrection of Latin American democracies.[43] After the collapse of the Eastern Bloc and the breakdown of the apartheid regime in South Africa, the Latin American discussions on transitional justice were transferred to these countries in transition and their legacies of a repressive past. These conferences were sought to facilitate a transfer of Latin American experiences of dealing with the past to post-socialist countries.[44] One important conference in this regard was "Justice in Times of Transition" which was organized by the New York based Charta 77 Foundation in Austria in March 1992 and conceptualized as the inaugural meeting of a new transitional justice organization with the same name as the conference title. In the foreword of his "Transitional Justice" compendium, Neil Kritz summarizes his impressions from this conference that inspired him to compile this book:

"In word spoken and unspoken, in skeptical glances and general body language, the Latin Americans and Europeans seemed to be expressing the same thing to one another: the suffering of our people during the old regime and the difficulties resulting from our legacy is far worse than any hardship you endured. Ours is the greater pain;

---

41 But there was a debate on "truth vs. justice". See Rotberg and Thompson, *Truth v. justice*; *The Politics of Memory: Transitional Justice in Democratizing Societies*, ed. Carmen González Enríquez et al. (Oxford: Oxford University Press, 2001); Ellen Lutz, Transitional justice: Lessons learned and the road ahead, in: *Transitional justice in the twenty-first century: Beyond truth versus justice*, ed. Naomi Roht-Arriaza and Javier Mariezcurrena (Cambridge: Cambridge University Press, 2006), 325-41.
42 Arthur, How Transitions reshaped Human Rights, 353.
43 Arthur, How Transitions reshaped Human Rights.
44 Timothy Phillips, The Project on Justice in Times of Transition, in: *The New Humanitarians*, ed. Chris E. Stout (Westport, Connecticut: Praeger Press, 2008), 2-22.

there is little we can learn from your experience. [...] And yet. By day two of the proceedings, there was a gradual but palpable recognition that many of the details and dilemmas were not so different."[45]

After the breakdown of the apartheid regime in 1994, another important conference was held by the title "Dealing with the Past" in South Africa. It was organized by the Institute for a Democratic Alternative for South Africa and supported by the Project Justice in Times of Transition. At this conference, experts from Argentina and Chile introduced their experiences of a truth commission to South African politicians and human rights activists. Until today, as the Tunisian conference shows, organizations such as the ICTJ or the Project Justice in Times of Transitions hold conferences in order to transfer transitional justice knowledge and experiences to countries in political transition.

Altogether, these conferences facilitated an exchange of experiences as well as the discussion on a broad range of possible ways how to deal with the past after political transitions. This had a strong impact on the worldwide diffusion of transitional justice and in particular of truth commissions. Based on a collectively shared reservoir of knowledge about different organizational forms, procedures, and practices of transitional justice, an epistemic community,[46] i.e. a network of professionals consisting of practition-

---

45 Neil J. Kritz, The Dilemmas of Transitional Justice, in: *Transitional justice*, xix–xxx, here: xix.

46 Haas defines an epistemic community as "a network of professionals with recognized expertise and competence in a particular domain and an authoritative claim to policy-relevant knowledge within that domain or issue-area". Peter M. Haas, Introduction: epistemic communities and international policy coordination, *International Organization* 46, 1 (1992), 3. In the realm of human rights, Keck and Sikkink suggest to talk about transnational advocacy networks instead of an epistemic community. They define transnational advocacy networks as a network of "actors working internationally on an issue, which are bound together by shared values, a common discourse, and a dense exchange of information and services." Kathryn Sikkink and Margaret E. Keck, Transnational Advocacy Networks in International and Regional Politics, in: *International organization and global governance: A reader*, ed. Friedrich V. Kratochwil and Edward D. Mansfield, 2nd ed. (New York: Pearson Longman, 2006), 162-176, here: 162.

ers from the field, academics, politicians, and policy consultants who advised governments or intergovernmental organizations (IGOs) all over the world, started to form. This epistemic community contributed to institutionalizing transitional justice as a widely shared expectation in the context of regime transitions and introduced this paradigm to the United Nations.[47] Furthermore, this epistemic community also provided members to following truth commissions. Human rights activists like the Chilean José Zalaquett or the South African Alex Boraine became members of truth commissions in their home countries.

Oettler interprets this process as the development of a "global transitional justice design", which these experts promote as a "hegemonic truth".[48] Through workshops, conferences, and direct support of NGOs and governments, this epistemic community not only spreads its transitional justice expertise. It also promotes its normative assumptions about the right way of dealing with the past. The members of this epistemic community are also members of research institutes, consulting agencies, NGOs or IGOs. The International Center for Transitional Justice (ICTJ) soon became one of the most prominent non-governmental organizations of this kind.[49] The

---

While they stress the identification with values as the important factor for cooperation, which are nonetheless also included in the definition of an epistemic community, in this article, I want to stress the formation of expert knowledge and the development of transitional justice standards and their promotion. Thus, I will refer to the term epistemic community.

47 The term "transitional justice" appears in an UN document for the first time in 1997 in the context of the question how to stabilize new governments. While, on the one hand, transitional justice is recognized to be an important factor, the document demands, on the other hand, that "[f]or reconciliation, the actors in a post-conflict society must reach consensus on the issue of transitional justice and a balance must be struck between the needs for justice and for tolerance". United Nations, Economic and Social Council, E/1997/86, 27 June 1997. From the beginning of the 2000s onwards, the mentioning of "transitional justice" in UN documents increases continuously.

48 Anika Oettler, Der Stachel der Wahrheit. Zur Geschichte und Zukunft der Wahrheitskommission in Lateinamerika, *Lateinamerika Analysen* 9 (2004), 93-126, here: 120.

49 http://www.ictj.org, accessed June 2011.

ICTJ was founded in 2001 after the experience of the South African TRC. Its foundation members were two transitional justice practitioners, former TRC's deputy chairperson Alex Boraine and TRC's executive secretary Paul van Zyl. Additionally, Priscilla Hayner, a pioneer in the research on truth commissions, became a third founding member. This constellation already demonstrates the twofold mission of the ICTJ. It does not only research on truth commissions. It also advises NGOs and governments all over the world in how to establish a truth commission.

The before mentioned Tunisian conference on "Justice in Times of Transition", which was co-organized by the ICTJ, is thus another example which demonstrates once again the promotion of transitional justice and, in particular, truth commissions as appropriate action after political transitions. Truth commissions are now a commonly shared standard in the transitional justice repertoire. They have become the common enterprise of an epistemic community because they are expected to be an adequate solution for transitional justice. But why could, in particular, truth commissions develop as such a popular transitional justice practice?

FROM TRUTH TO RECONCILIATION

The political, cultural, and social background against which truth commissions have been established has varied across countries. While the Argentine *Comisión sobre la Desaparición de Personas* was set up against the backdrop of the "dirty war" against civilians by the military dictatorship, the *Comisión de la Verdad para El Salvador* tried to account for the gross human rights violations committed during the twelve years of civil war. The Chilean *Comisión Nacional de Verdad y Reconciliación* was introduced while former dictator Augusto Pinochet still remained the supreme commander of the military forces. The German *Enquête-Kommission* was established after a long-lasting socialist dictatorship that had confined its people not only in economic, political, and social but also in geographical terms within the borders of the German Democratic Republic. In contrast to the GDR, the apartheid regime had drawn borders within the country separating and repressing South African people due to their ethnical origins. And the Moroccan *Instance Equité e Réconciliacion* was the first truth commission that was installed in an Islamic country and inaugurated by the former oppressor's son, King Mohammed VI.

Also in terms of their establishment, personnel composition, and competences, truth commissions have differed distinctively from each other. They have been installed by a presidential or royal decree, a parliamentary decision, or a peace agreement. They have been executed by national or foreign human rights activists, churchmen, politicians, or academics. Some have been equipped with the right to name potential perpetrators or to grant amnesties, while others were limited to collecting information about individual suffering and were not allowed to investigate individual accountability. Nevertheless, no matter how much these truth commissions differed in practice, a closer look on their mandates and end reports reveals a striking similarity. The Argentine truth commission claimed: "[W]e are neither motivated by any resentments nor by the spirit of vengeance; we only ask for truth and justice, [...], because we think that there won't be reconciliation without contrition of the culprits and justice based on the truth."[50] The report of the Chilean *Comisión Nacional de Verdad y Reconciliación* stated that their "task revolved around two fundamental objectives: truth and reconciliation. As defined for us, our work was to come to a comprehensive grasp of the truth of what had happened, for it was utterly necessary to do so in order to bring about reconciliation among Chileans."[51] Moreover, the UN brokered truth commission in El Salvador hoped "that knowledge of the truth [...] will be a reasonable starting-point for national reconciliation and for the desired reunification of Salvadorian society".[52] The German *Enquête-Kommission* found that "the experiences of the Enquête-Kommission have emphasized the dictum 'No reconciliation without truth'. Particularly the victims of the former regime have a right to truth. Only when the truth has been disclosed and individual guilt has been admitted, reconciliation

---

50 *Nunca Más: Informe de la Comisión Nacional sobre la Desaparición de Personas* (Buenos Aires: EUDEBA, 1987), 10.
51 *Report of the Chilean National Commission on Truth and Reconciliation* (Notre Dame, Indiana: University of Notre Dame Press, 1993), 1118.
52 UN Security Council, *From Madness to Hope*, Annex, 176.

can be addressed."[53] And the until now most famous truth commission, the South African TRC, emphasized that "[o]ne of the main tasks of the Commission was to uncover as much as possible of the truth about past gross violations of human rights [...]. The Commission was founded [...] in the belief that this task was necessary for the promotion of reconciliation and national unity."[54]

Although these quotes result from very different contexts, they all show a similar account of legitimacy. In order to justify their establishment, these truth commissions refer to the same argument. They describe their aim as discovering, documenting, and reporting the truth about gross human rights violations in order to reconcile a fractured society.

In the early 2000s, influenced by the prominent South African truth commission, the establishment of truth commissions increased. In 2003, several truth commissions were at work in countries as different as Sierra Leone, Timor Leste, Peru, and Serbia and Montenegro. These truth commissions show that "truth" and "reconciliation" are key concepts that are not only used to describe and to justify their work across cultural and political differences, but which are even represented in the names of many truth commissions.[55]

The Moroccan *Instance Equité e Réconciliacion* presents a further example. Although, reconciliation is often believed to be a Christian concept, this truth commission, inaugurated in 2004 in an Islamic country, referred to the establishment of the truth about gross human rights violations as important "[t]o develop and promote a culture of dialogue and set up the basis of a reconciliation process oriented toward the consolidation of the demo-

---

53 Bericht der Enquête-Kommission *Aufarbeitung von Geschichte und Folgen der SED-Diktatur in Deutschland*, ed. Der Deutsche Bundestag, Drucksache 12/ 7820, 31 May 1994, 281.

54 Truth & Reconciliation Commission of South Africa, *Report*, Vol. 1 (Basingstoke: Macmillan, 1999), 49.

55 Translated into the national idiom the commissions were called *Comissão de Acolhimento, Verdade e Reconciliação* (Timor Leste), *Comisión de la Verdad y Reconciliación* (Peru), Truth and Reconciliation Commission (Sierra Leone), *Komisija za istinu i pomirenje* (Serbia and Montenegro).

cratic transition in our country, the strengthening of the rule of law and the propagation of citizenship and human rights values and culture."[56]

These examples show that starting with the "right to know" about the fate and the whereabouts of victims of human rights violations, a new idea of transitional justice has surfaced. With the establishment of first truth commissions in the early 1980s, a new rationale has become part of the transitional justice practice and discourse. Besides ideas of justice through punishment, establishing the "truth" is related to "reconciling" societies. To publicly acknowledge the individual suffering of victims in the context of its structural and historical background has become recognized as an indispensable contribution to political transitions. This counts for the countries that have yet established a truth commission. But also beyond national boundaries, this practice has gained recognition. International NGOs as well as IGOs as the United Nations are now promoting truth commissions as a reasonable solution for dealing with past human rights violations, thereby contributing to its further diffusion. The rationale that truth leads to reconciliation has been institutionalized.

THE MEANING OF RECONCILIATION

However, truth commissions have also always been contested. Their global diffusion across different countries around the globe as well as their international promotion by a number of national, transnational, and international NGOs or IGOs proves that truth commissions are recognized as one possible way to exercise transitional justice, although, their results are often criticized. Critical evaluations show a lack of actual efficacy in various ways.[57]

---

56 Approving Statutes of the Equity and Reconciliation Commission, Dahir No 1.04.42 of the 19th of Safar 1425 (10 April 2004), The Kingdom of Morocco, http://www.ier.ma/article.php3?id_article=1395, accessed June 2011.

57 *Commissioning the Past: Understanding South Africa's Truth and Reconciliation Commission*, ed. Deborah Posel and Graeme Simpson (Johannesburg: Witwatersrand University Press, 2002); Rosalind Shaw, *Rethinking Truth and Reconciliation Commissions: Lessons from Sierra Leone*, Special Report 130 (Washington, DC: United States Institute of Peace, 2005); James L. Gibson, *Overcoming apartheid: Can truth reconcile a divided nation?* (New York: Rus-

In Argentina human rights activists also first refused the CONADEP, because they had opted for a parliamentary commission of inquiry with more judicial powers. Some members of the *Madres de Plaza de Mayo* even never accepted it.[58] They wanted to discover the truth about the gross human rights violations in order to punish the guilty. Hence, they were not interested in reconciliation at all.

However, despite of contestation and critical evaluation, truth commissions have become more and more popular for dealing with past crimes, albeit the urge for accountability never ceased. Initially, truth commissions had not been thought of as a substitute for trials.[59] However, due to (self-)amnesties, still powerful former elites or an insufficiently working judiciary, in many countries the truth-seeking process was not followed by trials and sentences against perpetrators. As a consequence, the establishment of truth commissions became accompanied by the fear of impunity. In countries where no trials were held before or in the aftermath of a truth commission, they were thus often considered to have facilitated impunity.

In particular, the term "reconciliation" was criticized. Already in the debates about "punishment or pardon", amnesties had been justified as an important factor for reconciliation. In this context, "reconciliation" became soon to be seen as a "watchword for impunity".[60] With the emergence of truth commissions and, at the same time, with the lack of trials, the goal of truth commissions to achieve reconciliation also got a bad aftertaste. Human rights activists as well as victims expressed their concern that the aim of reconciliation could end the search for the guilty and draw a line under the human rights violations of the past, which then would lead to impunity.

---

sell Sage Foundation, 2006); Audrey R. Chapman and Hugo van der Merwe, *Truth and reconciliation in South Africa: Did the TRC deliver?* (Philadelphia: University of Pennsylvania Press, 2008).

58 Strassner, *Die offenen Wunden Lateinamerikas*, 87.
59 The Argentine mandate insisted on transmitting information to the courts, Decreto 187 "Comisión sobre la Desaparición de Personas, Constitución, Integración y funciones", 15 November 1983. This also happened until the "full stop law" in December 1986. See Kathryn Sikkink and Carrie Booth Walling, Argentina's Contribution to Global Trends in Transitional Justice, in: *Transitional justice in the twenty-first century*, 301-324.
60 Orentlicher, Settling Accounts Revisited, 13,

It is important to notice though, that the consequence has not been a complete abandonment of this transitional justice practice. Instead, the Ecuadorean truth commission from 2007 explicitly decided not to apply the term "reconciliation", because it was regarded as opposite to justice. Justice in this case was defined as accountability for committed crimes. Therefore, the truth commission – called *Comisión de la Verdad para Impedir la Impunidad* (Truth Commission to Impede Impunity) – was set up to gather information in order to prosecute the perpetrators of severe human rights violations.[61] Reconciliation was not mentioned at all. But what does "reconciliation" actually mean?

In addition to the debates "in the field" about reconciliation, this term was also discussed in the epistemic transitional justice community. These debates show firstly that reconciliation is not limited to truth commissions. In discussions about retributive versus restorative justice, both sides have claimed to reach for reconciliation.[62] Furthermore, other transitional justice approaches such as social justice[63] are also seen as a means for reconciliation. Nevertheless, no matter whether punishment, reparations or truth were assumed to be the prerequisites for reconciliation, there was a growing awareness that it was necessary to get a clearer picture of what the term reconciliation actually addressed. After all, in post-conflict societies, where the former conflict still latently persists, transitional justice and its justifications are always based on morally loaded concepts. Different interpretations and applications of reconciliation are therefore bound to arise due to political interests and personal needs.

---

61 Gobierno Nacional de la República de Ecuador, Madato "Se creó la Comisión de la Verdad 'para impedir la impunidad'", 3 May 2007, http://www.usip.org/files/ROL/Mandato%20de%20Ecuador.pdf.

62 Franklin Oduro, *What do we understand by 'Reconciliation'? A Review of the Literature on Reconciliation. Emerging Definitions of Reconciliation in the Context of Transitional Justice* (Ottawa: The International Development Research Centre, 2007).

63 Bloomfield adds a third form of transitional justice. Social justice implies that all the "goods" of a society (economic, political and social) are shared in a fair way. David Bloomfield, *On Good Terms: Clarifying Reconciliation*, Berghof Report 14 (Berlin: Berghof Research Center For Constructive Conflict Management, 2006), 21.

Several organizations have actively engaged in clarifying what reconciliation could be. The International Institute for Democray and Electoral Assistance (IDEA),[64] the Berghof Research Center for Constructive Conflict Management,[65] the Institute for Justice and Reconciliation (IJR),[66] the South African Centre for the Study of Violence (CSVR),[67] and the Canadian International Development Research Centre[68] have tried to evaluate the meaning and concept of reconciliation.

Focusing on the South African Truth and Reconciliation Commission, Hamber and Van der Merwe from the CSVR define five different "ideologies" of reconciliation which do not only apply in this specific context.[69] These interpretations range from restoring individual relationships to rebuilding social bonds and political trust on the national level. Furthermore, they identify religious interpretations of forgiveness with references to human rights and the rule of law as well as the overcoming of racial discrimination for a peaceful co-existence as the content of reconciliation.

Additionally to the distinction between an individual and a collective level of reconciliation, Minow stresses different degrees of reconciliation. On the basis of truth, reconciliation can reach from a "minimal agreement to coexist and cooperate" to "a stronger commitment to forgive and uni-

---

64 David Bloomfield, Terri Barnes and Lucien Huyse, *Reconciliation after violent conflict: A handbook*, ed. International Institute for Democracy and Electoral Assistance (Stockholm: International IDEA, 2003); Mark Freeman, *Making reconciliation work: The role of parliaments,* Handbook for parliamentarians 10 (Geneva: International IDEA, 2005); Luc Huyse, *Traditional justice and reconciliation after violent conflict: Learning from African experience* (Stockholm: International IDEA, 2008).
65 Bloomfield, *On Good Terms*.
66 Charles Villa-Vicencio, Erik Doxtader and Richard Goldstone, *Pieces of the puzzle: Keywords on reconciliation and transitional justice*, ed. Institute for Justice and Reconciliation (Cape Town South Africa: Institute for Justice and Reconciliation, 2004).
67 Brandon Hamber and Hugo van der Merwe, What is this thing called Reconciliation?, *Reconciliation in Review* 1, 1 (1998), http://www.csvr.org.za/wits/articles/artrcbh.htm.
68 Oduro, What do we understand by 'Reconciliation'.
69 Hamber and van der Merwe, What is this thing called Reconciliation.

fy".[70] Villa-Vicencio et al. find that "different kinds of conflict require different forms of reconciliation".[71] But to talk and to listen are from their point of view the essential capacities on which reconciliation is built.

In order to evaluate the effects of the TRC on the South African society, Gibson operationalizes reconciliation in terms of four dependent variables.[72] Defined as social (interracial) trust, political tolerance, the acceptance of human rights, and the support of political institutions, these variables focus on the effects of reconciliation on the macro-level and present reconciliation as a goal of transitional justice practices. The outcome of the TRC is measured according to these norms and attitudes in order to draw conclusions about its efficacy.

Bloomfield regards it as important to predefine reconciliation as a harmonious end-state of working social relationships. From his point of view, this future vision could then become a "motivating ideal" for all actors involved.[73] However, he also stresses that reconciliation is a process and points to Huyse who describes the process of reconciliation as a three-stage model from "non-violent coexistence" to "building confidence and trust" towards "empathy". Starting from "looking for alternatives to revenge", in a second step he sees the "acknowledgement of the humanity of others" as "the basis of mutual trust [which] opens the door for the gradual arrival of a sustainable culture of non-violence". As a last step towards reconciliation, Huyse defines empathy as the "victims' willingness to listen to the reasons for the hatred of those who caused their pain and with the offenders' understanding of the anger and bitterness of those who suffered".[74]

This brief overview of the term "reconciliation" shows that it comprises many different interpretations. Altogether, these concepts, definitions, and interpretations demonstrate that reconciliation is an umbrella term, which

---

70 Martha Minow, The Hope for Healing: What Can Truth Commissions Do?, in: *Truth v. justice*, 235-260, here: 250.
71 Villa-Vicencio et al., *Pieces of the puzzle*, 3.
72 James L. Gibson, Does Truth Lead to Reconciliation? Testing the Causal Assumptions of the South African Truth and Reconciliation Process, *American Journal of Political Science* 48, 2 (2004), 201-217.
73 Bloomfield, *On Good Terms*, 6.
74 Luc Huyse, The Process of Reconciliation, in: *Reconciliation after violent conflict*, 19-33, here: 19-21.

contains a wide range of different dimensions. There are individual acts of building relationships as well as societal efforts to reduce conflicts and tensions by constructing a tolerant, peaceful, and inclusive environment. On the political level, reconciliation can stand for (re-)building political trust as well as political tolerance, but it can also encompass even broader ideas of peace-building and democratic reconstruction.

However, while this discussion about the content of reconciliation continues, it reveals some interesting insights that go beyond definitions and typologies. On the one hand, the term "reconciliation" has become part of a symbolic language of transitional justice. To aim for reconciliation is a legitimate goal used to justify transitional justice practices. As there is no explicit definition of what reconciliation implies, many ideas, procedures, and actions have been integrated into various concepts of what reconciliation actually implies. But regarding the efforts to define what reconciliation is about, there is a commonly shared understanding that reconciliation can be understood as restoring social relationships. Nonetheless, the particular demand for reconciliation in terms of who has to be reconciled with whom under which circumstances and by what kinds of efforts is always influenced by political and social pressures. As a consequence, not only the fear of its abuse has increased; sometimes – as e.g. in Ecuador – it has led to the complete rejection of reconciliation.

On the other hand, the goal to restore social relationships and to (re-)integrate victims as well as perpetrators into society can be found even in countries where the term "reconciliation" was opposed. Although the Ecuadorian *Comisión de la Verdad para Impedir la Impunidad* did not refer to reconciliation, the Ecuadorian end report stated that human rights violations, which were discovered by the truth commission, had to become part of a public memory in order to help to restore social relationships.[75] They did not talk about "reconciliation", but they nonetheless applied the same

---

75 Comisión de la Verdad Para Impedir la Impunidad, Sin Verdad No Hay Justicia. Informe de la Comisión de la Verdad, Vol. 5, Conclusiones, 2010, http://www.coverdad.org.ec/informe-final, 433; "The consequences of the human rights violations, like the pain, the fear, and the suffering of the victims and their families, must be regarded as part of the country's history; they must be known by the entire society and must be considered in the policies for reparations and for the reconstruction of social relationships which had been fractured by the violence".

characteristic idea in the truth commissions that truth leads to the reconstruction of society and thus to their reconciliation.

Reconciliation as a symbolic term as well as a concept of restoring social bonds is therefore an integral part of truth commissions. However, it remains quite vague. It does not specify how this rationale of truth and reconciliation is interpreted in a specific context by human rights activists, victims, perpetrators, politicians, or policy consultants.

At the same time, the findings suggest that it is exactly the ambivalence of reconciliation that enables the diffusion of truth commissions and their promotion across the world. Truth and reconciliation are an integral part of truth commissions' legitimacy account that is applied across various contexts. Because the content of the symbolic terms "truth" and "reconciliation" remain vague, the rationale that truth leads to reconciliation facilitates a fictional consensus,[76] within which various interpretations about what should be done and what should be reached can co-exist. This fictional consensus enables and ensures the formation of truth commissions. Against the backdrop of political and societal pressures to somehow "manage" past human rights abuses, the argument about truth and reconciliation provides the least common denominator for a consensus that allows for the establishment of a truth commission. Every participant can apply his or her own subjective interpretation to these commonly shared and legitimized goals. The ambiguity inherent in this argument, which links fact-finding and the public acknowledgement of its results to the aim of restoring a fractured society, is a necessary precondition for the establishment of truth commissions worldwide. Consequently, it can be applied to various contexts despite political divides and cultural diversity. And as the involvement of the multitude of international NGOs and IGOs shows, this argument is not only applicable in various national contexts, but also at the international level. The United Nations as well as a variety of (I)NGOs are now promoting truth commissions as a legitimate answer for dealing with the problems of

---

76 The term "fictional consensus" and its underlying concept, that collective action can be based on an unquestioned illusion of mutual understanding, were developed and defined by Roland Eckert, Alois Hahn and Marianne Wolf, *Die ersten Jahre junger Ehen. Verständigung durch Illusionen?* (Frankfurt a.M.: Campus, 1989).

past human rights abuses after political transitions, thereby contributing to their diffusion.

Conclusion

In this article, I have shed light on the phenomenon that truth commissions have been installed across the world in spite of different cultural contexts and political situations. From a global perspective, attention is drawn to the fundamental question why truth commissions have been accepted as a legitimate solution to the problem of massive human rights violations after political transitions worldwide. Truth commissions have been established in very different contexts. The political conflict, the level of violence, or the cultural environment always differed distinctively from the context of other truth commissions. Thus, every truth commission has been adapted to the respective conditions regarding its composition or competences. Nonetheless, although there is variation in the political and cultural context as well as in the formal conditions of their establishment, many countries across the world have decided to install this particular practice in an effort to come to terms with the past.

In order to answer this question of the global diffusion of truth commissions, I have taken a look behind their particular context and formal structure. Focusing on the mandates and end reports of truth commissions, I have highlighted the normative expectations on which their establishment is based. While the national context always affects the conditions under which a truth commission is established, the rationale behind their establishment is the same across cultural and political differences. Truth commissions are expected to disclose the truth in order to facilitate reconciliation. The "right to know", i.e. the public disclosure of human rights violations has become a transitional justice standard. States in political transition are expected to comply with it and thus to establish and publicly acknowledge the severe human rights violations committed by the former regime. Reconciliation as the restoration of society has become prominently linked to this process of fact-finding and acknowledgement. Thus, the "right to know" has prevailed over the fear of "re-opening old wounds". Instead, it has become positively related to societal restoration. The rationale that truth leads to reconciliation has become a standard assumption in the realm of transitional justice.

This article shows that the global spread of truth commissions comes along with the institutionalization of this rationale. The establishment of truth commissions by national parliaments, presidential or royal decrees or via peace agreements reflects not only a growing awareness that past regime crimes have to be addressed after political transitions even if they have been committed already years ago. Furthermore, their establishment responds to the widely shared assumption that the public disclosure of truth will help to reconcile societies as a precondition for democratic consolidation. A multitude of national and international NGOs, among many others the ICTJ, and intergovernmental organizations such as the United Nations promote and support this rationale based on the expectation that truth leads to reconciliation. Accordingly, they contribute to the global diffusion of truth commissions.

At the same time, I have suggested that the worldwide spread of truth commissions and their promotion are related to the ambiguity of this rationale about truth and reconciliation. The focus of the investigation and hence what part of the "truth" is addressed is always point of debate. But the term "reconciliation" is even more contingent. It comprises a wide array of different interpretations. In the case of Ecuador, where the claim for reconciliation was regarded as providing impunity to the perpetrators, it has even been rejected and replaced by the aim of restoring society. This aspect of restoration is also the least common denominator of the scope of interpretations of the term "reconciliation". At the same time, it does not define the persons that are sought to engage in this process and the conditions under which reconciliation should be reached. The ambivalence of reconciliation thus allows for the co-existence of multiple meanings and interpretations without the need for addressing the differences among them. It provides a fictional consensus about what should be reached by establishing the truth via a truth commission. This fictional consensus based on the rationale of truth and reconciliation enables the establishment of truth commissions because it provides legitimacy across political and cultural differences. As a result, this rationale bridges not only national divides but also allows for their global diffusion.

The rationale of truth and reconciliation is now a collectively shared normative standard about coming to terms with the past within the epistemic transitional justice community. Based on this assumption, they advise countries in political transition all over the world in how to deal with their pasts and promote truth commissions as an adequate answer to this problem. The Tunisian conference on "Justice in Times of Transition" is a further but certainly not a last example of this ongoing process.

About the Authors

Marco Duranti received his PhD in history from Yale University in 2009 and is currently Lecturer in History at the University of Sydney. His work examines the development of international human rights institutions, movements and norms in twentieth-century Europe. He is writing a book on the genesis of European human rights law.

Ayda Erbal is a Politics Instructor at the Department of Politics at New York University. Currently she is working on her dissertation titled *Black Turks, White Turks and the Minorities: The Limits of Transitional Justice and Civil Society in Contemporary Turkey*. Her research interests include democratic theory, democratic deliberation, the politics of 'post-nationalist' historiographies in transitional settings, mass violence and the politics of apology.

Andrea Erkenbrecher graduated in contemporary history and social psychology at the Ludwig-Maximilians-Universität of Munich. From 2003 to 2011 she was awarded a scholarship by the *Evangelisches Studienwerk Villigst e.V.* She is currently preparing her PhD thesis titled *Oradour and the Germans. Dealing with a war crime and its memory: Criminal prosecution, indemnification, revisionism and gestures of reconciliation in the FRG and GDR, 1949-2011*. In 2003/04 she was working at the *Centre de la Mémoire d'Oradour-sur-Glane*. Her research interests include the history of Nazi concentration camps and the coping with the National Socialist Past in the FRG and GDR.

Reinhart Kössler works at the Arnold Bergstraesser Institute, Freiburg, Germany, and is Professor of Political Science at Freiburg University. His interests include development theory, politics and sociology of development, the postcolonial state, ethnicity and memory politics. His regional focus is southern Africa. Among his publications are *Entwicklung* (1998), *Globale Solidarität?* (2002, with Henning Melber) and *In search of survival and dignity. Two traditional communities in Southern Namibia under South African Rule* (2005/06).

Anne K. Krüger studied sociology, political sciences and contemporary history in Dresden, Madrid, and Berlin. She was awarded fellowships at the Berlin Graduate School of Social Sciences, the Centre for Contemporary History in Potsdam, and the Stanford University School of Education. In 2012, she received her Dr. phil. in sociology from the Humboldt University Berlin for her dissertation titled *The global diffusion of truth commission as a collective learning process. A contribution to the microfoundation of organizational research*. Her research interests include world polity research, cultural and organizational sociology.

Charlton Payne is postdoctoral fellow at the University of Erfurt. His current book-length project investigates postwar and contemporary refugee narratives in German literature. He has published essays on narrative sovereignty in Wieland, cosmopolitanism in Goethe, the politics of sensus communis in Kant, and hospitality in Kleist. Book publications include a co-edited volume on *Kant and the Concept of Community* (2011), as well as *The Epic Imaginary: Political Power and Its Legitimations in Eighteenth-Century German Literature* (2012).

Ulrike Schröber graduated in history from the University of Mannheim, Germany, in 2008. From 2009 to 2012 she was PhD-student in the Graduate School *Die christlichen Kirchen vor der Herausforderung 'Europa'* which is organized by the University of Mainz and the Leibniz-Institute of European History, Mainz. Currently she is a Research Fellow in the Department of History at the University of Mainz. She is preparing her PhD-thesis about Marcel Sturm and Robert Picard de la Vacquerie, the two chief military chaplains of the French occupied zone in Germany, and their engagement within the Franco-German rapprochement.

Birgit Schwelling is currently the Academic Director of the Research Group on 'History and Memory' at the University of Konstanz, Germany. From 2000 to 2008, she has been Assistant Professor at the Cultural Studies Department of the European University Viadrina in Frankfurt an der Oder, Germany. She is the author of numerous books and articles on European memory cultures and politics, the cultural history of politics, transitional justice, and the integration of veterans into postwar societies, including *Heimkehr – Erinnerung – Integration. Der Verband der Heimkehrer, die ehemaligen Kriegsgefangenen und die westdeutsche Nachkriegsgesellschaft* (2010), *Politikwissenschaft als Kulturwissenschaft* (2004) and *Wege in die Demokratie* (2001).

Robert Stock graduated in European Ethnology from Humboldt University of Berlin in 2009. He has been a Research Fellow of the Research Group on 'History and Memory' in 2010/11 and was awarded a grant from the Gerda Henkel Foundation. Currently he is a PhD candidate at the International Graduate Centre for the Study of Culture at the Justus Liebig University Gießen, where he is preparing his dissertation on *Decolonization and Documentary Film. Filmic Representations of the Mozambican-Portuguese Decolonization*. He is also a Research Fellow in the Department of Media Studies at the University of Konstanz. His research interests include visual culture, postcolonial studies, memory politics, and disability studies.

Melinda Sutton graduated in History from Newcastle University in 2008. She is currently a PhD candidate in the Department of History at Newcastle University where she is preparing her thesis on *The British Labour Party and Northern Ireland 1969-2007*. Her research interests include the politics of memory and commemoration in contemporary Ireland and aspects of British government policy towards Northern Ireland throughout the Troubles.

Christiane Wienand is a Research Fellow in the interdisciplinary research project *Reverberations of War* at University College London, Department of German. In her post-doctoral project she pursues research on the 'young generation' as reconciliation activists in Europe and Israel since 1945. Her research focuses on the history of memory in Germany and Europe after World War II. She currently prepares the publication of her PhD thesis on

Performing Memory. Returned German Prisoners of War in Divided and Reunited Germany.

Jay Winter is the Charles J. Stille Professor of History at Yale University and is a specialist on World War I and its impact on the twentieth century. His other interests include remembrance of war in the twentieth century such as memorial and mourning sites, European population decline, the causes and institutions of war, British popular culture in the era of the Great War, and the Armenian genocide of 1915. He is the author or co-author of a dozen books, including *Socialism and the Challenge of War. Ideas and Politics in Britain, 1912-18* (1974, reprint 1993); *The Great War and the British People* (1985); *The Fear of Population Decline* (with Michael S. Teitelbaum, 1986); *The Experience of World War I* (1988); *Sites of Memory, Sites of Mourning: The Great War in European Cultural History, 1914-1918* (1995); *The Great War and the Shaping of the 20th Century* (1996); *Remembering War: The Great War between History and Memory in the 20th Century* (2006); *Dreams of Peace and Freedom: Utopian Moments in the 20th Century* (2006).